Management for Professionals

The Springer series *Management for Professionals* comprises high-level business and management books for executives. The authors are experienced business professionals and renowned professors who combine scientific background, best practice, and entrepreneurial vision to provide powerful insights into how to achieve business excellence.

Martin Pfiffner

The Neurology of Business

Implementing the Viable System Model

Springer

Martin Pfiffner
Fondation Oroborus
Altendorf, Switzerland

Translated by
Mark Kyburz
English Projects
Zürich, Switzerland

ISSN 2192-8096 ISSN 2192-810X (electronic)
Management for Professionals
ISBN 978-3-031-14259-8 ISBN 978-3-031-14260-4 (eBook)
https://doi.org/10.1007/978-3-031-14260-4

This Springer imprint is published by the registered company Springer Nature Switzerland AG
The registered company address is: Gewerbestrasse 11, 6330 Cham, Switzerland

Preface

As a rule, it takes 50–60 years for groundbreaking, seminal innovations to spread to the point where they create real benefits in the economy and society. This book concerns such a basic innovation, first because we urgently need it, and second because it is available, waiting to be used, after 50 years of practical testing and technological development.

Almost 50 years ago to this day, the British scholar and top manager Stafford Beer presented his solution to a problem that, at least in most people's minds, did not yet exist. While the technology already existed in rudimentary form, it was far from mature. Beer was way ahead of his time because the question at hand was how to make complex enterprises work.

A few years earlier, during World War II, a group of scientists in Mexico City had discovered a new science that would change the world as no discipline ever had: cybernetics, the science of control and communication in complex systems—or, simply put, the science of functioning. It enabled the unprecedented technological revolution of the postwar era, which led to today's Industry 4.0 and digitalization. Beer was the first to systematically apply the science of functioning to the management of enterprises—which he was directly involved in as a top manager. He revealed the structures that need to be in place for an enterprise—regardless of size and complexity—to fulfill its purpose and achieve its goals.

If cybernetics is now applied not only to technical systems but increasingly also to social systems, that is, our organizations, this could revolutionize the world a second time. Because as this book shows, the functioning of organizations is the core problem as well as the solution to the challenges of our time. Poorly functioning organizations cause the crises facing our world. Today, most organizations are overwhelmed by the complexity and dynamics of their environment, and unnecessarily waste a lot of energy and time in their paralyzing and incomplete internal mechanisms. If we want to regain our freedom of action, we need better solutions. But can we really find these in even better anatomies or organizational charts of the enterprise—even though we have been optimizing them for over a hundred years and have already tried out all conceivable forms? Or will we really find better solutions in an even better physiology of the enterprise or in process design—although we have also been using and optimizing this technology for 30 years? Or should we instead focus on a third dimension of organizing, that is, what an organization does to manage its internal and external complexity: its neurology? Without neurology, there can be no complexity management, no agility, nor intelligence and creativity. So what other lesson can we learn from neurology for control and communication in the enterprise? As we will see, a neurological perspective resolves many perennial questions of organizing, such as autonomy versus hierarchy, agility versus cohesion, and flexibility versus continuity.

Stafford Beer has given us a model that for the first time enables measuring, comparing, and assessing the quality and performance of various organizational structures. The yardstick for this is the question of how well these structures deal with complexity and dynamics. On the other hand, as long as we remain trapped in the first two dimensions of organizing, we will be taken in by fads, solving one problem and creating another. Dealing with complexity and dynamics is the main challenge of our time, and designing the third dimension of organizing is therefore *the* management issue of the future that affects every manager personally.

Beer's "Viable System Model" is the only model to date that comprehensively addresses the third dimension. After more than two decades of practical experience, I have decided to share that experience, and thus to contribute to the growing international community of practitioners and scholars. This book is for those managers who want to put Beer's model into practice. A book like this, therefore, needs to be understandable and useful. But if it is not well-founded or boring, readers will put it down. So the challenge was to manage a threefold balancing act: between practical usefulness, scientific thoroughness, and fascinating reading.

I am grateful to many people. First and foremost, I thank my wife Sibylle, who has encouraged and supported me for 25 years. She has contributed much to this book. I thank Mark Kyburz for his translation and for all his support throughout the project. I also thank Claudia Zürcher and Franziska Hubmann for creating the hand-drawn illustrations. Barbara Bethke at Springer, who supported the project from the outset, was a pleasure to work with. Thank you.

I am grateful to the many colleagues in the field of cybernetics I have been privileged to work with, and who became friends in many cases and role models in many ways: Allenna Leonard, Vanilla Beer, Roger Harnden, Joe Truss, Chris Cullen, David Komlos, David Benjamin, Angela Espinosa, Joe Walker, Stephen Davies, David Beatty, José Perez Rios, Markus Schwaninger, Jan Kuiper, Swanette van der Vegt, Mike von de Wijnckel, everyone at Liverpool John Moores University, and many others.

I am most grateful to the entrepreneur Bernadette Langenick-Pfister and her late husband Willy Pfister who created the Fondation Oroborus, which promotes the dissemination of management cybernetics in the business world, and which has also supported this book.

I thank the thousands of executives in business and nonbusiness organizations around the world for the opportunity to discuss application issues, to try out new ways of doing things, and to learn from them. They, along with my former colleagues at the Management Zentrum St. Gallen, are the foundation on which this book stands.

Finally, I thank my two teachers and mentors. Working with Fredmund Malik for nearly 30 years has shaped my thinking. He introduced me to the practice of systems-oriented management theory and management cybernetics as a student in the 1980s and later introduced me to Stafford Beer. From Fredmund Malik I learned what right and good management is and how to use it to create real benefits in practice, a concern always particularly close to his heart. Finally, my greatest thanks belong to Stafford Beer himself, who introduced me both to his thinking and to the application of his models and methods with such patience and affection during many long conversations in the last 3 years of his life. He did so on the condition that I pass on the knowledge I had gained to others, which gave me the best possible impetus to write this book.

I bow to the pioneers of cybernetics, most notably Norbert Wiener, Warren McCulloch, Heinz von Foerster, Ross W. Ashby, Walter Pitts, John von Neumann, Claude Shannon, Margaret Mead, and Gregory Bateson, on whose shoulders we stand. So let us see what we can make out from the vantage point they have given us.

Altendorf, Switzerland
May 30, 2022

Martin Pfiffner

Prologue: Why This Book Matters

Abstract
During World War II, a group of scientists in Mexico discovered a new discipline: the science of functioning. In it, they found the recipe for success, which was first applied in technology and led to the third industrial revolution (automation), and subsequently to the already proclaimed, fourth industrial revolution of digitalization, which today encompasses the economy and society as a whole. The problem is that technical systems have left social systems behind. Our ponderous and expensive organizations can no longer keep up with technology-driven complexity and dynamics. Only when the recipe for success is applied to our organizations will we experience a new way of functioning. This recipe lies neither in organizational charts (anatomy) nor in organizational processes (physiology), but rather in the third dimension of organizing: the neurology of the enterprise, that is, in its control and communication.

> Ever tried. Ever failed. No matter.
> Try again. Fail again. Fail better.
> (Samuel Beckett, *Worstward Ho!*)

A World-Changing Discovery: The Formula for Success

One evening, somewhere in 1940s America, when the first computers were being built, Warren McCulloch steps into a common room at a convention center. He spots Norbert Wiener sitting in an armchair, deeply immersed in a book. "Norbert," he says, "Walter Pitts and I are working on a machine that will enable blind people to read with their ears." The ensuing events led to one of the most far-reaching and crucial discoveries of the twentieth century. In our present, twenty-first century, this discovery will play an even more important role than ever.

Wiener looks up from his book with interest. "The advantage," McCulloch continues, "is that books will not need to be printed in braille. But there is one matter that I'd like to discuss with you. Our machine scans the text. The problem, though, is that it doesn't recognize individual letters because of their different sizes and fonts. We could of course print standardized letters, but braille already does that. Our machine must thus be able to recognize the shape of a letter 'n' in any size and shape. I have an inkling of how we could teach the machine." McCulloch draws a technical diagram on a piece of paper and explains the design of scanners, photoelectric cells, and oscillators to Wiener. The two scientists discuss and argue for a while. Later McCulloch pours another whiskey and goes to bed. He leaves the diagram on the table. Shortly afterward, Gerhardt von Bonin enters the common room. A leading expert in neuroanatomy, he knows everything about the nervous system, its structure and processes. Von Bonin sees the drawing on the table, studies it briefly, and asks Wiener: "Who was trying to draw a diagram of the visual center of the brain?"[1]

Wiener is overwhelmed. Could the blueprint for how the brain recognizes shapes look like McCulloch's drawing? Did the brain and the machine really work the same way? The next evening, Wiener told the other conference participants what had happened. About twenty people were present. What was special about the conference was that participants came from different subject areas and were world leaders in their field. Wiener was one of the six best mathematicians of his time and was also known as "the American Leibniz." McCulloch, the conference leader, was a world-famous neurophysiologist and a neighbor of Albert Einstein's, with whom he was good friends.

Wiener's excitement quickly spread to the other participants. Did an engineer eager to build such a machine need the same blueprint as nature had already developed in four billion years of evolution? Can we learn from organisms how truly difficult things, such as recognizing shape, work? The scientists gathered in that 1940s common room discussed the technical diagram and tried to quantify it: What speed must the machine operate at in order to function? The result was their next big surprise: They calculated a rate of ten vibrations per second—which corresponds to an alpha brainwave when we daydream in a relaxed posture. Our brain, then, scans the world at the same speed as a scanner capable of recognizing letters.

Evidently, recognition in the brain involves the same ingredients as in the machine. The scientists around Wiener instinctively sensed that they were on the trail of a potentially world-changing discovery. If the same principles applied in two worlds as different as the machine and the organism, might they also apply in other disciplines? Has focusing on our specific areas of expertise blinded us to discovering universal principles? And who says that God knows the difference between biology and engineering, or between physics and chemistry?

Dating the birth year of a new science mostly proves elusive. Nobody knows when exactly physics or philosophy emerged. In our case, however, matters are different. From 1943, at the height of World War II, McCulloch, Wiener, and the

[1]Norbert Wiener, *Cybernetics: Or Control and Communication in the Animal and the Machine*, 2nd ed. (Cambridge, MA: MIT Press, 1948), pp. 22 ff., 133 ff.

physiologist Arturo Rosenblueth founded an interdisciplinary discussion group in Mexico City. That is unusual because normally, only representatives of the same subject convene. This interdisciplinary dialogue continued from 1946 to 1953 in a series of ten conferences sponsored by the Josiah Macy Jr. Foundation. With only the best from each field admitted, participants neither had to prove their credentials nor adopt a defensive stance, as so often happens. They were meant to open up to each other. Careful to maintain an interdisciplinary balance, McCulloch, as conference chair, handpicked participants. Many were eager to participate, yet only a few were accepted. They included the anthropologists Margaret Mead and Gregory Bateson, the physicist Heinz von Foerster, the mathematician and father of computer science John von Neumann, the sociologist Paul Lazarsfeld, the psychiatrist Ross W. Ashby, the information theorist Claude Shannon, and the electrical engineer Julian Bigalow, who helped von Neumann build the MANIAC—one of the first universally programmable computers.

In the course of the Macy conferences, a key question soon emerged: Could what matters most in science and for humanity fall exactly between the established chairs at university departments? After all, biologists and engineers speak different languages and investigate different phenomena. If they met at all, then most likely in university refectories. Back in 1943, Wiener and his colleagues discovered "*Control*" as a universal topic. Or phrased as a question: "How must things be controlled to succeed?" This question concerns every specialist area, and yet none, because "control" is an interdisciplinary phenomenon. It occurs everywhere, in astrophysics as in biology, in anthropology as in engineering, in politics as in management. It is about the structuring forces, requirements, and principles that must be in place for things to work. And it is about the formula for success.

Cybernetics: The Science of Control and Communication

Wiener first happened upon the question of control in 1943, when the U.S. Army commissioned him to study the problem of "anti-aircraft artillery." His brief: To establish how field artillery could strike more enemy bombers. The underlying question about control was (and remains): How to hit a moving target? At the time, the state-of-the-art answer was that the shooter should raise his sights a little. But pilots perform all kinds of evasive maneuvers when they come under fire. As a mathematician and specialist in statistical methods, Wiener used radar information to predict the most likely position of aircraft at any given time and connected these data electronically to the gun-laying (i.e., target) mechanism. The aircraft and the cannon now "communicated" with each other in a closed loop, so to speak: If the aircraft changed direction, the cannon fired in a different direction, prompting the pilot to perform a new maneuver.

At the time, control was also being investigated and debated in other scientific fields. However, each participant at the Macy conferences had a different (i.e., specialist) view, and hence a different understanding, of control. Accordingly, 3 years lapsed before they began to understand each other and to establish what control is. The more they understood, the more unifying principles and laws they found that applied across all areas of science. Control problems follow the same pattern: In a dynamic environment, without causal relations being known, and despite ambivalent information, decisions are made, consciously or automatically, and things are changed such that a target value is attained and remains stable. For instance, control mechanisms distributed in our body keep its temperature constant at 36.6 degrees Celsius, even if the environment is much warmer or colder.

From the Macy conferences emerged a general theory of control, in which the principles of functioning began to be examined and systematized. Why does not a chestnut turn into an oak? And why does the oak need an acorn? How must something be designed to achieve a specific goal? Considering these questions, the "Macy" scientists turned the previous logic of causal relationships upside down: An earlier event is explained by a later one, that is, by its future purpose rather than by its past. The control process is not determined by past events, but by future ones. In an ever more complex society, in which ever less can be deduced about the whole from studying the parts, and in which we know increasingly less what exactly is happening, this teleological reversal is a helpful trick. Not the past, but the future determines the present. How does that work?

The most important findings of the Macy conferences included the *feedback principle* and the *principle of self-organization*: Design a system so that it can organize, control, and learn itself. Each unit controls itself using the feedback principle: It takes aims at a target, continuously measures the extent of its absence, and feeds this signal back into the input. In this way, target values are attained even in highly dynamic and complex environments. Hence, the word "control" might be misleading: It refers not to the explicit control that stands opposed to a system, but the implicit self-control built into that system. Self-control arises when we think in cycles and attribute the consequences of an action to its causes. This circularity is a universal principle. Still unknown in this form in the 1940s and 50s, it has long been evident in old folk wisdom: The way we treat others is the way we will be treated. We reap what we sow.

In 1948, Norbert Wiener published his findings and those of the Macy conferences and announced the discovery of a new, universal science: a "*science of everything*." In search of a name for the science of control, he used the image of a helmsman bearing toward a lighthouse. Constantly driven off course by the currents and winds, he needs to keep readjusting his bearings. He does not know exactly what is going to happen, nor what is coming. He knows neither the exact facts nor the connections, and yet still achieves his goal (Fig. 1). The Greek word for helmsman being *cybernetes*, Wiener called the new science *"Cybernetics."* In Latin, the helmsman is the *gubernator*—a word still preserved in terms associated with control or steering such as government, governor, or corporate governance. Wiener gave his

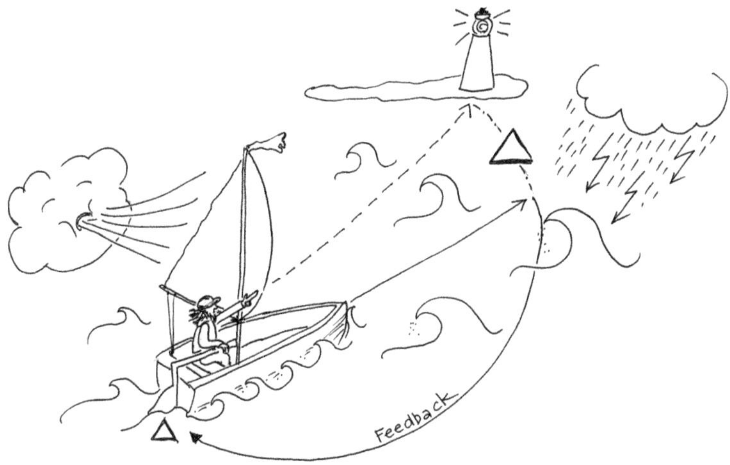

Fig. 1 Kybernetes: The Helmsman

book an amazing title: *Cybernetics: Or Control and Communication in the Animal and the Machine.*[2]

The first part of Wiener's title acknowledges that control depends on communication, which in turn affects control. "Control and Communication": When you cut the wire, nothing works anymore. Wiener thus highlighted the fundamental importance of information. Meanwhile, mathematical communication theory, largely developed by Claude Shannon, had also emerged: information theory. Control and communication belong together and are interdependent. If something difficult is to succeed, *circular communication loops* or "feedback loops" are required.

The second part of Wiener's title—"in the Animal and the Machine"—shattered the worldview prevailing at the time: The animate and the inanimate world have much more in common than was taught at schools and universities. Biology and engineering were now linked through common principles, despite being studied and taught as distinct disciplines. The previous Cartesian separation of these worlds was obviously mistaken, now that the biologist suddenly got along with the engineer, the anthropologist with the physicist, or the sociologist with the mathematician. "In the Animal and the Machine": The second part of Wiener's title contains a provocative statement: The laws and principles of functioning are universal. Success always occurs according to the same pattern, which can and must be applied to all types of complex systems. Wiener's book and its discoveries caused great excitement in science and philosophy.

[2]Norbert Wiener. *Cybernetics: Or Control and Communication in the Animal and the Machine*, 2nd ed. (Cambridge, MA: MIT Press, 1948).

Application to Technology

Pioneering discoveries are as a rule first reflected in technical applications. As happened in this case: From the 1950s, cybernetics and advances in information theory began impacting almost all areas of life. They boosted automation and robotics, helped develop new products and services, and created new industries. Radio, telephone, and television continuously improved and became affordable for more and more people. In England, America, and Germany, under the influence of Alan Turing, the first, universally programmable computers were built—so-called "electronic brains." These machines were no longer used to strengthen muscle power, but intelligence. Thinking machines emerged that independently powered the production lines of automotive plants. Cars, airplanes, ships, railways, and space travel developed further with the help of cybernetics and reached new levels of performance.

In the 1950s, the science of control and communication began spreading across the world. After the Americans, the Soviet Union began harnessing the new science to its advantage. The 1957 Sputnik crisis epitomized Soviet success. At the same time, the word cybernetics became negatively connotated in the anti-Russian America of the Cold War. With the Soviets using the term increasingly, the Americans opted for others, including Artificial Intelligence (AI) and Information Technology (IT). These, however, eroded the original universality and interdisciplinarity of cybernetics.

In the subcultures of the late 1960s, terms such as cyborg, cyberspace, cybersex, or cyberwar were coined in the western United States. Yet these new designations no longer bore any relation to the idea of cybernetics as a science of control and communication. Irrespective of terminology, cybernetics in the postwar period led to a technological and economic upswing that has continued to this day and is now culminating in the digitalization and networking of things in the context of Industry 4.0. Reality has caught up with the most utopian ideas.

There are always phases in the development of societies in which change is particularly dramatic. Major transitions are sometimes only recognized as such much later, through the historian's lens. The exploration of information, communication, and control that began in the 1950s heralded such a seismic transition. Besides matter and energy, information now became used as the third basic parameter of nature, while communication became recognized as a binding factor in operations as well as in society. The preoccupation with matter had produced the agricultural society, that with energy the industrial one.

Today, we are experiencing the development toward an information or knowledge society, as it is sometimes called. In this society, the systematic use of information is crucial to success. Also, knowledge is becoming more important than capital—because today's society is changed by knowledge and controlled by information. Or as McCulloch put it in the mid-1960s: "Power resides where information resides."[3] Organizations that have been successful for centuries, such as the Catholic Church, political institutions, the military, or even the mafia, have used this principle ever since they were established.

The transition from an agricultural to an industrial society, as well as the two industrial revolutions, in which mechanization was first initiated using water and steam power, followed by assembly line or mass production using electricity, were marked by major social and economic shocks. The current transition to the information society is causing as much turbulence and likely even more in the future. New technologies are leading to new solutions, which are making what exists today obsolete tomorrow. Schumpeter's mechanism of creative destruction has made entire industries disappear and new ones emerge. These are what Fredmund Malik calls the "birth pangs of a new world." He describes the "Great Transformation 21" as one of the greatest transformations ever experienced by the economy and society, one that will change almost everything we do, how we do it, and why we do it. An old world will pass and a new world will emerge.[4]

Figure 2 shows how, driven by cybernetics and information technology, new technical solutions, products, and services are spreading in the form of a new S-curve and replacing the old solutions on the lower curve: The combustion engine on the lower curve is giving way to electromobility on the upper curve, the printed encyclopedia to Wikipedia. But what about the quality of the organizations that should control all of this? Has their quality developed as quickly? Or are we not still on the lower curve in this regard?

Application to Organizations (Social Systems)

The great technical successes achieved by means of cybernetics led to the science of control and communication being equated with technology in some quarters and also to a somewhat uncritical faith in technology. This contrasted with the debates at the Macy conferences, whose participants understood cybernetics as a cross-disciplinary science, and who emphasized the universal validity of its "unifying principles," which corresponded to systems science. Besides technical applications, advances were made in other branches of science, yet were less visible to the general public.

In 1959, Stafford Beer published *Cybernetics and Management*.[5] He applied the science of control and communication for the first time to social systems, that is, to all types of economic and social institutions: How can managers achieve goals in a complex, constantly changing environment despite insufficient information? How must they design their organization so that it works reliably and permanently? Beer was way ahead of his time: In the 1960s, executives still believed that experience,

[3] Warren McCulloch, *Embodiments of Mind* (Cambridge, MA: MIT Press, 1965).

[4] Fredmund Malik, *Strategy: Navigating the Complexity of the New World* (Frankfurt and New York: Campus, 2013), p. 23 ff.

[5] Stafford Beer, *Cybernetics and Management* (London: The English Universities Press, 1959).

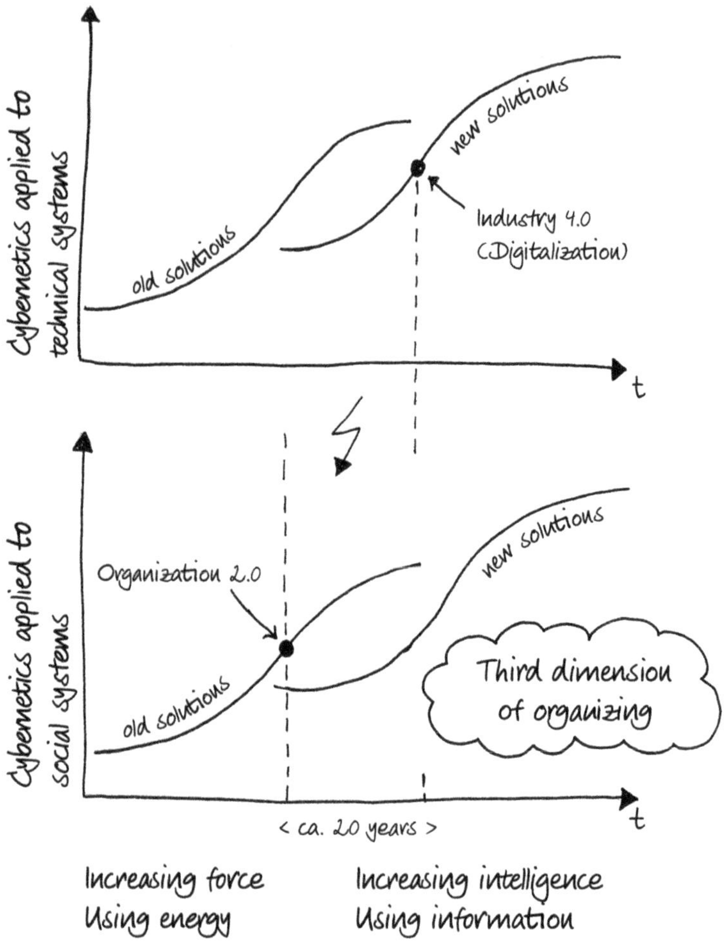

Fig. 2 From the Old World to the New World

talent, and gut feeling were the formula for success; science, moreover, was probably best applied in technology, yet had little to do with management. Complexity and dynamics were not yet an issue, and what were still relatively simple organizations could be managed without cybernetics.

After leaving school at the age of 17, to study philosophy at University College London, Beer was drafted into the army to fight in World War II. Soon afterward, he was sent to India as the commander of the 9th Gurkha Rifles, an elite British-Indian unit. During the war, he began exploring operations research, that is, finding scientific and interdisciplinary solutions to practical problems. After the war, he became "Head of Operations Research and Production Control" at a steel mill in Sheffield, and was later appointed "Head of Management Science" at United Steel, one of the first companies to install a computer, a Ferranti Pegasus, in the 1950s. Besides serving as a company executive, he delved into various areas of science.

Beer was only 22 years old when Wiener's *Cybernetics* appeared in 1948. Considering himself a cyberneticist, he contacted Wiener. Shortly afterward, McCulloch accepted him as one of several prodigies at the Macy conferences. McCulloch visited Beer in Sheffield and was so excited about his applications of cybernetics to management that he became his personal mentor. Beer later became "Development Director" at IPC International Publishing, one of the world's largest publishers at the time. He began publishing on management cybernetics, ran a large consultancy, and advised top managers and governments. To this day, he represents a rare combination: that of an experienced practitioner, who knows the world and the realities of management, and an outstanding scientist. His primary concern was to understand how organizations—no matter how complex—need to be structured in order to work.

Important Cybernetics is the science of effective Organization ... of which management is the profession. (Stafford Beer)

In the late 1960s, Beer's approach was taken up at the University of St Gallen (HSG School of Economics and Social Sciences) in Switzerland and became the basis of the St Gallen Management Model, giving the university an excellent reputation across Europe. Under the direction of Hans Ulrich, a small, practice-oriented team of researchers, including Walter Krieg, Fredmund Malik, and Gilbert Probst, began exploring what proved to be the most difficult problem for practitioners: navigating the unknown, dealing with the unexpected, and taking decisions under conditions of uncertainty. In sum: Confronting complexity and dynamism in all its forms.

The St Gallen researchers did not find answers in business studies and economics, but rather in systems science and cybernetics. Just as medicine was the science for physicians, cybernetics became the science for managers. In St Gallen, cybernetics became the science and practice of a functioning society and its organizations, which encompass, yet extend beyond the economy. It concerns the functioning of complex and productive social systems.[6]

The St Gallen Management Model was very well received in practice, because it better met the challenges of everyday life than what managers knew at the time from classical business studies. The idea that the core problem of management is mastering complexity fell on fertile ground in Europe. It corresponded to the nature of Europe with its diverse cultures and regulations. Occasionally, cybernetics was also applied to management in America. For example, in 1954 Peter Drucker put the principle of feedback and self-control into practice with his "Management by Objectives and Self-Control."[7] Nevertheless, the initial success of cybernetics in social systems, contrary to technical systems, remained a rather local phenomenon.

[6]Hans Ulrich, *Gesammelte Schriften*, vols 1–5 (Bern, Stuttgart, Vienna: Haupt, 1968).

[7]Peter Drucker, *The Practice of Management* (New York: Harper & Row, 1954).

Economy 4.0 with Organization 2.0 Leads to Turbulence

By the turn of the millennium, technology was already well advanced (Economy 4.0, increasing digitalization and networking on the upper S-curve). What was missing, however, was corresponding progress in designing social organizations. These have tended to remain in mode 2.0. Their performance capacity lags behind, is too sluggish, too inefficient, and too expensive. Moreover, they still exert control via authority and power instead of via information. They have become stuck on the lower S curve (see Fig. 2). Social development lags behind technological development by at least 20 years. The challenges of the new world therefore should be mastered by old-world organizations. And thus, we keep stumbling from one crisis to the next.

Rapid technical progress is leading to ever higher levels of functioning in the form of even greater performance capacity, complexity, and dynamics—at ever-increasing speed. Organizations become overwhelmed unless they, too, function on a higher level. They are also pressured by the turbulence of technological substitution: Companies are trying to gain a foothold in new markets or are struggling in saturated markets for market shares and returns that disappear as quickly as new markets emerge. In addition to technologies, customers, and suppliers, companies must also keep track of ever more stakeholders and regulations. Many are reaching their performance limits.

Another challenge is global interconnectedness. What began in 2008 as a banking crisis, with the collapse of Lehman Brothers, has developed into an international financial crisis. Since the financial and real economy are linked through debt, this crisis has quickly become an economic one. This crisis will eventually become systemic because individual banks and entire states cannot cope with the challenges on their own and need help. Trouble continues to brew. The real underlying crisis is the *crisis of our organizations*. Why? Because they still fail to use the principles of organizing and the formula for success that have spurred technological developement. They have yet to follow suit.

Even governmental and non-governmental organizations seem unable to contend with the major challenges of our time: massive debt (despite economic growth over the past 70 years), negative interest rates, migration problems, climate change, terrorism, the widening gap between rich and poor, demographic challenges. Jointly resolving problems across national borders is proving increasingly difficult, even leading the then president of the United States to predict the end of globalization in 2018. Wholesale reforms have therefore been demanded, so as to prevent the members of the international community from only pursuing their own interests.

In the same year, UN Secretary-General António Guterres also painted a bleak picture of the world. The UN, the embodiment of a multilateral world order based on rules and law rather than power, was in deep crisis. This, so Guterres, was due to the dwindling faith in finding international solutions to the world's problems. Citizens and governments, he added, were relying increasingly on national recipes, going it alone instead of together, and on populist responses. Guterres diagnosed an acute lack of trust in international institutions.[8] Large treaties were falling apart and nationalism was flourishing again. Not because nations function better than higher-level, international institutions, but because they do not function. Besides, their own unsolved problems and grievances matter more to them than more complex, overarching problems. For the first time since the last great war, the world once again seems to be unraveling. National and international organizations are more or less out of control.

How, though, can we get social systems to also perform on the upper S-curve and thus on a par with technology—such that technology serves humans and not vice versa? I mention this because people's fear of technology is linked to their justified fear that our institutions will be unable to control it. In practice, there is a certain lack of guidance and orientation. Essentially, we have two options: Either we get the most out of existing organizations with even better managers, or we give the managers we have more efficient organizations. Although, or precisely because true leaders are repeatedly called for in such situations, the second option seems to be more realistic. Organizations need not make work difficult; if designed correctly, they can also make it easier. This explains why managers have again become interested in organization in recent years, and why we are experiencing something like a rebirth of organizing.[9] The search for new solutions has made new organizational forms fashionable in business and industry. These forms are seeking to create better conditions for knowledge workers in a dynamic environment. They include the constantly flaring and ideologically charged idea of freedom of hierarchy, and thus the unsolved problem of autonomy versus cohesion.

Metamorphosis not "More of the Same"

To date, however, we lack a unifying and clarifying theory of organization. Much of what the new models propagate works in one organization, yet not in another. Or it works on a small scale, but not in an enterprise with 200,000 employees. New solutions are sought in the wrong place, because the common denominator of all organizations is neither size, nor character, nor industry, and least of all ideological questions. No, it is their complexity. How, then, does complexity emerge and proliferate? And how is information used to control it? These questions affect all enterprises, because *complexity and information are the core issue and the substance of modern management.* They challenge us just as physical matter and energy challenged our ancestors, who invented the horse plow and the steam engine.

---

[8] SFR, Echo der Zeit. 2018. Ein akuter Fall von einer Vertrauensstörung (September 9, 2018). https://www.srf.ch/news/international/trump-vor-der-uno-ein-akuter-fall-von-einer-vertrauensstoerung. Last accessed September 25, 2019.

[9] Martin Pfiffner, " The Rebirth of Organization," *M.o.M. Malik on Management* 18 (2010), pp. 21–33.

This, I suggest, makes cybernetics, the science of control and communication, the place to find answers: Because information is as informant and as relevant in management as in technology. Regarding the functioning of modern organizations, the focus lies on the flow of information, no longer on that of goods or finance.

Hence, the universal principles of control and communication must also be applied to management. We embrace these principles in technology but neglect them in our social systems. And yet, the laws of structuring forces remain the same—and are worth studying. As long as we try to improve our management systems without a knowledge of cybernetic control, we will cling to the principle of "more of the same." But as Einstein said: "We cannot solve our problems with the same thinking we used when we created them." Twentieth-century methods are only of limited use for solving twenty-first-century problems. People do not want reorganizations if these merely lead to shifting responsibilities around. We do not need a new organizational model with more of the same, but instead a real leap into a new dimension of functioning. We need something that transcends what we have. We need metamorphosis.

If we use the organism as a metaphor, then organization charts (Organization 1.0) were used to design the anatomy, business processes (Organization 2.0) the physiology of organizations. We have come a long way with this approach, but it no longer suffices. In today's new world, the information age, we need to shape the neurology—the organization of control and communication, and thus the management of organizations as a whole. This is the *third dimension of organizing*. We cannot cope with complexity without neurology. This concerns the informative connection and interleaving of the whole organism including its environment. The old ways of thinking and methods have not become superfluous. But without the third dimension, our organizations can no longer keep pace with economic and social turbulence—and in some cases even cause it themselves. Thus, I am not thinking of a few sophisticated organizational tricks. I believe we need to revolutionize organizational thinking. The science of control and communication has enabled technical progress toward Economy 4.0. Now, it is changing the world a second time, toward the controlling of social systems.

Important Communication is the binding factor in societies as in operations. (Norbert Wiener)

Which enterprises and institutions can claim that their control and communication work well? In the next two to three decades, we will likely see many organizations hit a brick wall due to their sluggish or overly complicated control system during the turbulent emergence of the new world. Just as communication is a perennial issue in most organizations. It is mostly understood as a cultural or interpersonal issue—only for perplexity to spread immediately, because everything has already been tried out. Communication and other supposedly cultural problems are more likely symptoms of a poor control system. Communication problems are far less about interpersonal relations than about an organization's nervous system being wrongly wired. If things are properly wired, many problems vanish into thin air. That, however, also means that control and communication need to be organized. Fine, but how?

The Third Dimension of Organizing

I began this Prologue with Wiener and McCulloch pondering a letter-recognition device for the blind and discovering that certain functional principles apply equally to machine and organism. Should not it be possible, then, to learn from the organism how to design an efficient control system? After all, our nervous system is the most powerful control system we know. Stafford Beer asked himself this question in the 1960s. In 1972, after about 10 years of research, his *Brain of the Firm* presented his model for control and communication in a social system that enables "viability."[10]

Viability is far more than "agility," which is just one of many features produced by an organization that is properly designed in the third dimension. Beer showed how the nervous system of the enterprise needs to be designed so that its anatomy and physiology function even when it is normal for things to keep changing and require fast response. Moreover, he explained how an enterprise remains controllable when it becomes more complex, as well as how control and communication channels need to be organized.

What makes Beer's model so interesting is its applicability to any type of organization, large or small, be it a public administration, business, association, or large-scale project. Second, it includes those elements that an organization needs to function. And it describes all relevant control elements and relationships in a single model. This contains what is really needed, but nothing more. To this day, it remains the only generic model of control and communication in a social system. As such, it provides the only starting point for the third dimension of organizing.

In the first few decades, Beer's so-called "*Viable System Model*" established itself primarily in science, where it has been tested and discussed worldwide. The subject of over a hundred books, it initially attracted only modest interest in practice. While increasing complexity already became evident in the late 1990s, managers were not yet concerned with designing an efficient nervous system. Now, in the new millennium, when control and communication problems are surfacing in all types of organizations, Beer's model is beginning to become relevant. Wherever it has been used in practice to diagnose and design organizational structures, precise and quick results have been achieved. Long-standing questions of organizing have been solved, and organizational pathologies, often only recognized with the help of the Viable System Model, have been laid bare. Interest among practitioners has soared in the new millennium. Increasing practical experience and a growing interest in new organizational solutions have resulted in the first books and speakers at international conferences reporting on practical applications.

The ingredients are now available for the first time: an increasing, global control problem evident at all levels and in all types of social and economic organizations; the search for new solutions; a model that has proven its merits in practice and in scientific discourse; as well as the technology needed to bring it to life. Now that all

[10] Stafford Beer, *Brain of the Firm*, 2nd ed (Chichester, New York, Brisbane, Toronto and Singapore: Wiley, 1972).

the prerequisites are in place, it is time to catch up with technology. Better functioning organizations give us a realistic chance of shaping a better functioning society. We are not at the end, but rather at the beginning of our possibilities. It is time to apply the insights of cybernetics, which have brought technology so far, to social systems. It is time to step into the third dimension of organizing.

So, let us begin. . .

Contents

Part I

Necessity and Benefits of the Third Dimension

1 Introduction

There are many possible manifestations.
There is one cybernetic solution.
(Stafford Beer)

1.1 Why We Need Good Structures

Today, we live in a world of organizations. Nothing happens in a modern society without at least one, although normally many organizations, some of them interconnected in supply chains, being involved. Not only the private sector, but also municipalities, associations, hospitals, educational institutions, ministries, governments, and supranational institutions (e.g., EU or UN) consist of more or less complex organizations, which function more or less effectively. We are directly affected by the quality of the many organizations that we deal with every day: We live in a family structure, in a community; we work in a company and deal with suppliers and customers; we spend our leisure time in associations (e.g., the local football club) and other institutions (e.g., the volunteer fire brigade). In all areas of life, whether we are sick, pursuing education, travelling, eating, or enjoying ourselves, numerous organizations are involved. Thus, the functioning of a modern society and our perceived quality of life depend directly on the functioning of these organizations. We are happy when they work, yet also annoyed when they do not.

This has not always been this way. A hundred years ago, people still took care of many things themselves—even in industrialized nations. If they wanted to cook soup for dinner, they fetched the vegetables from behind the house and fired up the stove with wood from their own forest. Afterwards, they read, or played cards or music together. They did everything themselves. Today, dozens of organizations are involved in one way or another in our cozy evenings at home: The greengrocer and his entire supply chain (often extending abroad), the electricity company, television and broading corporations, and so on. A hundred years ago, only a few

M. Pfiffner, *The Neurology of Business*, Management for Professionals,
https://doi.org/10.1007/978-3-031-14260-4_1

people were involved in organizing, and much worked without explicit organization. If we go back another few hundred years, the church, the state, and the military were the only large organizations. They were created and shaped by the brightest and most talented minds in society. Organizing was a matter for *the few*, not the many.

Over time, organizing has come to concern the *many*. Today, almost every manager needs to organize, be it a team, a project, a department, a division, a business, or an entire corporation. For a long time, the quality of organizations did not play a decisive role because good managers could largely offset almost any organizational weakness. They worked a few extra hours, convened a few extra meetings, perhaps ran a tighter ship, and became involved in a few more conflicts. Today, on the other hand, we can barely afford to spend management capacity on compensating for organizational weaknesses. In today's competitive environment, managers must focus entirely on their business and customers.

This makes the organization a bottleneck: Does this make it easy or difficult for people to succeed? Alfred P. Sloan reportedly said that "A good organization lets people do their job." He turned General Motors into one of the world's largest companies of the twentieth century, because many organizations obstructed rather than promoted work already back then. They spent much time and effort on matters little related to what people were paid to do. Matters have grown worse with increasing environmental complexity and dynamics, because organizations themselves need to become more and more complex. The pressure and demands are increasing. We have become accustomed to the idea that managers need particularly thick skin to endure the tensions of working life, that they clock up excessive overtime, sacrifice weekends for the company, neglect their families, and eventually their health, in favor of their job. We now seem to consider this normal. Often, discipline and good working methods still enable mobilizing personal productivity reserves. Ultimately, however, the question arises as to whether it really needs to be like this? Would it not be possible to build organizations so that it becomes easier to be successful again?

Organizing has meanwhile attracted even the attention of those executives who previously tended to delegate the issue to staff units and experts. In previous decades, other general management issues were pivotal: strategy, costs, corporate governance, finance, or culture and leadership effectiveness. In the next 10–20 years, however, organizing could well become the most important aspect of top management: For here enterprises have their greatest weaknesses, or rather the greatest potential for improving effectiveness and for tapping their greatest performance and capacity reserves. Organization is crucial for aligning the enterprise with the customer and thereby gaining market share, for shaping its productivity and innovativeness, for attracting good employees, and for making it profitable. After decades of not addressing organizational issues, this is where both the need and the opportunity for new and better solutions are greatest. Executives are realizing that they need to address this issue themselves. They can no longer delegate it, any more than they can leave strategy (and its development) to a staff unit. Enterprises will not outperform their competitors with even better executives, because these, too, will be in short supply for today's countless enterprises. Rather, they will beat their competitors by better unleashing and utilizing the existing potential through better functioning organizations characterized by less friction loss and higher efficiency. To properly design these organizations, we should not rely on experiences of the past decades. Nor is there enough organizational talent in our world. Instead, we need to rely on systematization and method.

1.2 Organizational Structure and the Process Organization at Their Limits

Essentially, we still organize today as we did a hundred years ago: We draw organizational charts. I call this pattern *"Organization 1.0"* and mean the focus on *organizational structure.* In 1855, railroad manager Daniel McCallum designed what was probably the first modern organizational chart for an American railroad company. McCallum was also a major general in the Union army during the American Civil War. He used organizational charts to organize the logistics of the Northern states by railroad, which could prove decisive in military operations: "No food, no battle." Roughly 50 years later, the term "organizational chart" emerged and, from 1920 onward, organizing by this means spread throughout the business world—more or less in the same way as we still organize today. In addition, issues such as efficiently designed production processes, automation, and mass production began to be addressed. In the wake of Taylor's "scientific management" and Ford's successful assembly line manufacturing, processes became systematically optimized. Later in the 1950s and 60s, the human relations movement, based on Elton Mayo's Hawthorne experiments and on Abraham Maslow's and Douglas McGregor's approaches to motivation theory, led to theorizing employee management and ways of influencing human behavior, although these remained largely academic. Other approaches were also developed at universities during this period. They were reflected in management training and led to modern human resource management. Little of this, however, entered the practice of organizing. The 1970s saw the emergence of matrix organizing, which gained widespread acceptance in business. In essence, this merely represented old-style organizing (i.e., with organizational charts), albeit now in two or more dimensions.

In the 1990s, business process reengineering once again focused attention on *workflow organization and processes*, initiating a phase I call *"Organization 2.0."* In contrast to conventional business process optimization, already applied in Taylorism and Fordism, Michael Hammer and James Champy, the two driving forces of this new approach, were busy rethinking and redesigning processes now that every enterprise had computers and information technology at its disposal.[1] They no longer viewed companies hierarchically, but from a 90° angle, as an end-to-end process from customer to customer. Process reengineering has become widespread,

[1] James Champy and Michael Hammer, *Business Reengineering: Die Radikalkur des Unternehmens*, 5th ed. (Frankfurt, New York: Campus, 1995).

and accordingly processes are dissected, analyzed, and redesigned in almost every organization today. The systems for performing such work are well developed. Applying other methods (e.g., Kaizen, CIP, or Six Sigma) turned the continuous optimization of the process organization itself into a process. The focus lay on improving the quality, costs, and time of business processes.

Compared to governance, strategy, culture, and leadership, which have attracted many studies, or compared to specialist fields such as finance, marketing, or law, almost nothing new was published about the proper organization of the enterprise as a whole until a few years ago. Business practice is still largely oriented toward old procedures. Organizational structures and the process organization seem to have been sufficiently well researched and tried out in practice. And yet, will we really come to grips with the new problems with even better organizational structures and processes—after decades of continuously optimizing these two established dimensions? No significant progress in organizing seems to exist. When we consider how many billions are spent on designing products and services, it is astonishing how little effort is invested in designing the organizations that produce these products and services. We remain stuck in Organization 1.0 and Organization 2.0. That would be fine if leaders were happy with their organizations. However, four symptoms indicate that this is far from true.

1.2.1 Barely Anyone Is Satisfied

If you ask managers whether their enterprise functions more "because of" or "despite" its organization, most of them raise their eyebrows and grimace as if they were facing an alien: "Thank goodness it also functions in spite of its organizational structure. We have organizational manuals and process descriptions, yet no one looks at these, let alone reads them. If the organization puts barriers in our way, we work around them. Rules and official channels are there to be circumvented. Without a healthy dose of pragmatism, no one survives in our organization." The good organization does not seem to exist in real life—only bad and less bad ones. Thus, people grow accustomed to the weaknesses of their organization, come to terms with them, learn to deal with them, and get by with a bit of thick skin, and a good internal network. Yet barely anyone is satisfied. Many believe they have tried everything, and some give up hope of finding solutions that work better.

1.2.2 Work-to-Rule as a Threat

"Work-to-rule" has become a popular threat among employee representatives and work councils. A paradoxical one because it means that employees will work exactly as intended by the organization! This threat makes the hair on any experienced manager's neck stand up. They know that if this happens, nothing will work anymore. If employees work-to-rule, the organization comes to a standstill. Trains stop running, trucks arrive late, planes cease operating at airports, and patients die in hospitals. This is symptomatic of the fact that organizational elements such as organizational charts, job descriptions, process descriptions, or sets of rules do not sufficiently reflect and support everyday business reality. Often, attempts are made to counter the growing complexity of the business with even more rules and standardization. This approach soon turns out to be mistaken. We are used to applying logic and common sense to deal with unplanned situations and to solve problems themselves. This explains why trains run on time, trucks arrive on schedule, airplanes take off, and patients survive, despite the odds. Often, organizational structure impedes rather than fosters success.

1.2.3 "Organisitis" as Chronic Disease[2]

Many managers seem to suffer from a particular reflex (or knee-jerk reaction): No sooner do they enter a new enterprise than they start reorganizing. Perhaps because changing things proves easiest. Especially taking up a new post, managers want to make their mark and implement change. They often start with a new organizational chart, because anyone can draw organizational charts, and hope this will resolve certain organizational weaknesses. Often they are disappointed because instead of solving old problems, so many new ones appear. The number of organizational problems seems to remain constant before and after reorganization. Friction and inefficiency simply shift from one place to another. In other cases, something changes on paper. Yet even if staff doorplates read differently afterwards, their tasks remain the same. Almost every enterprise suffers from too much reorganization. "Organisitis" even seems to be a form of hypochondria, because organization is a highly sensitive issue, because it affects everyone, and because change ushers in fear. More radical interventions lead to entrenched behavior among employees. They first go into hiding, and during the entire reorganization phase, they are concerned chiefly with themselves rather than with the customer. Productivity is often slow to increase again after a reorganization, which therefore should not be approached lightly. Peter Drucker compares reorganization to surgery—yet without anesthesia and with the patient fully conscious—and highlights that even minor procedures involve risks. It is often unclear when an intervention is really (not) necessary.

1.2.4 Fashions and Disorientation

A fourth sign that something is wrong with organizing is the dependence on fashions. These seem to change faster in management than in fashion. On the one hand, these are attempts to find answers to increasing environmental dynamics and to make organizations more agile. On the other, the unresolved perennial issues of

---

[2] Peter Drucker, *Management: Tasks, Responsibilities, Practices* (London: Butterworth-Heinemann, 1974, pp. 462–465.

organizing are dug up again decade after decade: autonomy versus hierarchy, centralization versus decentralization, staff versus line, flexibility versus size. The current fad involves a mixture of influences from agile software development, self-management methods, and the ideas of sociocracy (i.e., self-organized circles interlinked via representatives and favoring integrative decision-making). Whether the concepts of Scrum, Holacracy, or Agility will also establish themselves lastingly in organizations remains to be seen. At one point, small, agile, and autonomous is preferred, while 10 years later, the pendulum will swing back to collaboration and strength through size. Nor does the old problem of autonomy versus cohesion of the whole seem to have been solved either. And whether the currently propagated forms really lead to more innovative organizations also remains to be seen.

The basic problem, however, is that we have *no binding standards* to fall back on when organizing. We lack orientation about what is right and what is wrong, about when an organization is fully organized and when only incomplete. Lacking a reliable yardstick, we are disoriented and susceptible to fads. For the rest, we are left only with the individual experiences that leaders have made over the course of their careers. It is then argued that a solution has been tried before and either failed or worked very well. Yet every enterprise is different. What may be right for one enterprise may still be wrong for another.

Our organizational thinking still rests on the *model of the machine*. At university, we learned to first analyze tasks and activities, and then to pack everything that is the same into organizational units: Everything to do with money goes into finance, everything to do with people into personnel, and so on. This model is designed to reproduce processes. This works as long as the same tasks are performed and as long as everything can be organized and timed down to the last detail. However, when matters become complex and dynamic, and when tasks change from one situation to another, as in a soccer game, for example, the model of the machine no longer works. We would group all forwards, all defenders, and all wingers into teams, requiring team leaders to call meetings during the game to agree their plans and coordinate their next moves. They would lose every game.

Models are important because they help us compare organizations and discuss what is right and what is wrong. But the deterministic model of the machine loses its explanatory power in our highly complex social systems. An automobile plant functions differently from a hospital, a commercial enterprise, or a magazine publisher. Experience from one area can be transferred to another area only to a very limited extent. And a small company must be organized differently than a large one, even if they are both in the same industry. This makes it difficult for practitioners to figure out what constitutes the right organization for their company. They must find their bearings among different, competing organizational theories, current fads, and diverse experiences of colleagues in other organizations. They lack a unified, general organizational theory to which they can adhere and orient themselves. Such a theory would need to start from what is the same and decisive for all organizations, be it an automobile plant, a hospital, or a newspaper publisher.

1.3 Complexity as Common Denominator

How, then, might we compare different organizations having different purposes, characters, and scales? And how can we determine how well they function? We know how to measure the quality of products and services, as much as assess the quality of a strategy or that of managers. We know the standards by which we need to do this. But when it comes to assessing organizational structure, we struggle. Normally, we would take results as the yardstick. But even these need to be evaluated very differently depending on the enterprise. Is it a start-up or an established organization? A business or a nonbusiness enterprise? And what counts as a result? Short-term profits or long-term viability? Even if the performance is right, we cannot necessarily derive structural quality from this, because a good organizational structure, while a precondition for good performance, does not guarantee it. A poor structure, on the other hand, massively pressures performance. But, of course, in a thriving market, even the blind man is king. Even with poor structures, good operational results can be achieved for a time and under the right conditions.

At some point, accountants began making the classic four "Ms" measurable and comparable for managers by quantifying everything in financial terms: Men, Machinery, Materials, Money. And yet, not even this approach is suitable as a universal measure for assessing the quality of an organization, because it reduces the entire variety of enterprises and industries to just these four variables. The importance of money or machines, however, varies greatly from one sector or industry to another. What we need to manage, moreover, goes beyond the four Ms.: It is the enterprise as a whole, including all its interactions and interrelationships, which themselves include its environment. What threatens enterprises is the increasing complexity and dynamics within and around them. Every organization faces this proposition, regardless of industry, whether private or public, whether large or small. Except that complexity and size are two different categories: On the hand, large yet relatively simple organizations (e.g., McDonalds, the world's largest restaurant chain, which essentially multiplies the same processes and products; on the other, small yet highly complex organizations (e.g., a newspaper publisher or a hospital).

Complexity, therefore, is better suited as a universal metric than the four Ms. Not only is it the common denominator of all enterprises in all sectors, but also their greatest challenge. It is the right *measure for what we actually want to measure: The disorder we need to put in order.* After all, the purpose of organizing is to bring order to disorder. Organizational structure is the vehicle by which we create stability in an unstable world and enable ourselves to achieve a particular purpose or goal despite the odds. However, no one has yet managed to bring complexification into the fiscal picture. Therefore, it continues to be ignored in management equations. Unmanaged complexity manifests in dissatisfied customers, declining productivity, information overload, failing collaboration, internal friction, dissatisfied employees suffering burnout, or untapped business opportunities. The symptoms and manifestations of unmanaged complexity are manifold. And many of them cannot be expressed in money or numbers.

So if we want to make a statement about the quality of an organization, we have to assess the extent to which it is able to *master complexity*. "Mastering," however, is a word that easily leads to misunderstanding. In our context, it does not mean beating down forces, because complexity can be performance at the same time. Or as the German physicist and geneticist Carsten Bresch has observed: Higher capabilities always emerge from more complexity.[3] It is therefore important to use complexity and to deal with it in the right way. It is like a wild animal that gives us power when we have it under control, but can also kill us when we do not. Just as we know that in complex systems, there are always things that we do not have under control.

By mastery, then, I rather mean how we master a language or how our body masters the complexity of our internal processes so that we stay healthy. It does so neither on command nor by order, but by creating suitable structural conditions. It organizes its self-organization. There is no other way, because complex systems function like children, plants, or spouses: They react badly to commands and orders. There is no use in ordering a child to sleep or not to be afraid. We can, however, create the conditions for it to sleep or for it not to be afraid. Similarly, we cannot command plants to grow beautifully. Under the right conditions (sun, water, fertilizer), however, they do it by themselves. Thus, if we create the right conditions, the momentum of complex systems develops by itself in the right direction—and an acorn becomes an oak. I discuss these conditions in more detail later in this book.

Only assessing complexity enables us to compare and judge highly diverse organizations and to make clear statements on the seemingly perennial, yet insoluble questions of organizing. Instead of ideologies and fads, we will have the *tailor-made organization* for which we can determine exactly.

- How much autonomy and how much hierarchy and cohesion it needs
- How much we can flatten it and what its maximum leadership span can be
- How much flexibility and how much stability it needs
- What needs to be decentralized and what centralized

On the other hand, trying to introduce off-the-shelf, ready-made organizational models into enterprise is doomed to fail because every enterprise is different. *Organizational structures, like tailor-made suits, must be tailored.* Considering complexity as a measurable variable makes this possible.

[3] Carsten Bresch, *Zwischenstufe Leben: Evolution ohne Ziel?* (Munich: Piper, 1977).

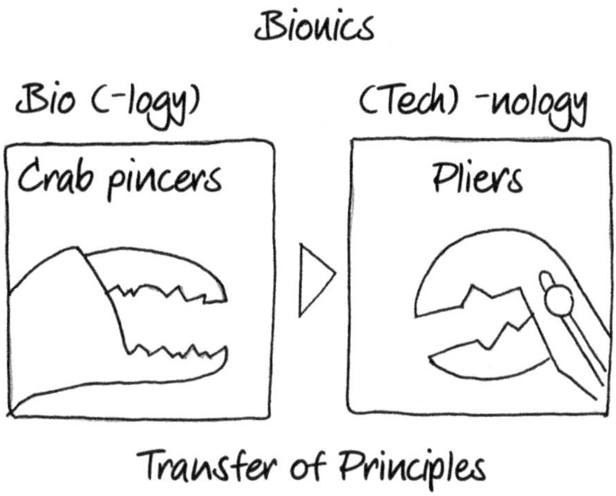

Fig. 1.1 Learning from nature: bionics

1.4 The Organism as a Model of Organizing

If it is simple, you do not need organization. But how do we make a complex organization function reliably? A functioning organization is robust, fast, adaptable, efficient, and effective, no matter how complex the environment. The entire history of our world is the story of permanently increasing complexity and ever greater capabilities. Organisms have learned throughout evolution how to deal with this complexity and how to use it to their advantage. So what if we could structure our enterprises the way organisms are structured, so that we could acquire capabilities and characteristics similar to theirs? As humans, when we want to go jogging, we make a decision, and millions of cells start working to implement that decision. And if we suddenly want to change direction, we have no problem doing so. While designing an enterprise like an organism may sound like science fiction, the foundations have long existed.

Not only *cybernetics* moves at the interface between "the animal and the machine." Also in the 1950s, *bionics* emerged as a new branch of science. It explores what we can learn to solve our problems from the solutions that nature has produced over four billion years of evolution. Bionics, then, combines bio(−logy) and (tech)-nology (Fig. 1.1). Like cybernetics, it has been applied primarily to solving technical problems. There are many successful examples:

- Dirt-repellent surfaces used as paint or as textiles (lotus flowers)
- Flow-optimized surfaces and shapes in ships and airplanes (shark skin, dolphin fuselage, eagle wings)
- Self-sharpening knives (rat teeth)
- Aircon insulation (polar bear hair or termite mounds)

- Lightweight construction for vehicle manufacturing (organic skeleton patterns)
- Bulletproof vests (spider silk)

Interestingly, the solutions developed by nature are optimized and exhibit the greatest possible efficiency. This does not mean that we should generally take nature as a model or use it as a blueprint. We neither want to nor can we. On the other hand, we can learn from nature's design, process, or development principles and transfer them to technical systems or even to social ones. This is the basic principle of bionics.[4] So what can we learn from the organism for designing a social system?

The organism is the biological model of an organization, for example, an industrial company and its interactions with its environment. The body represents the physical buildings and organizational units. It changes, grows, and shrinks organically with new internal and external demands. The organism eats up capital, labor, and raw materials. Its internal services energize and condition its body parts like blood flow and glands do the body. Its internal communication is a means of controlling and integrating the whole. It is in this last area, communication and control by the nervous system, that the great potentials for improving organizations emanating from cybernetics and bionics lie. Why? Because the level and quality of this communication in today's organizations compares to a sponge.[5]

A model based on the organism rather than on the machine opens up new horizons (Fig. 1.2). It shifts our attention from the idea of an organization that is designed for an unchanging purpose and functions as planned in detail. Organisms are not "single-purpose machines" but adaptable and able to serve multiple purposes. They are flexible, agile, and yet relatively robust in that they are constantly renewing themselves. This model also shifts our attention from parts to relationships and relations. And it shifts our attention from blue-collar workers, who perform unchanging, manual tasks, to knowledge workers, who already account for roughly three-quarters of today's workforce.[6]

Modeling organizing on the organism, we first discover that, besides *anatomy* and *physiology*, there is *neurology* (Fig. 1.3). This third dimension seems to have been forgotten in organizing so far, or has been designed based on talent and experience. In contrast, the systematic and complete design of neurology is missing in previous organizational theory. Yet this control organization is the main mechanism for managing complexity. We act as humans because of the foresight that neurology gives us, and we react with lightning speed because of built-in reflexes. *Neurology links and integrates the building blocks of our anatomy.* In the organism, these organs include the liver, heart, skin, or kidneys. In the enterprise, they are the

[4]Werner Nachtigall, *Bionik: Grundlagen und Beispiele für Ingenieure und Naturwissenschaftler*, 2nd ed. (Berlin, Heidelberg, New York, Hongkong, London, Milano, Paris, Tokyo: Springer, 2002), pp. 3–15.

[5]Stafford Beer, *Cybernetics and Management* (London: The English Universities Press, 1959), p. 132.

[6]Martin Pfiffner and Peter Stadelmann, *Wissen wirksam machen: Wie Kopfarbeiter produktiv werden*, 3rd ed. (Frankfurt, New York: Campus, 2012), pp. 39–57.

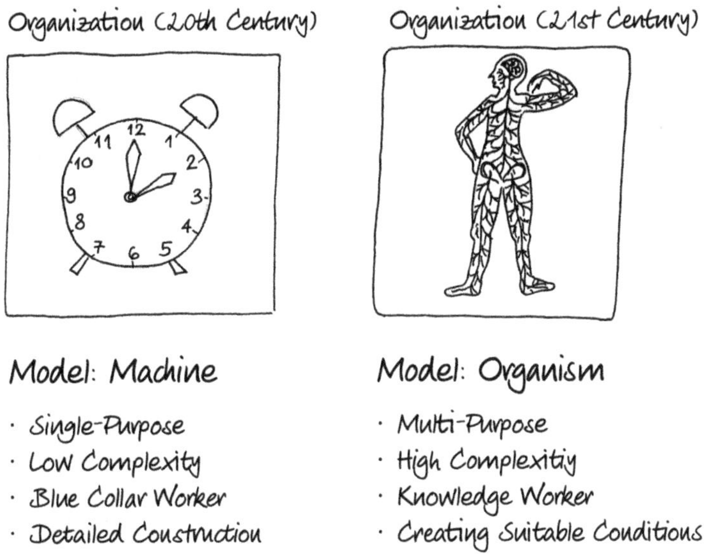

Fig. 1.2 From the model of the machine to the model of the organism

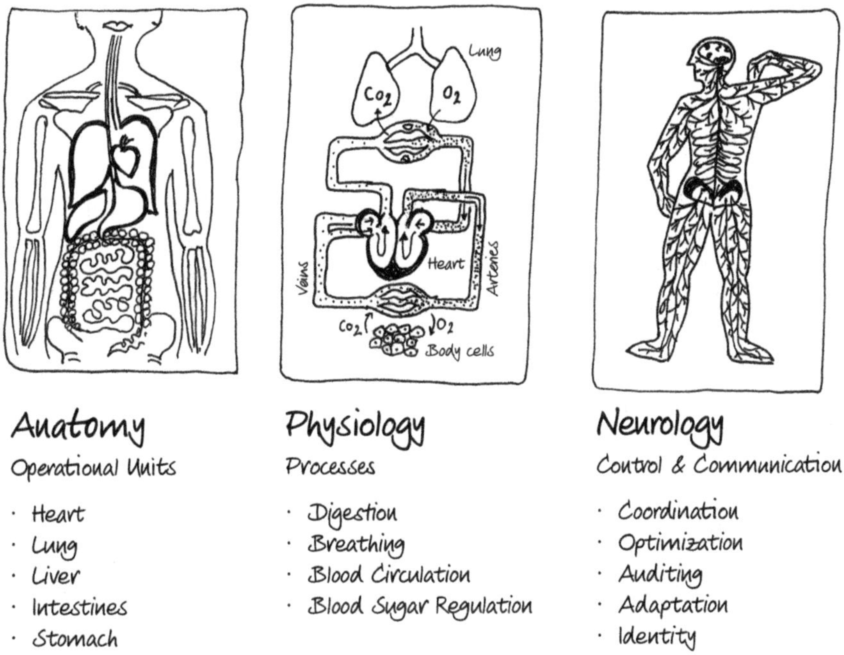

Fig. 1.3 Anatomy, physiology, and neurology

Table 1.1 The Third Dimension of Organizing

	I Organizational structure	II Process organization	III Control organization
Topic	Organizational units	Business processes	Control and communication processes
Analogy	Anatomy	Physiology	Neurology
Diagnosis & Design	VSM	Business process reengineering	VSM
Representation	Organizational charts Function diagrams Job descriptions	Flowcharts	VSM

Note: VSM stands for "Viable System Model"

organizational units that we find on the organizational chart. The anatomy cannot do anything on its own. Nor does physiology, that is, bodily processes (e.g., digestion or the cardiovascular system), or an enterprise's business processes, enable the whole to function. Only the interconnection of all elements generates the properties of organisms, and only this produces performance and viability. In systems science, we speak of emergence: The whole is something other than the sum of its parts. How these elements are brought together is crucial. For example, we can bring hydrogen and oxygen together in such a way as to create an explosive mixture. But we can also bring these elements together to create H_2O—with emergent properties, that is, ones not found in the individual elements themselves, because neither hydrogen nor oxygen is wet.[7] The proper interaction of elements requires the proper relation of the parts and the proper flow of information between them. Thus, with the right neurology, the whole becomes not simply something other than the sum of its parts. It becomes *more than the sum of its parts.* The result is performance.

If we apply the model of the organism to the organizational structure of an enterprise, we discover two gaps in the practice of organizing. The so-called Viable System Model (VSM), introduced and applied in this book, closes these gaps (Table 1.1):

(a) The methodology for diagnosing and designing the right organizational structure
(b) The methodology for diagnosing and designing as well as presenting the control organization

Table 1.1 shows that the classical division into organizational structure and process organization is not obsolete, but incomplete. Designing organizational

[7] Fredmund Malik, *Corporate Policy and Governance: How Organizations Self-Organize*, trans. Jutta Scherrer (Frankfurt, New York: Campus, 2011), p. 90.

units and business processes is necessary, yet not sufficient. If only the organs and physiological processes such as the cardiovascular and digestive systems were to function in our bodies, we might even be able to survive for a while. But it is only by designing the higher-level control and communication processes that we become viable. This applies to the organism as much as it does to the enterprise. The neuron and the manager must only fulfill one core task: decide. In order to decide, both need the right information. And in order for something to happen, a decision needs to be communicated at the right places. Ultimately, then, organizing is about three core questions:

- Who decides (or controls) what?
- Based on which information?
- And must inform whom?

Some of these questions can be clarified via the anatomy (i.e., the grouping of tasks into organizational units), others by defining business processes. In order for a manager to also be a good helmsman of the whole, the third dimension of organizing is needed: *The control organization, which also includes the communication processes.* Now that we have the necessary communication technology at our disposal, we should not simply use it to siliconize what has happened. Rather, we need to ask ourselves what the enterprise must look like if it is to be managed in real time and in sync with the increasingly dynamic changes taking place within and around it. Designing information, communication, and control processes becomes critical to success (i.e., mission-critical).

Important
We do not enhance organizing potential through even better organizational structures or even better business processes, but by making the neurology of the enterprise work.

To do this purposefully, we need a suitable model of the neurology of the enterprise, a model that generates the properties of a nervous system: speed, efficiency and effectiveness, adaptability, robustness, and even self-healing. Which information needs to be connected and which, by contrast, needs to be disconnected? Where is hierarchical control needed and where self-control?

It was long assumed that the brain, being the central authority, controlled everything. Today, we know that central control, which regulates everything in detail, only works in a plannable, deterministic environment. It is mistaken, however, to apply methods and models that work in a controllable environment.

in a complex environment. This is exactly what we are still doing by applying the model of the machine—precisely because it has worked so well in the past. Chess programs have been beating every opponent since IBM's Deep Blue first defeated the then world chess champion Garri Kasparov in 1997. But a game of chess follows rules, with both players having full visibility of the situation and all variables, and the game remains the same. As soon as this is no longer the case, central control no longer suffices; one example is the end of the communist (planned) economy. What we need are subsystems that control themselves. If our brain had to control the processes that take place in our liver every minute, the problem of overpopulation would be solved.

Artificial Intelligence (AI) researchers have also found that robots with centralized control can walk nowhere near as elegantly as robots with decentralized sensors and actuators. In the end, the point is that more sophisticated systems need both: A central hierarchical control axis that provides optimization and cohesion; and distributed, decentralized, and autonomous control that provides effectiveness and agility. The critical attitude toward hierarchy in this sense is rather a criticism of the model of the machine, because hierarchy also exists in natural systems. This is not bad in itself as long as it is defined by the logic of superior and subordinate control systems rather than by people, power, and prestige.

The *Viable System Model* developed by Stafford Beer, the subject of this book, is not a model of a nervous system. Nevertheless, it distills the factors that a control and communication system must have in order to be viable. It focuses on "viability," that is, the ability to sustain one's own existence over time. This

corresponds to the principles of good, entrepreneurial management and good corporate governance[8]:

- *Viability* before profit maximization
- *Competitiveness* before increasing corporate value
- *Customer value* before shareholder value

Money, then, is not the ultimate goal, but a marginal condition and the yardstick for how well the customer is served and for how competitive the enterprise is. Viability includes adaptation and progress, but also robustness against shocks from outside or inside. The model goes beyond the profit maximization thinking that has become state-of-the-art and is therefore equally interesting for business enterprises, as well as for public administrations, nongovernmental organizations, or any other type of institution needing an organizational structure.

[8]Fredmund Malik, *Die richtige Corporate Governance. Mit wirksamer Unternehmensaufsicht Komplexität meistern* (Frankfurt, New York: Campus, 2008). See also Malik, *Unternehmenspolitik und Corporate Governance. Wie Organisationen sich selber organisieren* (Frankfurt, New York: Campus, 2008), p. 156.

1.5 Structure and Benefits of this Book

1.5.1 Purpose

Since Stafford Beer's first publications on the *Viable System Model*, much has developed in the direction he foresaw. At that time, only a few firms owned computers, which also looked like giant monsters fed with punch cards. And every firm was wondering how best to use the new, groundbreaking technology. Even then, long before business process reengineering, Beer asked the opposite question: Now that we have the new technology, what might our firms look like? What do we need to rethink now that we have all the opportunities this technology opens up? Today, companies are full of computers, so that not having one on your desk has become a status symbol. But as long as we use information technology only to support our traditional organizational and management structures, to make existing things faster, easier, and cheaper, we will remain trapped in the first two dimensions of organizing: organizational structure and especially the process organization.

This book is about how we can develop the third, neurological dimension in our institutions and use new technologies to that end. As mentioned, the field of organization needs to take a great step forward, because the crises of modern society are not caused simply by greed for money, as is often claimed, but primarily by mismanagement. The book is intended to enable readers to create their own third dimension of organizing with the help of the Viable System Model, so that leadership can once again become simpler and more effective, and thus perhaps even more enjoyable.

In this sense, this book is not about the Viable System Model per se, but *about putting the Viable System Model into practice*. It takes readers through the diagnosis and design process and answers questions about application with practical examples based on my own experience. I have applied the model as a management consultant and entrepreneur on all continents and in all types of institutions for over 25 years. Enough has been written about the model itself (see References). This book, on the other hand, is about how to go from knowing about the model to using it in your own enterprise. *It is about application*. In fact, it is part of the cybernetic tradition of dealing with practice, because it is only in practice that application issues become apparent, and thanks to which we learn and innovate. Only application promises benefits. Without innovation, the best invention remains ineffective.

The reader must be willing to rethink the subject of organization and to throw familiar ideas and concepts overboard for the time being in order to make room for a new way of looking at things. This is what the future expects of us: That we constantly question our certainties and discover new ways and possibilities to better shape our lives. This new perspective does not simply fall into our laps. It needs to be devised and worked out. Unfortunately, there is no "One Minute Manager" for applying the model. Also, it encompasses more than the famous handful of principles found in the literature on how to achieve success. It is about actively engaging with the model. And yet: The prospective rewards justify the effort.

This book is aimed at *practitioners who are responsible for a unit that must deliver results*, whatever that unit may be, and who are no longer willing to accept the shortcomings of classical organization. It is also aimed at the general manager, not merely the organization expert, because organizing is a general management task. Every manager today has to organize if the whole is to work. Just as every manager needs to tackle things themselves if they really want to utilize the great potentials. Today, no one can avoid the organizational issues of the third dimension nor the findings of management cybernetics. Nongovernmental organizations will be able to cope with their tasks less and less without actively designing the third dimension. Just as those firms who design that dimension sooner than their competitors will gain decisive competitive advantages.

1.5.2 Working with the Viable System Model: Personal Experience

I first came across the model toward the end of the 1980s, in a lecture by Fredmund Malik at the University of St. Gallen. His lectures were very popular with students because they were concerned with practice yet were scientifically sound. At that time, Malik was already managing director of the Management Center St. Gallen. He expanded the Center, originally part of the university, and established to disseminate the St. Gallen Management Model as an interface between science and practice, into a large management consultancy and training company. In the late 1990s, thanks to Malik, I met Stafford Beer in Toronto, who became my mentor during the last years of his life. Besides training me during many long personal meetings in Canada, England, Wales, and Switzerland, Beer also served as a tutor in Viable System Model application projects. In subsequent decades, on this basis and as a member of staff at the Management Center St. Gallen, I tutored about a hundred companies in applying the VSM and trained thousands of managers. This enabled me to study and learn from practical application issues in all kinds of firms and institutions in Europe, America, and Asia. The success achieved in these organizations justifies this book. I will intersperse examples and accounts from these practical experiences wherever they serve the purpose of illustration.

Stafford Beer published three related companion volumes on his Viable System Model in a series titled "The Managerial Cybernetics of Organization":

- *Brain of the Firm* (1972):[9] Develops the Viable System Model, based on insights from studying the nervous system.
- *The Heart of Enterprise* (1979):[10] Interprets the model as applied to an enterprise.

[9]Stafford Beer, *Brain of the Firm: The Managerial Cybernetics of Organization*, 2nd ed. (Chichester, New York, Brisbane, Toronto, Singapore: Wiley, 1972).

[10]Stafford Beer, *The Heart of Enterprise: The Managerial Cybernetics of Organization* (Chichester, New York, Brisbane, Toronto, Singapore: Wiley, 1979).

- *Diagnosing the System for Organizations* (1985):[11] Offers a detailed description of the diagnosis and design process.

My procedure here largely corresponds to that in Beer's *Diagnosing the System for Organizations*. For practical reasons, however, I have sometimes abbreviated or chosen a more pragmatic approach in my applications. Where new questions about application need to be solved, I have also incorporated my own ideas in some places. I have been inspired in particular by Fredmund Malik and Peter Drucker. Stafford Beer's books also contain more advanced content that I have not used in practice.

"Absolutum Obsoletum," said Beer: "If it works, it's out of date." It would be highly uncybernetic to claim: This is how it is done. The approach in this book constitutes one possibility among others—one, however, that has proven itself in practice. As Beer observed:

> There is no "correct" interpretation of the VSM. We have spoken instead of more or less useful interpretations. Even so, there may well be incorrect interpretations, in the sense that the model's power to account for viability may become denatured by their use.[12]

By the latter point, he meant trivialized applications by people who use the model like an organizational chart and thus remain trapped in the first dimension of organizing. However, as long as we do not misuse the model, we may well used it creatively and experiment with it. The basics are rich enough. Accordingly, this book serves neither "prediction" nor "prescription." It does not claim to be complete, but it does claim to be useful.

1.5.3 Practical Experience and the Benefits of the Model

For decades, the Viable System Model (VSM) has been applied and used in firms of all sizes, but also in hospitals, schools, universities, public administration, federal offices, and countries. Application has demonstrated the model's great diagnostic power. Used as a brief diagnosis to assess an organization, the VSM enables detecting the neuralgic points more quickly and more accurately than any other procedure that I know of. Where it is used to clarify specific organizational issues (e.g., business unit segmentation, de/centralization, or maximum flattening), consensus is reached more swiftly because discussions no longer need to revolve around feelings, opinions, and experiences. And where it comes to diagnosing and shaping the entire organization, the model helps arrive at tailored solutions that often burst

[11] Stafford Beer, *Diagnosing the System for Organizations: The Managerial Cybernetics of Organization* (Chichester, New York, Brisbane, Toronto, Singapore: Wiley, 1985).

[12] Stafford Beer, *Brain of the Firm: The Managerial Cybernetics of Organization*, 2nd ed. (Chichester, New York, Brisbane, Toronto, Singapore: Wiley, 1972), p. 122

the corporate bottleneck. In working with practitioners for 25 years, I have made five key experiences[13]:

First Top executives' interest in organizational issues has increased dramatically. They appreciate having binding orientation points with which to distinguish a right organization from a wrong one, as well as a consistent language with which to communicate effectively about key organizational issues. They also appreciate the transparency that the model brings to the enterprise—for themselves, but also for employees.

Second The VSM is a language of its own. As with learning any new language, it takes determination and patience to get into things. However, because the model is close to the way our body works, this language is quickly absorbed, and, because it is useful, retained over time. This helps avoid misunderstandings, because especially where organizational topics are concerned, people very often talk at crossed purposes without realizing this, until emotions run high. Establishing the model in the minds of managers at all management levels leads to a kind of "genetic code" that has a self-organizing effect. Establishing the same model in all fractals of the organization, and logically joining these models with each other, creates a functioning overall organization. Many organizational problems then no longer need to be solved because they resolve themselves.

Third The model creates an unfamiliar way of looking at things, because it brings to light how things really work. It fills the white spaces in the organizational chart. Thinking in terms of communication channels rather than "boxes," and in terms of cycles rather than linear processes, is new and unfamiliar to many practitioners, and sometimes even to engineers. The focus shifts from what the firm is to what it does. Relationships and relations become more important than the elements themselves and than the physical organizational units in which we are used to thinking. This may cause irritation at first.

Fourth The unfamiliar perspective generates relevant and often quite different and new insights. I have often seen executives locate the problem in the people they are dealing with, for example. After illumining matters with the Viable System Model, they recognized the underlying, structural problem that was forcing these people into their behaviors. Whether we recognize the cause or just the symptom depends on the model through which we view the world. The data remain the same, but the interpretations can be fundamentally different. Copernicus looked through his telescope at the same stars as his predecessors and contemporaries—and yet, his findings were fundamentally different because he had a different model for

[13]Martin Pfiffner, "Five Experiences with the Viable System Model," *Kybernetes*, Vol 39, No 9/10 (Emerald, 2010), pp. 1615–1626.

interpreting what he saw.[14] Through the lenses of the third dimension, things become unmistakable that we would not even have perceived through the lenses of our classical models of structure and sequence. In this sense, the Viable System Model is suitable as a "model in the background," which enables quickly diagnosing the neuralgic points in an organization with minimal effort.

Fifth I have spent many long evenings discussing the VSM's practical benefits with executives whom I was applying the model with. They highlighted five benefits in particular:

1. The VSM creates organizational conditions for gaining market share by clearly anchoring responsibility for customer benefits.
2. The VSM relieves senior management. It frees up time for senior management to perform their actual tasks and thus increases their effectiveness many times over. This in turn increases the power of innovation and implementation.
3. The VSM reduces costs and increases productivity by accelerating, decluttering, simplifying, and flattening the organization.
4. The VSM makes the organization more flexible and designs self-adaptation mechanisms to dynamic markets. Distributing control is attractive for good people in the firm and helps to create management trainees. Problem-free growth or shrinkage.

From an executive perspective, what the VSM accomplishes can be condensed into five points:

1. Its methodological clarity reassures us that we have organized correctly and completely; it frees us from the feeling that we perhaps ought to have done things differently after all.
2. Its diagnostic procedure is fast and accurate. We recognize the need for action in terms of causes instead of symptoms, and thus obtain a thorough roadmap.
3. It brings clarity, transparency, and commitment to the organization and ends the endless discussions and conflicts associated with it.
4. It makes structure the "enabling link" between strategy and culture. It resolves many communication problems.
5. It integrates outside and inside, present and future, organizational structure and process organization, leadership and performance organization, lower and higher management levels in a systematic, holistic model.

The usefulness of this book can only be derived from understanding the model as a whole rather than from studying individual chapters. The model helps us see any organization through different eyes.

---

[14] Fredmund Malik, *Navigieren in Zeiten des Umbruchs: Die Welt neu denken und gestalten* (Frankfurt, New York: Campus, 2015), pp. 17–19. English edition: *Navigating into the Unknown: A New Way for Management, Governance and Leadership* (Frankfurt, New York: Campus, 2016).

1.5.4 How This Book Is Structured

The *Prologue* outlines the basic theme and emphasizes that technical systems still perform far better than social systems (i.e., our firms and social institutions). I argue that this advantage must be cut if business and society are to function better. Further, I show that cybernetics, which initiated technical (yet also technological) success, is the same scientific basis that will enable social systems to succeed. Control and communication are the central issues in our information society, and information is the basic variable with which management must primarily deal. The third dimension of organizing involves designing these control and communication structures, and the template for doing so is our own nervous system.

Part I shows, on the one hand, that a modern society depends on the quality of its organizations and that today every manager must organize. I examine the current state of organizing and argue that twenty-first-century organizations must discard the model of the machine and turn to the model of the organism. I identify complexity as the common denominator of every organization, whether business or nonbusiness. I posit that using rather than reducing complexity is a decisive competitive factor. Organizational structure and the process organization represent the first two dimensions of organizing, analogous to the body's anatomy and physiology. The third dimension is neurology, that is, the communication and decision-making processes that enable control. It is through these that complexity is mastered. Based on four billion years of experience, the best template is the nervous system of organisms. Next, I examine the practice of organizing, which is the focus of this book. I highlight and discuss the cardinal errors of organizing.

Part II introduces the Viable System Model (VSM). I apply it by way of example to very different systems: a family, a project, a firm, and a state. This demonstrates the general validity of the model and enables more comprehensively understanding it. The model, as we will see, is recursive: The same structure is repeated at every level of management. Thus, organizations, regardless of size, can be designed with one and the same model. Finally, I focus on the people in organizations. Considering why they usually "wear different hats," I argue that hierarchy is nothing bad, yet necessary for reasons of logic, as long as it results from the relevance of information rather than from a need for status and power.

Part III concentrates on application and takes readers through the diagnosis and design process. Every chapter concludes by inviting readers to apply what they have read to their own area of responsibility, be it organizing a team, a project, a department, a business, or an entire corporation. Only application and experimentation lead to deeper understanding. We will learn how to tailor the organization starting with the customer, as well as which control and communication structures need to be tested and developed and how. Part III also sheds light on properly dealing with complexity: It introduces the most important laws and considers communication performance and security.

Part IV focuses on implementation. How can the organization be represented intelligibly so that the organizational structure, process organization, and control organization can be interconnected? Which approach has proven successful in practice for implementing reorganization projects, and why should one proceed in this way? In addition, I consider some typical patterns of "sick" organizations in terms of the Viable System Model and show that the underlying pathologies would go unnoticed if organizational charts or process representations were used. Sometimes, anatomies lead to neurological crisis, that is, to overloading the nervous system; at others, it is the gaps in the nervous system itself. Finally, I highlight two additional methods developed by Stafford Beer in connection with the Viable System Model. They concern balancing the needs of today's business with the needs of the future business. This is where the most existentially important decisions take place and where the greatest risk lies for extrapolating past success factors into the future, thereby undermining the organization's ability to adapt. Team Syntegrity is a cybernetic communication structure for will-formation; the Operations Room is an architectural leadership and decision-making structure, as already used today wherever life and death are at stake and where systems must therefore function.

Later in the Bar At the end of every part of this book, I critically reconsider selected contents and clear up typical misunderstandings. The discussion between Sandra, Rachel, Marc, and David is a proxy discussion between the reader and the author, a technique also used by Beer in *The Heart of Enterprise*. I always enjoyed reading this part and having my attention drawn to particularly relevant points. I have therefore used this didactic device here as well.

1.5.5 Language

I deliberately avoid scientific language and use the language that I speak with executives. As I focus on application and practical benefits, I have avoided details that might confuse or slow the reader. I use terms that explain bodily functions without going into detail. Nevertheless, the Viable System Model is more than merely a metaphor. I only discuss its theory as much as is necessary for understanding. I refer readers interested in the scientific foundations of the VSM to Stafford Beer's writings, which discuss the axioms, theorems, laws, and principles in depth.

In this book, the word *"organization"* can always mean both, the institution and the instrument. An enterprise is an organization and has an organization. Language is not really clear here. I use "organization" predominantly for the instrument and sometimes supplement it with *"organizational structure."* Strictly speaking, organization (as an instrument) and structure are two different things. The structure of something is understood to be the constituents and the relations that constitute an entity and realize its organization. Organization, on the other hand, means only the relations between the constituents.[15] For our practical concerns, however, we can overlook these academic subtleties and use organization and structure

[15] Humberto Maturana and Francisco J. Varela, *Autopoiesis and Cognition: The Realization of the Living* (Dordrecht: Reidel, 1980).

synonymously. If, on the other hand, organization means institution, it refers to all types of institutions in the economy and society: firms, associations, communities, NGOs, public administration, and so on. The term *"social systems"* encompasses all of these entities, yet sounds a bit cumbersome and theoretical. I use the word *"enterprise"* instead, because this strikes me as the most comprehensive and clearest term.

Finally, researchers also distinguish "controlling," "steering," and "regulating." Once more, I have slightly simplified matters. I use *"control"* as the core term, in reference to the *gubernator*, the helmsman Kybernetes, from whom the word cybernetics is derived, and sometimes also mean steering or regulation.

"Leaders" or *"managers"* in this book are *people*, young or old, male or female, who bear a relevant responsibility for contributing to the enterprise. *"Senior management"* does not mean the old authoritarian boss, but the higher-level (meta-) control system, as we will see. For the rest, I refer to the glossary (at the end) and agree with Warren McCulloch:

Don't bite my finger—look where I am pointing.

The Ten Cardinal Mistakes of Organizing 2

2.1 Beginning with Organizational Charts

When executives talk about the appropriate organizational structure, they always do so in the same way. They meet in the boardroom, grab a flipchart, and start drawing organizational charts. Using boxes and hierarchical lines, they consider how they want to organize the enterprise in the future or how they want to integrate their latest acquisition, which unit should be located centrally and which decentrally, as well as where "solid" and where "dotted lines" are needed. Over their careers, all executives have gained a bit of experience with different organizational forms, which they bring to the table for better or worse. This approach is problematic for three reasons.

First, organizational charts are purely descriptive. They serve neither diagnosis nor design. They resemble maps of the organization and merely provide rough orientation. They depict the chain of command and the distribution of responsibility. And they describe who is to blame when things go wrong. That, however, is not why we build organizations. We build them so that things *do not* go wrong, and that requires proper design. Organizational charts show how the whole falls into its building blocks, but not how they interact. Dissection itself is not difficult: To make fish soup out of fish, we put the fish in a pot and put the pot on the stove. Soon afterwards, the fish is broken down into its components. But turning fish soup into fish is an utterly different proposition. What we lose in dissection is crucial information: *How do the building blocks work together* to make the fish function?

Hence, organizational charts tell us nothing about how things actually work, about whether an enterprise is organized functionally, as a matrix, or divisionally. No one with relevant experience would expect that from an organizational chart. In reality, the enterprise functions crisscross through the organizational chart. The white space between the boxes is often more important than the boxes themselves. Several essential things are missing from the organizational chart:

M. Pfiffner, *The Neurology of Business*, Management for Professionals,
https://doi.org/10.1007/978-3-031-14260-4_2

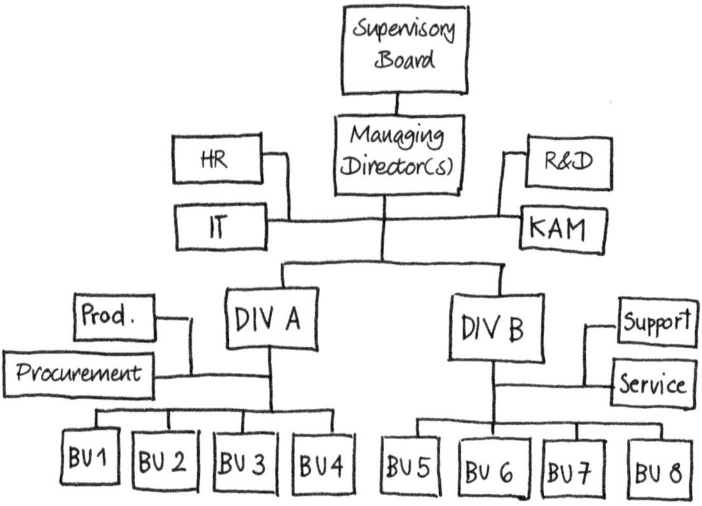

Fig. 2.1 Organizational charts

(a) Customers, with whom the enterprise fulfills its purpose.
(b) Committees, where decisions are prepared or communicated and through which managers coordinate and exchange information.
(c) Projects, through which most things are accomplished in an enterprise.
(d) Offices, which keep daily business up and running (if office staff went on strike, many enterprises would grind to a halt in next to no time).
(e) Meetings, through which almost everything that takes place in the enterprise is discussed, decided, and communicated.
(f) Traditional rules, which every employee knows and that are not written down anywhere. They are part of corporate culture. Staff know what to do, how to do it, and what not to do.

Organizational charts (Fig. 2.1) are like "Windows" on our computer—a surface structure accessible to our senses. They do not, however, show the underlying deep structure, the operating system that makes everything work. Therefore, they are useless for diagnosing and designing an organization. In terms of the metaphor of the three dimensions of organizing, organizational charts represent the anatomy of an enterprise—the organizational structure. They describe which organizational units exist, who is responsible for them, and who reports to whom in disciplinary terms. They show each person in the enterprise where they "belong," how the reporting lines run, and whom to turn to for information, decisions, or support. They do this quite well, as long as they are not overloaded. The organizational charts of large corporations, on the other hand, sometimes create the impression of mapping the entire Habsburg family—including its illegitimate sons. Organizational charts need not be simple, but they must be clear so that they provide orientation. For this purpose, we need them only at the end, rather than at the beginning of organizing.

Important
Organizing does not start with organizational charts but ends with them.

Second, when it comes to organizing, everyone seems to automatically and naturally consider themselves competent. After all, we all live in many organizations and therefore believe that we know a lot about organizing. This is only true to a limited extent. To really speak of having experience with organizing, we would have to have actively designed many organizations ourselves and then have experienced their functioning long enough to be able to judge the results. Very few of us have that experience. Most managers have truly in-depth, utilizable experience with perhaps five different organizations over the course of their careers. Importantly, they have not designed most of those organizations themselves. Moreover, experience with one organizational form does not easily transfer to another institution, even if it is active in the same industry.

Third, the notion of transferring organizational forms by means of an organizational chart is problematic anyway. Apart from the fact that organizational charts describe merely a very small part of the organization, we should not treat the organization a priori as an object and select the supposedly appropriate organizational form, as if we were choosing a ready-made suit off the rack, so to speak. As I have argued, in the context of complexity as a metric, organizing is like tailoring a custom suit: We start with the customer. Everything else we do results, inevitably, from fulfilling their needs. These are central to any good strategy. Apart from our goal to satisfy these needs better than our competitors, they are the fixed star by which we must orient our approach toward properly designing our organization. These needs tell us what the right measure and the right form are in terms of organization—for this specific enterprise in its current situation. We will consider how to do this from Chap. 8 onward.

2.2 Organizing Past Customer Benefit

"Put the customer first": Almost every corporate mission statement includes this assertion. Nevertheless, only very few executives can judge whether an enterprise is actually putting its customers first. Focusing on the customer means focusing on what the customer is willing to spend money on (this principle also applies to the service recipients of nonbusiness organizations). Now this differs from what we can deduce from customer satisfaction studies. Customers may be very satisfied with our services, but might never be willing to pay for them if they had to. They will only pay for what really matters to them—and will simply take the rest. What they are willing to spend money on is the target. This is where enterprises need to score points—and outperform their competitors. In the Swiss army, soldiers take their rifles home. Once a year, they are required to prove that they can still hit a target at their local shooting range. Time and again, someone scores ten points—on the wrong target—earning the shooter zero points. Likewise, many enterprises score ten points on the wrong target, by being particularly good at things that their customers are not paying for.

Important

Organizing starts by asking how to place center stage what the customer pays for so that it cannot vanish from sight.

Have we anchored responsibility for precisely these things in our organization? Or who else is responsible? And do we even know what the customer is really paying us for? If you ask five executives in the same enterprise, you will get seven different answers. And what about noncustomers? Because even if we have a 30% market share, 70% of potential customers are buying from our competitors. So it is worth looking hard and long at this question. Never be satisfied with one answer. Always question this point—also because it changes over time. It determines what must be considered the result and the performance in this enterprise.

We therefore need to judge whether the "customer is first" in terms of the customer benefit achieved compared to competitors. This is decisive for gaining market share, as longitudinal, empirical studies have shown: In the long run, those enterprises gain market share that exhibits higher relative customer benefit.[1] Customer value is the price-performance ratio, with performance defined by the *customer's purchase-decision criteria.* Typically, a potential buyer considers little more than five to nine different criteria before deciding whether to buy from this or that enterprise. When buying a car, for example, these criteria might be engine performance, safety, comfort, fuel economy, environmental friendliness, image and, increasingly in the future, social media capability. On the other hand, when executives are asked which criteria make people buy their company's products, their list is usually far too long. For them, not only are these important features of their products and services but they are also proud of them. Few buyers, however, consider more than a handful of criteria.

Sometimes executives also say that price is the most important criterion, or that price is almost all that matters to customers. Perhaps. And yet, we need to consider both sides of customer value separately. The question is: What is the customer paying for? Nobody just pays for a price. We always pay for a service. What this performance comprises interests us for the right organizational design. Whether this performance can be provided at a competitive price sooner or later always raises the question of an enterprise's size compared to its competitors. Larger enterprises, in accordance with the laws of the experience curve, have greater opportunities to work

[1] Robert D. Buzzel and Bradley T. Gale, *Das PIMS-Programm. Strategien und Unternehmenserfolg* (Wiesbaden: Gabler, 1989), pp. 91ff. English edition: *The PIMS Principles: Linking Strategy and Performance* (New York: Free Press, 1987).

on their costs.[2] The lowest achievable cost limit, which depends on this size, ultimately determines how competitive one's own price can be so as to still achieve the necessary margin. This brings us full circle: Because precisely when market share is still too small to offer a competitive price, superior customer benefit must arise even more from superior performance as regards purchase-decision criteria.

Thus, strategy and structure are closely related dimensions of the same question: How to serve customers even better exactly where it matters most to them? However, I have often seen executives instead design the organization *"inside-out."* They don't start with the customer's view, but with their own inside view. They start with the existing products and services and think about the best structure for bringing them to the customer. Sooner or later, this almost certainly leads to scoring ten points on the wrong target—at the latest when customer needs have changed. A good organization begins with the results it is meant to deliver, that is, with what should be understood as performance. Crucially, this is always defined by the customer or the service recipient, that is, *"outside-in."*

Good organizational structures do not simply emerge by themselves, through evolutionary growth. Only disorder, friction, and poor performance arise by themselves in an organization. They need to be actively designed. This requires much thought and a systematic approach, starting from a key question: What are customers really paying for? The better we anchor responsibility for customer benefits in the enterprise, the greater our competitiveness and chances of gaining market share. Section 8.3 discusses how to put the customer first.

2.3 Copying Competitors

Typically, executives grow somewhat nonplussed after discussing organizing for a few hours at the flip chart. By now, everyone has expressed their views and made suggestions for improving the organization. But how do we judge which suggestions are useful and which are not? How do we measure the quality of suggestions? In my experience, here is what usually happens: Someone suggests that we study the organizational structure of the most successful competitor before discussing matters further. The rationale being that if this competitor is successful with this particular structure, it cannot be that wrong. The suggestion is accepted with relief, and a study is commissioned. The idea is to study *"best practice"* in one's industry, in order to perhaps copy it. But "best practice" is not always the same as *"right practice."* In this case, this approach even systematically leads to *"wrong practice."*

Organizational structure can never be considered on its own. First, it is linked to strategy, which defines where the company wants to go. "Strategy is a big word for knowing what to do," Peter Drucker reportedly said. Thus, structure is the vehicle to get us there. Depending on where we want to go, we need a completely different

[2] Bruce D. Henderson, *Die Erfahrungskurve in der Unternehmensstrategie* (Frankfurt, New York: Campus, 1974). English edition: *Perspectives on Experience* (The Boston Consulting Group, 1972).

vehicle: If we want to drive to a mountain hut, we need an off-roader; but to win at Long Beach or Monte Carlo, we need a Formula 1 racing car.

Important
Structure follows strategy! (Alfred J. Chandler).

A good strategy starts with the current and future customer. It defines who this customer is. It also defines the service that the enterprise wants to provide based on its own strengths, and with which it can be slightly better than its competitors. In the long term, this can be achieved only if the enterprise optimally utilizes its own strengths. Such competitiveness defines success in a market economy. Customer benefit and competitiveness are the two fixed stars for managing the enterprise. Strategy, however, also includes the thrusts with which the enterprise wants to strengthen its market position, innovative strength, productivity, attractiveness for good people, liquidity, and profitability.[3] Structure, then, is the logical derivation. It must enable the interplay of enterprise strengths and customer needs and help to implement strategic thrusts.

If you copy your competitor's structure, you also copy their strategy. In other words, you try to beat your competitors where they have their strengths and where they are focusing their resources. But nobody really wants such a strategy, nor can anybody succeed with long term. Therefore, you cannot succeed with your competitor's structure, unless that strategy and structure have been poorly designed. So there is even less reason to copy them. Even if your organizational diagnosis results in the same basic structure as your competitor, it does so for other reasons. It is important for further organizing to know these reasons.

When we talk about organization, we need to remember that structure is linked to strategy, and to enterprise culture. The arrow in Fig. 2.2 shows that "Structure follows Strategy." But a logical connection also exists in the opposite direction: What a strategy is made for always depends on the existing organizational entities. A strategy process is therefore often not linear, but iterative. One starts with the cornerstones of a strategy, then adjusts the structure, and from this, new strategies emerge. The circularity—the interdependence of strategy and structure—thus becomes visible.

The connection between structure and culture, that is, people and their actions, is equally important. Structure determines and guides these actions in a certain sense. An authoritarian enterprise with a steep hierarchy and narrow scope for action produces a different culture than a flat hierarchy in which "entrepreneurs within the enterprise" enjoy great autonomy. Just like the type of leadership, structure also determines whether managers behave in a more active or in a more passive, wait-and-see manner: Do they dare advance? Or do they shun risk? Do they act creatively? Or more administratively? Are they quick or rather sluggish? Is

[3]Fredmund Malik, *Unternehmenspolitik und Corporate Governance: Wie Organisationen sich selbst organisieren* (Frankfurt, New York: Campus, 2011), pp. 152 and 172 ff. English edition: *Corporate Policy and Governance*, trans. Jutta Scherer (Frankfurt, New York: Campus, 2011).

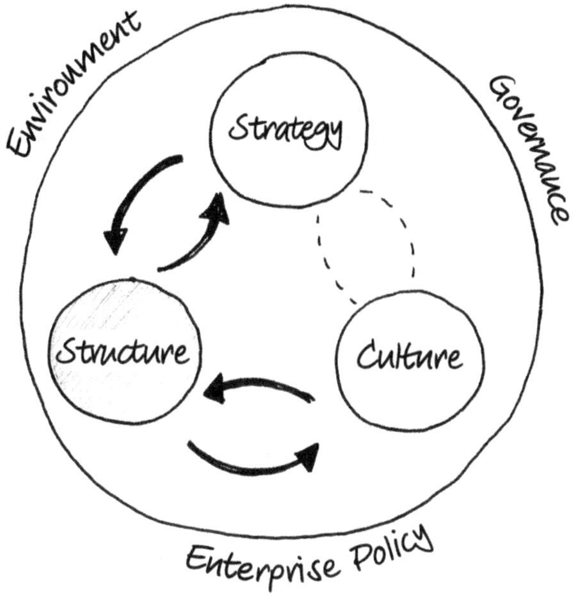

Fig. 2.2 Structure in connection with strategy and culture

implementation strong or weak? We are familiar with these questions from our private lives: Anyone who has children knows how strongly the structures of living together impact family culture. Even if these structures are not written down anywhere.

To repeat: Not only structure affects culture. Vice versa, culture affects structure: Structures and cultures grow together. We should not underestimate the resistance of existing cultures to change. Not every structure will be able to be implemented within the existing culture. For this reason, too, we should not copy our competitors' structure. Often, we need to make compromises because of people—and because of a very simple question: Do we have not only enough people but also the right ones to implement our ideal structure? That is the arrow from culture and people back to structure. Most of the time, the lack of human resources—the lack of enough qualified managers—forces us to compromise, not the lack of financial resources. Section 2.6 discusses how to reach the right compromise in such situations, and how to distinguish a good compromise from a bad one.

2.4 Optimizing Weaknesses

Above I mentioned that the processes for shaping structure are not always as linear as we imagine. Sometimes they are cyclical. Management teams often go through a psychological loop. During the design process, they suffer mental and emotional crises in which they lose sight of the understanding and certainty they have gained so far and start questioning everything all over again. They know the weaknesses and problems of the current organization, but do not yet know the future organization. They can guess its advantages, but when they imagine how things might pan out in practice, they have doubts: "Yes, but how are things going to work?" Lacking a robust yardstick to judge right and wrong, we are tempted to abandon or drastically cut back the design process: "Shouldn't we perhaps keep our present organization and just solve its most acute problems?" Although we should only change our organization if we really have to, this might be the wrong path. This is a common mistake.

That said, it helps to distinguish two types of problems: Those we must live with and solve; and those that would probably not exist if the enterprise were structured properly. The second type of problem *should not be solved—but dissolved.* Because solving such problems would mean doing those things better that are wrong and that present an obstacle.

Unnecessary weaknesses arise where areas of responsibility overlap and where therefore a constant need for discussion and conflict exist. Hence, an enterprise whose operating units are highly interdependent, and where many interfaces need to be coordinated, should not seek to optimize these interfaces. Instead, it ought to eliminate them, even if this requires drastic structural change. If another enterprise segments its business into product areas, but aligns its management structures with the legal entities of sales and production companies, it will not improve its problematic interfaces. These do not need to be improved, but avoided, because management dimensions intersect where they should not. This creates escape routes from responsibility, and conflicts become unavoidable. The enterprise must decide whether the heads of the product areas or the heads of corporations should be responsible for success and then align its management structure with the chosen dimension. Solving current problems will lead anywhere. Hence, the overall organization should always be diagnosed before addressing individual weaknesses. On the other hand, after the primary management dimension has been established, a residue of interfaces and problems will remain. Solving these, however, is no longer unnecessary, but about doing our homework. It is only when we have gone through a diagnostic process that we can be certain that the remaining problems are the right problems. Simply solving the current problems leads to great effort and little return.

Important
It is about having the right problems, not the wrong ones!

Alas, every organization has problems: The present one and the future one. New problems will highly likely appear in new places after reorganization. There is no such thing as a conflict-free organization. Because conflicts depend not only on which people meet to discuss an issue, but most of all on what kind of people they are in concrete terms: Do they understand each other? Can they rely on each other? Do they work together productively? Above we saw that culture impacts an enterprise's structure. But even more than corporate culture, our personality impacts our encounters with other personalities. Enterprises have all kinds of personalities: cholerics and "quiet types"; disciplined and undisciplined people; good communicators and those who will never learn. There will be some role models, whom everyone likes working with, as well as some sociopaths, whom no one can work with. Most of all, though, enterprises consist of *average, ordinary people*, with average communication and team skills. Thus we need to accepting that friction and conflict are part and parcel of the organization.

The trick (or rather the art) is to structure the organization so that it works well even when we just have average people and when staff are not saints. To function, a good organization needs neither outstanding interpersonal or team skills, nor emotional intelligence or other qualities that tend to be fashionable from time to time. It works with the average people it has. Not that we can dispense with developing those skills. We should, however, make it easy for employees to be successful, and therefore ought to build organizations that are customer- and people-oriented. In principle, this means reducing interdependencies to a level that is healthy and beneficial for the enterprise. This in turn requires diagnosis and design before we simply optimize the weaknesses.

2.5 Escaping into the Matrix

Of all organizational forms, the matrix generates the most interfaces. In a matrix, no one can do anything on their own without first quizzing five other people. Hence, this organizational form demands the most from its employees as regards what they are normally not very good at working methods, discipline, consensus-building skills, and robustness. The matrix maximizes the number of interfaces, and thus entails tremendous coordination and alignment effort. In practice, those interfaces that do not work because of personality clashes are simply disconnected and human bypasses are fitted. I have rarely experienced a matrix that worked as intended.

The matrix provides a popular yet only an apparent escape from the complexity trap. If, for example, an enterprise has succeeded in its traditional home market and then expands abroad, all of sudden it must optimize regions *and* products. Complexity increases. Besides, different customer groups may also have to be served differently. Before we know it, we have three management dimensions. Although they overlap, every dimension needs to be optimized separately. In the matrix, someone is responsible for every dimension. The dimensions intersect because a product manager can only be successful in regions and with customer groups, while a regional manager needs products and also addresses the same customer groups, while finally a customer group manager must be successful with products and in regions.

Thus, no single manager is responsible for business as a whole. Every manager's success depends on every other manager. This produces, first, meetings and, second, friction. Sooner or later, therefore, matrix organizations cause anti-market delays in the decision-making process and *productivity loss*. Second, they lead to a *loss of transparency*, because no one knows who is actually responsible for what. Third, they lead to a *loss of responsibility*, because everyone has excuses if the results are not right: The product managers blame the regional managers for not getting things right. The regional managers complain about not receiving the right products. No sooner do regional and products agree than they blame the customer group managers. This lack of transparency and wide-open escape routes from responsibility are deadly for an organization—at the latest when its business has become so complex that it overwhelms the interfaces. Complexity grows exponentially, as Chapter 9 shows, and therefore most matrix organizations are surprised by these dynamics. One consequence of overwhelmed interfaces is that tasks are delegated back to senior management. Any conflict at the interfaces unable to be resolved independently by managers now becomes an issue for senior management. All of a sudden, coordinating and optimizing the operational units requires so much effort that senior management is inevitably drawn into operational micromanagement. It must now spend its time solving urgent problems in daily business. Rather than solving complexity, the matrix merely maps it.

Important
Minimize the number of necessary—not "possible"—personal contacts.[4]

Ideas about what a matrix is varied. As soon as management lines intersect, we normally already speak of a matrix. In a real matrix, not only do the responsibilities of the organizational units overlap, but this organizational form also leaves unresolved the *priority rule at the interfaces.* Everyone is equally responsible, and therefore needs to discuss matters until a solution is found. This only works in "fine weather." Just as we should not build organizations for saints, we should not design them for fair weather alone. They must function primarily in rough weather. Before that, we do not necessarily need them. This is the problematic—and the most widespread—form of the matrix. It is also the *genuine matrix* because, unlike the *apparent matrix*, it does not clarify the interfaces but leaves them on an equal footing.

If, on the other hand, priority (i.e., the right-of-way) at the interfaces is clear, we still have interfaces but no longer a genuine matrix. The interface problems may not have dissolved but at least they are solved. An enterprise may decide to manage itself primarily via customer groups. Group managers then still need to coordinate with regional managers and product managers—but they decide and, just as importantly, are solely responsible for their decisions. Customer groups thus become operational units, while regions and products become supporting functions. This distinction is important for an enterprise to function (see Sect. 2.9).

Matrix organizations often emerge after an enterprise has been functionally organized. A functional organization also faces the problem of many interfaces. No function can really be successful without the other. Moreover, every function is solely responsible for its subarea, yet never for optimizing the whole. As the business

[4]Fredmund Malik, *Führen, Leisten, Leben: Wirksames Management für eine neue Zeit* (Frankfurt, New York: Campus, 2006), p. 199. English edition: *Management: The Essence of the Craft*, trans. Jutta Scherer (Frankfurt, New York: Campus, 2010).

becomes more complex, these interfaces typically also become overwhelmed. Once an enterprise has grown large enough, the business can be divided into several wholes. Business areas (business units, strategic business fields) are now superimposed on the existing functions and should be responsible for this part of the business across all functions. Business unit managers must therefore have clear priority (right-of-way) at the interfaces over functional managers. Otherwise they can neither make decisions nor be held responsible for results.

In practice, however, I have sometimes observed that existing functional managers are left in their current roles while new managers are appointed to lead the business units without further addressing the interface. In theory, this makes the business unit managers responsible. In practice, however, they keep working as before, because employees do not listen to theory but to the established and successful figures in the enterprise and to their superior. This maximizes bureaucracy but not customer value. Matrix organizations are created when it is impossible to decide which business dimension should determine strategy, and therefore which dimension should determine leadership. Moreover, matrixes are created when synergies are weighted more heavily than the autonomy of the operational units and their agility and self-control.

2.6 Starting with People

Very quickly, organizational projects focus on people and positions. No sooner do discussions begin (and are points written down on the flip chart) than matters get personal. What will happen to "Franz"? What about "Sonja" and "Walter"? Knowing that each of them matters for the future of the enterprise, we consider the social compatibility of the various organizational options. Sooner or later, we have to face this question. It involves a balancing act between what is right for the individual and what is right for the enterprise. Managers who consider specific employees too quickly are making a mistake. After all, the *purpose of the enterprise* is not to *satisfy* the employee but *the customer*. If you think of your customer, you will also satisfy your employees, because they will be working for a successful and reputed enterprise capable of appealing to good employees and offering them good prospects. This does not work the other way around: Just because employees are satisfied does not mean that customers are also satisfied. The "pursuit of happiness," propagated by the human relations movement in the 1960s, has not proven itself in practice. It works as an academic scenario, but anyone who has run a business knows that it takes more than satisfied employees to satisfy customers—however important they are.

Important
Only compromise in favor of people if you know what would be ideal.

Consequently, the logical sequence is: Don't start with people. First ask what is right for your business and for your customers. This ideal structure serves as a reference point for distinguishing good and bad compromises: The former are always closer to the ideal. But we first need to know what would be ideal. Because only if we do can we consider whether key people might consider themselves losers in a new organizational structure, and whether we still have enough good people even if we would have to do without them. Now we never simply have enough good people. Nor do all key people see a personal advantage in the new solution. Now that we know the ideal structure for our business and for our customers, we can make the right compromises. We can now change the structure in the right direction and then compromise because of the people. But compromising first, even before knowing what would be ideal, would be mistaken. Section 16.2 discusses this point in more detail.

It is equally important to question *historically grown structures*. Over time, every organization adapts its jobs to the strengths of postholders. Such personalization enables matching tasks and strengths. But people come and go. Your successor will unlikely succeed if the job was tailored solely to your strengths. Simply because an organizational structure worked in the past, with and for certain people, does not mean it is right for your enterprise. The managers at the time played to their strengths with that structure and therefore may have disguised or offset many of the organization's weaknesses and failures. However, as argued in the Introduction, today we can ill afford to waste leadership capacity on compensating for organizational mistakes. This is another reason why we should not start with people; we always need some idea of what the right organization looks like from a factual perspective.

Section 2.4 maintained that an enterprise must also function with average employees. It should not depend on outstanding talent. Truly robust enterprises go one step further. They build *organizations that, on the one hand, function perfectly well with normal people and, on the other, continue to function even when their weaknesses become decisive*, when they make mistakes and fail. "You must allow room for mistakes." This was one of American General Norman Schwarzkopf's recipes for success in the Gulf War in the early 1990s. He was not concerned with "creating an atmosphere in which people can learn from mistakes," as he has been misrepresented, but rather with building an organization that works despite its flaws. We cannot eradicate mistakes from our enterprises, but we can build them so that mistakes do not have a critical impact.

This principle was demonstrated as early as the 1950s by John von Neumann, a Hungarian-American mathematician and computer science pioneer, who also attended the Macy conferences.[5] He asked himself whether and, if so, how reliable systems (or machines) could be built from unreliable components. His discovery marked a milestone in the "theory of computing": Errors can be kept under control by correctly arranged components. Consumer advocate Ralph Nader used the same principle to shake up the American automotive industry in the 1970s. He forced car

[5] John Von Neumann, "Probabilistic Logics and the Synthesis of reliable organisms from unreliable components" (1952), In: *Automata Studies*, eds. J. McCarthy and C.E. Shannon (Princeton: Princeton University Press, 1956).

manufacturers to shift from the principle of "safe if used correctly" to that of "safe even if used incorrectly." A good organization does the same. While it uses its employees' special talents and skills as best it can, it does not depend on them. It remains robust, despite their shortcomings and mistakes, which occur every day.

2.7 Overlooking Nesting

Organizations can grow, reaching sizes and complexities that overwhelm managers. This happens for the first time when a small enterprise, whose entrepreneur or founder is still doing everything themselves, transitions to a functional organization, in which they must delegate individual tasks because there is simply no other way. Previously, they were doing the purchasing themselves, now they have hired the best buyer they can find. The same applies to the workshop, accounting, or sales. In principle, the entrepreneur divides the company into segments, each of which performs a specific function of the whole. Often, this leads the enterprise into a further growth phase, because experienced specialists are now occupying every important position. The disadvantage, however, is that now no one is responsible for the whole. Everyone primarily optimizes their function (i.e., the one for which they are responsible). This creates a typical problem: silos. The segments separate responsibility, but also cooperation. New problems arise as a result.

The alternative is a *different kind of segmentation*. Instead of dividing the whole into functions, it can be divided *into smaller wholes*. We can observe this principle in nature: A cell grows until it reaches a certain size. Then it stops growing and divides into several smaller cells, which in turn start growing again as a whole. In this process, every cell is a relatively autonomous whole rather than a function dependent on other functions. A healthy organization utilizes this principle. It segments the whole business into several business units (strategic business units). These comprise not merely one function but a business as a whole. This creates the entrepreneur in the enterprise. Dividing the whole into several self-organizing units has several advantages. It enables the enterprise to grow without becoming overly complex. It enables agility and robustness. And it enables easily integrating or shedding individual business units. This explains why many enterprises adopt this *principle of fractal organization*.

One mistake is that we only partially understand the principle of cell division, and therefore apply it incompletely. For example, many enterprises segment into individual business units but fail to equip these units with the vital functions and competencies needed to really organize and control themselves. For example, when the blame game starts between functional silos (see above), we often segment into wholes. These, however, are still too small to be equipped with their own functions. We therefore leave the existing functions as they are and superimpose the business segments—thus creating the first type of matrix organization (see Section 2.5).

Genuine nesting, on the other hand, requires that at least functions, competencies, and resources become the responsibility of the business segments, which influence the customer's purchase-decision criteria. The cell must have what is critical to success in its own hands. Otherwise, it can neither be held accountable for results nor can it achieve them. This much we know from organizations that must function as a matter of life and death (e.g., emergency services or military operations). All mission-critical resources and competencies are in the hands of the mission commander, who can thus make the necessary decisions on the spot and depending on the situation. Otherwise, the air ambulance pilot would not take off, or the infantry commander would not go to war. They are responsible for those belonging to their operation. Therefore, their cells are robust and largely independent of other cells or functions. While they want to rely as little as possible on others, they want to and can take responsibility for themselves.

Important
Create the smallest possible units but ensure they are large enough to have the mission-critical competencies in their own hands and are largely able to control themselves autonomously.

The other mistake lies in how we equip the management system of each cell. Rather than having one single management, a properly segmented enterprise has many managements at many levels. Besides having the necessary resources and competencies, each cell also needs a complete management system to be able to self-organize and remain capable of acting. *Thus, each cell needs its own operational, strategic, and normative leadership.* Not that each cell needs a large office with many managers: In extreme cases, the same person can perform all management functions.

In practice, however, this nesting is often corrupted or overlooked. This happens, for example, by defining strategy at the group level and tasking divisions (or business units) solely with implementation. Or vice versa: The divisions develop their own strategies while group strategy is no more and no less than the sum of divisional strategies. However, using the principle of cell division and self-organization means that each cell has its own strategy and independently aligns this with the needs of the enterprise. Each cell is given its own management at every level, which keeps in view which environment is relevant for that cell. It makes the cell fit for the future by noticing environmental changes, which in turn necessitate adaptation. Divisional strategy should emerge at the divisional level, where managers have the relevant information for *that* division's environment. The group level also needs a group strategy. This is more than the sum of divisional strategies, because the group's environment always extends beyond that of the divisions. The levels (group, division, department, etc.) are nested like Russian (matryoshka) dolls and always need their own normative, strategic, and operational management if they are going to function as a whole (see Chapter 5). Keeping track of nesting is not always easy. Managers often perform different tasks at different levels of nesting. They wear different hats, so to speak, and do not always exactly know on which management level they are operating.

2.8 Organizing the New in the Old

Sooner or later, every enterprise must ask itself how it organizes the new. Where should innovation—in the form of a new business field—be positioned organizationally? Consider an enterprise that is planning to expand abroad. Its strategy is to conquer new regional markets such as South America or China. Currently, it comprises regional business units in Europe, the largest of course being Germany, its home market. Who should be responsible for developing the new markets in South America and China? Should two new business units be formed for these regions? That, however, would require offices, a legal entity, and capable managers in these regions, which the enterprise lacks today because its current managers are reluctant to relocate to these regions with their families. Not to mention the huge expenditure and risks. The enterprise decides to organize the new in the old. The two new regions will report to the Business Area Manager Germany. "A proven and experienced business unit manager can be expected to handle this," managers tell themselves, or "it's feasible." The idea being to let the new units work with a small budget at first, to watch how they develop, and, if they prove themselves, to expand them into fully fledged, independent business units.

This approach invites failure. Successful innovation is one of the most difficult managerial tasks, because everything is new and uncertain. No networks exist as yet. Nor do we know the customers or the legal rules and regulations. We still need to test the product in this market, as well as develop and adapt it to local needs. That said, expenditure and investments are very high from the outset. Conquering a market is not easy. In any event, it is far more difficult than succeeding in an existing, well-known market with a proven product. Besides, the executives whom I have met in the past 25 years have too little time. They can never attend to everything they should be. Many feel guilty most of the time because they are constantly neglecting either their professional obligations, their family, or their health. To be successful, managers must set priorities. They do "first things first—and second things not at all," as Peter Drucker said. Most likely, they will not prioritize what is new, risky, uncertain, and bound to cause nothing but problems. They will instead prioritize what has made them successful: the established market and the familiar product. *The new thus starves in the old.* It receives neither the resources nor the attention nor the impetus it would need to thrive.

Important
Separate the new business from the existing business and position it at the top organizationally, or it will starve in the existing business.

Once more, observing nature proves interesting: How does it organize the new? A baby is "designed" as an independent organizational unit, which essentially is equipped from the start with everything it needs to be viable (i.e., able to lead a separate existence). Even in the embryonic state, its eyes, ears, and all other organs are innate and exist, rudimentarily or fully. As a rule, however, we do things differently in our enterprises: We decide that the baby will not have its own ears until aged four (it is not meant to hear everything at first). Nor will have its own eyes to begin with (the mother can look at things on its behalf). Also, the mother will look after the baby herself, allowing someone else to do so only when the little one is stable and independent enough. Thus: Task the *best managers full-time* with innovation. They must be able to focus entirely on innovation until it has become stable.

We should also judge novelty by completely *different standards*. Profits, sales, and costs are not as important to begin with as they are in the established business areas. In the first few years of innovating, we should focus more on customer benefit and gaining market share. It takes very *different people* to gain market share and increase customer value than optimizing profits and leveraging productivity do. Making novelty successful requires people willing and able to innovate because this requires other strengths. They must have their own resources. Initially, we may restrict their autonomy, just as we grant our children more freedom only as they grow older. Innovators must have direct and impeded access to top management and be given sufficient attention. They need special treatment and priority until they have established themselves.

2.9 Not Distinguishing Supporting and Operational Units

I began this chapter by noting that organizational charts have very limited explanatory power. What they fail to distinguish, for example, is whether an organizational unit is operational and thus fulfills its purpose, or whether it is supporting. However, operational and supporting units are two very different things. Operational units are responsible for success and for results. Based on the targeted customer benefit, these units determine what the enterprise should and should not do. They are the dominant management dimension in that they determine the business strategies and operational plans with which the enterprise intends to succeed as a whole. Supporting units, on the other hand, serve the operational units and perform an internal function. They are not responsible for results but for performance. They create the conditions for the operational units to work and help them succeed. This distinction is often not taken into sufficient account in practice.

Typically, supporting units include human resources, marketing, information technology, finance, compliance, and so on. They may look the same on the organizational chart as the operational units. But they have a very different task. Like innovation, they need to be measured and assessed against different yardsticks. While operational units should grow and enjoy as much autonomy as possible, supporting units should only be as large as necessary. They should not work autonomously but serve the operational units. In the first case, growth is positive; in the second, it is pathological.

Important
Distinguish operational units, which are responsible for results, from supporting units, which are responsible for performance, because they must be managed and assessed according to different criteria.

In one enterprise, IT might be a supporting unit that enables the operational units to sell vehicles. In another, IT is an operational unit because it is an IT firm in its own right, its purpose being to bring IT to market. Thus, the distinction between operational and supporting *depends not on the type of activity but on whether that activity concerns the enterprise's actual purpose.* In an IT firm, unit managers will develop their own business strategies, operational goals and budgets with which they believe they can succeed in the market. As a supporting function at our automotive manufacturer, IT is precisely not meant to do those things. Like the distinction between new and old, that between operational and supporting places very different demands on managers.

As part of a reorganization, an automotive manufacturer merged its used-vehicle department with the department responsible for allocating company cars to employees and to be sold later as year-old cars. The underlying idea was that both units dealt with used cars, with the company thus seeking to eliminate this interface. However, managers overlooked the fact that, in one case, used cars were a business the manufacturer wanted to grow and make money with, while in the other case, they were a supporting function having to perform as cost-effectively as possible and that should therefore not grow. Employee culture and managerial qualities in the two departments were completely different: Business-oriented and active in one case and administrative-reactive in the other. Before long, further reorganizing was needed.

Another company (in financial services) had turned a large supporting unit into an operational unit literally overnight. Having established an efficient facility management team comprising over 200 staff to operate and maintain its offices, the company decided to provide this service not only internally but also externally. Facility management was meant to become a business and thus (suddenly, in fact) part of the company's purpose. Whether this is right or not, or whether one wants to or not, are normative and strategic questions. In organizational terms, however, a clear decision needs to be made as to whether a unit should be purpose-fulfilling or supporting.

For the facility management team, this decision also immediately changed the standards for assessing the department, its accounting system, and the requirements to be met by its managers. However, the company management did not impose the usual overheads of a business unit on what was now an operational unit, nor had it adjusted the assessment standards or the management team. And thus, years later, the facility management team was still generating 80% of its sales with internal services and was satisfied with that. While the term "internal customer" was now used, real customers are defined by their ability to say "no," which internal customers cannot. On paper, facility management became an operational unit but essentially remained a supporting function.

Supporting units are *cost centers* that should not develop a life of their own. This is not always clear to their managers. I have experienced enterprises in which IT has been allowed to develop a life of its own as a supporting unit. As a result, it grew increasingly larger and more costly. At the same time, the operational units began complaining that while receiving a lot from IT, it was not what they needed. IT managers cannot be blamed for trying to develop what they believe is the best possible IT. But their strategy always needs to serve the strategies of the operational units and help them realize those strategies. Care must be taken to ensure that a functional IT strategy really supports the business strategies. Because an R&D manager, if they applied themselves and are granted a free hand, will develop the best possible "Rolls Royce technologies." This is called "happy engineering." Developers take pride in their latest technologies but may be developing past what the regional operational units need to satisfy their customers. The operational units, on the other hand, are *profit centers*. They are responsible for making so much profit through satisfied customers that the enteprise can invest in and prepare its future development. Operational units make money for IT and should therefore have a say in how this money is invested in IT.

Thus: Should a unit be operational or supporting? Should it be largely autonomous and viable? Or should it serve the whole with as little effort as possible? Phrased in the figurative language of this book, this distinction is part of the anatomy of the enterprise. This anatomy must be clear before the enterprise can be innervated and its neurology established so that the right units are properly controlled and the decision-making and communication processes properly designed.

2.10 Neglecting Neurology

This brings us to the core topic of this book and to the largest "construction site" in most organizations: control and communication structures. In addressing these kinds of structures, we are also talking about the leadership or management processes that optimize, coordinate, audit, and guide the enterprise into the future. After all, the core task of management is to make decisions and thus to control and communicate.

One of Germany's largest medium-sized enterprises, active worldwide in the high-tech sector, had adapted its organization following a strategy decision. Whereas in the past the regions had played the most important role in creating superior customer benefits, that responsibility was now assigned to the product. Accordingly, the company adapted its anatomy: Global business units were created in the form of product areas, which were to determine the company's strategy and operational success in the future. Organizational charts were adapted, the new organization communicated, and new product area managers appointed. Immediately setting to work, they contacted the previous regional managers worldwide, coordinated their plans with them, and agreed on targets. Two years later, not only regions were still optimizing themselves but the business units had failed. What had happened?

Well, the management process between product areas and regions had been adapted so that the product areas now set the goals. However, the "regional lords" still had direct access to the board of directors, which assessed and rewarded their performance according to the same standards as in the past. Employees also continued to recognize the "centers of power" in the regions. According to the new organizational model, they should have become supporting units (i.e., cost centers). In actual fact, however, they were still profit centers. They had to optimize themselves to achieve their goals because they were organized as legal entities required to produce an income statement and a balance sheet. These figures were looked at—as in the past. The employees in the regions did exactly what was required of them by the managers determining their salaries and promotions—the latter were the same regional managers to whom staff were subordinate, contractually, and disciplinarily. In case of doubt, the goals agreed with the product area managers were neglected if they conflicted with regional interests. The consolidated result per product area was also reviewed and assessed by the board of directors. But as long as regional companies delivered acceptable results, the board was prepared to overlook quite a lot. Soon, however, the product area managers gave up, frustrated, because organizational "eunuchs" had been created. They were fighting a losing battle from the start. After the strategic decision to switch to product areas and create the corresponding business units, the management structure should also have been changed. This proved difficult for managers as they were thinking primarily in terms of organizational charts and legal entities. Also, they weighted the interests of individual employees as more important than those of the company and the customers. If you change the anatomy, you must adjust the neurology. Or your enterprise will develop various "mental disorders" (see Chap. 17).

Important
An anatomy comes to life only when it is also properly innervated.

The problem with the third dimension of organizing is not so much that mistakes are made but rather that a clear idea of what the overall control and communication processes should look like is missing. In detail, many things are done right. For example, most enterprises have long implemented functioning target agreements or budgeting processes. The control and communication processes needed to optimize today's business seem to work in most enterprises. Often, they are also aligned with legal requirements for accounting and corporate governance. However, neurology involves more than managing today's business. It is also about recognizing when adaptation is needed to stay in business for the long haul. It is about ridding ourselves of things in time and building new potential for success. And it is about preventing conflict rather than resolving it. And about much more, as we will see.

Because the idea of a complete and functioning control and communication system of the whole is missing, many of its parts remain unfulfilled or piecemeal. While some management processes are fulfilling their task, they are not integrated into a management system that works together as a whole. Part II, however, shows that some areas in the neurology of an enterprise must function. Period. In the short term, one or the other area might be dispensed with. In the long run, however, the errors and shortcomings will appear, whether frustrated employees, dissatisfied customers, lack of innovation, or various other symptoms, including inertia and overwork.

A functioning neurology aims to absorb the complexity inside and outside the organization, the complexity of today's and tomorrow's business, and the complexity of lower and higher levels of the organization. As we will see in Part III, "absorbing" does not mean destroying or dismissing complexity—even if at times we might feel that ignorance works perfectly. What it does mean, however, is *"coping with complexity,"* as Stafford Beer called it. It is about coping with complexity, using it, and managing it. This capability will become a crucial success factor in the future.

The model and process for diagnosing and designing an organization presented in Part III aim to develop this capability—to cope with complexity—and to avoid the mistakes discussed in this chapter.

Later in the Bar

Sandra: Now that's totally new!

Marc: What? That we should also learn from nature how to run a firm?

Sandra: No, that you're watering down your whiskey with ice.

Marc (laughs): Oh—I just like it that way. Are you a purist?

Sanda: Yes. I don't like diluting things. And I think the thing about learning from nature is nonsense, by the way.

Rachel: Am I interrupting?

Marc: Not at all. Cheers, Rachel. We're just talking about learning from nature. As an engineer, what do you think about copying nature?

Rachel: Well, I've been thinking about that too: Can we and do we even want to? First of all, I question our ability to do so as long as we aren't even able to recreate a single blade of grass. Secondly, I don't think we should copy nature at all—after all, there are also human achievements.

Sandra: Exactly! I learned how to run a business from my father, not from nature. Nature would have simply starved our employees in 2009 when the going got tough.

Rachel: But if I'm not mistaken, bionics wants something different.

Marc: Like what?

Rachel: It doesn't use nature as a blueprint, but is looking for principles and laws to apply to its technical application problems. I think that's fine. Laws can be transferred because they always apply. And thus also to technical application areas, like antennae.

Marc: Really? Antennae?

Rachel: Yes, the old American radios that were used in Vietnam. They had bionic antennae like that. The engineers learned from insect antennae how to gain stability while remaining flexible. Before that, their antennae were constantly snapped off by branches in the jungle. I read that in a magazine.

Sandra: But as we've heard, it's not about more technology, but about more intelligence. It takes smarter organizations to clean up the mess in the world.

Rachel: Yes, digitization doesn't seem to be taking us away from nature, but back to it—if that's true about bionics.

Sandra: It would be great if now, in our information society, we managed to amplify our intelligence as massively as we did with our muscle power in the industrial revolution.

Rachel: The greatest efficiency we've achieved with engineering is around 50%. That's what our powerful marine engines are capable of. The rest is hot air and exhaust fumes. A simple thing like a firefly, on the other hand, converts 90 % of its energy into light, and only about 10 % into heat. No one has ever burned their fingers on that.

Marc: So, if I do the math ... We've strengthened our muscle power from about 0.1 horsepower to a thousand horsepower. If we amplify our intelligence by the same factor, my IQ would be about—one million ...

Rachel: I'll drink to that! Cheers.

(to Sandra:): Then at the latest he'll hopefully have his whisky without ice. Shouldn't be long now. With industry 4.0 and digitalization, the fourth industrial revolution has already been proclaimed.

Sandra: ... And for the first time in history, before it has even taken place ... So that's all very well with bionics for antennae and machines and so on. But in a company? To me, that sounds too much like management books like "The Mouse Strategy," "Harvesting Together," or "Saving with Hamsters." I don't read that kind of stuff.

Rachel: Give me a break! Sure, some people will always water down an idea and think it's great. Just look at Marc with ice in his whisky. ... Obviously, things immediately get arbitrary ...

Marc: You're moving on very thin ice yourself, my dear!

Rachel (laughs): But from a scientific point of view, it's absolutely fine to transfer principles from one field to the other. That's what science is all about: Finding the general in the specific. Bionics is a recognized science. Some of its approaches are worth taking seriously. The approach we're discussing doesn't strike me as implausible at first glance.

Marc: You mean the Viable System Model?

Sandra: Designing a company like an organism? Sounds too much like science fiction to me.

Marc: I can imagine that we can learn something from the nervous system. Why not? After all, humans have learned everything they can from nature somehow.

Sandra: Pacioli!

Marc: What?

Sandra: Luca Pacioli. He invented double-entry bookkeeping in the Middle Ages, in the very early Renaissance. I don't think he copied that from nature.

Rachel: Who knows. But it's not about copying. The Viable System Model was not simply copied.

Sandra: Yes, it was! From the human nervous system.

Rachel: No, it wasn't. If it had, it would be a model of the nervous system. But it's a model of viability, which was found in the structure of the nervous system. But the nervous system contains so much else that has nothing to do with viability.

Marc: So the nervous system is just a study site and a metaphor. I've already asked myself what exactly is meant by the three dimensions of organizing: If I remember my school days correctly, neurology is the study of the entire nervous system, anatomy that of the internal structure of the organs, and physiology that of life processes. But surely there's also a neuroanatomy and a neurophysiology? Vice versa, my digestion also has an anatomy and a control system. This is confusing.

Rachel: Stop being clever, Marc. It's a metaphor. Not every metaphor that doesn't work is a comparison. What matters is that the focus is on neuro, that is, on information flows and control. You're the computer scientist among us! But you're just thinking like a guy again. For once, it isn't about what controls your metabolism or your digestion, Marc, but about controlling the whole. If you want to climb Mount Matterhorn, controlling your digestion won't help.

Sandra: You've obviously never gone climbing in the mountains.

Rachel (laughs): Yeah, okay, but if you're halfway up and need to relieve yourself, you've just planned badly overall. It's not the fault of the process controlling your digestion.

Marc: Alright, I see what you mean. So the recipe for success, as the Prologue tells us, lies in the structure of this overall control, as Rachel says.

Sandra: … So that eventually I reach the Matterhorn summit, energized and jubilant, despite difficult conditions, incidents and last-minute changes of plan—and return safely to base camp again.

Rachel: Exactly. Because this recipe allows you to design something so that it works in a volatile environment until it has achieved its purpose. We engineers also call this a "teleological machine."

Sandra: I'm bailing out!

Marc: Very simple—it's a machine that doesn't just keep doing the same thing, but one that achieves a goal, like a robot scoring a goal. So it's a much more complex machine. I know this from my IT studies. We were also studying information circuits.

Sandra: Okay, I've got that. So this question is: How is my nervous system built so that I could spontaneously climb the Matterhorn tomorrow? And how do I need to design my company so that it can keep scoring goals? Because that's what I promised my father when I took over from him.

Marc: Of course, it should be viable so that you can pass on a healthy company to the next generation, even if the economic environment becomes even more difficult.

Sandra: Well, I'm excited to see what's next. In this book, I mean. I'm still skeptical.

Marc: How come?

Sandra: If this Viable System Model is really so helpful, why doesn't anybody know about it? I, for one, have never heard of it. Have you?

Rachel: No, me neither.

Marc: Well, we need neurology now because the world has become so complicated and everything has become so fast. We need neurology to work very well today. Our companies probably had one in the past. It wasn't as efficient, but it was sufficient. I can understand that.

Sandra: Well, if you look at the state of the world, a little more neurology wouldn't hurt.

Rachel: The third dimension of organizing. So are you saying that nobody knows about that yet because nobody's had to deal with it until now?

Sandra: Well, after all, it took several hundred years for double-entry bookkeeping to really spread as a standard—even if it was invented long before that.

Rachel: Not by Pacioli, by the way. He only described it. It was invented much earlier, as far as I know.

Marc: That's what I'm saying. Invention alone is not enough. There also needs to be a real need for it on the market. Otherwise, no one will be interested. That's when the first big banks, the Medici and so on, emerged in Italy. For a long time, most companies were satisfied with simple bookkeeping. All of a sudden, everything became far too complicated, so that double-entry bookkeeping was needed. Before, one could do without and so, at the beginning, everyone probably asked themselves whether double-entry bookkeeping—doing everything twice—was necessary ... You don't make the effort until you have to. It seems to be similar with the model of neurology.

Rachel: Viability.

Sandra: What?

Rachel: Exactly, it's a model of viability, not of a nervous system! But you may be right about the need. Big hits take time to become known. It took 80 years for Einstein's theory of relativity to be taught at universities. I read about Stafford Beer receiving an innovation award for his model—a medal with Prometheus on the front. At the ceremony, he was asked if he knew why it had Prometheus on it. Beer said, "Perhaps because Prometheus brought fire, that is, knowledge, to mankind?"—"No, because vultures will pluck your liver for the rest of your life!"

Marc (laughs): He probably meant the critics, whiners, and skeptics. As with everything new, all they ever see is the problems. They're gung-ho to prove that things don't work. Basic innovations have a hard time.

Rachel: For a long time, people didn't dig Einstein because they "knew" that parallel lines can't cross.

Sandra: Yes, it's one of these things with innovations. The status quo is always the enemy of novelty. For me, the question isn't really whether it's old or new, but whether it's useful. What I don't feel like doing, however, is introducing a new organizational model in my company. We reorganized 2 years ago—and you're not supposed to reorganize all the time, as we've been saying.

Marc: As I understand it, you don't need to reorganize, you just need to check the third dimension and, if necessary, get it right. That's different from switching from one organizational model to another; for example, from a functional organization to a matrix, as our insurance company did. And it's true, by the way: Our communication problems have since increased. Everything has gotten cumbersome and complicated—difficult to control. We probably just forgot about the third dimension and are wondering about it now.

Sandra: And do you really think you wouldn't have problems if you were using this model of neuro- . . . Of viability?

Marc: Basically, I'm also always skeptical if things sound too theoretical, scientifically based, and whatever. Mind you, what I find interesting is that unplannability is the credo of cybernetics. It seems to accept that things will always go wrong, and that there will be disruptions and unforeseens. It also believes its formula for success is particularly good at dealing with just that. I find it exciting that it accepts real-life conditions and not laboratory conditions.

Sandra: Did you also read that this guy Beer was not only a scientist, but also a special forces captain in the Second World War, and later a successful manager in industry? He ought to know what it's like to have to make decisions and not have time to wait for studies and research.

Rachel: . . . And employees get on your nerves, the phone rings constantly, and everyone wants something from you at the same time. Apparently, he owned a Rolls Royce and frequented gentlemen's clubs before opting for a simpler and freer life. He's an interesting guy. So I'm curious about his model. If someone knows the reality of managers and is also a good scientist, which is extremely rare, that promises something exciting. Something robust.

Marc: A robust organization works reliably even when its individual parts don't work. I found that interesting: John von Neumann is reputed for showing how to build reliable machines from unreliable parts.

Sandra: I need that machine. We have a lot of unreliable colleagues in our company.

Marc: Alan Turing and von Neumann are credited with demonstrating that machines themselves can design and build other machines that are more complex than they are. Who knows where all this will lead.

Sandra: Looking at my children, as biological machines we're already able to do that.

Rachel: We're viable, but still die.

Marc: So what? Do you want to live forever?

Rachel: Good question. What does "viable" actually mean? How long should something be viable?

Marc: Perhaps until it fulfills its purpose?

Rachel: So when I die, does that mean I've fulfilled my purpose?

Marc: Probably.

Rachel: And, vice versa, if a project has fulfilled its purpose, it should die.

Marc: Exactly. But in our insurance company, most of the time they continue to be artificially ventilated.

Sandra: The purpose of our company is to bring machines, or rather solutions, for the woodworking industry to market. So our purpose is fulfilled when nobody needs those kinds of machines anymore.

Rachel: Because there are no more forests and therefore no more wood because of climate change.

Sandra: So hopefully the company will remain viable for a while.

Marc: That's why in English the word "viable" also means "fit for purpose." A "viable idea," for example, is an idea that is useful and works. I didn't study in England for nothing.

Rachel: We know that. Drink up.

Part II

The Viable System Model

A Model of Control and Communication 3

The purpose of a system is—what it does.
(Stafford Beer)

3.1 Organization: The "Enabling Link" Between Strategy and Culture

For all three dimensions of organizing, we first need to consider the model discussed in Sect. 2.3. The question there was "why can't we simply copy our best competitor's structure?" Fig. 2.2 showed the connections between a enterprise's strategy, structure, and culture. It also highlighted that the three elements are interconnected in all directions and influence each other. When we talk about organization, we need to realize that we do not organize in a vacuum. Instead, *we always organize in the context of an enterprise's very specific strategy, its specific people and their behaviors, which are usually summarized as "culture."* Before we delve into the model of control, let us revisit Fig. 2.2.

It reminds us, first, that we want the organization to achieve a certain performance for a certain customer and that structure should focus our attention on this performance. It must be strategy-driven, that is, help us to implement the strategic thrusts. It should enable us to be successful by leveraging our strengths. Before we start organizing, therefore, we need a clear idea of who this customer is, what they are paying for, and what strengths will enable us to outperform our competitors in these criteria. We also need to know what we intend to do with our enterprise in terms of market position, innovation, and productivity; how we can attract good employees; what liquidity and profit targets we need to achieve these goals. Only when these core questions have been clarified can we discuss strategy.

So much for theory. In practice, I have often seen boards that are unclear about strategy at the outset of an organizational project. Strategy papers exist, but closer scrutiny reveals these are long-term operational plans. They describe how *turnover*

M. Pfiffner, *The Neurology of Business*, Management for Professionals,
https://doi.org/10.1007/978-3-031-14260-4_3

and profits should develop over the next few years. *Operational figures*, however, are systematically misleading for strategic planning, because they only enable looking back (rear-view mirror). Besides, their extrapolation into the future is nothing but hopes and forecasts. They are useless for strategy because our world has become too complex and too dynamic to base important decisions on forecasts. Nor do they capture the essential changes in our specific business. However, starting to work with a board often reveals that its members do in fact have a shared vision of what the enterprise needs to do in strategic terms. Thus, strategic questions answer themselves in the course of discussions. That suffices for organizing, because *we do not need completed strategy forms, but strategic content.* Sometimes these are only formulated when working on organization.

Strategy influences structure, just as structure influences strategy. Why? Because structure determines which organizational entities we need to develop strategies for in the first place. And also because sometimes legal structures limit the scope for design, or at least seem to. While designing strategy and structure, information, perceptions, and ideas from both elements converge, so that strategy and structure evolve together until they are mutually coherent.

In addition, structure impacts culture, that is, people's behavior (as observed). An enterprise that needs to become more responsive and adaptable due to increasing market dynamics may change its structure to do so. It provides market-facing units with the necessary resources and competencies so that they can act in an agile manner and assume responsibility. Structure influences people's behavior by opening up or closing down room for maneuver. It determines how much self-organization and self-control are possible. And it influences how authoritarian managers and superiors must appear (see Sect. 17.3).

Conversely, culture also influences structure: Do we have the *right people and enough managers* to implement the desired structure? Will we lose employees who are critical to success if we change our structure? Moreover, *unwritten laws, informal networks, and practiced behaviors* impact the enterprise far more than any organizational manual. They have a tremendous impact on functioning, but are screened out by standard organizational methods rather than addressed coherently. The organization remains one matter and culture another, and hence are dealt with separately. *If, on the other hand, we look at culture from the perspective of control and communication, it suddenly becomes relevant to organizing.* Why? Well, because behavior and communication are not different things. Paul Watzlawick suggested that we cannot communicate and that behavior is always a form of (sometimes nonverbal) communication.[1] Likewise, we also need to understand cultural factors such as symbols, shadow structures, or implicit rules of the game and traditions as structures. Although they do not feature in organizational charts and

[1]Paul Watzlawick, Janet H. Beavin and Don D. Jackson, *Menschliche Kommunikation* (Bern, Stuttgart, Vienna: Hogrefe, 1969), p. 53. English edition: "Some Tentative Axioms of Communication," P*ragmatics of Human Communication: A Study of Interactional Patterns, Pathologies and Paradoxes* (New York: W.W. Norton, 1967).

process descriptions, these structures are very much a part of the third dimension of organizing, the neurology of business (see Sect. 4.3).

The ordering structures implicit in an enterprise become visible via *symbols*. They regulate, for example, who gets to sit by the window and who drives which car. As a consultant, you deal with roughly 20 new enterprises a year and over time learn to spot these cultural symptoms. They are interesting because they quickly reveal what makes an enterprise tick: What does the parking lot tell you? For example, if boardroom parking is located right next to the main entrance, whereas visitor parking is hidden somewhere behind the building? What about reception atmosphere? Do staff run for cover when the boss walks by with a visitor? How do people interact with each other? How are they dressed? Are meetings prepared?

Enterprise culture also includes *shadow structures*. These determine who really has a say. There are soccer clubs in South America, for example, where supporters groups rather than not the club's management decide transfers. In one large enterprise, the choir was the real center of power: Because although it did not make important decisions, it discussed and prepared them. Sometimes the owner's partner also plays an important role. Or assistants become gray eminences with great influence and little responsibility that hardly anyone can get past.

All this is structurally relevant. It tells us much more about enterprise culture than the snazzy catchwords printed in the glossy mission statement. This contains the values to which the enterprise adheres, often resembling Christian moral theology. For example: "We want to deal honestly and openly with each other." Which makes us wonder, involuntarily, whether some enterprises expect their employees to lie to each other? Not that a corporate policy should not contain norms and values. However, culture is not shaped by guiding principles, but by concrete action in daily exchanges.

Cultures per se can hardly be changed. What distinguishes German or Swiss people remains more or less the same over the centuries. What can change in Germany or Switzerland, however, are very specific behaviors. These may be necessary or useful depending on the circumstances, including the requirements of a changing environment. So instead of trying to change corporate culture, we should ask which *concrete behaviors* need to be changed and which structures, whether written down or not, favor these behaviors. In this regard, we can learn a lot from good school teachers. They excel at establishing implicit structures and at shaping a certain culture in the shortest possible time; not through guiding principles, but through repeatedly demanding concrete actions. By looking at behaviors, we more quickly grasp the real organizational and management issues, as well as the levers through which change can be brought about. Culture itself, on the other hand, cannot be tweaked. Culture slogans fizzle out at the appellative level; they are not taken seriously by employees and, at worst, are perceived as sarcastic when reality and expectations diverge.

3.2 What Can a Model Do?

The model in Fig. 2.2 applies to all three dimensions of organizing: the organizational structure, the process organization, and the control organization. In turn, each of these dimensions has its own model. We know what an organizational chart looks like as a model of organizational structure. We also know what a flowchart looks like as a model of a process organization. These two models serve very different purposes. The purpose of the organizational chart is to show the management hierarchy and the organizational entities. The purpose of the flowchart is to describe a relevant process in the organization. Every model, then, has a certain purpose. It is suitable for showing certain things—those on which it focuses—and not others. For example, the London Underground map does not depict the city's political landscape. But it is useful if you are looking for the fastest route from Paddington Station to the Tower of London.

A model can only ever be an abstraction of reality for a particular purpose. Vice versa: *"The map is not the territory,"* as Alfred Korzybski put it.[2] We can survey a territory with our retina or with a scale and then present our observations on paper. Reality, however, is always more complex than the model. Every "map" can only be a colored, filtered image and a section of reality with which an observer pursues a certain interest and intention. The observer always influences knowledge. This has been described not only by cyberneticists, Gregory Bateson in *Steps to an Ecology of Mind* or Heinz von Foerster in *Second-Order Cybernetics*.[3] It is also a general insight of twentieth-century humanities and natural sciences. It has changed our understanding of objectivity. We find this insight not only in modern epistemology, philosophy, or sociology, but also in quantum physics, for example, in Heisenberg's famous "uncertainty principle" or Schrödinger's "cat experiment." Observers and their intentions always need to be factored into the equation.

Thus, every model helps every observer to pursue a certain purpose. It contains what is relevant for that observer, so that they can recognize, diagnose, try out, simulate, and take something back to reality with the model. To do this, a model must omit whatever is not purposeful (i.e., not relevant to purpose) and focus on what matters to gain insight. Otherwise, we would injure ourselves in the flight simulator if we crashed. A model can very much abstract and reduce reality, as is the case, for example, with a child's drawing of an airplane. A wooden airplane model, on the other hand, already contains much more information than a drawing. We can look at it from every angle, as well as feel and smell it. A model airplane really able to fly represents reality even better. The best model would be reality itself ("the territory"), or as Norbert Wiener put it: "The best material model for a cat is another,

[2] Alfred Korzybski, *Science and Sanity: An Introduction to Non-Aristotelian Systems and General Semantics* (Institute of General Semantics, 1933).

[3] Gregory Bateson, *Steps to an Ecology of Mind: Collected Essays in Anthropology, Psychiatry, Evolution, and Epistemology* (Chicago: University of Chicago Press, 1972); Heinz Von Foerster, *Cybernetics of Cybernetics: The Control of Control and the Communication of Communication*, 2nd ed. (Minneapolis: Future Systems Inc., 1995).

or preferably the same cat."[4] Good models help us to make complex things as simple as possible—but not simpler.

Epistemology teaches us that models are important because we think through them. We understand how the economy works according to the model of how an economy works. We understand how our partner or our children function according to our mental picture of them. But beware: The map is not the territory! Models sometimes oversimplify. Then we see certain things in black and white or fall prey to our own prejudices by pressing reality into our model. Hence, the Danish Military Manual states: "If the map and the territory are not the same—follow the territory!" Sometimes we need to check and update our models. And sometimes different models lead to misunderstandings and conflicts, because they prevent us from understanding why others see the world differently than we do. Especially with management issues, people often talk at crossed purposes—because everyone has a different model of a good strategy or a good organization in mind. However, in my experience, the best-managed enterprises have a common understanding of management, at least in the key areas of strategy, organization, leadership, and the desired culture. Also, they underscore the importance of having *shared models of management* and ensuring that new staff understood this thinking.

Even more important than having common models is the *quality of these models*. Sometimes our solutions remain ineffective because the underlying model is not fit for purpose. It focuses on the wrong variables (i.e., ones lacking leverage), or it misjudges relationships. As Chap. 9 shows, the outcome of any kind of management cannot be better than the model on which it is based—except by chance. This explains why such enterprises carefully considered which models to include in their management concept. The quality of these models is part of the recipe for success, because it determines the quality of the solutions and decisions that are made with them—and thus the fate of the enterprise. The British neurophysiologist W. Ross Ashby, one of the child prodigies at the Macy conferences, studied modeling in depth. He also called cybernetics *"the science of simplification."*[5] As the science of correct or permissible simplification, it teaches us that recognizing the *"essential variables"* is critical to success, as is studying their connections and interplay.[6] In this sense, the best models are not the complicated ones (i.e., with as many variables as possible) but the simple ones (i.e., with a few yet essential variables).

[4] Norbert Wiener and Arturo Rosenblueth, "The Role of Models in Science," *Philosophy of Science*, Vol. 12, No. 4 (Chicago: University of Chicago Press, 1945), pp. 316–321.

[5] W. Ross Ashby, *Design for a Brain: The Origin of Adaptive Behaviour* (New York: Wiley, 1970), pp. 41–42.

[6] W. Ross Ashby, *Mechanisms of Intelligence: Ashby's Writings on Cybernetics*, ed. Roger Conant (Seaside, California: Intersystems Publications, 1981), p. 142.

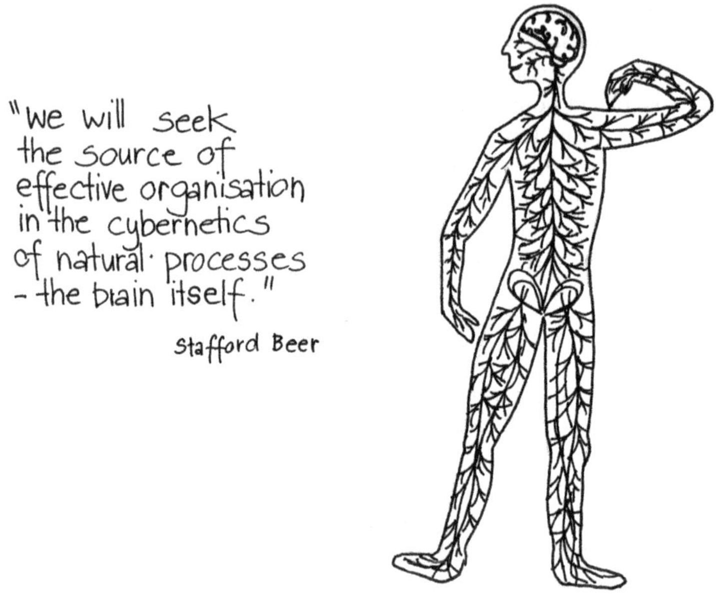

Fig. 3.1 The best practice model of control

3.3 The Invariant Structure in the Best Practice Model of Control

What we can find out and show with a model thus depends on three factors: (1) the purpose of the model, (2) its quality, and (3) the observer applying it. This book is most interested in a *model of control and communication*. Rather than modeling an enterprise, or a nervous system, it seeks to model the necessary control and communication. Stafford Beer developed this control model in the 1960s and 70s. He designed it to meet scientific standards, have general validity, and be applicable to whatever needs a control structure: animals, machines, and social organizations. The latter could be large or small enterprises, ministries, teams, projects, or countries. The model had to be independent of what the organization does. It also needed to include everything needed for powerful control, yet be simple enough to maintain an overview. Does such a control and communication system exist, one capable of satisfying these high standards—*"a model of any viable system,"* as Beer called it?

Beer's discovery led him to develop his own organizational model for the third dimension of organizing. His celebrated breakthrough earned him numerous awards. As a cyberneticist, he looked to the living world for ideas for his control model. This makes sense because over several millennia of evolution organisms have learned to do enormously complex things—be it a hummingbird buzzing around a flower, a school of fish escaping its hunter, or a swift remaining airborne for almost its entire life. Beer, however, found the most powerful and complex of these control systems in the human nervous system (Fig. 3.1). Our brain contains roughly 110 billion

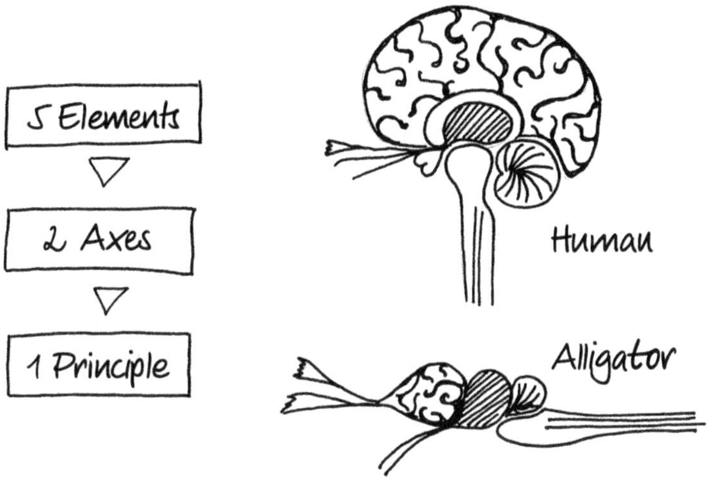

Fig. 3.2 Ingredients of control

neurons, which in turn are interconnected up to tens of thousands of times. It is an electrochemical computer weighing one-and-a-half kilograms, powered by glucose at 25 watts, operating at a rate of ten cycles per second, and possessing a storage capacity of approximately 10^{15} bits.[7] Humans thus possess an incredibly complex control capacity, which enables us to cope very quickly with the unforeseen, to plan in advance, to perform an elegant ballet, or to scale a mountain in adverse weather. The human central nervous system is so complex that it can even generate consciousness for itself—something no other control system has yet managed to do.

In his search for a model, Beer discovered that the highly developed brains of humans and the less complex animal brains are similar in many respects. He thus asked himself: What remains unchanged in all organismic control systems? And what does this teach us about the control structures of an enterprise? From the various nervous systems of different organisms, he distilled those elements that are essential for viability. Which left five elements, two control axes, and one principle that occur in living creatures—be it an alligator, amoeba, bird, horse, or human being (Fig. 3.2).

Over four billion years of evolution, nature seems to have found a universal structure that produces such fantastic properties as flexibility, efficiency and performance, foresight and adaptation, reproduction or renewal, healing, consciousness, and even self-awareness. Beer showed that these five elements, two axes, and the principle in the mathematical sense are necessary and sufficient for viability. *Necessary*, because in the long run nothing can be omitted without causing damage. *Sufficient*, because nothing else is needed for control to function. Thus, this model

[7] Stafford Beer, *Brain of the Firm: The Managerial Cybernetics of Organization* (Chichester, New York, Brisbane, Toronto, Singapore: Wiley, 1972), p. 97.

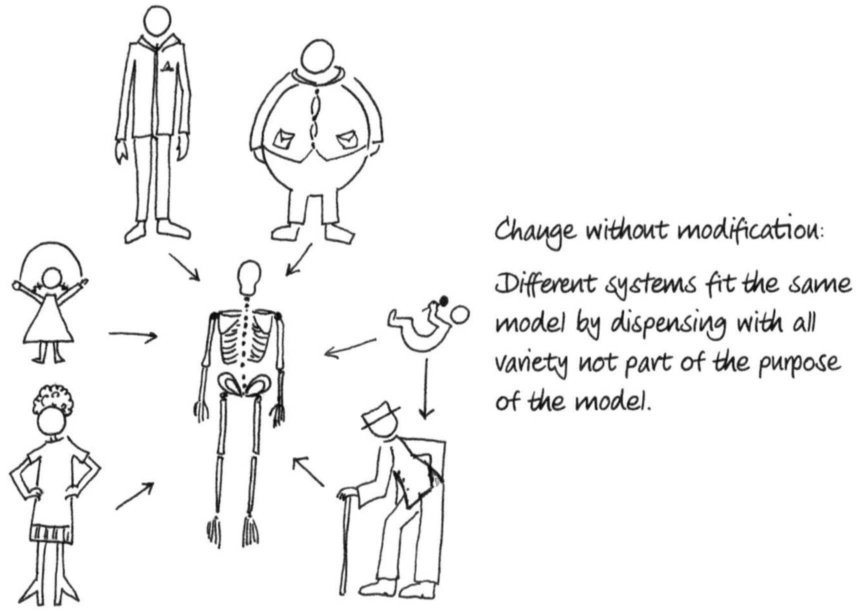

Fig. 3.3 Invariant structures

provides a language that, on the one hand, is rich enough to talk meaningfully about the third dimension of organizing without, on the other, requiring 10 years of study to first understand the language.

This structure exists in every organism, just as, for example, our skeleton exists in the same form in every human, whether obese or lean, small or tall, female or male. This structure also grows with the organism from cradle to grave (Fig. 3.3). While the ratios of bone lengths change a little with age, with the bones becoming more brittle, the structure remains the same. In our enterprises, we always seem to have to reorganize just because the enterprise has grown. The organism, on the other hand, grows without changing its structure. We will see that the discovered control structure can be used to represent *enterprises of any type, size, and complexity.* These properties, moreover, grow with the enterprise. When President Allende sought his help in the early 1970s, Beer applied the model to the entire Chilean state.

The model consists of two dimensions: *a lateral (or horizontal) and a vertical control axis.* The lateral axis provides relative autonomy and agility. It allows an organ to regulate its affairs independently while bringing this local activity into organic balance on the vertical axis. The vegetative nervous system, comprising the sympathetic nervous system and its counterpart, the parasympathetic nervous system, ensures the coordinated up or down of our heartbeat, respiration, digestion, and so forth. It ensures the *autonomous, involuntary regulation* of our internal organs while we listen to a lecture, for example. However, we can intervene at any time by getting up, inhaling, and running to catch the bus. Our vertical axis makes this possible via the somatic central nervous system. The vertical control axis provides the voluntary control of the whole, thus enabling its meaningful interaction. It comprises the nerve cords of the spinal column and converges at its end in a walnut-like brain with two hemispheres: the cerebral cortex. This sits atop other parts of the brain like a wig. Put simply, these are the brainstem (the oldest part of the brain, the so-called "reptilian brain"), the cerebellum, and the midbrain or diencephalon (the so-called mammalian brain). The cerebellum, diencephalon, and cerebrum function as a "triune" brain. Together with the spinal cord, they form the central nervous system.

Communication between the control elements takes place electrically, via the nerve cords and synapses, as well as biochemically, as messenger substances in the blood, known as neurotransmitters, transmit information. Interestingly, the sensory part of our organism functions largely digitally: Visual stimuli, for example, stimulate millions of cells in the retina, causing them to be either active or inactive. These perceptions are then processed from digital to analog until they participate in the higher operations of the brain. Modern-day industry does the opposite: It mostly uses analog sensing equipment and processes this information in digital form for the higher control centers.

3.4 The Viable System Model (a Model of Viable Systems)

Stafford Beer called the structure he found the *"Viable System Model" (VSM)*. He used the word "system" to emphasize that the VSM applies to whatever needs a control organization. That it should be a "model of any viable system" is a strong claim, scientifically speaking. We can refute this assertion, or even ignore it. As a management consultant, I often hear people say: "Oh, everything's so different around here." That is, they believe they are different, that things are not valid in one's own industry or at least have a completely different significance. Mostly, this thinking attempts to avoid potentially unpleasant insights. Let us remember that Beer's model contains only those elements that are invariant in all viable structures. In over 20 years of practical experience, I have not dealt with an organization, business, or nonbusiness, to which the Viable System Model did not apply. And only one organization out of about a hundred turned out to be correctly and seamlessly organized after diagnosis.

While metaphors like the three dimensions of organizing always remain somewhat ambivalent, models like the Viable System Model are very precise. But what exactly does "viability" mean? First, we need to distinguish *"viability"* from *"survivability"* because these terms tend to be confused. Many people are still alive in hospitals solely because they are kept alive artificially: They survive even though they are not viable. We also see this in business and public administration: Such organizations have outlived their purpose or are so poorly designed that they could not function at all unless they were kept alive by subsidies (as a rule to protect jobs). Conversely, an organization can be fundamentally viable and still not survive. The structural conditions for viability may exist, but a legal case hits, a factory burns down, or patents are stolen, that is, events able to drive an enterprise into insolvency. Even as human beings with a basically viable structure, we can walk across the street and yet still not survive: We might be hit by a car or a flowerpot.

Business people are most familiar with economic viability. As they know, this is defined by the fact that, in the end, someone has to pick up the cheque. If an enterprise lacks liquidity, it will not survive. Although viability encompasses this economic viability, it extends beyond it, because *life is more than survival.* We need money to implement strategies, to enable innovations, and to pay employees. In this sense, *money is an indispensable condition, a conditio sine qua non.* Viability, however, also requires an identity and a purpose to which we can dedicate funds. We must also have the necessary adaptation mechanisms to ensure that we do not stray from our goal despite the storm.

Definition
Viable = Able to maintain a separate existence.[8]

Viability thus describes an existence that can sustain itself in its environment, regardless of origin, until its purpose is fulfilled. The necessary foundations of viability are not concerned with the energy it takes to propel a system, but with the dynamic structure that determines the adaptive interconnection of its parts. This structure contains the principles of effective organization that we came across in Chap. 2 in their negative manifestation in the form of practice errors. This enables us to quickly and accurately diagnose and remedy organizational errors in an enterprise, or to avoid these errors from the start. The axioms, theorems, principles, and laws of the viable organization, as contained in the Viable System Model, help us to properly and completely design the enterprise individually, that is, according to its environment and situation.

In summary, the Viable System Model provides a flexible and scalable organizational design for whatever should be a viable system. The design does not change during the life cycle, but remains the same from cradle to grave. It leverages the principle of cell division by creating agile operational units that can control, organize, and coordinate themselves. It leads to a robust organization that is easy to manage, yet capable of complexity. It ultimately serves us as a reference point for proper organization without falling victim to ideologies and paradigms. As such, it is also an alternative to the fads, arbitrariness, and shortcomings of previous organizing.

[8] Stafford Beer, *Diagnosing the System for Organizations: The Managerial Cybernetics of Organization* (Chichester, New York, Brisbane, Toronto, Singapore: Wiley, 1985), p. 1.

Introduction to the Model 4

We tend to think in terms of objects. We ask ourselves what an object is and what it is like. Only later do we discover that as a rule not objects themselves are difficult, but their relationships. Likewise, in the Viable System Model, not only the five control elements are important, but also the connections (communication channels) between them because control does not work without communication. This introduction to the model also begins with objects, that is, the *control elements*. It considers communication lines between these elements later, during diagnosis and design in Part III. I explain the meaning of the two control axes and the *principle* mentioned above at the end of the introduction.

Let us begin with the elements: What does it take for control to work? Well, not the obvious organizational units such as marketing, finance, human resources, or sales, because these are specialist functions. We find these in the organizational chart, as part of the anatomy. They vary greatly depending on the type of enterprise: Finance in a publicly traded company works differently than in a local government. We, on the other hand, are looking for the invariant elements for controlling an entity. To do this, we need to view the organization differently and ask: What must the control of a complex whole actually do? We need to think in terms of control functions instead of specialist functions (Fig. 4.1).

Viability requires *five control functions*:

1. Operation (Purpose Fulfillment Through Self-Control)

These are the operational units that do what the company is there to do. They belong to the anatomy of the organization and feature in the control model because they are the self-controlling units in the control system. They are the building blocks of the organization. In the human body, they are the organs (e.g., muscles, kidneys, skin) that collectively fulfill its purpose. In social organizations, they are responsible for service provision. The operational units are located on the lateral axis of control, which enables autonomous action.

M. Pfiffner, *The Neurology of Business*, Management for Professionals,
https://doi.org/10.1007/978-3-031-14260-4_4

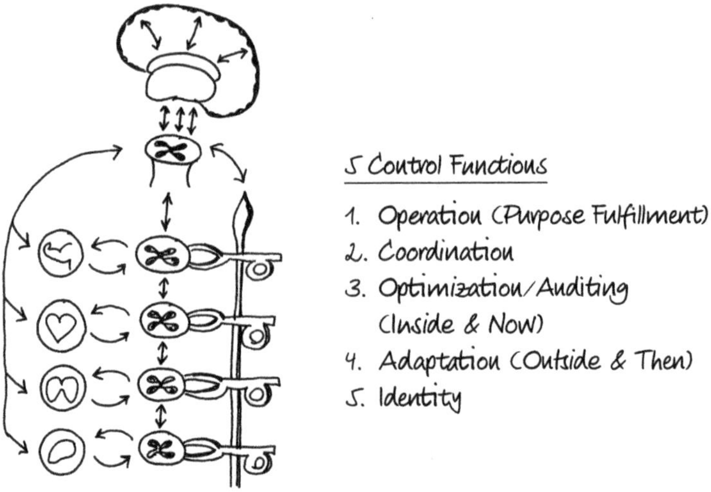

Fig. 4.1 Five control functions (elements of the control system)

2. (Self-)Coordination

At the interface between the horizontal and vertical axis lies the second control function. It enables the (self-)coordination of the operational, purpose-fulfilling units and ensures smooth cooperation where necessary.

The superordinate management system, referred to subsequently as *"senior management"* because the operational units have their own management, ensures that they achieve more together than they are able to individually.

3. Optimization and Auditing

Coordination alone does not create added value in collaboration. "Achieving more together" as a rule means limiting the autonomy of operational units for the good of the whole. This is the third control function. It makes decisions to optimize the whole.

4. Adaptation and Development

Viability requires adaptability to a changing environment. The fourth control function ensures that we know what lies ahead and therefore how we should behave. It communicates with the overall environment of the enterprise.

5. Identity (Defining Values)

The fifth and final control function ensures that the whole has an identity, knows what it is and what it wants to be. As a normative function, it establishes a framework for everything else. It is also the final decision-making authority.

Everything takes place in an *environment*. This also needs to be integrated into the model. The system fulfills its purpose in its environment. This is where the

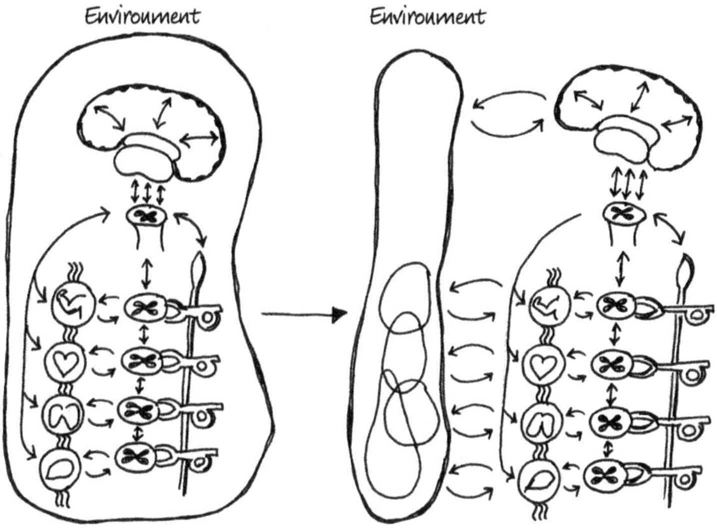

Fig. 4.2 The environment is part of the whole

system must act, and to which it must adapt. In our model, this environment resembles a cloud, because we never know exactly where it begins and where it ends. Nobody can say exactly where Bosch ends today and where BMW begins. We draw the environment around the control system because it is part of the environment. Everyone working in this enterprise is part of this environment and familiar with it. But the environment also includes customers or service recipients, non-customers, competitors, authorities, the media, and whatever is relevant for this enterprise. In an economic enterprise (i.e., firm), we use the environment to map the addressable market. To be able to say more about the information flows between the environment and the control system, let us position the environment to the left of the control system instead of around it (Fig. 4.2). This convention makes working with the model easier and clearer.

Figure 4.3 shows the Viable System Model as a whole, with its five control functions and its two control axes (lateral and vertical). The lines between the boxes are the communication channels. These connect and interlock the control functions. Working with the model often reveals that the lines demand more attention than the boxes. Some control elements may not be evident enough or too weak. Even more often, however, adequate communication channels are missing, because in practice designing these channels is rather left to chance—probably also due to a lack of orientation. Consequently, these channels are often overloaded. Or they are too slow, ambivalent, fail to convey content, or missing completely. Chapter 14 discusses how to diagnose and design these communication channels. Every control function is a subsystem of overall control, which itself consists of several elements. Hence, the five control functions are simply called *"System 1, 2, 3, 4, and 5."*

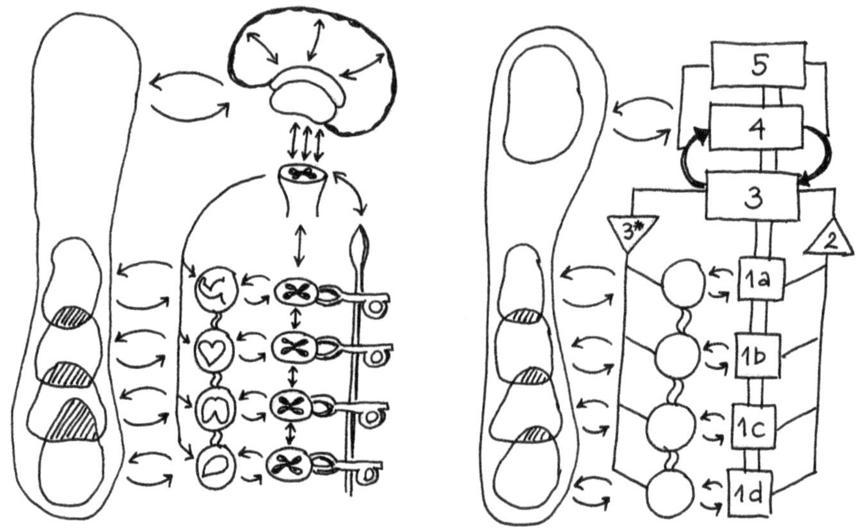

Fig. 4.3 The viable system model in the nervous system

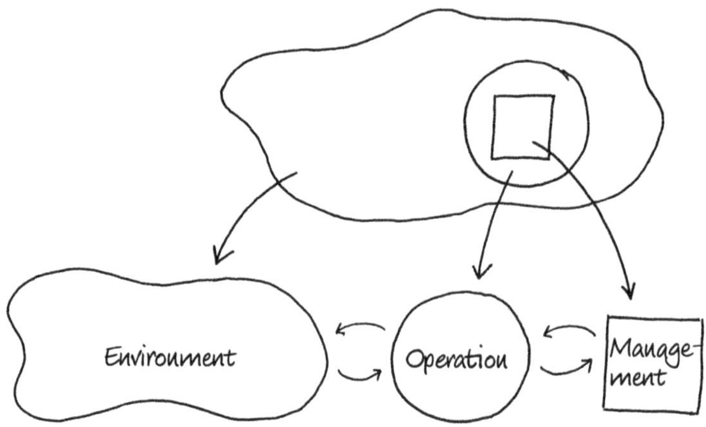

Fig. 4.4 Environment, operation, and management in an operational unit

4.1 The Basic Elements: Environment, Operation, and Management

The foundation of the organization consists of building blocks, so-called *"operational units."* Figure 4.4 shows an operational unit interacting with its outside world. The unit can be a corporate division, a team in a large project, or a federal state in a country. It consists of three basic elements: *A management that is controlling an operation that is doing something in an ever-changing environment.* Together, environment, operation, and management each form a building block of the foundation. Again, let us imagine the environment as a cloud surrounding the whole. For example, it represents the relevant market in which the division operates. Or it defines the scope of work in the project. Or it is the geographic area of the federal state with all its citizens and landscapes. Within the environment is the operation, for example, offices and buildings, machines and workshops, and the employees working in that operation. Let us draw every operation as a circle. Finally, inside the operation is the management box, which controls everything. Let us draw that as a rectangle. Again, to better represent the connections between environment, operation, and management, let us separate the elements out horizontally. This helps us recognize how environment and operation interact in a dynamic cycle. The operation serves its customers in the environment, just as customer expectations affect operational activities. Operation and management interact likewise. For these interactions to be effective, the operational unit needs maximum flexibility, freedom of action, and autonomy.

For each of the three basic elements—environment, operation, and management—the enterprise needs a vision of how it wants to do things. With its entrepreneurial policy, it determines the enterprise's fundamental orientation, normatively and permanently. Entrepreneurial policy comprises a concept for each of the three basic elements: an environmental concept, a corporate concept, and a management concept. The latter must contain a concept of how to organize the basic features of the enterprise. The starting point is the *three basic questions of organizing*:[1]

How Do We Organize so That...

(a) ... *what customers pay for is the focus of attention, from which it cannot disappear (environment)?* Who are the customers? And what are they paying for? How well do we satisfy these criteria? And what structure of our enterprise enables us to satisfy them even better? The better we answer these questions, the more firmly we will anchor genuine organizational responsibility for customer benefits (see Sect. 2.2).

(b) ... *our employees can do what we pay them to do (operation)?* You might think it goes without saying that people do what they are paid to do. My management training programs and discussions with managers show that they spend 70% of their time doing other things (meetings, phone calls, e-mails, or administration). At the hospital where my brother was a senior physician, nurses spent at most 30% of their time on patient activities. The rest of the time, they wrote reports, attended meetings, transported patients, or changed flower vases. If you ask yourself what you really pay your own people to do, and from time to time check what they are actually doing, you will probably reach similar conclusions.

[1] Fredmund Malik, *Führen, Leisten, Leben: Wirksames Management für eine neue Zeit* (Frankfurt, New York: Campus, 2006). pp. 195–196. English edition: *Management: The Essence of the Craft* (2010).

(c) ... *managers can perform their actual task (management)?* This, too, is not as self-evident as it seems at first. The core task of managers is to shape the future of the business, to seize opportunities, and to tackle what matters. Again, however, most executives spend about 70% of their time doing the opposite: dealing with the urgent instead of the important, solving problems instead of seizing opportunities, and addressing today's business instead of the future. Often, this malaise results from pathological organization. Structural failures force managers into these activities and prevent them from doing their actual jobs. A well-designed organization frees up its top executives for the core tasks of corporate governance: It gives them their time to implement strategic projects, and to identify and seize opportunities.

Together, the three basic elements (environment, operation, and management) form an operational unit. Several operational units form the first control function, which we will call System 1. What follows discusses the *five control functions* and provides some examples to help better understand Systems 1–5. Since we are talking about a model "of any viable system," we can (and will) examine very different examples.

Therefore, to demonstrate how broadly the model can be applied, at one end of the scale let us choose an example with relatively low, yet sometimes overwhelming complexity: the family. Families also function because of structures—or do not function because there are no structures—even if these are not written down in organizational manuals, organizational charts, or flowcharts. Our second, already more complex example is the *project*. A large project, in fact, such as introducing new software in an enterprise involving a hundred people for more than a year. The third, even more complex example is the enterprise. And finally, at the other end of the scale, let us take an enormously complex system, involving millions of families, projects, and enterprises: an entire state.

4.2 System 1: Operational Units

Let us begin introducing the Viable System Model at the very "bottom" of the organization, where the enterprise fulfills its actual purpose: the operational units. In our metaphor of the organism, this is the primary part of the control system and contains the anatomical organs that need to be innervated. The operational units therefore always appear as organizational entities in the organizational chart. Supporting units, on the other hand, which also feature in organizational charts, are not part of System 1 because they do not fulfill their own purpose. It is imperative that we distinguish purpose-fulfilling and supporting functions in the Viable System Model because otherwise we will incorrectly innervate, communicate, and control (Sect. 2.9 and Chap. 8).

Each operational unit in System 1 comprises its own environment, operation, and management. Together, all operational units form the enterprise as a whole.

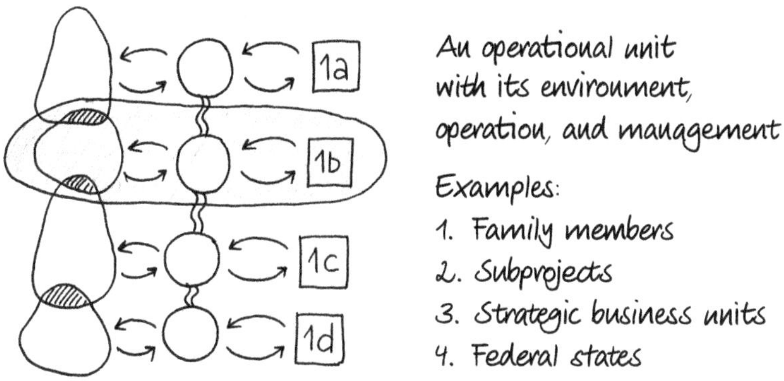

Fig. 4.5 Purpose fulfillment by the operational units

Figure 4.5 shows four such units, albeit quite randomly. The number of units can be very different. There must, however, be at least two units, or there would be nothing to organize. Remember: Operational units organize and manage themselves.

Thus, if we consider only a single unit, its control requires no more than what is given: its own management box. Two units or more, on the other hand, create a higher management level, on which things need to be coordinated and optimized by a senior management team. Any other number of operational units is also conceivable. The largest System 1 that I have encountered comprised 172 units: the Canton of Zurich (Switzerland) with its many municipalities, some of which are very small. The usual rule of thumb for the largest possible span of control does not seem to make sense in this case. Chapter 10 ("Manageable or Not?") will return to this question.

The operational units fulfill the enterprise's purpose by doing what customers or service recipients pay for. These units are meant to independently manage the complexity and dynamics of their own environment and must be granted great autonomy and their own resources (budgets) to do so. Because they want to be part of the whole, they abide by agreed rules of the game and accept that their autonomy is restricted to the extent necessary for the good of the whole.

Ideally, the operational unit should be able to maintain its own independent existence with its own identity. That is, it should be viable, able to lead a separate existence. Yet how exactly do we recognize life? As Chilean biologists and cyberneticists Humberto Maturana and Francisco Varela have shown, self-production defines life, not self-reproduction, as most people think.[2] Our body produces itself anew every 7 years, maintaining order among all the organs and pieces of the puzzle, thus ensuring that we remain the same person even if our cells

[2] Humberto Maturana and Francisco J. Varela, *Autopoeisis and Cognition* (1980).

are different. At age 70, then, we will have reproduced ourselves ten times. The human body does this self-directed, aided by a blueprint in its DNA.

In scientific terms, the body is an *autopoietic system, a self-producing and self-controlling system.* Only the operational units in System 1 should possess such autonomy. As Beer observed: "... any viable system developing autopoiesis in any of its Systems Two, Three or Five is pathologically autopoietic; and that entails a threat to its viability."[3] In practice, however, we repeatedly see organizational units that are not operational and purposeful, yet nevertheless develop a life of their own. They uncouple themselves from their actual support task and do what they think is right. This leads to costly and unproductive bloatedness, for instance, IT, marketing, HR, controlling, or R&D units that have become independent. This can affect units across all disciplines and is symptomatic of shortcomings in the control organization.

Only operational, purpose-fulfilling units should be viable systems in their own right and be given a high degree of autonomy. They need this autonomy to manage the complexity of their environment so that they can act quickly, agilely, and purposefully around the customer. In addition, operational units become freely combinable due to their extensive autonomy, which increases the flexibility of the whole. A unit can be removed or a new one integrated with ease. This is not so simple with a functional or matrix organization, where operational units exhibit strong overlaps and interdependencies.

Conversely, we test matters (and ourselves) by asking whether we could sell a unit and whether it would still be viable without much support. An affirmative answer means that we are dealing with an operational unit. The autonomy enjoyed by these units is always relative. In principle, no absolute autonomy exists because nothing is completely independent. Every existence depends on other existences. If you think of yourself as totally independent, hold your breath for a minutes. Just like our enterprise, we are part of an environment, thanks to which and with which we live. *We are autonomous, yet not independent.*

Chapters 6 and 10 discuss how great this *relative autonomy* can be. Already a fetus (i.e., a pregnancy) can be considered a new operational unit. Autonomy is still very small at this stage, and yet viability already begins here. It increases continuously from embryo, to baby, to child, to adolescent, to young adult. Out of love, we strengthen our children to think and act independently and to take responsibility for themselves until they become capable of maintaining an existence of their own. And even then, they must continue to abide by the rules of their environment. In a children's hospital, patients are already relatively independent and viable beings but they are strongly dependent during admission.

We also find the principle of relative autonomy in our bodies: If, for example, our heart or liver were fully autonomous, they could decide to function differently and we would fall ill. On the other hand, if they could not operate with some degree of autonomy, we would constantly need to instruct them what to do—and would die

[3] Stafford Beer, *Brain of the Firm: The Managerial Cybernetics of Organization*, 2nd ed. (Chichester, New York, Brisbane, Toronto, Singapore: Wiley, 1972). pp. 338 ff.

within minutes. Similarly, an enterprise cannot function if it fails to give its operational units some autonomy. Because otherwise, first, top management would be overwhelmed, and second, the managers of the operational units would quit.

Let us start with the simplest example: the *family*. What are its operational units? Some might say the family home and its rooms. Others would rather call the family's shared experiences operational units. Remember: Models are always shaped by the observer's interest(s). It may make sense to define a house or shared experiences as operational units, depending on what we want to model with their help. If we are interested in how a family functions, it probably makes sense to consider the individual family members operational units. In a traditional nuclear family, for example, these are the mother, father, son, and daughter. Every operational unit has its own environment. The daughter attends school during the day while her father might be working abroad. Environments overlap where family members have in common friends, places, or experiences. Every operational unit also has its own operation. The mother digests her food independently of her husband, whose respiratory system does not rely on his wife (Romantic poetry aside). Nature has provided each of them all with everything necessary for life. This includes the self-management of each operational unit: The mother has her own mind, the daughter hers. This does not always make things easy but it is the prerequisite for mother, daughter, father, and son to be able to control themselves and manage their own affairs to a large extent. The family as a whole would be overwhelmed by this. Its members, however, are there to strengthen each other so that the whole can be more than the sum of its parts.

In a *project*, several options exist for dividing the overall project into operational modules. Typically, a project is divided into subprojects or project modules, each having to perform its own task(s) in its own environment and in turn possessing its own resources (operation) and subproject management. The environments of the subprojects overlap to a greater or lesser extent, depending on how well the tasks have been delineated from one another. Dependencies may exist between operations, for example, when individual employees work on several subprojects at the same time.

In an *enterprise*, we speak of departments, strategic business units or divisions, or entire businesses in a group, depending on their "flight altitude." Systems 1 may or may not be legal entities. Whether something is a legal entity or not is relevant for public authorities and taxation but not for controlling the enterprise. Alfred Sloan, the former president of General Motors Company, whom we already came across in Sect. 1.1, is said to have invented a classification of strategic business units. For Sloan, a strategic business unit corresponds to what we mean by an operational unit in the Viable System Model: An entity capable of sustaining its own existence in the long run.

In Sloan's case, the Buick brand had its own environment (i.e., Buick customers, competitors, and suppliers), its own operation (i.e., Buick plants), and its own Buick management, which was not meant to care about anything but Buick. The same was true for the other GM brands. Every operational unit catered to a portion of the total market, enabling customers to enter the GM world with low-cost brands like

Chevrolet and to work their way up to the prestigious Cadillac brand in the premium customer segment. Again, the environments overlapped because more or less the same customers were buying the most expensive Chevrolet or the least expensive Pontiac in the marginal segments. Interdependencies existed between operations when brand autonomy was limited in order to take advantage of synergies, for example, in development or purchasing.

To keep the last example—the *state*—understandable, let us look at a European, democratic state (e.g., Germany or Switzerland). This usually consists of federal states (in Switzerland, cantons), whose environment is defined by geographical borders. It is clear where Bavaria begins and where it ends. Nevertheless, environmental overlaps occur, for example, when enterprises operate in several countries and thus belong to several environments. People are also part of the environment. They also move between countries but act mainly in one country, where they also participate or collaborate in the operation in one way or another. Operations include cities, utilities, airports, educational institutions, the police, and plenty more that is managed at the state level. Every state, moreover, has its own management box (i.e., government and parliament) that primarily manages the interests of that state internally and externally. Every federal state enjoys a relatively high degree of autonomy in a federal state system and would in principle be viable without the state—as the Bavarians, for example, rightly emphasize time and again. Nevertheless, they also accept the common rules of the state and its restrictions because they want to be part of this state. This balance—between freedom of action on the one hand and its restriction by a higher level whole on the other—is an age-old problem, which Chap. 6 discusses in the context of autonomy and hierarchy.

4.3 System 2: Coordination

How are operational units interconnected? Depending on how the overall enterprise has been designed, the environmental overlaps and operational dependencies are greater or smaller. As in set theory, an environmental overlap means that, for example, the same customer appears in two environments. This kind of overlap may also arise from common competitors, suppliers, stakeholder or interest groups, affiliations, or geographies. Operations are also more or less interdependent, depending on organizational design; for example, when they need to access common resources or pursue common strategies. In our diagram, let us draw the *environmental overlaps as shaded areas* and the *dependencies* between operations as *vertical squiggly lines* (Fig. 4.6).

These overlaps and dependencies are problematic because they can lead to conflicts. The freedom of one operational unit ends where another's freedom begins. If two units serve the same customer, they need to coordinate, to prevent two salespeople from standing on the customer's doorstep at the same time oblivious to each other. They need to coordinate not only deadlines but also customer development strategies, procedures, pricing, communication channels, and lots more. When two operations access the same resources, as often happens with large

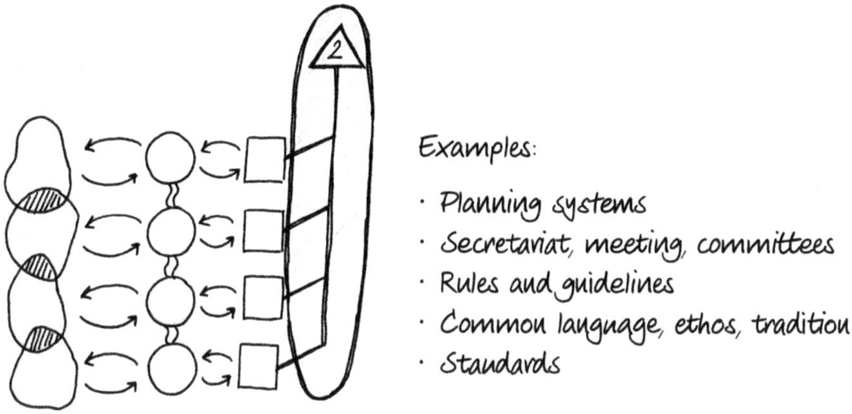

Fig. 4.6 Coordination and oscillation-damping

projects, there must be rules, or one operation will always profit at the expense of the other.

This is the core task of the next control system: System 2. Represented in the model as a triangle, it ensures the smooth cooperation of the operational units in System 1, where they have to work together. It regulates the problem areas and coordinates activities wherever overlaps and dependencies exist. Cybernetics calls this *"oscillation-damping"*: When two or more systems are connected via feedback, they can develop each other's momentum. In technology, this leads to practical problems such as whistling loudspeakers. But even among people, conflicts can take hold and eventually be hugely damaging. Even if it amounts to "much ado about nothing," conflicts are still time-consuming and nerve-wracking. We must deal with them, in order to avoid major damage, including smoldering fires, and to ensure they do not stop us unnecessarily from focusing on our customer and business.

It is better to prevent conflicts than having to resolve them. Sections 2.4 and 2.5 have already addressed the problem of interfaces and dependencies, among others, in the matrix organization. Remember: Do not optimize but avoid them as far as possible. Thus, when you segment the enterprise, ensure operational units overlap as little as possible in their environment and that each has its own resources as far as possible. Amid today's digitalization, where everyone is focusing on *networking* (interconnecting) everything with everything, we therefore also need to increasingly reconsider where *de-networking* is right and important because it makes things robust.

Now, "de-networking" has not (yet) entered today's dictionaries. It will, however, become important for the future organization because factors such as agility, flexibility, speed, motivation, and drive all emerge from the ability to de-network. The more de-networked things are, the more self-directedness, freedom, and ultimately robustness become possible. The so-called Year 2000 Bug (i.e., the worldwide collapse of all IT systems due to the changing of dates at the turn of the millennium) failed to occur because systems were far more de-networked than we believed.

Interconnecting what does not belong together, or incorrect networking, generates high costs and blockages. It is also dangerous. In the future, we will have to learn to neatly and tidily network what really belongs together and to eliminate the rest as far as possible. Even the best segmentation as a rule entails unavoidable overlaps or intentional dependencies, which must now be managed by System 2. Normally, this is still more than we would like. In practice, today's Systems 2 today tend to be too weakly developed, creating many unnecessary sources of conflict as a result. Cleanly regulating all overlaps and dependencies is therefore an important control element and an important ingredient for success. Regulation should not be confused with regimentation because regulation is also possible without paper and regulations.

System 2 comprises all functions, services, systems, and mechanisms having a coordinating, harmonizing, and oscillation-damping effect. It includes a school timetable, which ensures that only one class occupies the same classroom at a time. It is the fire department's operational plan, which ensures that firefighters needn't argue over who will hold the hose today if there is a fire. It is the right-of-way rule that keeps traffic flowing. We could, of course, station a police officer at the intersection to ensure traffic flow. Well-designed two-way systems, on the other hand, ensure extensive *self-coordination*: They require no coordination but self-coordinate. They create the prerequisite for units to coordinate themselves among themselves. Coordination need not be enforced top-down in the form of rules. Ideally, the managers of operational units will design their mechanisms themselves.

Let us return to our examples: What are the System 2 functions in a *family*? If we ask ourselves where environmental overlaps and dependencies need to be coordinated in a family of four, we will likely not first think of family law but of the spat at seven in the morning when everyone wants to get into the bathroom at the same time. So: We need a rule. Perhaps a weekly schedule (posted on the refrigerator), which coordinates the activities of family members and records who needs the car when, when they are visiting Auntie Emmi this weekend, or who will away in the evening and for how long. Being socialized with the family's rules for living together and childraising teaches its members consideration and tolerance. Take the family dinner, a sacred principle in many families: Members eat together instead of alone gazing at their smartphone. System 2 is excellent for coordinating a family because members ask and tell each other what is going on, as well as listen to each other.

In a *project*, environmental overlaps and operational dependencies exist between subprojects. We have already considered the problem of individual colleagues working on several subprojects at the same time and therefore being permanently absent either here or there. Good resource planning is therefore an important element of System 2 in a project. Other elements include the project plan (with milestones), project coordination meetings, possibly a project software (to be used by everyone), or rules of conduct (to be set out by the overall project manager). Subproject managers who recognize dependencies with other subprojects will independently exchange ideas and information and coordinate with their managers, and thus design their own System 2.

In an *enterprise*, many things belong to System 2: First of all, formal matters such as coordinating meetings, boards and committees, offices and secretariats, joint service centers, planning and control systems in computers, company policy (guidelines and directives), employee contracts, or professional standards. Coordination can also enable novelty, just as sheet music enables an orchestra to perform music. In the enterprise, this can be competence centers or conferences that enable mutual learning or initiate innovative ideas. In addition, the informal dimension may also have a coordinating effect: People know the company's traditions, speak a common language, and exchange ideas at business lunches. The unexpected also happens: I once experienced a Swiss medium-sized company where the CEO and the divisional heads were always well informed about each other. In the 1990s, the divisional heads were still smoking, as was the assistant to the managing director. Problems began when the latter stopped smoking. Before, they had met several times a day in the smokers' corner and had discussed matters. These informal gatherings involved sharing information that would otherwise have been lost in reports or memos. These meetings also helped resolve misunderstandings and clarify issues. Thus, even a smokers' corner might be part of a functioning control organization, even if unconsciously. Moreover, we have described corporate culture as a part of the organizational structure in the third dimension of organizing. This is where it becomes effective because culture coordinates human behavior. It concerns what people do or ought better not do in an enterprise.

In 1960, the Austrian physicist, philosopher, and cyberneticist Heinz von Foerster, who also attended the Macy conferences in the 1950s, before becoming director of MIT's Biological Computer Laboratory, formulated the principle "Order from Noise": Under certain conditions *order may arise from disorder by itself.*[4] Normally, the opposite is true. Disordered elements self-organize to form a pattern, for example, when crystalline sand is shaken on a glass plate and the parts converge to form a recognizable shape because of their own structure, as if controlled by an invisible hand.

A well-working System 2 tries to exploit this effect by ensuring that all employees have the same understanding of what constitutes a good meeting, for example. When all employees have the same expectations about a meeting, self-regulation begins to take effect, and order emerges over time as if by itself. This means leading without leading. Companies create such crystalline structures by embedding the same understanding of leadership in every single employee like a genetic code. That suffices. Everything else happens on its own to create order. This also includes making public the implicit rules of the game. They might only become clear when we consider what advice we would give a friend newly entering this enterprise: How to achieve success as quickly as possible? What blunders should be avoided at all costs? As long as they remain implicit, the rules favor those in the enterprise who know them. If, on the other hand, everyone knows them, then

[4]Heinz Von Foerster, "On self-organizing systems and their environments." In: M.C. Yovits and S, Cameron (eds.), *Self-organizing systems* (London: Pergamon, 1960), pp. 31 ff.

everyone is bound by them, even the CEO. This enables everyone to achieve great self-organizing power as part of System 2.

In a *state*, its confederated states share certain tasks in special-purpose associations and cooperations, while cross-state coordination exists in ministries and offices. The required bodies and legal entities are part of the country's System 2. Here, too, we are reminded of a common language. Of course, laws and regulations also have a strong, coordinating, and oscillation-damping effect, as do customs and culture. However, those unable to communicate will struggle to find their way around. Socializing children is important, not only by their parents but also by schools, recreational associations, teachers, and bosses. In the past, more than today, a common religion damped oscillation (i.e., mitigated diversity). Given the increasing diversity of languages, cultures, religions, and traditions due to globalization, a functioning System 2 is probably one of the greatest challenges of politics—especially in highly diverse Europe.

4.4 System 3: Optimization and Auditing

We have now developed our model to the extent that several operational units can organize, control, and optimize themselves (System 1). Moreover, wherever they are interconnected, they can also coordinate themselves independently (System 2). These first two control elements are necessary for a viable system. But are they sufficient? Neoliberalism seems to answer this question in the affirmative: If everyone takes care of themselves, everyone is taken care of. This may be the case with certain exceptions, such as a pure financial holding company, whose sole aim is to invest in interesting businesses. We can exclude this case here because there is little to control, since the individual businesses have nothing to do with each other.

If, however, we consider a holding company, or any other form of social organization where interaction is important, it takes more than Systems 1 and 2. The old liberal thinkers, the eighteenth-century Scottish Enlightenment thinkers, were thinking of a different liberalism: Every unit should optimize itself and take care of itself. And yet, they also knew that the sum of all partial optima is never equal to the total optimum. Instead, it is either smaller or larger, depending on unit interaction. Thus, a higher level function needs to controls interaction. In poorly managed organizations, the overall optimum is smaller, and every operational unit would be better off on its own. Often, such organizations end up disintegrating back into their component parts, as in the case of the former Yugoslavia, when the state dissolved into several countries again. This may also happen when a corporation is sold off, or when a family goes through a divorce.

The whole does not become more than the sum of its parts of its own accord. It needs the right organization and control to do so. In the Viable System Model, System 3 ensures the optimization of the current business. This internal function deals with existing products, customers, employees, technologies, and activities. Beer therefore calls this function *"Inside & Now."* Its task is to ensure that synergies are exploited by looking at the whole "from the top down," so to speak, and thus

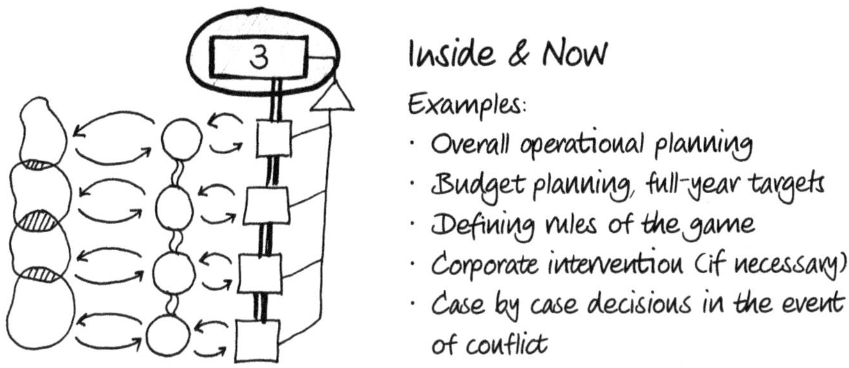

Fig. 4.7 Optimizing today's business

recognizing where and how we could be stronger together. The operational units cannot see this because they are busy optimizing and maintaining themselves. They may not even want overall optimization because it may contradict their own interests. Thus, we need System 3's higher level control function. This can implement measures for the good of the whole even against the interests of individual units if necessary. In doing so, it never interferes in issues that can and must be resolved by the management box of an operational unit itself. Instead of engaging in micromanagement, it concentrates on overall optimization.

For this purpose, System 3, which we can also call *"operational management,"* needs information about the status and plans of the operational units. It must be able to communicate with them. The management boxes of System 1 are all located on the vertical control axis, which connects them to System 3. The vertical lines in the model are the communication channels, through which they report to higher level management and, vice versa, through which they receive their instructions. Figure 4.7 shows two such vertical communication channels. Hence, there are two types of communication between System 3 and System 1:

(a) A *"Resource Bargain and Accountability"* communication channel, through which planning is coordinated and optimized, budgets or goals are discussed and agreed, and responsibility for the distributed resources is handed over and demanded.
(b) A *"Corporate Intervention"* communication channel, through which the autonomy of the operational units can be restricted at any time due to corporate requirements. This channel must also be able to act as a command channel, as a last resort when circumstances demand a higher level decision. In well-organized enterprises, this command channel is used only as little as necessary—yet remains available when needed.

Through these two channels, System 3 optimizes cooperation between the operational units in System 1. To this end, it manages and optimizes the portfolio of its operational units. It can decide to reduce or sell one unit and to develop or purchase another. It allocates available resources in the interests of the whole and thus sets priorities. It identifies and realizes synergies. And it ensures that experience is used and that people learn from each other. Put more comprehensively: It ensures that the whole becomes more than the sum of its parts.

In a *family*, the System 3 function is usually performed jointly by the parents. They discuss, plan, and decide what is good and necessary for the family as a whole and then implement these decisions. They decide how to divide tasks between each other, how to raise the children, and whether to have separate or joint property. They determine who would support whom in the near future. They define the rules of the game that should apply to the whole and which, once defined, will take effect in System 2. Since they are also units of this family, they must also abide by these rules. In another family, the System 3 function may be performed by the husband or wife alone, and perhaps the children will also be involved in certain decisions.

In terms of viability and functioning, it is not relevant who performs a function but only that it is performed. Which and how many people perform a function may vary depending on the organization and situation. *A function can be performed by one person or by several persons.* Vice versa, a single person may also wear several hats, that is, perform different control tasks in different systems. While the persons can change, the control tasks remain the same. Therefore, in terms of the Viable System Model, it makes sense to speak of System 3 management rather than of a manager, that is, a person.

In a large *project*, System 3 tasks are performed by the operational project management. Again, depending on project size roject, this may be just one person, that is, an overall project manager, or a body consisting of several people. Here, too, project management makes decisions to optimize the whole. It lays down the overriding rules of the game and defines the methods and resources to be used, also making these available via its System 2. It agrees targets and deadlines with the subproject leaders in System 1 and allocates the required resources to them. It monitors progress in achieving the defined goals and intervenes supportively if required. An operational unit may need to forego or limit its activities in favor of another, for example, because the particular competencies of an excellent project employee are needed more urgently in subproject B than in subproject A.

In an *enterprise*, operational management is performed by a managing director or a committee (e.g., an executive board or a board of directors) with the support of specialist departments. Depending on the legal form, other organizational entities are also possible. The task of a COO (Chief Operating Officer) is a typical System 3 task. It includes overall operational planning, budget planning, setting annual targets, and ongoing monitoring of target achievement, solving acute problems, and overseeing the overall productivity of the current business. Decisions made by specialist departments, for example, on personnel or IT issues, are also part of System 3, provided they affect overall optimization. System 3 is responsible for ensuring that the enterprise's existing success potential, such as a large market share, is effectively translated into economic success. With a large market share, this means converting economies of scale into cost advantages. This is achieved, for example, by System 3 limiting the autonomy of System 1 such that purchasing is centralized or other cost-reducing synergies are exploited. Size is useful only if turned into strength. System 3 analyzes profitability issues and manages them in advance. If the egotism of individual operational units becomes detrimental to cooperation, System 3 intervenes through the intervention channel.

In a *state*, the System 3 function is mainly performed by the executive branch, (i.e., government and public administration). It is the executive power, which, rather than enacting laws, at most requests (or demands) them and, above all, implements them. It guides the state through operational matters, for which it establishes various ministries and federal offices to handle different issues. Their functions also belong to System 3, insofar as they contribute to optimizing the "Inside & Now" in the state.

4.4.1 System 3*: Real-Life Information and Auditing

System 3 therefore optimizes the overall internal performance of the enterprise and makes decisions for the good of the whole. On what information are such decisions based? How does System 3 inform itself and how can it know what is really happening and what is relevant? As mentioned, the two vertical reporting channels between the management boxes of the operational units and System 3 are available. As a rule, these two channels work very reliably but also very selectively because, first, they only report what the lines themselves can see and, second, because they only report what they want to report. In addition, another communication channel is available through System 2. This comprises automated reports, retrievable from the systems and computers. However, neither the reports of the operational managers nor computer data represent reality, but only ever filtered and selected content. The picture remains incomplete, which can be dangerous for higher level decisions.

Natural systems teach us that System 3 opens up another communication channel to give itself a better information base: This so-called System 3* belongs to System 3 and is represented in the model as an upside-down triangle. It delivers *unfiltered information directly from the operations* in System 1 to System 3 so that better decisions can be made there (Fig. 4.8). The operating principle of System 3* is *"Go & See."* It is thus an internal audit of sorts, not only financial and administrative but also driven by specific issues and interests. It can be used by the higher level management in System 3, for instance, to discover potential synergy effects in which operations managers might have no interest at all. It sees what no one else sees because this becomes relevant solely from the perspective of the whole. The number of different screws or electric motors installed in the group is not relevant for the individual business unit. However, reducing this complexity can create significant cost benefits for the group as a whole.

System 3* is *not an intervention channel* but a pure *information channel*. People establish a sense of things on the ground. If anything needs to be corrected, this is done in the normal way via the "corporate intervention" channel between System 3 and System 1 mentioned above. It is also advantageous for operations managers if higher level management has some "grip on reality" and is aware of what is going on

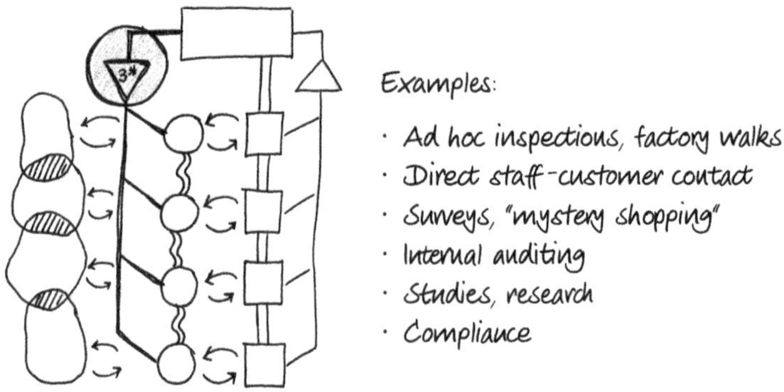

Fig. 4.8 System 3*: real-life information and auditing

"outside" (i.e., daily business). No operations manager wants to deal with management that does not understand its own challenges. That would be frowned upon as an "ivory tower" mentality and, more importantly, would lead to poor decisions and faulty management. On the other hand, if management knows what is going on, messages on the vertical communication axis are more likely interpreted and understood in the right context. The System 3* channel also ensures that agreements and requirements are adhered to, that processes work, and that performance and quality meet expectations. In this sense, System 3* also builds trust on both sides.

In a *family*, a System 3* function is performed, for example, by the representatives of System 3 participating in the activities of other family members from time to time in order to find out how they are doing. This is different from involving your child or partner in your hobbies so that you can be together. It is about obtaining unfiltered information from the other family members to better understand them. Even a parent-teacher meeting about our child's behavior at school, or an occasional phone call during the day is a System 3* channel: We want to know how others are doing, whether they need support, and perhaps whether they are adhering to agreements.

In a *project*, the overall project manager, or representatives of the overall project management, delve into subproject activities, perhaps attending meetings unannounced and talking to project staff. Again, this should never be about intervention but always about information. What is being talked about? How are deferrals (or shifted deadlines) handled? Where do employees recognize unused opportunities or unsolved problems?

In an *enterprise*, the enterpreneur's classical walk through the factory is part of System 3* before heading to the office at eight in the morning. They talk to employees and by chance learn a lot that no one would have told them. They see for themselves whether everything is tidy and which orders are ready for dispatch. They can listen to individual employees. And since this walk is part of a daily ritual, sometimes conversations are substantial and important. At the other end of the scale, on the formal side, regular auditing functions such as internal audits are part of

System 3*, institutionalized primarily in larger enterprises. In between, management may obtain unfiltered information in all sorts of ways: unannounced visits to construction sites, direct customer contact, internal surveys or studies. A large Swiss telecommunications company, after discovering that senior managers had not seen a customer first-hand for a long time, sent them to work at outlets for a few days to once again experience what makes real customers tick, which they would otherwise merely know from reading marketing reports. A British television station even dedicated its own reality show to System 3*: In "Undercover Boss," board members work undercover in their enterprises with their employees to gain an unbiased view of work processes. Alfred Sloan, the former president of GM, reportedly amazed his managers with an in-depth, even intimate understanding of their business. He even systematically established several System 3* information channels to remain well informed even at the top of the corporation. This included visiting a dealership once a year, unbeknownst to his employees, and spending a week on the shop floor and in sales—less to sell cars than to learn directly from customers what mattered to them and what did not, and what they did and did not pay attention to. Back at headquarters in Detroit, he used this knowledge in conversations with engineers, developers, and marketing managers. He was notorious for not being bluffed by reports and empirical studies from staff departments. He went and looked for himself.

In a *state*, finally, an uncensored media landscape exerts an enormous System 3* effect. This is probably the systemic reason why media freedom is so highly esteemed in democracies. In a state, very many people in different functions and with different perspectives work together in System 3. They all inform themselves through the media about what concerns citizens and what discrepancies have been uncovered. In particular, critical scrutiny of how the government and its agencies work at all levels of the state, provinces, and municipalities is one of the basic tasks of the media. The more important public offices become, the greater the danger that information will be fed to them tainted and filtered.

How do political leaders know what really concerns citizens? They are themselves citizens, of course, but their life differs greatly from that of other citizens. While they may have friends, staff, and staff units, their position means that the information they receive becomes ambivalent as it is colored by particular interests. Political leaders in particular must therefore build their own System 3* channel. Konrad Adenauer, for example, did so apparently by traveling a lot by taxi—less to get from A to B than to hear from cab drivers what people were talking about. What were they worried about? What arguments were they making? Presumably, Adenauer learned what no one else would have told him. The national audit office, the secret service, citizen surveys, and so on also perform System 3* functions in a state.

4.5 System 4: Intelligence and Adaptation

Once again, we must ask whether we have meanwhile sufficiently developed the control system. We have established that Systems 1–3 are necessary. But why does our model need a System 4? Figure 4.9 shows an environment that is larger than all the environments of System 1 put together. These are embedded in an overall environment of the enterprise that encompasses much more than the existing business. Within this overall environment lie all the present and future *opportunities and threats, of both the known world and the still unknown world.* This includes untapped markets, unexpected acquisition opportunities, new technologies and applications, or changes in legislation. We need a control function that has these changes on its radar and helps us prepare the enterprise for the future in this environment. We can call this intelligence and adaptation function in the enterprise's control system *"strategic management."* Someone equipped only with functioning Systems 1–3 would walk elegantly across the street but without System 4 would not see an approaching vehicle.

The structural division into (1) a System 3 for today's business and (2) a System 4 for future business is a proven solution of nature and an alternative worth considering to the customary distribution of business (e.g., into administrative and disciplinary leadership) in the management box. Today, this division arises less from the logic of functioning than from the logic of professional specialization, in order to exploit expertise, or from organizational history, such as acquisitions. It tends to lead to reductionist behavior because people bury themselves in their silos and end up interfering with each other rather than supporting each other. Ultimately, we need both: expertise and an overall view of the current and the future business. Even the classical division into staff and line no longer makes much sense. Staff members are now so highly specialized that, as experts, they are already making the

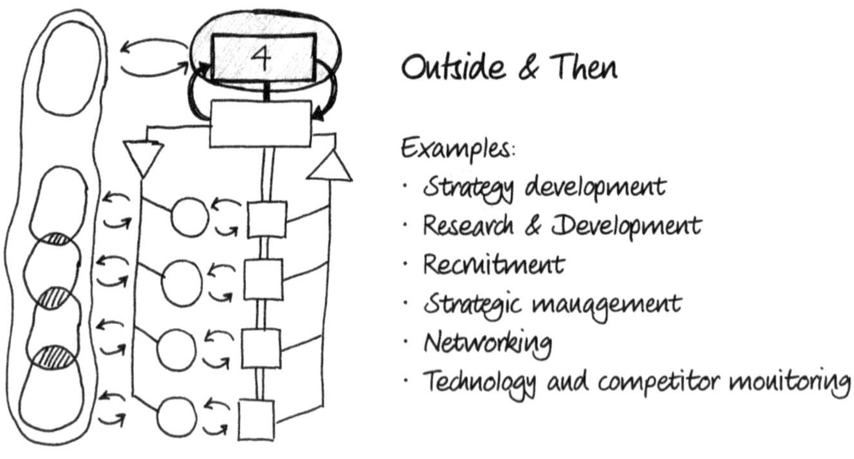

Fig. 4.9 System 4: external communication, intelligence, and adaptation

decision when they present option A, which is likely to win, or option B, which is more likely to lead to ruin. This is the kind of recommendation that management expects from them today. Thus, they should be just as accountable as line managers.

Nature has found a better way of dividing labor in the management box than specialist functions or staff and line. It favors an *overall view* because that is the task of control: to control the whole in all its dimensions and interrelations. It therefore divides the whole into an autonomic nervous system (System 3), which is concerned with the *"Inside & Now,"* and into a system of sensors linked to the midbrain and limbic system (System 4), which is concerned with the *"Outside & Then."* In humans, this System 4 is highly developed. It gives us greater foresight and ability to plan than animals are capable of. This biological subdivision is a clever, reasonable, and understandable trick of nature—one we are not yet using systematically in our businesses. It focuses control on what matters for viability: *integrating outside and inside, present and future*.

System 4 works like a "crow's nest" on a sailing ship. When the lookout discovers things on the horizon that do not fit the normal pattern, he or she reports this. It is the same in our organism: Even when we are asleep, all control systems are still somewhat active, and when we hear a sound that does not fit into our known patterns, System 4 wakes us up. The design of a functioning control system for intelligence gathering and adaptation in the enterprise, whose attention is directed outward and into the future, is most important when this environment is changing rapidly—that is, today! Jack Welch, the successful former CEO of General Electric, was a System 4 talent. One of his most famous statements highlights what he really believed in: *"If the rate of change outside exceeds the rate of change inside—the end is in sight."* Welch was a successful, albeit controversial, change maker. The more change outside, the stronger System 4 must be. Otherwise, normative System 5 (to be discussed below) collapses into and identifies with System 3. Instead of operating in the *mode of self-determined adaptation*, the enterprise sooner or later operates only in the mode of permanent crisis management.

Like System 3, System 4 also fulfills its tasks on the *vertical control axis*. Unlike in an organizational chart, we do not enter somewhere on the side or in the margin. If it is not given the same importance and responsibility as operational management, nothing will change in an enterprise. Take, for example, social and political organizations: If changes cannot also be brought about on the vertical line of command and via jointly established laws, little will change. The discussion about the disadvantages of democratic states compared to dictatorships concerns precisely this point. Although our European states also undergo permanent change, via the enactment of laws on the vertical axis, this happens much more sluggishly than, for example, in China at the beginning of the new millennium, where a stronger vertical axis of control is evident.

Either way, many countries seem to miss making the necessary adjustments, even though their necessity could have long been recognized, for example, due to demographic developments, and certainly has been. The problem of today's aging society, for example, could have been foreseen 50 years ago. Nevertheless, not much has happened. On a global level, too, the vertical axis of the United Nations seems to function quite weakly, as argued in the Prologue. Unsolved problems at home pull states back from multilateralism, leaving overarching challenges unresolved. Firms also often struggle with vertical axes that are too weak. This is the main reason why many are struggling with digitization. Although aware of the potential and determined to exploit it, they soon become disillusioned by the modest practical success. As studies have shown, this is due to a lack of leadership, not of ideas and opportunities.[5] They lack the reduction gearbox to put the horsepower on the road as well.

Thus, while System 3 focuses on exploiting existing success potential, and is interested in operational performance, System 4 ensures the timely development of *new, future success potential*. Existing markets can disappear if they migrate to new technologies or business models that better solve the same customer problem. Then, even a 70% market share suddenly loses its value: There is no use having a large market share in an in exceedingly small market. The last remaining supplier of encyclopedias, whose spines once adorned bookshelves in every living room, will eventually have a market share of 100%—but almost no market anymore. And the major manufacturers of photographic cameras (e.g., Leica, Minolta, Pentax, Canon, or Nikon) lost most of their market to a competitor suddenly emerging from a completely different industry: By integrating a camera and a telephone into a single device, Nokia conquered the global camera market as a telecommunications company at the beginning of the millennium. The most comfortable size is useless when circumstances demand change. Entire corporations have collapsed because they failed to transition from the old to the new business in time.

As the horizontal communication channels between System 4 and the overall environment of the company show, *System 4 communicates with this environment.* It informs its stakeholders about itself. It maintains important networks. It performs intelligence work. It identifies relevant opportunities and threats early on. It develops an understanding of the organization in its future environment. To do this, it thinks in the subjunctive: We could, would, or should. As such, it opens up the horizon of possibilities and highlights probabilities. It makes proposals for the development of the enterprise and coordinates them with System 3. This involves *balancing today's business with tomorrow's business.* Today's business, which is ultimately where money is made and from which all (ad)ventures must be financed, also has its needs: Customers like predictability and reliability, which operational units must also earn through continuity. Investments also need to be made in existing technologies, production facilities, or markets. Employees must have a share in success. Depreciation has to be increased or owners must be serviced. Hence, competing for resources to optimize today's business and build the future business always involves a tough yet necessary struggle to strike the right balance. This permanent struggle for the right answers is represented by the two thick, circular arrows on the left and right of Systems 3 and 4, which connect them in a balancing circuit (Fig. 4.9). This control

[5]Roman Stöger, "Umsetzung der Digitalisierung. Fazit 1.0 in der Neuen Welt." *Organisationsentwicklung* No. 1. (2017), pp. 58–84.

mechanism is important because it ensures *adaptability* (see Sect. 13.4 for details; see Chap. 18 for a discussion of the necessary instruments).

In a *family*, the System 4 function addresses key questions about the family's future: Do we want another child? Will we relocate to America for your new job? Where and how do we want to live in the future? Do we want to buy a dog? Will our retirement plans work out? A family might sit down together to discuss these and other issues (family council). The family's System 4 also communicates with its overall environment and maintains the family's network and social contacts.

In a *project*, a steering committee as a rule performs System 4 functions. It identifies environmental changes compared to the original project plan and discusses necessary and tolerable deviations. Together with the project manager (System 3), the committee weighs up and takes decisions to guide the project toward its goal. Continuously communicating the project's current status to the outside world, to stakeholders and employees, is also part of System 4 tasks in the project.

In an *enterprise*, corporate communications might handle stakeholder communication together with the board of directors. R&D departments will concern themselves with the technological future. Strategy projects will be carried out, research conducted, technologies developed, patents registered, and competitors observed. Strategic marketing designs concepts for the enterprise's future market orientation. IT designs functional strategy, and human resources development, along with recruiting, ensure the right people are hired to pursue organizational development in timely fashion. Complex environments are modeled and simulated to help understand megatrends. Decisions are made about whether to make an acquisition, forge an alliance, exit an existing business, or open a new one. How well Systems 4 are developed, and whether they are strong enough to be taken seriously by System 3, varies greatly from enterprise to enterprise. They tend to be too weak. Although they often function quite well in themselves, at the latest when systems need to be balanced, they are not sufficiently considered compared to System 3. They are often formalistic and not very effective. Less thought has been given to their design than to that of System 3. In particular, a decision-making mechanism between System 4 and System 3 is often lacking, which would enable redirected resources from the old to the new business in good time.

In a democratic *state*, the executive branch, as observed, is the essential (yet by no means the only) System 3 function. Ever since Baron de Montesquieu introduced the separation of powers in the eighteenth century, the second power, the legislative branch, has performed essential System 4 functions. Parliaments deliberate on the future and propose necessary legislative adjustments. Lobbies are created and relationships forged at home and abroad. Entire departments deal solely with the proper communication of the state to its stakeholders, through the media and official channels. The interaction between the government (System 3) and parliament (System 4) is an interplay between what is possible today and what is required in the future. Parties and individual citizens also participate in System 4 functions by determining the direction of their state at the polls. In the case of direct democracy, they even decide on factual issues, such as purchasing new fighter jets, adjusting tax laws, or whether or not cows should have horns in the future. Finally, the media

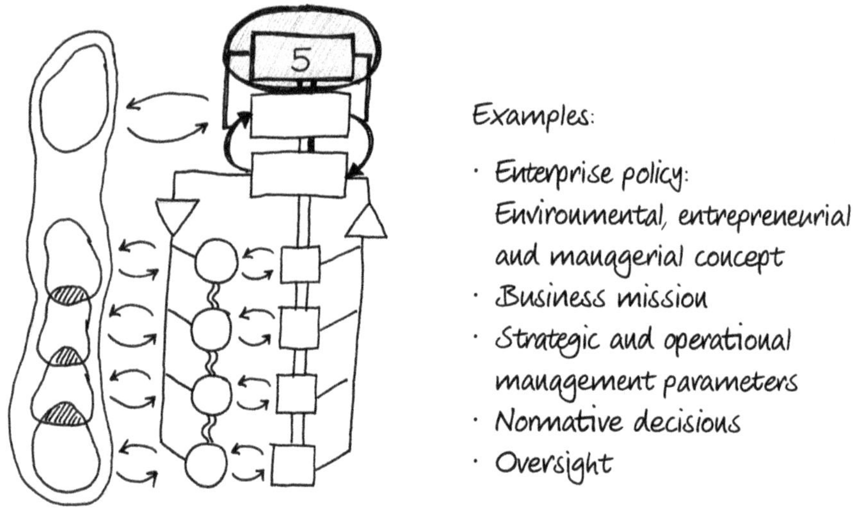

Fig. 4.10 System 5: identity and normative policy

perform not only an important System 3* function in the state, as argued above, but also a crucial System 4 function. They can strengthen opinions that can steer the views of a population and its politicians and government in one direction rather than another. The rise of artificial intelligence, and its manifold opportunities, will bolster this power even further than in the past, in a development that involves both opportunities and threats.

4.6 System 5: Identity

Our model now includes four different control functions. System 5 completes the control system as the last function and makes it self-referential. This *normative control* makes fundamental statements about itself: Who do I want to be? How do I want to function? What do I consider important and what not? This provides the enterprise with meaning, consistency, and identity, which hold it together. With these basic statements, System 5 flanks the work to be done in Systems 4 and 3. These statements may be written down or may simply take unconscious effect, just as our sense of self gives us an identity that distinguishes us from others. The sum of such fundamental decisions is called a policy while individual issues are called "policies." A policy is a basic decision that is valid for an unlimited period of time.

Figure 4.10 shows that, besides the two communication channels on the vertical control axis, which flank Systems 4 and 3, System 5 also has another communication channel. This connects it to the balancing circuit between Systems 3 and 4. System 5 is thus meant to ensure balance and intervene in case of instability. This may be necessary, for example, if no decision can be found argumentatively because there is too much uncertainty, but where a decision still needs to be made. In this case, System 5 steps in: It makes a normative decision, without further justification, yet with reference to its identity and mission. These decisions amount to a "That's enough!" Hence, they are often made by the highest authority, for instance, the company owners or the population. System 5, as the highest authority, absorbs the last remaining complexity, which has not been absorbed by the other, upstream systems, and decides, as the final authority, all remaining questions.

In a well-functioning *family*, such fundamental decisions are discussed between spouses: What kind of family do we want to be? What do we believe in? How do we envision our life together? What do we find meaning in? How important are children and how important is a career? By addressing such questions, a new identity is created, of partnership and family. All subsequent decisions are measured against this identity. It is the reference point for whatever will be undertaken together. Values, role models, and traditions play a major role in this process. These ideals orient the control system when finding the right compromises becomes difficult.

In a *project*, basic normative decisions are also made during setup: The purpose and goal are described in the project mandate, the project manager and steering committee are appointed, the project methodology and IT systems are defined, the communication rules to be followed, or how to proceed in case of conflict. Typically, either the project sponsor makes such decisions, perhaps together with the designated project manager, or a general project policy is applied. However, System 5 also includes an oversight function and a final decision-making authority if issues cannot be resolved by the project manager and steering committee. They may occur, for example, because irregularities have occurred or because basic assumptions have fundamentally changed.

In an *enterprise*, identity is defined by the business mission and the corporate policy. This contains an environmental concept, which defines where the company should operate, a corporate concept, which specifies the business model, and a management concept, which determines the *modus operandi* (i.e., the functioning of the company as a whole.[6] A company's System 5 not only ensures the existence of these normative parameters (flanking measures) but also supervises compliance with them. This also means that it can intervene if necessary or actively support Systems 3 and 4. The relevant supervisory bodies and their tasks are endowed with different powers and responsibilities in the various forms of corporate law. But if we consider function, once more it does not matter who made a decision, only that it could be made. After all, the most important fundamental decisions are reserved for the owners, for example, the shareholders or partners, depending on the legal form.

The *state* lays down these principles in the constitution, and the supreme judicial authority, the Constitutional Court, ensures their observance. The fundamental decisions are made by the supreme authority of the state. In a democracy, this is either the people or its elected representatives. The extent of a head of state's rights

[6]Fredmund Malik, *Unternehmenspolitik und Corporate Governance: Wie Organisationen sich selbst organisieren* (Frankfurt, New York: Campus, 2008), pp. 141–258. English edition: *Corporate Policy and Goverance* (2011).

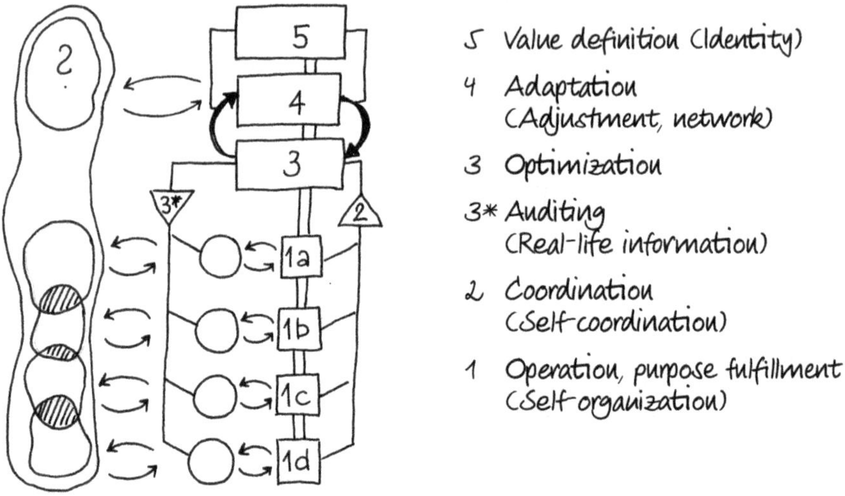

Fig. 4.11 System 5: the viable system model (VSM)

depends on the form of government and—as practice has shown time and again—on their self-image. Stafford Beer once told me how he explained the Viable System Model to newly elected President Salvador Allende in the early 1970s. Allende had contacted Beer because he was looking for an alternative to both Chile's feudalistic system, which had become untenable, and the communist system with its planned economy, which was functioning just as badly. As a trained physician, he understood very well Beer's explanations about the nervous system and the relation to the control system in a functioning state. When they came to System 5, and just as Beer was about to explain that he (Allende) was System 5, the president reportedly exclaimed with relief: "Ah, finalmente—el pueblo!"

Although the state constitution granted him extensive rights as an elected president, Allende saw himself exclusively as a representative of the people. What is interesting about this example is that the lowest authority in the organization, the citizen, toward whom the entire state is directed, is also the highest authority. This need not be the case in every state but it has interesting, self-regulating effects. Thus, in the direct, most immediate form of democracy, the citizenry often takes decisions that might be considered to oppose its own interests. For example, a few years ago, the Swiss electorate rejected an initiative to extend the mandatory minimum vacation from 4 to 6 weeks.

With System 5, all necessary and sufficient functions of the control system are now finally available. No another function is needed to make viability possible. The whole has now become a large, *permanently operating control circuit* that uses its communication lines to solve various tasks in different control elements and at different levels (Fig. 4.11). Together, Systems 3–5 form senior management, which acts meta-systemically to Systems 1 and 2 by solving those control issues that the operational units cannot solve themselves. It solves the higher level issues.

Thus, the term "senior" here does not mean a manager's personal seniority, but their higher level responsibility for System 1 as a whole. Even a young or inexperienced executive can assume senior management functions in this sense. He or she will do so with initially small Systems 1 to gain experience.

Task
Try drawing the Viable System Model from memory. Practice this until you can draw all the elements and especially the lines between them correctly. To be able to work with the model, you will have to have it in your head. Reading the instructions (in the car manual) on the passenger seat is not enough.

Russian Dolls

5

In the Viable System Model (VSM), System 5 is not followed by System 6 but by something else. Chapter 3 introduced the VSM by saying that a viable structure consists of five control elements, located on two axes, and one principle. Following the introduction of the elements and the axes, we now consider what this principle is all about. It is the principle of *recursion*, which occupies a key role in mathematics, logic, grammar, computer science, and art. Figure 5.1 illustrates the principle in the form of Russian dolls (*matryoshkas*). They are nested such that the same homomorphic structure appears on each level. In our context, recursion means that the same control structure always occurs on multiple, infinitely nested levels.

Recursion is a *problem-solving strategy for dealing with complexity*. It is a suitable framework for creating order in chaos or, vice versa, a trick for building a complex structure out of something that is simple in itself. In art, for example, we find it in compositions by Wolfgang Amadeus Mozart, or in fugues in general, where the same melody is repeated over and over at different levels, and where complex beauty is created through this fractal nesting. Having adopted this trick from the theory of formal logic, cybernetics has learned about it in practice from genetics. The genetic blueprint for the whole occurs in every single cell, just as every seed contains the information for the whole tree.

Important
The whole recurs in its parts.

According to Norbert Wiener, the idea that the world is a system and consists of smaller systems was the most important technological idea of the twentieth century.[1] Without this insight, technology today would still be at the level of primitive,

[1] Norbert Wiener, in: "Remaining Human. Norbert Wiener and the Lost Science of Cybernetics." Film by J. Mitchell Johnson and Robert M. Elfstrom (2016). Abamedia. http://norbertwiener.org/remaining-human.

M. Pfiffner, *The Neurology of Business*, Management for Professionals,
https://doi.org/10.1007/978-3-031-14260-4_5

Fig. 5.1 The principle of recursion

modestly performing automata. In its application to the structure of social organizations, on the other hand, the principle of recursion has by no means had the impact it could have had. Nevertheless, it is indispensable to the functioning of really large and complex enterprises. We are familiar with the principle in various manifestations, such as strategic business unit structuring (i.e., the division of the enterprise into self-controlling units), fractal organization, self-organization, or chaos theory. It also appears in the modern and most current organizational approaches such as agility, holocracy, or scrum. However, self-organizing units that are recursively nested do not yet result in a functioning system per se, because systems can also be nested such that they become uncontrollable. The self-organizing power of decentralized units can even become a problem if they gain too much independence or if the wrong units develop self-organizing tendencies. In the enterprise, this can lead to the pathological organizational pattern of "schizophrenia" (cf. Sect. 17.2).

The principle of self-controlling, recursive units is therefore not sufficient in itself. If we follow the recipe for success, we must first design the five control elements correctly, second make the communication channels between the elements work, and third transfer this control structure to all operational units at all levels of recursion. Only when these three conditions are fulfilled can we speak of a viable system. As with Russian dolls, the same control structure with the same five elements and the same communication channels can therefore be found in every operational unit in the Viable System Model.

The same invariant control structure recurs time and again in every operational unit at every management level of the enterprise. Therefore, every operational unit at every management level can also be diagnosed and designed with the same model. The organization thus carries within itself the *genetic code for effective control* in every cell of the enterprise.

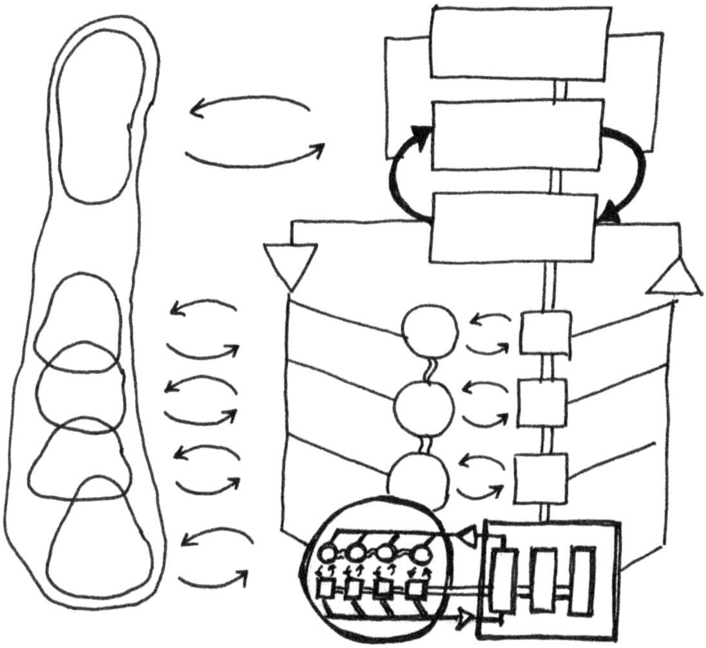

Fig. 5.2 Recursion in the Viable System Model

Definition

The Recursive System Theorem[2]

In a recursive organizational structure, any viable system contains, and is contained in, a viable system.

The recursive nature of the structure is clearly visible in the model below (Fig. 5.2). Let us first consider the management box of the lowest, operational unit in System 1: It controls its operation in its environment. From the perspective of senior management in Systems 3–5, this management is a black box: Senior management is not interested in what happens in detail in this *black box*. It is only interested in input and output. If, on the other hand, we want to know what is happening in this management box, we move down one level of recursion. In the management box, we again recognize the structure of Systems 3–5. In the operation, we again recognize a System 1, consisting of several operational units. We thus recognize how management works with its operations in its environment. If we move up another level of recursion, we lose sight of these details and see environment, operation, and management only as black boxes with inputs and outputs. We

[2] Stafford Beer, *The Heart of Enterprise: The Managerial Cybernetics of Organization* (Chichester, New York, Brisbane, Toronto, Singapore: Wiley, 1979), p. 118.

have returned to the original focus, in which these details are unimportant; that is, they do not belong to the *control task of this level of recursion.*

Definition

First Regulatory Aphorism[3]

It is not necessary to enter the black box to understand the nature of the function it performs.

We do not need to understand in detail why a car drives but we do need to know how it reacts. For the driver, the car is a black box, just as the operational unit is a black box for senior management. The principle of the black box allows senior management to focus on its own task. Indeed, controlling the higher level of recursion provides enough work because it is more than the sum of the lower levels of recursion. It has its own larger environment and therefore needs its own System 4, for example, to find its way around. R&D in Systems 4 on the lower level is not sufficient because that level has a different content focus.

How many and which levels of recursion we want to look at depends on our interest. In a *family*, we would probably start with the individual family members as the lowest level of recursion. The next higher level is the family. This in turn is embedded in a third level of recursion, which can be seen as part of a family tree, or as part of a neighborhood with other families, or even as part of a community. We are all part of very different dimensions of levels of recursion. Even an enterprise is always part of several higher levels of recursion. For example, a Swiss company can be a part of a German corporation while belonging to its Swiss industry association. Which of these many dimensions we want to shape or diagnose is up to us and depends on our interest.

In a *project*, we may start with the subproject as the lowest level of recursion. Several subprojects together make up the project, which in turn may be one of several projects in the company at an even higher level of recursion. We could move up another level and look at the group, of which the company is one of many operational units. However, our interest ends here at the latest. We want to look at project functioning, for which the corporate level is hardly relevant anymore. However, if the group has defined guidelines for dealing with projects and controls them, even this level of recursion can be relevant. Thus, how far we go down or up again depends on the situation and our interest.

In an *enterprise*, the nesting of the levels of recursion depends on strategy. For example, at the highest level, the company can be divided into regions, because regional responsibility is advantageous for strategy implementation. In turn, a region can be structured according to customer groups, and a customer group according to products, for example. This focuses managerial attention on different things at different levels. With the right cascading, the specific focus of each level does its part, so that in the end everything that matters to the customer is taken care

[3]Stafford Beer, *The Heart of Enterprise*, p. 40.

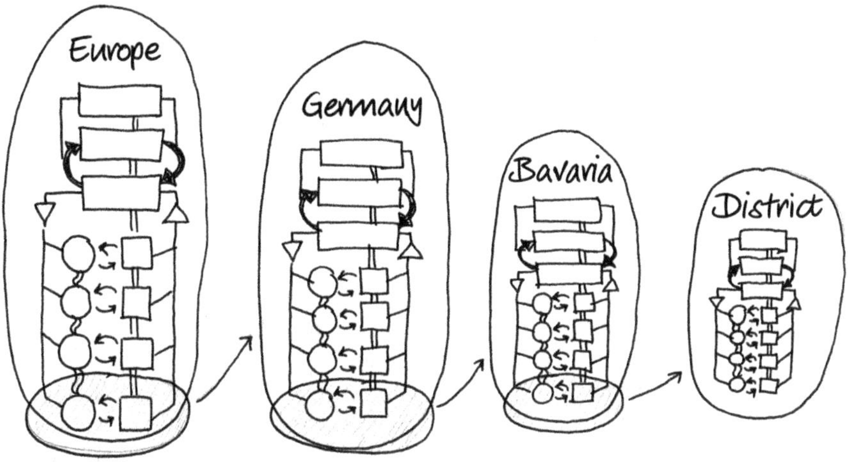

Fig. 5.3 Example of a recursive control structure

of. Countless combinations are possible, from which the company chooses the best possible one for its situation. Part III explores how to make the right choice when we start working with the Viable System Model (see Chap. 8, "The Basic Structure"; Anatomy).

In a *state*, municipalities are the lowest levels of recursion. As a rule, these combine to form districts, which in turn combine to form states, while states combine to form a country. Yet the country is again part of a higher level of recursion, for instance, Europe in the case of Germany and Switzerland—albeit in different forms. Whether municipalities first unite to form districts or immediately to form countries (cantons in Switzerland) is irrelevant, because ultimately these are simply different names for one level of recursion. Thus, the practical question is not what these levels of recursion are called but how many levels are needed for an enterprise to be manageable (see Chap. 10).

Above I called the principle of recursion a trick for coping with complexity. What is this trick? As every operational unit is supposed to be viable itself at every level of recursion and therefore has its own control system, in principle a *huge control capacity* (Fig. 5.3). However great, this capacity would nevertheless be quickly overwhelmed by the complexity of the whole if it had to control everything from a central point. The failed experiments with the planned economy show that this kind of centralized control cannot work.

In the early 1980s, I actually saw snowplows at an airport in the sweltering desert of Guinea, Western Africa, because the then-planned economy of the USSR had supported developing countries with entire airport equipment—in the USSR, this included snowplows. Nor can we use our brains to control the complex processes in and between our peripheral organs, such as the citric acid cycle in the liver after we have had a bit much to drink for a change. Even in our bodies, most of the complexity is absorbed by the individual organs themselves. What reaches the brain is merely residual. But even this is, besides all other "Outside & Then" tasks to be performed by the brain, still ample fodder. Even in our technical systems, as a rule more than the one central computer controls everything. In a modern car, for example, up to 100 peripheral computers and control units perform their tasks independently.

The trick, then, is to *distribute control.* When cells at all levels of the enterprise control themselves (i.e., by their own control system), *complexity is absorbed where it arises.* Every operational unit in System 1 absorbs most of the complexity in its environment and from its interactions with the other operational units itself. This means that higher-level, senior management in Systems 3–5 only needs to deal with the remaining complexity. As a result, management becomes faster, better, and more robust. It becomes *faster* because all units at all levels can react independently. If something relevant changes in their environment, they adapt immediately without first having to wait for other units or for decisions from above. Decisions become more substantive because the relevant unit is based on better information, and thus better understands the decision and its consequences. In addition, control becomes more robust, because distributing control is more than delegating responsibility.

Delegating means making someone your representative. In case of doubt, however, the delegator always has the final say. Their argument counts, even though they have delegated responsibility. In reality, however, only part of the responsibility is really passed on, and where exactly decisions are made is no longer clear in the end. True distribution of control, on the other hand, means that more decisions are made decentrally in the operational units than by senior management. It is only when *task, competence, and responsibility converge on one level of recursion* that we speak of distributed control. Then real responsibility for control is created, without escape routes and excuses. Regardless of whether this control is successful or not, it remains clear where the decision was made and where the responsibility lies. The effect is quite different and points to a form of self-disciplining. In a cybernetic view, this constitutes no more and no less than a properly designed *feedback loop*: The consequences of a decision are clearly and unambiguously fed back to the decision-maker. They bear the consequences of their decision, positively and negatively.

As discussing the recipe for success in the Prologue has shown, stabilization does not occur until the error signal is fed back into the input of the control system. This is the mechanism by which dynamic goals are achieved because it is the only way to genuinely learn from mistakes. In technology, feedback loops are natural elements of a control system. In business and society, we would have higher-performing organizations if this principle were taken more seriously. Instead, our organizations tend to learn very slowly, especially when they reach a certain size or complexity. This is evident in the administrations of some European countries, which have become unstable at the latest since the economic crisis of 2008, can hardly be reformed, and lack these feedback loops. The most impressive example that I have experienced was a Greek ministry during the euro crisis: The opposite of distributed control prevailed and seemingly no one was responsible for anything.

Distributing control is especially important in the age of brain or knowledge workers, who now make up the bulk of a modern economy.[4] Enterprises today pay a great deal for managerial expertise and knowledge. They must therefore use this knowledge, even if it is further removed from corporate headquarters. The productivity of knowledge has become a relevant variable in the information society because knowledge as a resource is as worthless as oil as long as it is not used. Distributed control makes it work to the enterprise's advantage. Managers can focus all their know-how on their operational unit. They are closer to the business, know the local context, and can therefore arrive at faster and better decisions.

Besides the advantages of distributed control in a recursive organizational structure, however, the enterprise also needs to balance the *cohesion of the whole* to a certain extent. This means that the centrifugal forces of a fractal, self-organizing organization must also be countered by centripetal forces that hold the whole together. *The more distributed control, the stronger the center must be.* In some cases, an operational unit cannot make decisions on its own because other units are also affected and therefore a higher-level decision is needed. In other cases, the plans of a unit are curtailed because, seen from the enterprise as a whole, priorities lie elsewhere.

Thus enters the question of *autonomy versus hierarchy*. Chapter 6 discusses this age-old, seemingly unsolved problem of humanity in depth. How far may autonomy go and where is cohesion needed? The law of cohesion formulates this relationship for the Viable System Model.

Definition

The Law of Cohesion (for multiple recursions of the viable system)[5]

The System 1 variety accessible to System 3 of Recursion x equals the variety disposed by the sum of the metasystems of Recursion y (for every recursive pair).

We sometimes struggle to keep recursive nestings apart. The levels of recursion actually correspond to the leadership or management levels in the enterprise. However, it is difficult to grasp them from organizational charts because it is difficult to represent recursion two-dimensionally. Figure 5.4 shows the Viable System Model in a mathematically correct fashion on three levels of recursion. The law of cohesion becomes slightly more understandable if considered in this figure: It applies on all levels of recursion because it connects all levels (always a recursion level x with a recursion level y). It also means that senior management in System 3 is only allowed to regulate (accessible variety) what the management boxes in System 1 could not regulate themselves and what therefore remains (disposed). In other words: *The autonomy of the operational units is limited to the extent needed to maintain the identity of the whole—and only to that extent.* This in turn also means that, as far as

[4]Martin Pfiffner and Peter Stadelmann, *Wissen wirksam machen: Wie Kopfarbeiter produktiv werden*, 3rd ed. Malik Edition (Frankfurt, New York: Campus, 2012), pp. 39 ff.

[5]Stafford Beer, *The Heart of Enterprise*, p. 355.

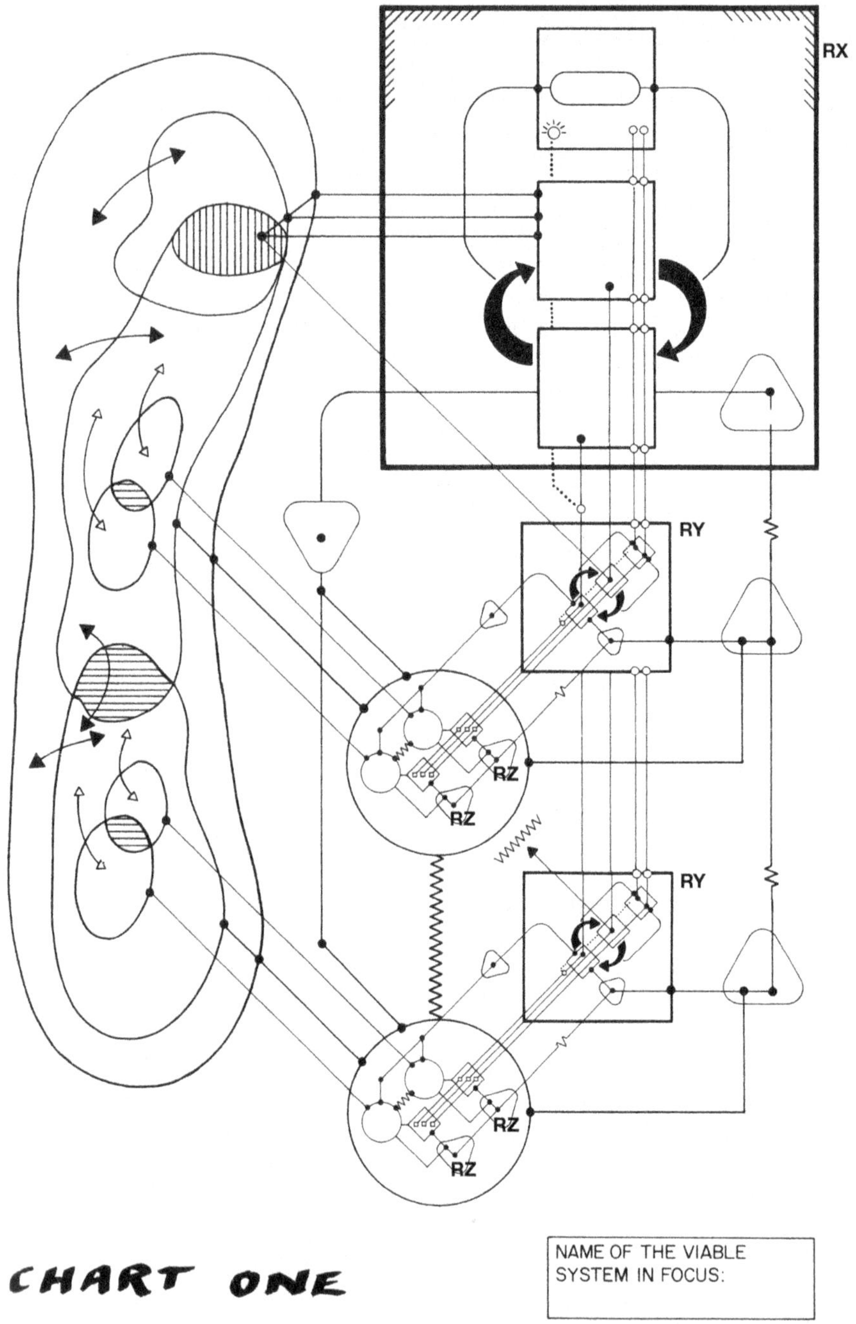

Fig. 5.4 VSM on three levels of recursion (RX to RZ). Source: Stafford Beer, *Diagnosing the System for Organizations* (1985), p. 139

possible, decisions must be made at the lower level, which is closer to the matter at hand.

This corresponds to the *principle of federalism*, that is, the merging of operational units (e.g., states) into an overarching whole (e.g., the country), in which the operational units retain a relatively high degree of autonomy and independence. It also corresponds to the *principle of subsidiarity*, according to which tasks are only performed by a higher level if they can no longer be performed by the subordinate, relevant level. The superordinate level intervenes only subsidiarily, that is, only in a supporting or substituting capacity. In terms of the Viable System Model, senior management in Systems 3–5 performs only those tasks that the operational units in System 1 cannot perform themselves. By performing these control tasks, however, it creates the cohesive glue that holds the whole together at its core.

6 Hierarchy and the Redundancy of Potential Command

Wars have been fought over the right balance between autonomy and freedom on the one hand and between hierarchy and authority on the other. In management, too, this is one of the trickiest and seemingly insoluble questions. To function, every viable system, as Chap. 3 has shown, needs *both a horizontal and a vertical control axis*. The enterprise also needs *agility and flexibility* on the one hand but also *continuity and cohesion* on the other. These factors restrict individual freedom to a greater or less extent.

So where does the right balance or compromise lie? Typically, opinions on this question are mainly ideological. Some say that humans want and need strong leadership; they refer to China to illustrate how successful a hierarchical structure is compared to our slow, Western democracies. Others vehemently oppose curtailing freedom because they consider this the highest good in a society. They recall the historical catastrophes that resulted from dictatorships. In fact, successful examples of both forms of control exist. Whether something works does not depend not on whether it is hierarchically or autonomously controlled but on whether the control system per se works. If it does, it finds the *right balance between hierarchy and autonomy* for its particular situation, because that is part of the functions of a control system. Nevertheless, there seems to be a tendency today to assume that, in the age of knowledge, hierarchy is rather a hindrance than a help, since it serves to control cannons and tanks. It also assumed that controlling intelligence and information functions differently from energy and matter. Is this really so? Do we need to free ourselves from hierarchy?

Undoubtedly, freedom and autonomy have been and are curtailed—unnecessarily, repeatedly, and often unfairly. This, of course, always involves some degree of hierarchical pressure, from soft authority to harsh repression. Resistance to the repression of freedom is an ancient theme of humanity. The word hierarchy is therefore fundamentally discredited, partly because it is associated with the ivory tower syndrome of delegated (rather than distributed) responsibility, as well as with bureaucracy and slowness. The manager-less enterprise is therefore a fascinating idea that flares up time and again. Current hierarchy-free models of organization also

M. Pfiffner, *The Neurology of Business*, Management for Professionals,
https://doi.org/10.1007/978-3-031-14260-4_6

promise agility, innovative power, and motivated employees. They focus on the horizontal control axis and promote the idea of self-control as an alternative to unloved hierarchical control. This is mistaken because *the two forms of control are not contradictory*. They complement each other to form a functioning whole.

So why is the vertical control axis also justified? Hierarchies are necessary for reasons of *logic* when large systems are being organized. This insight is undisputed in the natural sciences and philosophy. When, however, hierarchy is translated into human domains, everything suddenly seems to be about *power and dominance*. This leads to losing sight of the true nature and meaning of hierarchies in a system.[1] If we search for the reason for hierarchy instead of status and power in the relevance of information, all of sudden we begin looking at matters differently. In natural systems, decisions are made where the relevant information is, namely, in numerous places distributed in the organism. This makes sense, because a good decision requires a good information base. On a flight, for example, pilots have decision-making authority, despite being hierarchically subordinate to the airline manager. Only they know the situation on the ground and in the air well enough, and only they have relevant information so that the right decision can be made in a critical situation. When their aircraft approaches an airport, on the other hand, pilots follow the tower's instructions, despite air traffic controllers being clearly inferior to pilots in terms of status and salary. This is because at this moment the tower has the relevant information about how the pilot fits into the structure of the other aircraft arriving and departing. The controller decides, and the pilot follows this decision. The command center always shifts to the place having the most information.

Important
In a viable system, hierarchy results from the relevance of information (rather than from status and power).

When hierarchy arises from the relevance of information rather than from status and power, it assumes a different character. It is recognized as being necessary for something to function. We need to clearly distinguish these two types of hierarchy, that is, logical versus physical hierarchy. In organization studies, hierarchy falls into disrepute from time to time, with aim being taken at physical, social hierarchy. However, we should not throw the baby out with the bathwater. Hierarchy is not a priori evil, as long as it is established for the right reason and in the right measure. The question is not whether we need hierarchy but what we need it for and to what extent.

Cybernetics speaks of the *meta-system*. Hierarchically, this is located above other systems in a logical sense, because these systems can neither do certain things themselves nor answer certain questions themselves. Thus, in the Viable System Model, senior management in its Systems 3–5 has relevant information for making

---

[1] Stafford Beer, *Brain of the Firm: The Managerial Cybernetics of Organization*, 2nd ed. (Chichester, New York, Brisbane, Toronto, Singapore: Wiley, 1972), p. 4.

higher-level decisions that hierarchically limit the autonomy of its operational units in System 1. For example, a System 3 decision may shift priority from one operational unit to another and reallocate the necessary resources because this is appropriate from the perspective of the whole. System 4 information may prevent the enterprise from running into trouble because it considers a longer time horizon than the operational units. Or it may cause an opportunity to be seized that the operational units themselves would not have recognized because System 4 focuses on a larger environment. Hierarchy can save lives when a quick decision is needed to turn things around. Senior management in this sense always acts as a meta-systemic service provider for the enterprise, with the goal of ensuring synergy, adaptation, and cohesion of all units. This is different from the classical understanding of top-down hierarchy. The top manager is not the most important person but the enterprise's highest servant—serving the cause and the joint mission. Classical, traditional entrepreneurs have always understood themselves in this way.

The cohesion of the whole arises primarily from a *planning process based on recursive logic*. When a system at a higher level of recursion provides a framework within which a lower-level system can operate freely, it is acting in the logical sense of the hierarchy of relevant information. It is the logical purpose of that system to provide that framework. This is the case, for example, when the constitution of the federal state provides the confederated states the framework within which they can operate. In practice, these are ordinarily planning processes in which decisions are negotiated between levels of recursion. For example, corporate strategy provides the framework within which divisions can develop their divisional strategy. Or conversely, divisions submit their strategies to the corporate level, where they may be adjusted if they do not complement each other meaningfully to form a corporate strategy. The same applies to operational planning processes such as budgeting or target agreements between all levels of recursion.

From the point of view of opposing interests, hierarchy is always a double-edged sword and its discussion as a rule is no more than an ideologically motivated dispute. From the point of view of the functioning of a larger whole, however, this is plausible. In a viable system, it is embedded and distributed across the architecture of the whole system and across all levels of management, rather than concentrated in one place. It serves a logical and necessary function. As observed, the law of cohesion shows that autonomy may be restricted only to the extent necessary to *maintain the identity of the whole*. Identity and thus the *purpose* of the whole are therefore the first, legitimate reason for restricting autonomy. System 5 establishes this purpose: Why do we work together and why do we exist at all? Which needs do we want to meet in the marketplace? With what strengths and beliefs do we do this? In what do we see a benefit and meaning in our activity? What do we gain our self-respect from and mobilize our performance reserves if necessary?[2] This purpose, the mission of the enterprise, is the normative parameter (flanking measure) for every

[2]Fredmund Malik, *Management: Das A und O des Handwerks* (Frankfurt, New York: Campus, 2007), pp. 166 ff.

action. If actual action deviates from this purpose, System 5 should be able to notice this and act in the hierarchical sense.

Important
Autonomy is a computable function of the purpose of a viable system.[3]

The other reason for limiting autonomy is the *prospect of being stronger together*. This is the responsibility of System 3, which optimizes the whole and exploits synergies. However, pursuing a joint market, product, or design strategy or utilizing synergies may severely restrict autonomy. In the City of Zurich, after the turn of the millennium, each of the 80 service units in the nine city departments had its own IT. These units were largely incompatible: The city had a lot of information technology but no information with which to carry out its System 3 mission. It, therefore, had to limit the autonomy of the service units as regards IT, which would never have been possible without some hierarchical assertiveness; the city would still have no facts and figures today. Volkswagen, too, would barely have managed to implement its famous platform strategy with its Audi, Seat, and Skoda brands without any hierarchy. Whereas the overriding goal was to save costs, for the brands and their designers this was primarily an unpleasant encroachment on their entrepreneurial and design freedom.

In this sense, the Viable System Model is a logical and hierarchical system. Independent of ideological ideas or personal interests, it helps to find out where and to what extent individual autonomy may be restricted for the good of the whole. It helps to recognize how much force on the vertical axis of control is necessary in a specific situation and how much force on the horizontal axis of control can be transferred. There is no clear "the more the better" and no ideological solution but only a *suitable balance for the current situation*. Chapter 10 ("Manageable or Not?") will explore this perspective, starting from the question of how much autonomy an enterprise can maximally tolerate. *Complexity considerations* will help us to matter-of-factly and accurately assess a situation regardless of paradigms. They will also enable us to measure the maximum possible flattening of the organization and to know which tasks must be organized decentrally and which centrally. As with autonomy versus hierarchy, this question also concerns determining the right measure in the current situation. Wars of ideas, fads, and paradigms are unnecessary.

Hierarchy based on the relevance of information also includes that no system ever decides on the affairs of another system. A System 5, for example, does not decide on the affairs of Systems 3 or 4. *Actors, on the other hand, can be active in several systems* and take decisions there. For example, a manager may simultaneously have responsibility for an operational unit in System 1 while serving at the group level on

---

[3] Stafford Beer, *The Heart of Enterprise: The Managerial Cybernetics of Organization* (Chichester, New York, Brisbane, Toronto, Singapore: Wiley, 1979). p. 158; see also Stafford Beer, *Diagnosing the System for Organizations: The Managerial Cybernetics of Organization* (Chichester, New York, Brisbane, Toronto, Singapore: Wiley, 1985, p. 103.

the extended management board in System 3. Similarly, the carpenter in my village performs several system tasks at the same time. He has established a small company with about 15 employees. His operational units are customer projects, in which he is partly involved himself. Thus, he is active in System 1. He also fulfills all System 3–5 tasks in senior management as one and the same person. No one can do this for him.

If managers perform different control tasks in different systems at different levels of recursion, this easily leads to confusion. Section 2.7 ("Overlooking Nesting") has already touched on this problem. Managers do not always know which hat they are wearing and which one they ought to be wearing: What level of recursion am I on when I say this? Am I assessing the situation as I see it as the head of the operational unit? Or as I should see it as a representative of the extended management team? When I express a strategic opinion, do I see it from the perspective of the overall group? Or do I want to see it that way because it serves the strategy of my own operational unit? And finally, am I really making my decisions at the right level of recursion? Or am I mistakenly losing myself in micromanagement? This problem is also familiar from the so-called "Peter Principle": Successful people are promoted until they are no longer successful. They do what brought them success most recently, that is, what they needed to do on the lower level of recursion.[4] While the control functions are the same at all levels of recursion, the tasks and contents are quite different.

Dealing with different hats, and being able to distinguish levels of recursion, is a challenge that managers must face up to. Especially in more complex organizations, it serves cohesion when leaders are lifted out of the frog's perspective of their operational unit by also performing higher-level tasks. This gives them a better understanding of the whole. It helps them see why certain constraints are necessary from a bird's eye view. Also, we have seen that systems that function like brains are not built as pyramidal command structures that look like family trees. A recursive hierarchy with distributed control can instantly shift the command center to where most information is at a specific moment, if needed. In our brain, these information nodes are called *"a center of potential command."*[5] The flow of information determines which link is currently relevant and therefore provides the current command center. For example, a helicopter pilot of the Swiss Air Rescue (REGA) is such a center of potential command. He or she has the hierarchical decision-making power to call off a rescue maneuver on the Matterhorn because of a storm. In a critical situation, only the pilot has the relevant information to take such a decision. In an emergency, he or she therefore takes over command from the operations center. Once again, having information rather than the authority conferred on an individual entitles the pilot to act.

[4] Laurence J. Peter and Raimond Hull, *The Peter Principle* (New York: William Morrow, 1969).

[5] Stafford Beer, *Brain of the Firm: The Managerial Cybernetics of Organization*, 2nd ed. (Chichester, New York, Brisbane, Toronto, Singapore: Wiley, 1972), p. 232.

Definition

The Principle of Potential Command[6]

Power resides where Information resides.

The *redundancy* of such centers of potential comman is another massive source of protection for the organization and serves as a mechanism for its functional security. If one center fails, another center immediately takes over. Redundancy exists so that systems can become robust against errors and learn from them (see Sect. 2.6). Our organism therefore has *two* brain hemispheres, eyes, ears, lungs, respiratory tract, kidneys, legs, and hands each. If one element fails, the system can continue to function to a limited extent. In engineering, redundant systems ensure functional reliability. Eurofighter engineers explained to me that they maintain sixfold redundancy in the avionics computers in military aircraft so that an aircraft can remain airborne even if several systems fail simultaneously.

This principle—*the redundancy of potential command*—is applied not only in the brain and in technology but also in social systems. For example, Lord Nelson, the British admiral who inflicted a devastating defeat on the French-Spanish fleet at the Battle of Trafalgar in 1805, reportedly used this principle as follows: Because visibility was repeatedly lost in the channel between the British Isles and France due to dense fog, the Royal Navy's command ship could be out of action for an extended period of time. In this case, command automatically had to pass to that ship that was not in the fog at the time. Because only that ship had information, the command center was thus immediately shifted. This in turn meant that every naval captain also had to be trained in the control functions of an admiral as this would immediately enable them to command the entire fleet, not just a single ship. Vice versa, every officer on a ship also had to be trained in the control functions of a captain, so that they too could take over immediately. This dual training in different functions at different levels of recursion ensured, first, that the fleet's command center could be relocated immediately if necessary, and second that a fallen captain or admiral could be replaced immediately without jeopardizing the functioning of the whole.

Today, enterprises use the principle of redundancy of potential command by involving managers in the tasks of the next higher level of recursion early on so that they also familiarize themselves with the control issues of this level. In this way, managers become accustomed to wearing different hats, and the next generation of executives is developed in timely fashion. This potentially redundant command might suddenly be needed when the enterprise switches to crisis mode. Even in normal mode, an enterprise never seems to have enough managers: Most plans that never get implemented fail not because of a lack of funds but because of a lack of manpower. Therefore, building potential command cannot start soon enough.

[6]Warren McCulloch, *Embodiments of Mind* (Cambridge, Massachusetts: MIT Press, 1965).

Later in the Bar

Rachel: I don't think your Viable System is really working, Marc.

Marc: Oh yeah? How come?

Sandra: Ice in the whiskey again today? Despite the clear contradiction last night? There seems to be some sand in your System 4 gear.

Rachel: Exactly. It's also called: Unable to learn!

Marc: My System 4 works wonderfully, because first of all I'm talking to you and that's System 4 communication to the outside; secondly, my System 5 has decided that I basically don't listen to you two. As you know: parameters, flanking measures for System 4 and so on . . .

Sandra: Right. You should never listen to others on strategic issues. And certainly not to majorities. If the much-cited Henry Ford had listened to majorities, he would have bred faster horses.

Rachel: (Laughs) True. Back then, not only organization but strategy was still a matter of talent. Strategy didn't really become an issue until the 1980s. Nowadays, though, I think it's important to hear other opinions before you decide on something tasteless, Marc.

Marc: You sound like the Holy Inquisition: Interfering in things that don't concern you at all. Like System 3*.

Rachel: Why 3*? Isn't that an information channel, not an intervention channel? No one is being thumbscrewed. Besides, 3* operates with the consent of the operational unit.

Marc: Huh?

Rachel: For example, when Sandra, as the boss, visits a project site at one her clients in Spain and talks to people there and listens to them, she sees what's going on. She sees things that need to be corrected. But that doesn't mean she intervenes past the supervisor and makes corrections herself. Because that's the supervisor's job.

Sandra: Exactly. That would never occur to me. José, my manager in Spain, would lose face. I did that once—and was even wrong in the end. That caused trouble. Today, I take note of what I see, perhaps establish a more complete picture, and then discuss matters with José. If action is needed, that's José's job. He's always happy when I visit him.

Marc: Everybody's "happy" when the boss visits. Okay, so that means you're System 3 and your store manager José is System 1?

Rachel: What? Have you been listening? You can't say, "You're System 3." The Viable System Model is not an organizational chart. So you can't put a name in a box either.

Marc: What else?

Rachel: The model is not centered on people but on control functions. That includes everything through which things are optimized. It may be that only one person does System 3, or that hundreds do it together. In our company, for example, besides the two managing directors, we also have an extended management board, a committee with seven people.

Marc: Isn't that more like a body?
Rachel: If it decides, it's a body; if it just advises, it's a committee.
Marc: So the extended management doesn't make decisions at your company, only the management?
Rachel: That's right. But only after listening to our opinions.
Sandra: Are you part of the extended management team? I thought you were a business unit manager?
Rachel: Yes, and as of a few weeks ago, also a member of the extended management board.
Marc: Congratulations!
Rachel: Thank you. Marc: . . . and secondly, you can't say José is System 1 either.
Sandra: You mean he's just the management box of System 1?
Rachel: He's responsible for the management box in one of the operational units in System 1. That's the way to put it.
Marc: Right, because a System 1 always consists of several operational units.
Sandra: Well, but the beverage distributor in my village has only one store. So there seems to be only one operational unit?
Marc: That's not possible.
Rachel: Right, there always needs to be at least two operational units. Otherwise nothing would have to be coordinated or optimized in between.
Marc: Exactly. The operational units control themselves. So no higher control is needed until there are at least two units.
Sandra: As soon as there are two, trouble starts. Then it's a matter of being considerate, tolerant, coordinating and dealing with conflicts.
Marc: God knows! But it also means experiencing things together that you couldn't experience alone. The meta-system has its own magic.
Rachel: Things are getting too romantic for me. It's called synergy.
Sandra: Uuuhhh! Back to the beverage vendor: So what exactly are his operational units?
Rachel: It depends. Maybe soft drinks, fizzy drinks, and spirits?
Marc: Exactly, back to the topic: So, you see, my self-control works wonderfully. The liver is doing its job. Plus, my System 4 has wisely decided that it should be whisky on the rocks again today.
Rachel: You're right, the Viable System can't be held responsible for wrong decisions.
Marc: . . . Yeah, really funny!
Sandra: Why?
Rachel: Because it's a control system. It has to be fully fledged and has to work. But what gets decided with it depends on the people using it.
Marc: Right, then I'll have another beer.
Sandra: There's something about that. An airplane can have a perfectly functioning control system, and the pilot can still make bad decisions—or even decide to let the plane crash.

Rachel: Exactly. You can use a working control system well or badly, and for better or worse. You can use it to heal children, as well as for a terrorist operation.

Sandra: Which has probably happened. Do you think the mafia uses the Viable System Model?

Rachel: I don't know. But when I think about the 9/11 attacks, they seem to involve plenty of cybernetics: self-directing entities combining for a higher purpose, using existing forces, and so on.

Marc: That's right. To plan and pull off an action like that is a huge control task in a very complex environment. Behind an action that achieves its goal, there obviously has to be a functioning control system—whether you know it or not.

Sandra: That still puzzles me: Why have there been so many successful organizations if no one knew about the Viable System Model? If the model is so important, they should have known about it. Or today's organizations shouldn't be able to function without it.

Rachel: They don't work when I look at all the failures. But that's not the point. I don't think you have to know this model to get things right—in this case, to build a working control system. You can get things right without having to read a book first. Or did you have to read a book so you could be a good mom?

Sandra: Well, for some mothers, maybe a book like that wouldn't be a bad idea. I just did my best, which was certainly not always easy next to the family business.

Marc: I think I know what you mean now. Lots of organizations have been successful in the past without knowing the model because they were built by talented people experienced in organizing. They just did things the right way.

Sandra: But we don't have enough experience and talent available in society to be able to provide that to every single organization. That's why models are helpful because they can be taught and learned. They help cover the need.

David: May I interrupt?

Marc: Hey David, how are things?

David: Great. Just heard you guys talking about "models" and "needs"? That sounded kind of interesting . . .

Rachel: Haha, funny (rolls her eyes). Now's a good time for a pilot to join the discussion. We were talking about plane crashes and motherhood.

David: Oh, I think I'll need to nip out again in a minute . . .

Rachel: . . . We were also saying that you don't need to know models, theories, principles, and laws as long as you follow them.

Sandra: Anyway, I still have no idea how this model is going to be of any use to me. It's interesting but also confusing.

Rachel: That's how it is with good models: At first you're confused, and then you start seeing things clearly. It's the opposite with bad models.

David: Well, I always struggle with models. For airways, we use the best electronic maps in the world. But even those have to be updated all the time. The map isn't the territory—that's true. An art dealer once asked Picasso why he didn't paint the world as it was. Picasso asked him what he meant by that. "Well, the way it looks objectively," the dealer said. "Look here. Here's a photograph of my wife as she really is." Picasso looked at it, "Well, she's pretty. A little small, and also a little flat ..."

Rachel: (laughs) ... But think about it: People dealt with gravity before they understood the law behind it. And Lord Nelson certainly didn't copy his principle of potentially redundant command from the brain either. He knew what he was doing from experience.

Sandra: So it's even more impressive that what worked for Nelson also works in exactly the same way in our brains.

Rachel: Because it's a principle, and principles apply everywhere.

Marc: You stickler for principles.

Sandra: Okay, David: I'd like to know how you deal with responsibility on a flight? As a pilot, aren't you responsible for everything in the end?

David: Of course. But the cabin steward is responsible for what goes on in the cabin. I don't know anything about that. Just as other people are responsible for cleaning, loading and unloading. My co-pilot and I fly and control everything around the flight.

Rachel: So, in VSM-speak, you're running the operational unit of flying, and at the same time, in senior management, you're running the flight as a whole.

David: You could see it that way. Most of the flying is done by my co-pilot, though. So I can focus on everything else.

Marc: And so we have a redundancy of potential command! The co-pilot could fly the plane by himself.

David: Right, and he could also take over all my other duties if he had to. And sometimes we take turns with tasks, for training purposes.

Marc: So the command center can change as needed. That's also a safety aspect. It makes control robust.

Sandra: That's great for those who can afford it! The redundancy of potential command and control sounds like a lot of effort to me.

Marc: Yes, certainly. That's the price of functional reliability. Not paying it would be more expensive in the end. How much money do you think our insurance company invests in cybersecurity to make sure our technology works securely? How nice it would be if management worked that securely, too.

Sandra: So do delegate or distribute your overall responsibility, David?

Rachel: You can't delegate responsibility. Only the task and the competencies needed to perform it. But what you're responsible for, you remain at least partially responsible for. So it's about distributing responsibility. After all, not everyone has to be responsible for everything.

David: That makes sense. I couldn't do the cabin work or the loading myself. If that responsibility were delegated, I'd have to know something about it. If I told them what to do, we'd have adhocracy, which wouldn't be preferable to any hierarchy. The processes are always somewhat different depending on the airport.

Sandra: I'm beginning to understand the difference.

Marc: I also see it as distributed responsibility. But if I understand things correctly, you're also responsible for the next higher level of recursion, that is, the flight as a whole, and you have the final say there. On the one hand, you work with your co-pilot in the management box of the operational unit called "flying" and at the same time you also do Systems 2, 3, and 4 for the "flight" as a whole. And if a final decision is needed, you make it as a System 5.

David: Exactly. The recursion levels thing makes sense. But I've reconsidered that for my family.

Sandra: You're divorced, aren't you?

David: Exactly. I see three levels of recursion: the family member, the family, and the family around it. All three levels influence whether the family works.

Marc: Absolutely: an interconnected system in which everyone is also responsible for themselves.

David: I think that's the core issue.

Sandra: What?

David: That it's hard to separate these levels of recursion: What's important for me to function as David? What's important for the family to function? And what does it take to make it work with the parents and siblings as well, that is, with the family around it?

Sandra: Well, yes, we all primarily see our own current level of recursion. You need to be mature to recognize higher recursions. Do you know the story about the twins in the womb?

Marc: Let's hear it.

Sandra: They're having a conversation about whether there's a life after birth where everything will be different. One of them says that they will finally see a "mother" who will be around them all the time, who will love and nourish them, and whose heartbeat they will hear when it's very quiet. The other replied: "Can you see a mother around here somewhere?"

Rachel: Yes, part of growing up is discovering higher and higher levels of recursion. And as you get older, you go back, and the world gets smaller again.

David: Each level of recursion wants to be maintained and requires us to contribute. That can be exhausting.

Rachel: Well, people *are* exhausting. If you had to find a measure of love, it would be how much you strengthen the other person. I didn't realize that for a long time. That's why parents want their children to be independent.

Marc: When I told my father at sixteen that I would be self-employed from now on, he wasn't thrilled. I think he was thinking more in terms of delegated responsibility that he would have liked to have back.

Rachel: Autonomy increases gradually. Everyone has to get used to it first.

Sandra: As soon as the umbilical cord is cut, things happen quickly. First, they discover "no," then they're only out of the house during daytime, then in the evenings, and in the end they think they're adults because they know about civil law.

David: And then suddenly they want your car keys. That's relative autonomy. Where that ends is the question: What do I need? What does the family need? What do the families above need? If the family is going to function, the lower and higher level of recursions below must also function.

Sandra: And from time to time, we must actively readjust in both directions.

David: It's tricky with adults.

Rachel: You mean your ex-wife? Apparently you didn't find the right balance between freedom and cohesion?

David: Now that sounds very theoretical. But yeah, maybe in our family System 5 we never really talked about what we actually wanted together. And our System 4 was not aligned with that.

Marc: All control issues.

David: And communication issues.

Marc: Another beer? It keeps your system viable!

Part III

Diagnosis and Design

Overview of the Diagnostic Process 7

All happy families are alike; every unhappy family is unhappy in its own way.
(Leo Tolstoy, *Anna Karenina*)

Following the introduction to the Viable System Model, let us get to work. Once again, our diagnosis begins where the company fulfills its purpose: with the customer (or service recipient) and in the operational unit. This is where the entire organization is ultimately focused and where it must demonstrate its performance capabilities. It is the "place of truth" and the pivot around which organizing turns. Thus, the diagnostic process begins *"outside-in"* and *"bottom-up."* We should not lose ourselves in detail but focus on connections, cross-connections, and side effects. Therefore, we are not *"analyzing"* the control organization, that is, breaking it down into its elements for in-depth scrutiny. As argued in Sect. 1.4, performance arises from the connection and interaction of elements. This overall view, and functioning as a whole, is important because we are studying a control and communication system. Hence, the word *"diagnosis"* is more appropriate for our purposes. It concentrates on a comprehensive view and fits our metaphor of the organism, whose health and performance we intend to examine.

While diagnosing an organization, we will likely arrive at many affirmative findings yet even more pathological findings. The latter point out what is wrong with the organization at a certain point in time. In most cases, we simultaneously identify what needs changing. Therefore, during diagnosis, we are inevitably already shaping the organization. *Diagnosis and design take place concurrently in our thinking and in practical work* because diagnosis serves "action."

Figure 7.1 shows the diagnosis and design process of the third dimension of organizing in seven steps. Leo Tolstoy begins *Anna Karenina* with the observation that while all happy families are alike, the unhappy ones are all unhappy in their own way. As a rule, there are not many ways to do something right but very many more to do something wrong. I consider the diagnostic process proposed here as one way of doing things right. It has proven itself in practice, circumvents the threats of trivial and wrong applications, and helps prevent the classic mistakes and shortcomings of

M. Pfiffner, *The Neurology of Business*, Management for Professionals,
https://doi.org/10.1007/978-3-031-14260-4_7

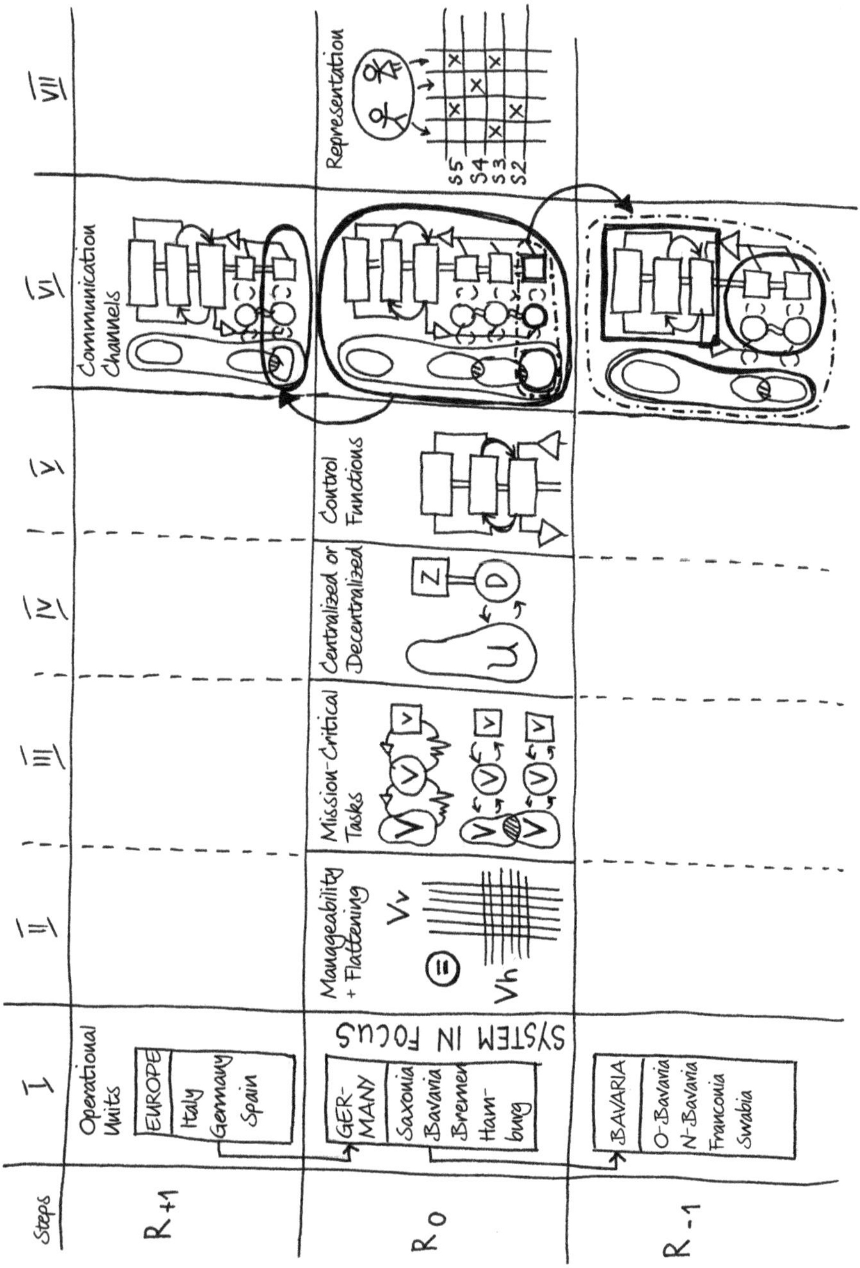

Fig. 7.1 The diagnostic and design process

organizing. Depending on the situation, we proceed through all the steps, omit some, or emphasize one step over another. This is fine. We should, however, more or less follow the order of steps because it follows a certain logic: Every step builds on the results of the previous one. Diagnosis can cover the organization as a whole or merely one level of recursion. It can also focus on a single organizational subquestion. It may take up 5 min in our own mind, be developed on a napkin over dinner for two, or require some executive retreats over several months.

Sect. 15.3 ("Implementing Successfully") discusses who ideally diagnosing and designing a larger enterprise will involve, when, why, and in what form. In principle, it is advantageous not to work alone at the beginning, nor to work with more than two to a maximum of five people. This means compromising between ensuring the necessary productivity and enough variety for good discussions. Before we begin, we need to gather some basic information that will frame our work:

(a) *Mission and parameters*: Are the purpose and mission of the enterprise defined? Is it clear which organizational options, if any, are excluded a priori for normative, corporate policy reasons?
(b) *Strategy*: Does it include strategic statements about market and customer, innovation, productivity, and the attractiveness of the enterprise for good employees? Or does strategy only contain operational long-term plans for developing sales and profit? Is the strategy written down somewhere? Who is or is not aware of it?
(c) *Culture and employees*: What makes the enterprise tick? What are its strengths? How is it managed? Where do managers and employees see the need for action? Who are the key people?
(d) *Organizational history*: What phases has the enterprise gone through and when was its organization changed and why? How successfully? How is the enterprise organized today?

If too little is known about these points, we should talk to managers and examine existing documents. The more we know about these four areas, the easier and clearer diagnosis becomes.

We call the unit to be designed the *"System in Focus" (SIF)* and its *level of recursion R0*. In the course of diagnosis, we will consider at least the two recursion levels above and below the SIF. These appear as lines in Fig. 7.1 and are labeled R +1, R0, and R−1. To prevent mistakes and misunderstandings in our discussion, we must always clearly indicate which level of recursion our diagnosis is focusing on. As Sect. 2.7 observed, one of the cardinal errors of organizing is mixing levels of recursion. According to Chap. 6, moreover, depending on the level, the control functions do not change but the contents of control do.

I. Diagnosing and Designing the Basic Structure (Anatomy, See Chap. 8)
Let us first gain a general sense of the operational units on all relevant levels of recursion. To do so, we establish (i.e., diagnose) whether a unit actually fulfills its purpose. We do not yet consider supporting units. We start with the CURRENT state of the organization, the current anatomy of the enterprise, so to speak. Basically, any anatomy can be innervated. However, some anatomies make "supplying nerves" easy while others make this difficult. In the first step, we want to be certain that we are dealing with the best possible anatomy of the enterprise for its future. For example, if the enterprise is currently divided into products, we diagnose whether it might also make sense to divide it into regions, customer groups, technologies, and so on. To do this, we start on that level of recursion that we can actually design because we are responsible for it. We define it as our SIF and label it "Recursion Level 0" (R0). For this level, we then check whether the operational units are viable, that is, can operate largely autonomously, and whether they focus on what customers pay for. We diagnose their strategic fit and elicit further segmentation variants. Finally, we select one variant and thus establish the primary control dimension for the enterprise on this level of recursion.

II. Manageable or Not? (See Chap. 10)
In the second step, we examine the span of control on every level of recursion that we include in our diagnosis. In doing so, we also test the maximum possible flattening of the organization: Can we omit one or more levels of recursion without overburdening management? Instead of using the usual rule-of-thumb to gauge the management span, we assess matters based on measuring complexity (see Chap. 9). On completing this step, we will have established the basic structure across all relevant levels of recursion. We will now know exactly which level of recursion comprises which operational units for the IDEAL organization.

III. Mission-Critical Tasks (See Chap. 11)
Next, we return to the level of our System in Focus (SIF). If the first two steps have led us to conclude that we need to change our System 1 (i.e., operational units) because, for example, we want to resegment it by customer groups instead of regions, from now on we will only consider this IDEAL organization. For each operational unit, we examine which of its tasks are mission-critical. Here, too, we do this based on considering complexity (see Chap. 9). We realize that we cannot organize everything and know that this is not necessary. We, therefore, focus on the 20% of all tasks on which 80% of success depends. Mission-critical tasks can also result from environmental overlaps and operational interdependencies. If we manage to neatly organize these tasks, much of the rest will take care of itself, or at least will no longer be difficult to organize.

IV. Central or Decentral (See Chap. 12)
After working out the mission-critical tasks in the SIF in Step III, we again consider several levels of recursion in Step IV. We ask which task should be performed at which level of recursion. What should be done centrally? What decentrally? We

examine which competencies the operational units must keep in their own hands to maintain their relative autonomy and satisfy their customers. Only secondarily do we examine which tasks can be centralized in order to achieve synergies. As a result of this step, we know for our SIF, as well as for the other levels of recursion, which mission-critical tasks should be performed on which level. These tasks are, so to speak, our raw material for designing the control functions in the next step.

V. Diagnosing and Designing the Control Functions (See Chap. 13)
By now, we know which operational units our SIF has, how large they are, and how strong their environmental overlaps and dependencies are. We also know which mission-critical tasks need to be performed on this level of recursion. We now ask what concrete contribution the individual control Systems 2–5 make to the functioning of the whole by distributing these tasks among them. For example, what tasks does System 2 have to perform very specifically for this enterprise on this level of recursion so that the operational units can work in a coordinated manner and receive the necessary support? We ask what System 3 must focus on to optimize the whole and what the mission-critical tasks are there. We also ask these questions for Systems 3*, 4, and 5. As a rule, 20–40 tasks are mission-critical and distributed among the five control functions. We consider this for the senior management of the operational units as a whole. Next, every department considers in-depth what its additional, department-specific control tasks in senior management consist of.

For operational management, we normally appoint someone to take care of System 3 as a whole. In a company, this is usually the CEO, who is also responsible for the annual accounts and balance sheets. Often, a responsible person is also designated for the System 5 function, for example, the chair of the supervisory board or the president of the board of directors. They gather all the concerns and perspectives of the departments and people involved and integrate them into decision-making in the control system for which they are responsible. They do this in the form of meetings, workshops, retreats, or projects. For control systems 2, *3, and 4, on the other hand, no responsible persons are designated as a rule—which explains why these systems are often neglected in practice and cause control problems. We therefore establish responsibility for every control function to ensure its functioning and communication channels.

VI. Diagnosing and Designing the Communication Channels (See Chap. 14)
As mentioned, the control functions are important but the communication channels between them are even more important. The Viable System Model shows us how the control elements must be connected and tests the effectiveness of the communication channels between those elements. Here, we use principles from cybernetics and information theory to establish that communication is comprehensible, timely, robust, and secure. The control system ends up being a large, self-contained communication loop.

At the end of Step VI, we again move beyond the level of recursion of our SIF and consider the communicative linkage with the management of the next-higher and next-lower level of recursion. Chapter 5 discussed the "Law of Cohesion" and what follows considers in detail how this works. Finally, we check how the "algedonic signal" is working. This signal alerts us across all levels of recursion to what requires our attention, negatively or positively.

VII. Making the Organization Understandable (See Chap. 15)
So far, we have considered what needs to be done yet not by whom and where. At the end of organizing, we need to bring the control tasks together with concrete positions and people in the third dimension of organizing. Doing so makes the organization implementable and understandable. We use the function diagram to connect the mission-critical tasks in Systems 2–5 with the organizational entities and their responsible persons. In a control function diagram, we define the key values of the individual control processes (who is involved in what and how?). This enables us to represent the entire control system of our SIF on a single page, from which we can derive organizational charts and job descriptions as required. The organizational chart, the function chart, and the job descriptions are ultimately used to communicate the organization.

Part III will consider these individual diagnostic and design steps one after another, explaining each in detail and providing practical examples. This will help us understand the Viable System Model even better. My experience with executives has taught me that they learn the most when applying the model to their own situation. Every reader can do this, because we are talking about a "model of any system." Every chapter, therefore, ends with a "Call for Action." The tasks included there invite readers to actively engage with the model, that is, to diagnose the organization that is relevant to them—their "System in Focus." The purpose is not to produce long lists and texts but rather to gain a systemic perspective by drawing the whole model as a diagram and by working creatively with its representation (not, however, with its precision and logic). This overview will help us focus on the essentials. It will save time and unnecessary work. The aim is to gain relevant insights. Ultimately, it is not simply about understanding but about holding our breath for a moment—and swallowing the medicine.

8 Diagnosing and Designing the Basic Structure (Anatomy, Step I)

We begin our diagnosis with a blank sheet of paper on which we first draw all the enterprise's operational units on all levels of recursion (Fig. 8.1). This provides a first, important overview of the organization as a whole. By the end of Step I, we want to know which levels of recursion to include in our diagnosis, which level to focus on, and how the operational units (System 1) on this level should be properly designed. That is, we begin with the most important part of the enterprise, its *building blocks, which lay its foundations*. Everything else serves these operational units. If we misdesign them, not even the best control system can offset these design errors. Vice versa, we can live with a patchy control system—at least for a while—as long as we correctly place the building blocks.

In laying the foundations of the house, we also design its purpose, because the enterprise fulfills its purpose through System 1. System 5 only thinks about what that purpose should be. The operational units fulfill their purpose by doing what customers or service recipients pay for. In this sense, they reproduce the enterprise every day. Successful companies often acquire businesses completely unrelated to their original purpose. They run these businesses as they run their traditional divisions, as part of the group. For example, some fashion chains operate seminar hotels, construction companies ski lifts, automotive suppliers wineries, or banks facility services. Normally, this is unproblematic, as there are no interfaces with the existing business, and because this does not become more complex as a result. Even if these businesses are only run out of opportunity or as a hobbyhorse, they still absorb management capacity, especially because people are not really familiar with them. Since such acquisitions also involuntarily expand the purpose of the enterprise—irrespective of and in contrast to what is stated in the mission statement—it is still worth asking whether this is the right thing to do.

M. Pfiffner, *The Neurology of Business*, Management for Professionals,
https://doi.org/10.1007/978-3-031-14260-4_8

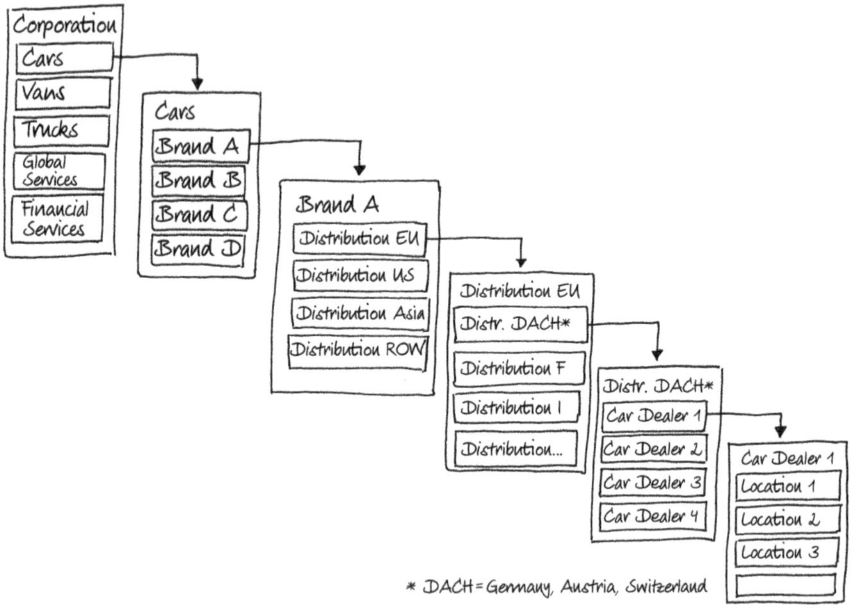

Fig. 8.1 Levels of recursion: the example of an automotive enterprise

Important
The purpose of a system is—what it does![1]

Stafford Beer's dictum contains a sober truth: The purpose of the enterprise is not what is written in any mission statement but what the enterprise actually does in its building blocks. This is exactly what it is perfectly designed for. If design does not match enterprise policy, the enterprise needs to be designed differently.

So what should be the building blocks of the enterprise? A whole can be broken down in diverse ways but which one is the right one? That is the first key question we need to answer. In breaking down the enterprise, we must focus on the right things and ensure that the parts can also be put back together to form a whole. Correctly designing the operational units also matters because it makes innervating the enterprise easy or difficult. Designing the operational units determines the requirements for the control system. Depending on how we segment the enterprise as a whole, smaller or larger overlaps will exist between the environments of the operational units and smaller or larger dependencies between their operations.

Sections 2.5 and 2.7 have already considered two anatomies with large overlaps and dependencies. The building blocks of a functional segmentation, which divides the firm into specialized functions such as production, development, and sales, have

[1] Stafford Beer, *Diagnosing the System for Organizations: The Managerial Cybernetics of Organization* (Chichester, New York, Brisbane, Toronto, Singapore: Wiley, 1985), p. 99.

little autonomy because each operational unit shares the same environment with all other operating units since they all address the same customer. No unit can succeed without the other because production needs sales and development to succeed, just as they need production. Segmentation into functions is possible and even quite common. It is also justified in certain growth phases, as this helps the enterprise to utilize expertise. But overlaps and dependencies make this anatomy challenging. Therefore, in a next phase, the organizational chart is normally rotated by 90°. Businesses are placed above the functions but are still too small to afford their own infrastructure. Nevertheless, they are now measured by their own success just like the previous functional units. The overlaps and dependencies of the functional organization have not disappeared as a result. Rather, how complexity works means that they are not only multiplied but also exponentiated. This explains why the advantages of the matrix organization are soon lost again: The numerous overlaps and dependencies will overwhelm corporate management again at the latest in the next growth phase. When the enterprise will be reorganized all over again…

Chapter 17 ("Quick Diagnoses") discusses these two particular anatomies and their implications for neurology in more detail. It examines why certain anatomies (basic structures) systematically lead to control problems and shows how these can be avoided or recognized with the Viable System Model. For now, however, it is enough to realize that by designing the operational units (System 1), we decide what business purpose will be fulfilled and how easy or how difficult controlling it will be. So how do we find the appropriate segmentation for our System 1? And which System 1 are we talking about anyway? Diagnosis follows a simple and clear procedure but requires observing a few rules.

8.1 Capture the Levels of Recursion

First, we capture all the levels of recursion of the *CURRENT organization.* These units are *responsible for results on all management levels*, those involved in controlling the enterprise today. Observing the principle of Russian dolls in our representation (Chap. 5) enables us to recognize how the levels of recursion are nested within each other.

In Fig. 8.1, this has been done for an automotive group. On the highest level, we find five operational units that are organized by product: Cars, Buses, Trucks, Spare Parts, and Financial Services. If we are interested in cars and move down one level of recursion, we find brands as operational units. Brand A, in turn, is divided into sales regions, these into countries, these into car dealerships, and these finally into locations. If we were to go down another level of recursion, we might find sales, workshops, and used cars as operational units for each location. Our interest ends here at the latest because on this level the organization no longer poses any problems. Figure 8.1 merely illustrates one of many possibilities. Step I aims to find out whether the enterprise should organize itself in this way or differently.

When we diagnose our own enterprise, we also start on the highest level that strikes us as relevant. Next, we draw all the levels of recursion beneath it, down to the last level in which we are interested. In doing so, we should not be tempted to simply draw an organizational chart. While this includes the operational units, these are only one part of the anatomy of the enterprise (the organizational chart also contains the supporting units). Our representation, however, should only contain the building blocks of the organization (i.e., the operational, purpose-fulfilling units).

In practice, this is a simple exercise—yet only in roughly half of all cases. In these cases, it is immediately clear what the operational units are on the various levels of recursion. In the other half, however, the first questions already arise here. Often, we encounter a hodgepodge of randomly nested organizational units, companies, holdings, or acquisitions that have grown in an unorganized way and follow no deliberate organizational design. These enterprises survive as long as the economic situation permits, and as long as they have sufficient managerial talent and experience, because managing them is essentially an "impossible job." In this second category of unclear cases, three considerations (a–c) help us search for today's operational units:

(a) *Through which units is the enterprise planned and controlled today by strategies, targets, budgets, and income statements?* Operational units are normally responsible for results. For us, however, it is not relevant whether a unit is a legal entity or not. Legal boundaries sometimes hinder functioning but are not decisive. The *management perspective, not the legal perspective* is relevant. For example, legal persons or entities often exist as private limited companies, public limited companies, and incorporations, whose sole purpose is to pay taxes, hire personnel, or purchase technology in a particular country. For example, a global logistics company was divided into five regions. The Africa region consisted of several well-equipped and well-managed market units. They handled business with offices located in various countries. Only because required by law, companies were set up in each country to which the offices then belonged. However, the managers of these national companies did not realize that they were not actually meant to perform any operational function, but only a janitorial one. So they started managing between two levels: the market units and the local offices. They developed their own ideas and strategies, making it difficult to implement any market unit strategy. They had created an unnecessary layer between the market units and the offices, which was eliminated after the organizational diagnosis by making it clear to managing directors what their real function was. They were allowed to keep their business cards, salaries, offices, and company cars but were no longer allowed to manage. This flattened and accelerated the enterprise. Thus, we are interested primarily in the functioning of the enterprise and only secondarily in legal requirements or ownership. For this reason, holdings are relevant for our representation only if they are really controlled by the Group, that is, if they are majority shareholders.
(b) *Have we really drawn operational, purpose-fulfilling units rather than supporting ones?* Supporting functions are not purpose-fulfilling. They are responsible for results, not performance. For example, the sales force of a pharmaceutical company is normally not an operational unit, but a supporting

unit. The distributor of an electrical wholesaler is an operational unit because the enterprise's purpose is to provide sales services. That is what it was set up to do. In both cases, we are talking about distribution. Distribution has a supporting function in the first case, as against an operational function in the second. The R&D department of a manufacturer of measuring instruments is a supporting unit whereas an R&D service provider in the chemical industry is an operational unit. Similarly, the IT department of a local municipality is not an operational unit, unlike an IT company based in the same municipality. Section 4.2 has already noted that supporting units often strive to be operational units in order to gain influence and power. As such they follow the natural tendency of self-preservation. This, as observed, is a pathological case of *autopoiesis* because a supporting function in a healthy system neither renews itself nor expands for its own sake. This form of "cancer" occurs in both business and nonbusiness sectors. A typical characteristic of rather formal and bureaucratically managed enterprises, it sooner or later inflates the organization and produces "red tape." Supporting units, on the contrary, ought to dissolve themselves rather than maintain themselves for their own sake in the long run—and yet, in practice, precisely this very often happens. If permitted to, these units develop a life of their own. It makes no difference to management whether a unit is productively supportive (e.g., sales or production) or nonproductively supportive (e.g., human resources or marketing). However, we must clearly distinguish operational from supporting units.

(c) *Which units can operate relatively autonomously?* As we are talking about relative autonomy, the question is not whether they are independent but how strong their dependence is: Which units could continue to exist on their own without much additional effort if we sold sell them, for example? Units capable of leading a life of their own are operational, viable units.

In representing the levels of recursion, we should not feel pressured to include units simply because they appear in the organizational chart, or because this is current practice, or because they are legal entities, or for other, possibly power-political reasons. If we are interested in the best possible functioning of the enterprise, we must not be hindered by conventional categories.

Tasks

(a) Take a blank sheet of paper and draw the levels of recursion of the enterprise you want to diagnose. Use the same type of representation as used in Fig. 8.1.
(b) Check whether the CURRENT situation really involves operational, purpose-fulfilling units with relative autonomy. If not, remove these.

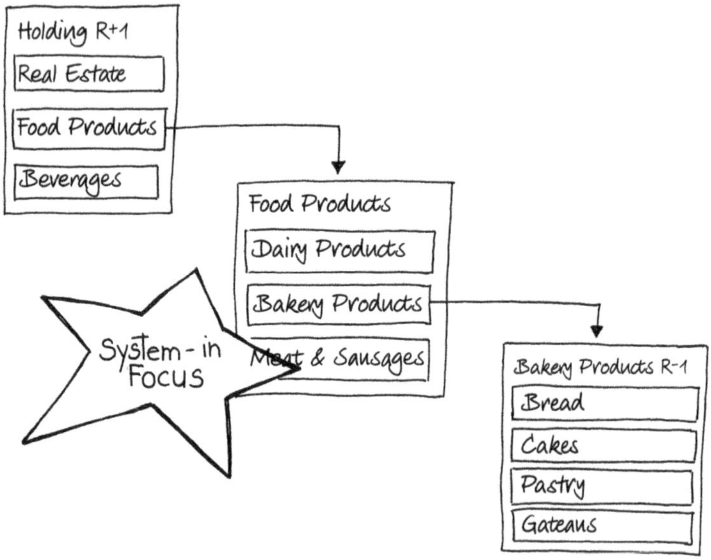

Fig. 8.2 Defining the levels of recursion and the system in focus (SIF)

8.2 Define the System in Focus (SIF)

After drawing the levels of recursion, we define our *System in Focus (SIF)*. This is the *level that we are particularly interested in*. Normally, we diagnose the level for which we are responsible ourselves and which we can therefore also design ourselves. In principle, every level can be selected as the SIF. In case of doubt, it makes sense to choose the level on which customers receive the enterprise's service, that is, where actual customer benefit is created, because this level is the only reality on which we can robustly build. Everything else is a construct that we can design one way or another. We refer to the System in Focus as recursion level 0 (R0). We denote the recursion levels above it as R+1, R+2, R+3, . . . and the recursion levels below as R−1, R−2, R−3, . . . (Fig. 8.2). This clear numbering will serve us later during diagnosis and discussion. It is sometimes harder than you think to stay properly focused, especially in discussions with professional colleagues.

There are *special cases*, of course. For example, the head of HR of a large enterprise wants to make an organizational diagnosis because his department, with 200 staff at 20 locations, has become so large and confusing that control and communication problems are occurring. However, HR is a *supporting function* and thus not meant to be a viable unit. Can we nevertheless apply the Viable System Model to diagnose it? The answer is yes, but . . . We need to realize that it is not supposed to maintain its own existence but only to perform the required tasks—at the lowest possible costs. Still, it also needs a control structure in order to function. For example, it needs a System 4 to develop the enterprise's HR strategy. It needs to know how many executives are needed, with which skills and competencies, and by when. And it must work out how these people can be recruited, internally or externally.

Thus, the HR strategy is not an independent but a functional strategy. That is, it contributes to business strategy, which specifies the need for human resources. Likewise, HR needs operational units, which as a rule are structured according to internal "customers" and thus reflect the actual operational units. HR also needs a System 2 to coordinate these units, and a System 3 to enable it to perform its tasks with maximum effectiveness. Thus, internally, we can also diagnose a department with the Viable System Model, even if externally it contributes to the enterprise as a supporting unit. When we have finished designing the inside, we must ask how all System 2–5 functions fit in and contribute to the whole as *part of senior management in the SIF*.

Task
Select your System in Focus and label it R0. Designate the other levels of recursions with ascending or descending numbering (as shown in Fig. 8.2).

8.3 Check Segmentation

Once we are clear about the levels of recursion and have chosen our SIF, the next question arises. We have captured the CURRENT state. In doing so, we may have already eliminated some ambiguities or discovered shortcomings. However, we are still looking at THINGS AS THEY ARE. The question now is: Is the current segmentation of the operational units also right for the future? Does this organization really anchor responsibility for customer benefits? Will it leverage our strengths and help us implement our strategic thrusts?

In my experience, most enterprises do not actively design this segmentation. It has simply emerged over time and therefore offers a glimpse into the history of the enterprise rather than how it operates. Many enterprises still get by (with their segmentation) for a surprisingly long time—well, more or less. In reality, however, at some point, these structures start slowing competitiveness and development because they focus on the wrong things. The symptoms manifest in larger or smaller trouble spots, which may even have been caused by control problems. If matters become too strained, and structure is again made to fit the enterprise, it may seem as if floodgates had opened. Business flourishes and strategy implements itself almost by itself. Testing whether the SIF is properly segmented is therefore hugely important. It is worth considering segmentation with a few trusted people because we develop better solutions if we can argue about matters a bit.

So the question is: Which segmentation will best serve our purpose? Enterprise purpose originates in the customer or the service recipient, making their needs crucial. Every segmentation impacts customers differently. We, therefore, need to clearly establish which effect we want to achieve. In peacetime, for example, an army is segmented into branches (e.g., infantry, artillery, air force, navy) because in this phase the focus is on ensuring the best possible specialized training. In wartime, segmentation can suddenly change from branches to frontline sections, because a different effect is now needed, namely, harnessing weapon types into a single combat unit.

In a business enterprise, we want to use the right segmentation first to ensure that we anchor responsibility for what customers pay for in the enterprise. We anchor *responsibility for customer benefits* and thus create the *precondition for gaining market share.* In a nonbusiness enterprise, this principle applies mutatis mutandis: We anchor responsibility for the desired effect on the service recipient, thus creating the prerequisite for the best possible fulfillment of the enterprise's purpose.

Second, we want to ensure that *structure is compatible with strategy*. A globally active ship classification organization, the technical inspection association of ocean shipping, as it were, had developed strategies for its various product groups. There was a strategy for passenger ships, another for cargo ships, another for bulk carriers, and another for tankers. So while strategies were based on products, operational units were based on regions. Every region represented all products. Consequently, regional managers had to implement four product strategies plus their own regional strategy. If strategic management (System 4) is based on products but operational management (System 3) is based on regions, this ensures that in reality no strategy is ever implemented and everyone simply does what best suits them. Exactly this happens in many enterprises: They may have filled whole files with strategy papers, perhaps satisfying stakeholder requirements, yet little happens as a result.

And third, with this diagnostic step, we want to ensure that we have ultimately created *self-controlling units* that we can give everything they need to succeed. In this way, we want to anchor autonomy and create the entrepreneur in the enterprise. We want to organize self-organization by designing viable, autonomous units.

We design viable, autonomous units by first asking what other segmentation possibilities exist besides the current one. Every business can be segmented in different ways (see Fig. 8.3). Every business:

- Reaches different customer groups
- Who have different customer needs
- Who are served by different solution technologies
- That generate different products
- That flow through different sales channels to the customer groups

Each of these dimensions could be used to manage the business. Other dimensions (e.g., materials, utilization conditions, or even regions) are also conceivable. The point of segmentation is to find the primary, *dominant* control dimension through which to manage the business. For example:

- A leading high-tech company will tend to be structured according to *technologies* because it wants to beat its competitors with innovative technologies. These are the focus of attention for the customer and therefore also for the enterprise.

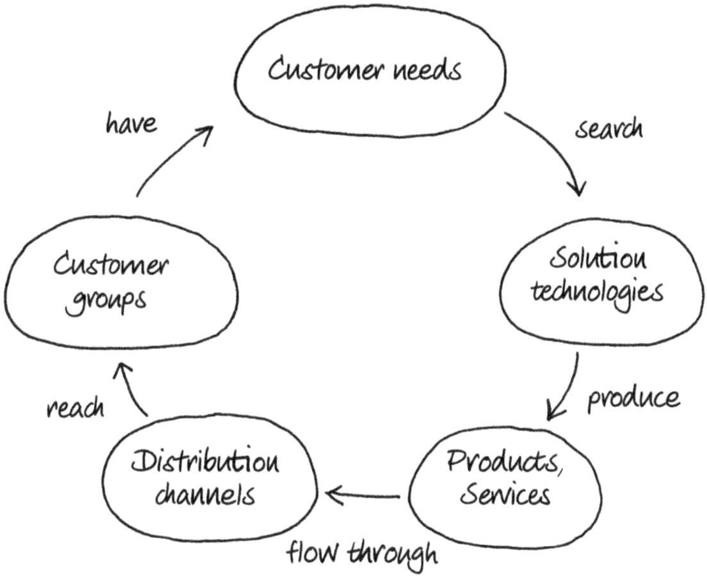

Fig. 8.3 Possible segmentations

- A travel agency, on the other hand, may be structured more according to *products* because its customers above all expect the best product knowledge. The agency also needs technology, for example, to book flights, but in the digital age we probably no longer travel agencies for that purpose. But a customer planning a diving vacation expects a travel agent to know a lot about diving and to provide up-to-date tips. Customers planning a city break or an adventure trip expect travel agents to have in-depth knowledge about such holidays.
- A retail company may be structured by *sales channels* because it wants to beat its competitors with its multi-channel capability, that is, by combining various stationary and online channels.
- Banks and insurance companies are often structured according to *customer groups*. While they too have technologies, products, and sales channels, having the best possible customer knowledge (knowing their financial situation and needs) is even more important.
- A former school friend of mine structured the bicycle store she took over from her father according to *customer needs* such as transportation, sports, or lifestyle. The product is always a bicycle. If, however, that bicycle is a lifestyle product, customers will pay for other things, in fact, ten times more than for a bicycle as a means of transport.
- A headphone manufacturer might segment by different *usage situations* (e.g., stage, studio, home, and mobile).
- Finally, companies producing food or white goods such as ovens tend to be segmented by *region*. I wonder why.

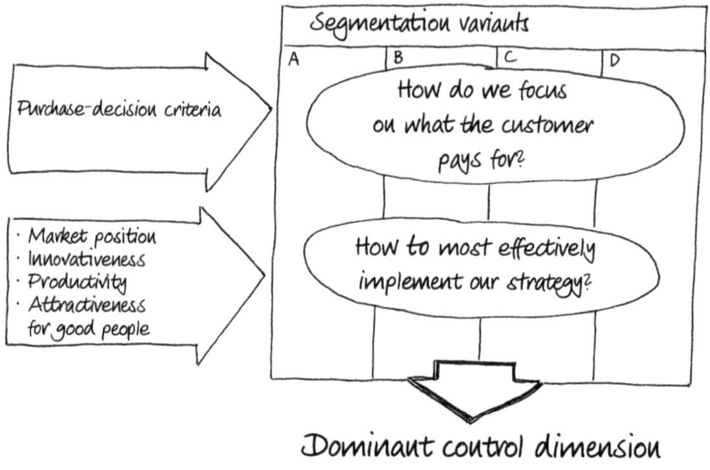

Fig. 8.4 What should be our primary control dimension?

By segmenting its business, an enterprise is saying which strengths it will use to beat its competitors and best meet customer needs. In principle, therefore, many segmentation options exist. But when we consider these for our own enterprise, as a rule there are only three or four possibilities. We enter these variants in the columns in our *segmentation diagram*, which we create according to Fig. 8.4. In doing so, we are describing for every variant how many and which operational units we would have, so that we can imagine these units as best as possible as we consider segmentation. Our first variant is always the current segmentation. Checking might confirm this variant. Or reveal that none of the other variants provides any significant advantage. To make our review broad enough, we should discuss at least three, yet also no more than five variants, including the CURRENT state.

In the rows of the segmentation diagram, we enter the criteria according to which we want to judge the segmentation variants. They consist of two groups. The first group is oriented toward the first basic question of organizing (see Sect. 4.1).

Important

How do we need to organize so that what our customers pay for is at the center of attention, and cannot disappear from there?

Thus, we need to consider *what our customers are (really?) paying for*. When I asked this question in a large insurance company, I was handed three files filled with marketing studies. These all examined how satisfied customers were with the company compared to its competitors. But that is not the question we are interested in. We want to know what our customers' purchase-decision criteria are. What are they willing to spend money on? We are not interested in all the other factors, regardless of how satisfied customers are with them. Of course, they will accept the advantages, perhaps even expect them, but would not pay for them. Ultimately, customers weigh up the price against the service they are willing to pay for. They choose that provider with the best price-performance ratio, that is, the greatest customer benefit.

Purchase-decision criteria can concern the product but also the service or the enterprise. These are what customers pay attention to when considering whether to buy from one provider or another. As George A. Miller demonstrated in the 1960s in one of the most cited articles in psychology, the human attention span normally limits this choice to the *"magic number of seven plus/minus two"* criteria.[2] Typically, no one pays attention to more than five to nine different things before purchasing a car, a smartphone, or anything else.

It is important to start with customers and their point of view—that is, with the person making a purchasing decision. This need not always be the service recipient. After all, not cats buy cat food but their owners. Marketers, therefore, design cat food so that we would like to eat it ourselves. Marketing translates the cat's needs into its owner's purchase decision. Aid organizations also have two types of customers: Those in need and donors. The impact needs to be achieved with the person in need, so marketing must identify their real needs and communicate them to donors.

Often, the customer's view differs significantly from how employees see their enterprise's products and services. If you ask employees, they will rattle off 20 attributes they believe are fantastic and essential for the customer. If, on the other hand, you ask the customer, they pay attention to fewer and often also completely different things. In a Berlin-based producer of washing machines and tumble dryers, I sent the engineers out to shopping malls—not to buy washing machines but to once again experience what interests customers and what does not, and what salespeople praise about the appliances. The engineers came back with tears in their eyes. No customer was interested in the elaborate "fuzzy logic" (with all the lights and options) that had taken years to develop. Instead, they wanted a machine that was robust, ecological, and easy to operate. But no customer satisfaction study had flagged this.

Thus: Do not be too easily satisfied with the answer and return to the question (what are customers really paying for?) at regular intervals. It is the most important question for an enterprise and central to every strategy. We have already talked about purchase-decision criteria in Sect. 2.2 ("Organizing past customer benefit"). It would be worth rereading that section again now. Remember: *No customer pays for a price.* Hence, price is not one of our criteria. It results from the market situation, from competition and, above all, from the enterprise's cost structure. This is defined by other, strategic factors, which we need to consider in the second group of criteria: the enterprise's market share, innovativeness, and productivity.

The second group of criteria concerns strategy as a whole. Our aim is to find that segmentation that *makes it easiest for us to implement our strategic thrusts.* Based on long-term empirical studies on the correlation of strategic success factors with actual

---

[2] George A. Miller, "The Magical Number Seven, Plus or Minus Two: Some Limits on our Capacity for Processing Information," *The Psychological Review*, No. 63 (1956), pp. 81–97.

enterprise success, we know which factors to pay attention to. Together, they determine about 70% of corporate success.[3] We need to develop strategic thrusts for these factors so that we can speak of a strategy in the first place. This is because a strategy consists of a congruent triangle of goals, means, and measures: What goals do we want to achieve with which strategic thrusts? And what resources did we need to achieve those thrusts? Only when we know what needs to be done, and only when we have the people and money to do it, can we speak of a consistent strategy. In total, a strategy needs to provide information about six factors:

1. *Market position, consisting of market share and customer benefit (relative to competitors):*
   Where do we want to maintain or gain market share? What arguments do we want to use to take how much market share away from which competitor? What do we use to strengthen our customer benefit relative to our competitors?
2. *Innovativeness:*
   With which products, services, or business models do we want to be successful in the future? How innovative must we be in which specific areas? What do we need to do today to achieve this and how do we need to adapt our enterprise to achieve this?
3. *Productivity:*
   How productively must we work to achieve a cost structure that allows us to offer our services at attractive prices compared to our competitors? How productively do we need to work to move swiftly enough, for example, from development to marketing? And how productively do we handle our investments? Vice versa, which investments enable us to best increase our productivity?
4. *Attractiveness for good people:*
   How are we going to make our company attractive enough for the people we need in the future? Which and how many people do we need and by when? And how do we want to retain or attract them?
5. *Liquidity and cash flow:*
   How do we get the financial resources we need to implement strategy? How large must these resources be due to investments or lean periods?
6. *Profit:*
   What profitability do we need to generate these financial resources in the long term? What is the minimum profit we need to be able to afford all this, and how do we achieve it?

Regardless of whether the enterprise to be diagnosed has formulated thrusts relative to these factors in its strategy, we need to know its intention. The order of

[3]Robert D. Buzzell and Bradley T. Gale, *Das PIMS-Programm: Strategien und Unternehmenserfolg* (Wiesbaden: Springer, 1987). English edition: *The PIMS Principles: Linking Strategy and Performance* (1987).

Table 8.1 Evaluating segmentation variants

No.	Evaluation Criteria	Variant 0 (IST) Region	Variant I Application	Variant II Customer Group
C1	Technical Quality	1	4	3
C2	Speed	4	2	1
C3	Logistical Performance	4	1	3
C4	Personal Relationships	4	2	1
C5	Quality of Sales Force	1	4	3
1	Market Position	4	2	3
2	Innovativeness	1	4	3
3	Productivity	3	1	4
4	Attractiveness for Good People	4	3	1
5	Liquidity and Cash Flow / Profitability	4	3	1
	Total	30	26	23

these six factors, which Malik calls the "Sixpack of Control," corresponds to their importance.[4] Depending on the enterprise's situation, we can therefore neglect the last two factors for our purposes. While segmentation may facilitate or impede implementing strategic thrusts in the areas of liquidity, cash flow and profit, in the long run they result from the first four factors, which control profit and liquidity in advance. Depending on the nature and character of the enterprise, we will also need to adjust the questions about the six factors.

After entering the segmentation variants in the columns of our table and the criteria in the rows, we start evaluating (Table 8.1). For each criterion, we ask ourselves which of the segmentation variants will help us be most successful. We evaluate the variants, rank them, and enter our ranking in the table. It is advisable to score every variant. With three variants, for example, the worst score should be 1 and the highest score 4, so that we can also clearly evaluate one variant as being better or worse than others. We must force ourselves to discuss scores until the order is clear. Do not be tempted to simply score variants equally. If we evaluate all variants as equal, as sometimes happens in the case of liquidity/cash flow or profit, we can delete the criterion.

Note that we are conducting an *assessment, not a scientific study*. When we have finished assessing, an overall picture will emerge. We can add up points, and if we

[4]Fredmund Malik, *Strategie: Navigieren in der Komplexität der neuen Welt* (Frankfurt, New York: Campus, 2011), pp. 96–100. English edition: *Navigating into the Unknown: A New Way for Management, Governance and Leadership* (2016).

are unsure we can weight certain criteria higher than others, or we can omit certain factors. We should not, however, decide mathematically. Normally, this is not even necessary because the picture is clear enough at the end of the assessment. Every organizational variant can only fulfill a certain number of criteria really well.

As experience from hundreds of cases shows, this approach resolves most questions and uncertainties. In a pan-European company for individualized photography products, for instance, the board of directors had long been discussing whether to segment and manage by regions or by product groups. After evaluating the two options based on the above criteria in a 2-h meeting, the case was as clear as daylight. But two variants may be assessed very similarly and no clear picture emerges, not even after weighting criteria differently. In this case, the variant requiring fewer changes to the current organization is chosen. If this includes the CURRENT variant, one simply keeps the present organization. After all, another variant would have to have a clear advantage, or reorganization could be dispensed with.

One may not agree on purchase-decision criteria. Of course, these are somewhat different for every customer. However, it is usually possible to agree on the criteria of the typical customer. If this is really not possible, this indicates that we are dealing with a priori different businesses. Different businesses appeal to different customers with different products and services and have different competitors. They need to be seen as independent operational units anyway, making segmentation a moot question in such cases. Innovations, that is, new businesses, should also be created as independent operational units as soon as possible (as explained in Sect. 2.8 "The New in the Old"). In an existing business, however, it should be possible to agree on the typical customer and their criteria. In case of doubt, it makes sense to ask both customers and noncustomers.

When we have agreed on that segmentation variant that best promotes the purchase-decision criteria and with which we will most easily realize our strategic thrusts, we have decided on the *primary control dimension of the enterprise*. This dimension has priority (right-of-way) when compromises need to be made between technology, product, distribution channel, customer group, or region. It is the leading dimension, and as such the first that needs to be optimized in the SIF. In the control system, this is the responsibility of System 1. All other dimensions are optimized via Systems 2–5 and serve System 1. Even with the best segmentation, overlaps and dependencies exist between the operational units and cause coordination needs and problems. However, these are now the right problems and no longer the wrong ones (as argued in Sect. 2.4 "Optimizing Weaknesses"). This is the homework that Systems 2–5 must do. That is what the control system is for.

Different levels of recursion can be segmented differently. An enterprise may be segmented by products at the top level and by sales regions beneath, which are then divided into customer groups. But enterprises may also be segmented across all levels of recursion, for example, by region. Both options are possible. If, on the other hand, we encounter different segmentation variants on the same level of recursion (a hybrid structure, so to speak), these can also be innervated. However, this will likely result in large environmental overlaps and operational dependencies that limit the scope and agility of the operational units. This is not what we want.

In about half of the cases in which I have taken this diagnostic step with executives from all types of enterprises across industries, federal agencies, or NGOs, the existing segmentation of the operational units was basically confirmed or, at best, only cosmetically changed. In the end, diagnosis led to improving the control organization of the existing units, which became relatively easy to implement without involving a larger number of employees. In the other half of the cases, reorganization began here. This means that the operational units have to be changed, and this necessarily involves a large number of employees. Section 15.3 ("Implementing Successfully") discusses these two possibilities in more detail. It also considers who should be involved in the design process and when. For now, it suffices to know that we have found the primary control dimension for our business. We now know what the operational units in the SIF look like, which we will build on in the next diagnostic step. We have started with the CURRENT state, but are already defining the IDEAL state for the future of the enterprise.

Tasks

(a) Consider alternative segmentation possibilities for your SIF and evaluate them based on the criteria described above.
(b) Decide on the segmentation that, in sum, best meets the criteria.
(c) Discuss these points with a few colleagues to reach better solutions.

Mastering Complexity (Excursus) 9

Before we continue our diagnosis, we need to familiarize ourselves with a few basics about how to properly deal with complexity. *Complexity is the raw material of control.* We, therefore, need to know how this raw material comes into being, behaves, takes effect, and how it can be managed. Our nervous system exercises control in a highly complex and dynamic environment. To do this, it uses some tricks and laws that we will also apply in the Viable System Model. So what exactly is complexity? This chapter digresses into as much theory as we need to understand these basics.

Some people argue that complexity cannot be mastered. That may be true, depending on what we mean by "master." In this book, it means correctly handling complexity, or what English calls "coping with complexity." Hence, we need to understand "master" in the same way as we "master" an instrument: We know how to handle it properly. For practitioners, the semantics are not so important. They are confronted with complexity, must cope with it, and therefore want to be able to grasp and measure it somehow. Just as we express weight in kilograms or length in meters, complexity is also measurable. The measure of complexity is called "variety."

Definition

Variety

The number of distinguishable states in a system.

Variety is thus the number of states distinguishable by an observer. The word "distinguishable" is close to "information," which, according to Gregory Bateson, is "a difference that makes a difference."[1] Or as Stafford Beer put it: "Information is, what changes us." Since variety is the distinction of states, and because these differences are information, *variety and information* are obviously somehow related.

[1] Gregory Bateson, *Steps to an Ecology of Mind: A Revolutionary Approach to Man's Understanding of Himself* (Chandler, 1972), p. 582.

M. Pfiffner, *The Neurology of Business*, Management for Professionals,
https://doi.org/10.1007/978-3-031-14260-4_9

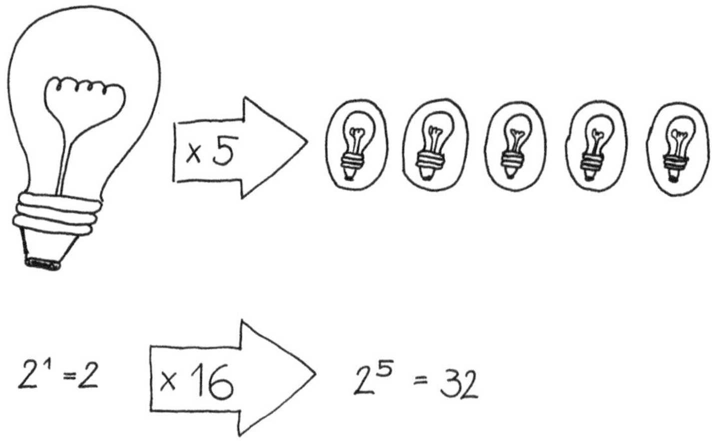

Fig. 9.1 Complexity is measured and expressed through variety

They are *related, yet different.* In the Viable System Model, variety is controlled along all communication channels by means of information. Information and mathematical communication theory, therefore, speaks of the "flow of bits" as the "flow of variety." Information theory, however, is not concerned with the flow of semantic meaning, that is, what the bits mean to the receiver.[2] For the manager, however, and for functioning in social organizations, this is just as important because the "flow of bits" and facts only become information when they mean something and when they can change something (see Chap. 14, "Diagnosing and Designing Communication Channels," for a discussion of successful communication and communication security). This chapter, then, deals with both aspects: the technical aspect of information as a bearer of variety; and with its social aspect as a bearer of meaning.

9.1 Measuring Complexity

If we want to measure complexity, we must examine the number of distinguishable states in a system. The simplest example is a light bulb (Fig. 9.1).[3] It can have two distinguishable states: "on" or "off." But is this correct? Besides "switched off," "off" can mean "broken" or "not energized" perhaps because a transistor in town has blown. Nor does a dimmer produce an infinite number of states, but once again the seven plus/minus two states that we are normally capable of distinguishing. Thus, here, too, the observer plays a role.

---

[2]Stafford Beer, *Brain of the Firm: The Managerial Cybernetics of Organization*, 2nd ed. (Chichester, New York, Brisbane, Toronto, Singapore: Wiley, 1972), p. 359.
[3]Ibid., p. 45 ff.

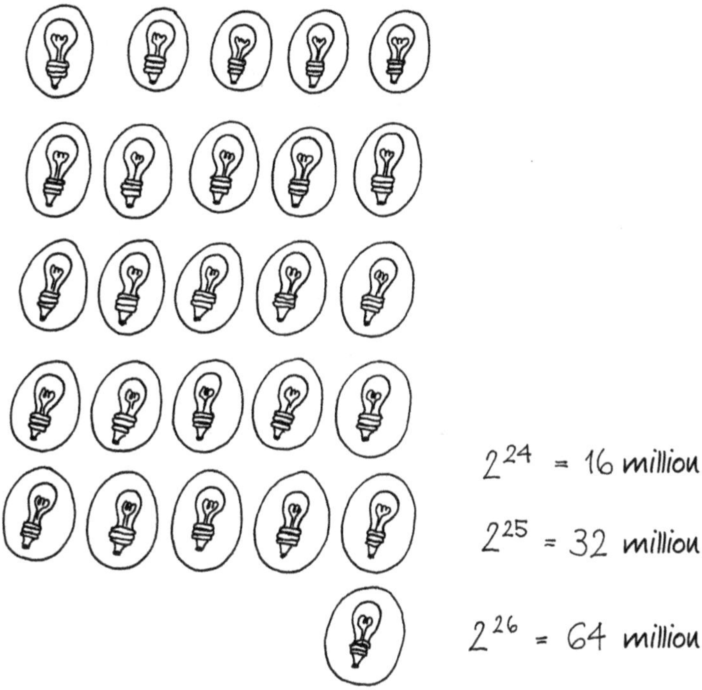

Fig. 9.2 Complexity proliferates exponentially

If we keep the system simple for the moment and only consider "on" and "off," we have two possible states per bulb. If five light bulbs are connected as disco lighting, this creates a system able to assume 32 possible states. Interestingly, the number of elements increases fivefold, while the number of states increases by a factor of 16. The formula for calculating variety is *"the number of states square the power of the number of elements"*—which means we are dealing with exponential growth. This is tricky. Managing 32 states may not be a problem for a manager. But if we now make the system a bit more sophisticated and, for example, connect 32 light bulbs, we recognize the explosive effect of complexity: It immediately increases to 32 million possible states needing to be kept under control (Fig. 9.2). From now on, if we switch on just one more light bulb, complexity doubles unexpectedly by an additional 32 million states. This *proliferating effect of complexity* overwhelms every control system sooner or later if that system is not designed properly.

As we are unaware of this feature of complexity in everyday life, we tend to add even more elements to a system, no matter whether they are products, variants, meetings, people, projects, or whatever. As growth is exponential, nothing happens for a long time, so we keep adding new elements without discarding old ones at the same time. Then, at some point, we add just one more element, and all of a sudden the whole thing blows up in our face—and we find ourselves scrambling to put out fires, working even more overtime, and still treading water. We have no idea what exactly has happened because we simply kept doing what we had long been doing: We just added a single, additional element. All at once, *what is possible* massively exceeds *what is desired*. Now, things can unexpectedly go wrong in twice as many ways. Security engineering at airports, nuclear power plants, or large sporting and musical events, for example, faces such situations.

We did not consider the *necessity of de-networking* without good reason in Sect. 4.3. Complexity arises because elements are interconnected. Only then do we speak of a system in the first place. Complex systems behave like a chessboard on which the pieces are connected with rubber bands. If we move one piece, all the other pieces move at the same time. It is therefore barely possible to attribute individual symptoms to individual causes. Causal relationships disappear in a circularity of the whole, generating previously nonexistent system properties. The horsepower of a car and the "joy of driving," as BWM puts it, cannot be traced back to individual elements and causes. Rather, they emerge from the interaction of 20,000 parts. So if we strip away the whole, we also sever the connections that produce such emergent properties as horsepower or joy. This is the *problem of reductionism*. In science, there is a tendency to reduce the complexity of the world by dividing universities into departments and by using the ceteris paribus clause to focus on a part of the whole. In economics, for example, this is how mathematical models are developed to answer partial questions. However, the economy as a whole cannot be explained in this way. It is too complex. Our schools and our ministries also function according to the reductionist principle. We have a ministry for health affairs, one for education, and one for labor and social affairs.

Practical problems, however, are not based on our categories. They are interconnected problems because it is the same citizen who is sick or poorly educated or unemployed and poor. And perhaps they are sick because they are unemployed or poorly educated. Edmund Stoiber, the former Bavarian Minister President, put matters in a nutshell when discussing the difficulties of holding political office: "Ois hangt mit oim zamm" (Everything is connected with everything else). In contrast to scientists, neither politicians nor managers can work with the reductionist approach. They are responsible for the whole and must cope with the entire complexity. Thus, how they de-network is crucial. In the last chapter, we used segmentation to *properly de-network* our business in the System in Focus (SIF).

We must also distinguish *complexity* from *complicatedness*. Complexity is an objectively measurable feature (see the example of light bulbs). Whether something is complicated or not, on the other hand, is a subjective question. A hundred-piece jigsaw puzzle can be complicated for a child yet simple for an adult. But it is not complex because there is only one state in which the puzzle makes sense. An instruction manual is not complex because it does not assume different states. It can, however, be complicated to understand. Nor is a mechanical watch complex, because it is always meant to function the same way. But watch lovers spend a lot of money on its complicatedness (i.e., complications).

The trick lies in creating *complexity through simplicity*. The black and white keys on a piano are highly simple. And yet, the whole world of music can be created with them, whether jazz, classical, pop, or folk music. Even the cockpit of a military aircraft is not complicated. This "human-machine interface" is carefully designed so as to perform very complex maneuvers without overwhelming the pilot's attention span. Essentially, as with modularization in building-block systems, the focus lies on a few elements whose possible combinations create a high degree of complexity, just as an infinite number of pieces of music can be created by differently combining no more than seven notes of a musical scale, or an entire book can be written with the same 26 letters (of an alphabet). *Focusing on a few, yet important elements and their circular connections* is a pattern that we find time and again in the *"science of simplification,"* as I called cybernetics in Chap. 3.

Important
"There is more to quantification than numeration" (Stafford Beer)

Let us return to the question of how we want to measure complexity. We cannot go around counting states, of course. Nor do we need to, because measurement is not an exact science. On the contrary, we measure most things in life quite naturally by applying our sense of judgment. For example, when we try on clothes or move furniture around our lounge, we gauge (size up) whether things fit approximately without having measured them beforehand. That is straightforward. When we want to overtake another car on the highway, we can judge from experience how hard we have to accelerate without knowing the kg/cm^2 necessary to do so. The simpler things are, the more likely we can measure them in the classical sense and write down a concrete number. The more complex and the more important they are for the enterprise, the less we can measure them, and the more we need to assess quantities. After all, not the number of varieties is relevant, but the *"matching" of varieties*, that is, *comparative evaluation*: What is greater than what? That is enough to decide. If you still have an old pair of scales and put some potatoes in one bowl and a weight in the other, you will quickly see whether things are balanced—without having to count the potatoes or know the weight. Varieties are measured without counting them.

Definition
Second Regulatory Aphorism[4]

It is not necessary to enter the blackbox to calculate the variety that it potentially may generate.

[4] Stafford Beer, *The Heart of Enterprise: The Managerial Cybernetics of Organization* (Chichester, New York, Brisbane, Toronto, Singapore: Wiley, 1979), p. 47.

9.2 Coping with Complexity

To correctly deal with complexity, we need to know that complexity is not simply negative and threatening. It is neither good nor bad. It is not undesirable per se, because complexity also generates performance. Section 1.3 already quoted the evolutionary biologist Carsten Bresch on this subject: "Higher abilities only arise from more complexity."[5] It is the problem *and* the solution. On the one hand, it makes everything difficult, but on the other, it makes everything possible. Hence, we can only agree to a limited extent with the KISS principle, developed in the 1950s and still popular among managers: "Keep it simple, stupid." In the 1990s, for example, many enterprises set up cost-cutting programs according to the lawnmower principle: All divisions had to cut their costs by 10% regardless of their specific situation. Accordingly, too little fat was cut where it could have been cut whereas too much was cut where actual performance fell behind costs. Because people wanted to make things easy for themselves, they curbed their own strengths. On the one hand, we need to eliminate complexity where it is superfluous; but on the other, we need to build it up where it leads to performance. Hence, *the new key competence of enterprises is not to avoid complexity, but to master it.*

Reducing complexity by abandoning the old and the unimportant, by de-networking what does not necessarily belong together, or, for example, by consciously selecting the market in which one (does not) want to operate, is thus one side of the coin. Aldi, the German discounter, for example, decided to only sell products that a housewife buys once a week. *Deliberately creating complexity* for more performance is the other side. The more performance capacity we generate, the less we need to reduce environmental complexity, for example, because this enables reaching and serving more or different customers. *Complexity is attenuated or amplified*, to use telecommunications terminology. Ultimately, all that matters is the matching of varieties—that is, achieving balance. Every form of control aims to bring the whole into a desired balance, into a *steady (i.e., homeostatic) state*, and to maintain this equilibrium long-term. The so-called homeostatic processes occurring in our body keep our body temperature constant between 36.3 and 37.4 °C. This self-regulating mechanism does not depend on knowing the causes of disturbances, but reliably deals with their effects. To control the enterprise, we also define targets that it should achieve and maintain in the long term.

Figure 9.3 shows such a steady state. We see the variety of the environment on the left and the variety of the operation on the right. The latter is smaller because there are always more environmental states than the operation can ever represent. The management of this enterprise can either become active and consciously attenuate environmental variety or it can strengthen its operational variety. It does so by following a permanent cycle until the desired steady state is achieved. In a company, for example, this may be a certain market share or profitability. But what happens if an enterprise does nothing?

---

[5] Carsten Bresch, *Zwischenstufe Leben: Evolution ohne Ziel?* (Munich: Piper, 1977).

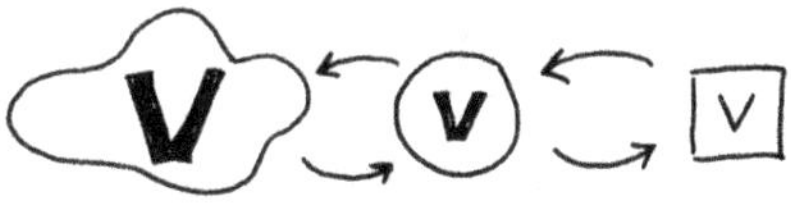

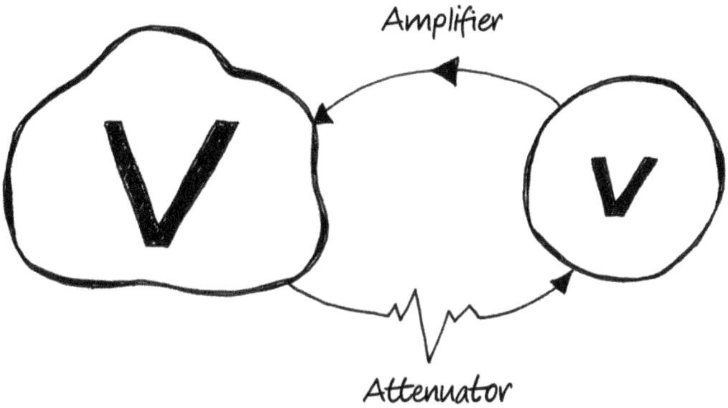

Fig. 9.3 Managing variety

Definition
Ashby's Law of requisite Variety[6]
Only Variety can absorb Variety.

Ashby's law of complexity is one of the most important laws of cybernetics. It acts like a law of nature, whether we know it or not. It is immensely important for managers because most management problems stem from ignoring it. "Low variety solutions" are applied to "high variety problems." *Ashby's law of requisite variety means that complexity can only be absorbed by an equal amount of complexity.* Thus, keeping complexity under control requires applying at least an equal amount of complexity. Eleven soccer players are kept under control by 11 other soccer players. If one player is sent off, the variety equation no longer holds and both teams immediately change their tactics.

Varieties always balance out in the long run. Environmental variety can only be as large as operational variety allows. For example, if ten customers (environment) enter a shoe store at lunch time, but only one salesperson is on duty (operation), then nine customers will leave the store again because they are not being served. So the store manager has to take action. He or she tries to increase operational variety during the busy lunch period, for example, by adding a second salesperson. But options are limited. Therefore, the manager also needs to attenuate environmental variety as much as desired. He or she determines what kind of customers to focus on and how to approach them.

[6] W. Ross Ashby, *An Introduction to Cybernetics* (London: Chapman & Hall, 1956).

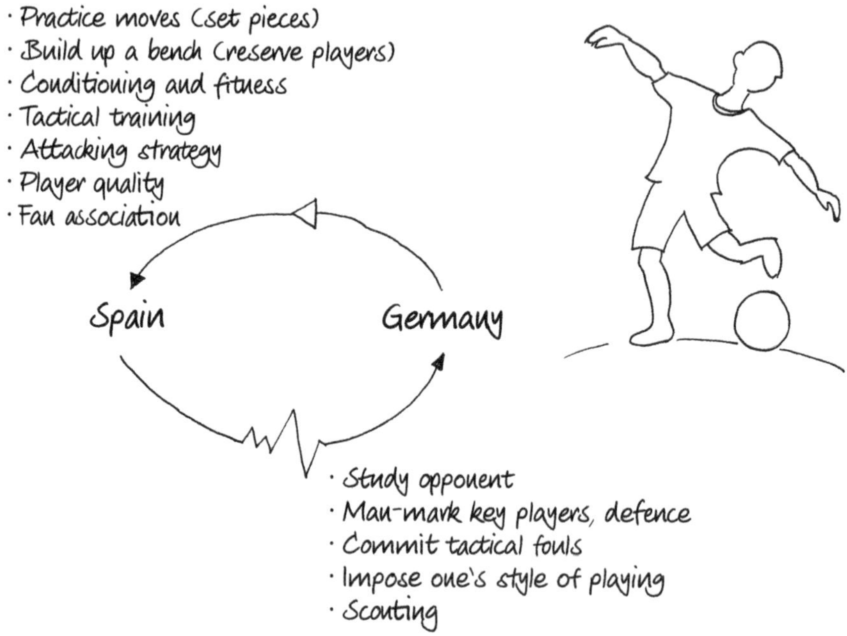

Fig. 9.4 Managing variety in soccer

The coach of the German national soccer team faces a similar problem. His team needs to control the Spanish team, which is known for its complex playing style. The coach has two options: He can either increase his team's variety or attenuate the opponent's. But how? He employs numerous techniques, having either an amplifying or an attenuating effect, or sometimes both at the same time (Fig. 9.4).

The chief of city police also needs to solve a complexity problem because the relevant environment—covert and overt crime—is highly complex and far exceeds the available human and financial resources. Thus, the chief must also consider which attenuators and amplifiers to use. In the 1970s, for example, the idea arose to use television, which had since become widespread, as a variety amplifier. The German television show *Aktenzeichen XY* (Crimewatch) was created for this purpose, and remained successful for decades. Police use many other techniques and tactics to actively fulfill Ashby's law of requisite variety. Figures 9.4 and 9.5 include enough free space for you to add your own tips for amplifying or attenuating variety for the chief of police or the soccer coach …

Ashby's law of requisite variety also applies to our model of control (i.e., Viable System Model): Does it have enough variety to enable effective control? Chapter 3 discussed the fact that the quality of management decisions cannot be better than the quality of the models on which they are based, unless by chance. Now that we know Ashby's law, we can also better frame the Conant–Ashby theorem:

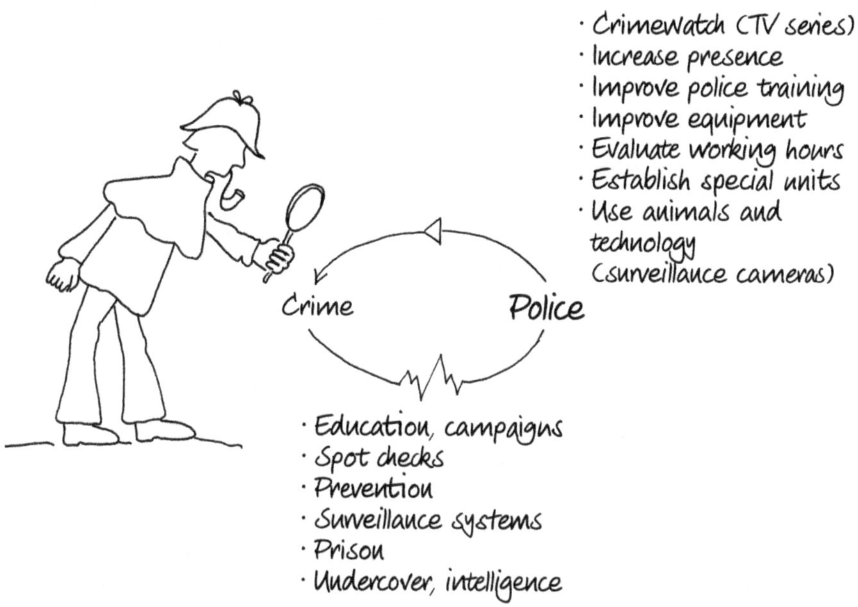

Fig. 9.5 Managing variety in police forces

9.3 Conant–Ashby Theorem[7]

Definition

Every good regulator of a system must be a model of that system.

That model must have requisite variety.

If our model had less variety than the system to be controlled, it could do things that the control system would not understand. A good model of control must develop the necessary control power for a complex enterprise. To do this, it focuses on the *essential variables and their interconnections*, as we have seen in the Viable System Model with *Systems 1–5* and the *communication channels* in between. We recall the principle of Russian dolls, the principle of distributed control, and the relative autonomy of the operational units in System 1. Through this structure, the Viable System Model cuts the overall complexity of the environment into digestible yet holistic portions, equips them with their own control, and reconnects them to achieve higher performance. It is almost part of the purpose of an organizational structure that it reduces environmental complexity and implements Ashby's law. Poorly structured enterprises, however, are sometimes more complex than demanded by

[7] W. Ross Ashby and Roger C. Conant, "Every good regulator of a system must be a model of that system," *International Journal of Systems Science*, Vol. 1, No. 2, (1970), pp. 89–97.

the market, and also more complicated than necessary. For example, a medium-sized construction company consisted of more than 30 different companies, which could be consolidated into half that number after diagnosis.

9.4 Negative Feedback and Self-Control

Probably the most effective principle of the Viable System Model to control an enormous amount of control complexity is to use distributed control capacity by establishing self-control. Not only because this makes the enterprise robust (see Chap. 6 for a discussion of the principle of redundancy of potential command), but because self-control, as a great variety amplifier, multiplies the number of control units. Self-control arises from establishing control loops. The Prologue has already considered the discovery of the feedback principle and its importance. More precisely, we need *"error-controlled feedback"* or "Negative Feedback" for self-control. *Negative feedback, like Ashby's law of requisite variety, is one of the most important ingredients in the recipe for success.* The trick is to feed the failure signal (i.e., by how much we have missed the target) back into the control system (Fig. 1.1). The Prologue has also considered how this principle is applied highly successfully in engineering. In our enterprises, this means that the consequences of a decision are traced back to the decision-maker. Whoever makes a decision must feel its effects—both positive and negative. It also means that someone holds a position long enough for the results of their decisions to become visible. This can sometimes take several years, which explains why enterprises should avoid "job hopping." For the same reason, a new decision should always be made only after the effect of the previous decision is known. This impulse of negative feedback is necessary for a control system to learn, recognize its error, and correct it. The better we design this feedback loop, the more self-control we create.

The principle of negative feedback was first discovered and described by James Watt in the form of the centrifugal governor of a steam engine (Fig. 9.6). When engine speed increases, the centrifugal force of the weights pulls up a lever which, via a linkage mechanism, reduces steam supply with a throttle valve. This mechanically creates a control loop with negative feedback, ensuring that the system can never run out of control. It controls itself. While our enterprises are not about mechanical or electronic control loops, they are also about control loops. The principle of negative feedback works exactly the same whether we are talking about an organism, a steam engine, a computer, or an enterprise. "Negative" does not mean that feedback must always be associated with punishment or some other negative consequence. It simply means that the measure of deviation from a target value is fed back (hence "negative") into the input. While positive feedback in this sense has a self-reinforcing effect in the form of a vicious circle, and hence a buoying effect, negative feedback has a stabilizing effect.

Establishing negative feedback structures means that *control no longer counteracts the system, but is built into it.* No one controls the system (from the outside). It controls itself. This principle can be used in many ways. Here are some examples:

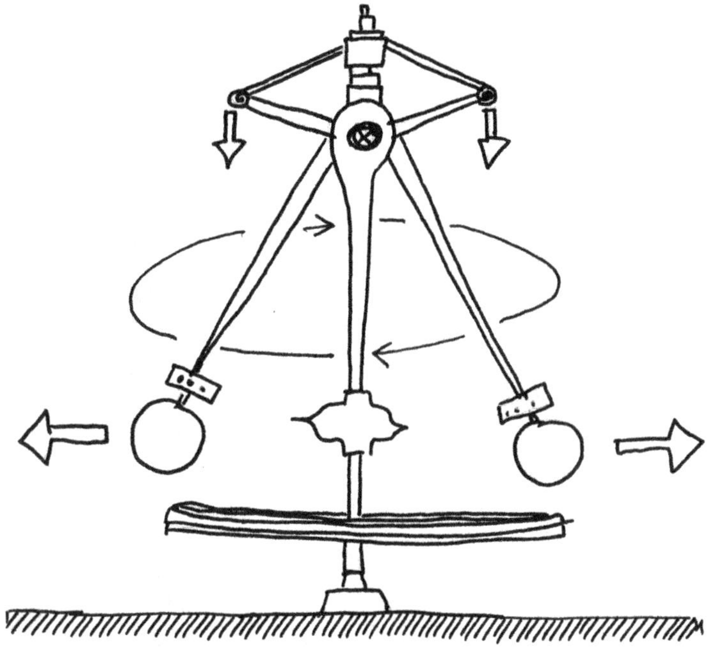

Fig. 9.6 Self-control: the system cannot run out of control

- One of the first adaptations was Peter Drucker's invention of "*Management by Objectives and Self-Control,*" adopted since in almost all enterprises worldwide (although not always in its inventor's sense).[8]
- Professional *parachute packers* in the Israeli army have to jump with self-packed parachutes in random checks. They, therefore, pack every single parachute conscientiously. Further checks are unnecessary.
- After a *prison riot* in Italy over bad food, the kitchen suddenly cooked much better meals on the same budget. It was decided that the prison warden and staff would get the same food as the prisoners.
- A *Lufthansa* manager told me how he trained Chinese engine maintenance crews. On the day of the practical test, after completing the maintenance processes, he gave the teams two choices: Either get on the plane and fly a lap, or remove and reinstall the engines again. "Hey presto, nobody wanted to fly . . ."
- If we only make a minor structural adjustment at an *intersection* and build a roundabout, traffic will regulate itself—at lower cost because we no longer need police officers or traffic light systems; performance will also improve because the adjustment has made red lights on empty roads at three in the morning unnecessary.

[8]Peter F. Drucker, *The Practice of Management* (New York: Harper & Row, 1954).

Fig. 9.7 Self-control instead of explicit control

- To my best knowledge, the example in Fig. 9.7 is from Edward de Bono. It shows a *paper factory* located next to a river flowing from left to right. The factory takes clean water from the river on the left and puts back the polluted water into the river on the right. This causes a control problem because the local community does not tolerate water pollution. Tolerance limits are set and regularly checked by a controller. If the limits are exceeded, the factory must pay a penalty. This is the usual procedure of explicit or extrinsic control, where this works against the system (the factory). It is an expensive, troublesome, and burdensome control system. Therefore, we now change the structure. We build in a negative feedback loop by requiring the factory to release the polluted water into the river at that point where it extracts the water from the river. Thus, from 1 day to the next, the factory has an intrinsic interest in releasing clean water into the river. Control is thus built into the system as intrinsic regulation—the system controls or governs itself.
- Negative feedback loops are partly responsible for the fact that Switzerland's *public finances* are comparatively healthy, even though the country has no raw materials worth mentioning other than stones and water. In accordance with the principle of subsidiarity, in Switzerland's direct democracy every municipality enjoys considerable autonomy. Their citizens also vote on motions. For example, they decide whether the village should build an indoor swimming pool. In addition, every municipality has tax sovereignty and must cover its own expenditure. Thus, local citizens know that approving the indoor swimming pool will increase taxes. Thus, not the typical Swiss virtues keep the country financially healthy but combining autonomy with a stabilizing feedback loop, which applies equally at the cantonal and the federal level.

The more intrinsic regulation we establish in our social systems, the less extrinsic, imposed control we need. Change becomes easier, the better we not only turn those affected into participants but also turn participants into those affected. *Such change takes immediate effect, from 1 day to the next.* In enterprises, however, change is often unnecessarily psychologized. We now have ever-expanding legal codes, which lag behind developments and always arrive too late. Whole professions (e.g., lawyers, tax advisors, and accountants) look for legal loopholes, and the cost of explicit control increases exponentially.

In the Viable System Model, self-control arises when we equip operational units with what they need to succeed in their environment, and also when we hold them accountable for that autonomy. In most enterprises, it has become difficult to hold anyone accountable for anything because their organizations create so many interconnections and interdependencies that every manager can make excuses. The point of a robust organization is to cut off these escape routes and to establish genuine autonomy with real accountability. Only this enables a complex enterprise to really perform in the long term in a complex environment. And only that attracts good people.

Successful managers, therefore, take the time to *work on the system rather than in the system.* They actively shape the enterprise in their area of responsibility and look for the self-control mechanisms they can establish in their sphere of influence to make their practical day-to-day work easier and to become more effective themselves. *They control what controls.* They apply the recipe of success, taking Ashby's law into account whenever they can. They decide only when they have to decide. But when they do, they do so only after thorough preparation, applying Heinz von Foerster's cybernetic imperative, which is related to Ashby's law: They decide so that, whenever possible, the options for action are increased.

Definition

Cybernetic or ethical imperative[9]

Always act so as to increase the number of choices.

[9]Heinz von Foerster, *Understanding Understanding: Essays on Cybernetics and Cognition* (Springer, 2003), p. 303.

10 Manageable or Not? (Step II)

In the first diagnostic step, we identified the levels of recursion, derived the System in Focus (SIF) from those levels, as well as tested and defined the System 1 segmentation in them. This segmentation results in a certain number of operational units. In the second diagnostic step, we want to check whether these units can be managed. Can senior management control and keep them under control? And if we were to eliminate one level of recursion, would the SIF still be manageable? If so, under what conditions?

Every level of recursion that we can eliminate makes the enterprise more agile, more robust, and more productive. In this step, we therefore want to find those recursion levels that are not actually needed, thereby making the enterprise *as flat as possible*. In Sect. 4.2, when we considered the basic structure, we said that a level of recusion needs to comprise at least two operational units, and that we would discuss the upper limit in this chapter. We also said that we cannot rely on the usual rule of thumb for the control or management span of seven plus or minus two direct subordinates. In many cases, a maximum of nine direct subordinates will suffice. However, the rule of thumb is not enough to assess potential flattening. After all, in practice, many organizations control many more operational units on one level of recursion. The Catholic Church, for example, despite its global dimension, consists of only three levels of recursion: The church as a whole with the pope, the dioceses or bishoprics with the bishops, and the parishes with the priests. Although the cardinals do not occupy their own level of recursion, they can be understood as a variety amplifier at the level of the pope. But how has such a large organization managed for 2000 years with so few levels of recursion? How can it keep the complexity of so many operational units under control on one level?

As this question concerns complexity, we need to assess it with Ashby's law of requisite variety. This states that only variety can absorb variety. Thus, in asking how many employees a superior can manage, we should include not only the employees but also their superior in the equation. How large is his or variety? And how does he or she amplify that variety? Presumably, for example, the superior appoints several line managers, thus significantly increasing his or her senior

M. Pfiffner, *The Neurology of Business*, Management for Professionals,
https://doi.org/10.1007/978-3-031-14260-4_10

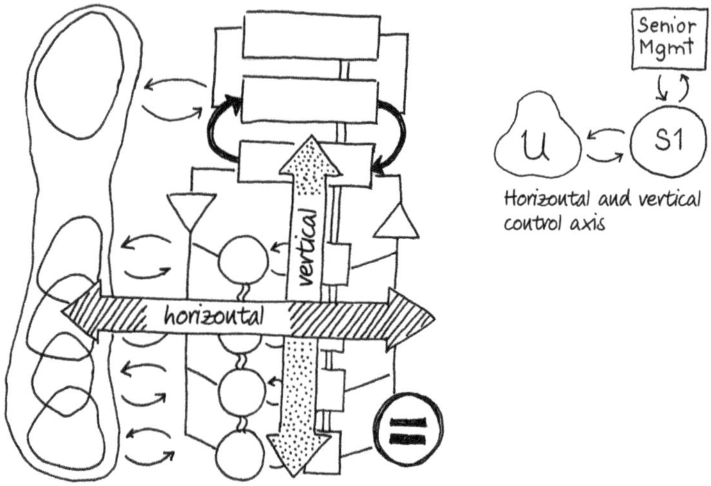

Fig. 10.1 Manageable or not? What is maximum flattening?

management capacity. We need to assess the overall capacity of senior management. Miller's magical number (seven, plus or minus two) does not help us in this respect.

Our model of control consists of two axes: lateral or horizontal control, corresponding to the autonomic nervous system; and vertical control, corresponding to the somatic, volitional nervous system. Both axes have their own complexity, with the horizontal axis providing autonomy and the vertical axis providing cohesion. Senior management controls the operational units in System 1 on the vertical axis, where those units can no longer exercise control themselves. The autonomy and allowed behavioral richness of System 1 can therefore only be as great as it can be compensated for by senior management. Put differently: *The greater the autonomy and decentralization of the operational units, the stronger senior management must be. The variety of the vertical axis must be equal to the variety of the horizontal axis for Ashby's law to be fulfilled* (Fig. 10.1).

But how do we measure, or rather evaluate, horizontal and vertical variety? As explained in the last chapter, such evaluation is not about counting but about fitting: Rather than needing to know how large the varieties are, it is sufficient to know that they are roughly the same size. First, we consider the *variety of the horizontal control axis* (Fig. 10.2) and assess it based on three aspects:

(a) *The number of operational units*
It is easier to manage 3 units than to manage 30 units. The more operational elements, the greater the variety of System 1.

(b) *Their dissimilarity*
If all operational units are alike, this results in less variety in System 1 in total than if they are different. For example, if a foreman has ten long-standing employees who speak English and have the same training, they are easier to

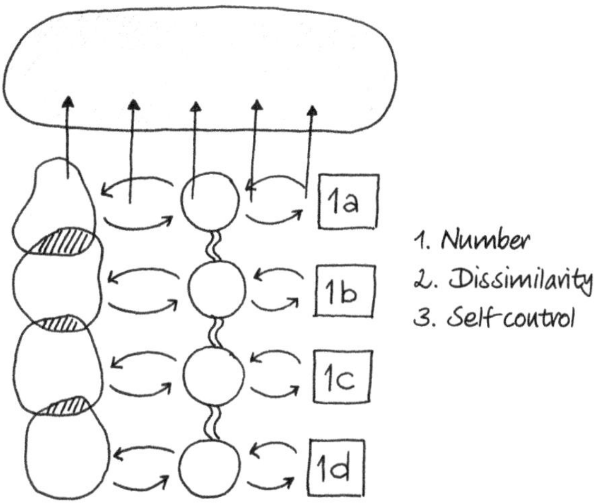

Fig. 10.2 The variety of the horizontal control axis

manage than if three employees are new, others are about to retire, each speaks a different language, and all have different training. For the same reason, corporate diversification strategies are problematic: They can massively increase horizontal variety.

(c) *Their ability to control themselves*
Operational units able to manage their environmental variety themselves are easier to manage than those always calling for support and help. Managing ten experienced employees is not difficult. Ten inexperienced employees, on the other hand, can generate so much variety that they push their superior to his or her limits if they constantly want something and constantly make mistakes.

It does not matter how high this horizontal variety is, as long as it can be absorbed by the vertical variety. According to Ashby's law, senior management must have at least the same amount of variety. So how do we measure the *variety of the vertical control axis*? There are six ways for senior management to absorb variety. In sum, these six ways must be strong enough to keep complexity under control in System 1. The channels absorb variety in different ways (Fig. 10.3):

(a) *Environmental Overlaps*
. . . absorb variety on the vertical axis because, for example, you cannot have an outstanding reputation in one part of the world and a different reputation in another part. Reputations spill over and absorb variety. And if units share certain customers, there will be fewer customers overall for the enterprise than if each unit has its own customers. The same holds true for all other stakeholders in the environment. The greater the overlap, the greater the variety absorbed, the less room for maneuver in System 1 (which we basically want to preserve).

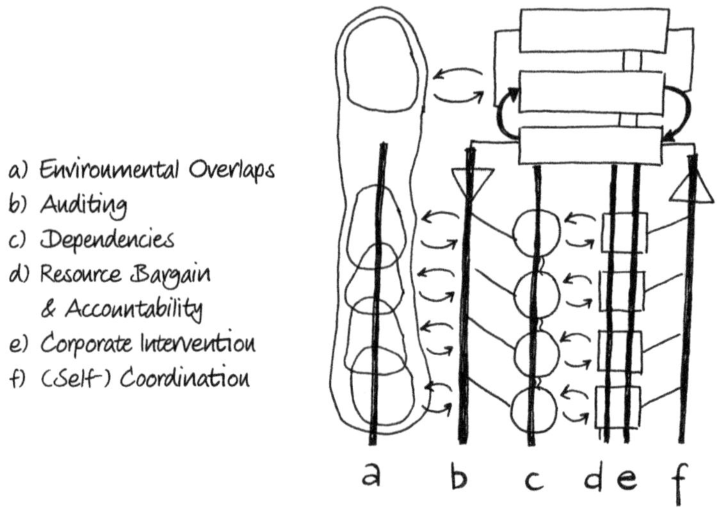

Fig. 10.3 The variety of the vertical control axis

(b) *System 3**
... turns uncertainties into certainties. The direct channel into operations absorbs variety because it reduces the world of possibilities to the world of reality. It tells you what is going on in operations, where something is wrong or could be improved, and thereby eliminates uncertainties. In this sense, it is not only an "audit channel" but also a means of balancing purpose (i.e., what the system does). It notices when operations are doing what does not correspond to the intended purpose.

(c) *Operational Dependencies (squiggly lines)*
... constrain each other's scope of action. In a steel mill, for example, whose operational units are individual value-creating steps, they are highly interdependent. If one process step falters, this affects the subsequent steps. The "squiggly lines" between the operations thus absorb behavioral freedom or variety. In a corporation like Unilever, on the other hand, where business units practically compete only for money, the squiggly lines are weak. The greater the dependencies, the greater the variety absorbed.

(d) *Resource Bargain and Accountability*
... is the first communication channel between the management boxes of Systems 1 and 3 and one of the most important channels on the vertical control axis. It concerns negotiating resources and taking responsibility for them. The operational unit says what it needs; based on its overall view, senior management decides what can be allocated on what conditions. Resources and targets are agreed. The operational unit reports back on what it has done and achieved with the resources. Its freedom of action is more or less constrained through this channel.

(e) *Corporate Intervention*
. . . is the second channel between the management boxes of Systems 1 and 3. It operates in terms of a command channel. Through it, the variety of operational units can be strongly restricted. Statutory, legal, or ethical obligations must be observed, while corporate policy provides binding guidelines. The enterprise must ask itself how much variety it wants to absorb through this channel in order to strike the right balance between autonomy and cohesion. In case of doubt, this is the channel through which a superior can also simply enforce something once in a while. However, the channel should only ever be used as far as necessary.

(f) *Coordination*
No other channel absorbs as much variety as System 2. It encompasses all the rules, guidelines, standards, coordination mechanisms, and culture of the SIF so that the operational units can perform their tasks as smoothly and as autonomously as possible, without System 3 intervening. At the same time, it is the most neglected channel in most enterprises—left to chance rather than actively shaped. The stronger System 2 is, the more variety it absorbs.

For most people, control occurs only through the corporate intervention channel (i.e., the command channel). In reality, the vertical control axis absorbs the variety of its operational units through all six channels. Three of these—Environmental Overlaps, Dependencies, and Resource Bargain and Accountability—depend on how we have segmented and designed System 1 in the first diagnostic step. The strength of these channels, and thus their variety-absorbing effect, is more or less given by this. The other three channels—System 3*, Corporate Intervention, and System 2—are more flexible and can be actively shaped (i.e., designed). See Chap. 13 ("The Control Functions").

It does not matter whether some of these six channels are weak or strong. *They can offset each other and only their sum total needs to be strong enough.* Very authoritarian systems with a heavily used command channel (corporate intervention) can be just as balanced as a "Society of Love," which manages variety via a strong System 2 with rules, principles, shared culture, and ethos. Both systems can function in their own way of dealing with the variety of operational units. What is right depends on the enterprise's purpose and current situation.

Thus, we evaluate the horizontal variety of our SIF and develop an idea of how complex this System 1 is. Next, we do the same for the vertical control axis. The required balance of the varieties of both control axes is described by the "First Axiom of Management":

Definition

First Axiom of Management[1]

The sum of horizontal variety disposed by all the operational elements equals the sum of vertical variety disposed on the six vertical components of corporate cohesion.

[1] Stafford Beer, *Diagnosing the System for Organizations: The Managerial Cybernetics of Organization* (Chichester, New York, Brisbane, Toronto, Singapore: Wiley, 1985), p. 89.

Here are two examples. I have already mentioned the Canton of Zurich (Switzerland) with its 172 municipalities. At first glance, that is an incredible number of operational units on a single level. For this reason, about 20 years ago there was a constitutional debate on whether a control level should be established between the municipalities and the canton. Let us assess this question ourselves. On the horizontal axis, we have 172 operational units. They are not very different because one municipality functions like another. Their tasks and problems are the same. Only the three larger cities in the canton differ significantly from the other municipalities. The third aspect remains: How well can the municipalities manage themselves? Do they solve their own problems largely autonomously? We have already established that, due to the combination of direct democracy, subsidiarity, and fiscal sovereignty, a stabilizing negative feedback loop is at work. In effect, the municipalities solve most of their tasks independently and control themselves. What at first glance appears to be a huge horizontal variety due to the 172 units is put into perspective with the other two aspects.

Let us look at the canton's six vertical channels. On the one hand, the environmental overlaps are small because there are clear regional boundaries. On the other, they are not insignificant because most residents and businesses are not active solely within one municipality. System 3* is very well equipped thanks to a broad media landscape with many public and private broadcasters and publishers. The canton's System 3 informs itself via these media. Operational dependencies are strong, as the municipalities share a great deal at the district level, such as utilities and waste disposal plants, courts, hospitals, and schools. The Resource Bargain and Accountability Channel works well because, in addition to financial equalization, there is a legal obligation to coordinate plans in quite a few areas with the canton. The Corporate Intervention Channel is effective because the canton has the ability to enforce its intervention rights if necessary. Finally, we note that the canton's System 2, with the supporting function of the districts, the laws and ordinances, and a common language, culture, and religion, is also strong in this nevertheless relatively small area. Overall, we seem to be dealing with an extremely strong vertical axis of control, one capable of absorbing the complexity of System 1, which at first seems very large yet is then strongly relativized. The same conclusion was reached after a 3-year-long constitutional discussion.

Let us look at a much larger political system: the European Union. Is it manageable? Again, we first assess the horizontal axis. After Brexit, the EU comprises 37 member states. That is significantly fewer entities than in the Canton of Zurich, yet still much more than what we would accept as a span of control in our enterprises. The entities are also all very different: Poland is very different from France, Bulgaria from Sweden, and so forth. Finally, EU member states are all barely able to cope with their own, national problems. Debt, pensions, health care costs, environmental problems, or migration issues pose challenges for which no solutions are in sight. What at first glance already appears to be a lot of variety due to the 37 units is multiplied by the other two aspects. This, however, is not a problem as long as the vertical control axis is strong enough. We remember, after all, that it is only about the "matching" of varieties.

The environments are separated from each other by national borders but the overlaps are large in many respects. System 3* is weak at the European level. The media focus on national issues and are tainted by political sensitivities in their own countries. Operational dependencies exist, for example, in terms of a common currency or economic dependencies (e.g., electricity production or foreign trade). Nevertheless, many states could also operate largely self-sufficiently if required. Next are the two channels that connect the EU's management box with that of the states. The Resource Bargain and Accountability Channel works as long as individual states are able and willing to co-finance the others. However, no effective processes seem to exist to align the plans of the various states with those of the EU. For example, there is no common fiscal policy beyond the 2012 fiscal pact, which is based on the equally ineffective Maastricht convergence criteria. The divergent interests of the many different states make it difficult to work within the common System 3. The Corporate Intervention Channel is therefore almost nonexistent on important issues. The states ratify restrictions on their autonomy voluntarily, which explains why there is still no European constitution. In contrast, the number of European laws on less important issues is increasing, as is the number of joint European institutions. In this respect, System 2 is increasingly expanded and even overregulated in some cases. Apart from laws and institutions, however, it remains weak: A pan-European cultural area, a European language or religion is missing: In the Balkans, significantly different rules apply than in the German Rhineland.

We might consider these points differently and reach different conclusions. It is therefore important to bring these considerations together in a discussion. In the end, not the individual consideration counts but the overall picture. And in the case of the EU, we may well conclude that Ashby's law is not fulfilled. The horizontal variety seems to be unable to be absorbed by the vertical variety at the latest after the EU's eastern expansion. Since Ashby's law ensures that these two varieties will sooner or later balance out, there are two possibilities. Either the EU will succeed in expanding its vertical channels in time (varietal reinforcement). Or System 1 will reduce its variety by individual units leaving again (see Brexit). Or the EU will split into several Europes, which in themselves are again less complex and therefore considerably easier to manage. This would be tantamount to introducing a new level of recursion between the states and the EU. Complexity proliferates exponentially but also dwindles as quickly.

Our first look at a level of recursion always checks whether the horizontal and vertical axes are balanced. A globally active supplier in the construction industry faced the question of whether its 40 national subsidiaries could continue to be managed directly by corporate management, or whether a level of recursion had to be introduced. After a thorough discussion of the two control axes, the conclusion was reached that the additional level of recursion was needed and that the national companies would have to be grouped into eight market units. The assessment was based on the assumption that while there would be around 60 companies in future, they would be very similar and each would be run by a strong local management team. After discussing the six vertical channels, it was nevertheless concluded that

Ashby's law could be fulfilled by expanding System 2 in the form of competence centers, coordination committees, training and IT systems, but that this expansion would take too long. If the level of recursion had not been established in time, the company would have imploded due to its growing internal complexity.

If, on the other hand, *the axes are balanced, we check whether we can flatten the organization by one level of recursion:* Would our SIF still be manageable if we eliminated the next level down? In a locally operating construction company, the turnkey construction division consisted of five branches, each running about 20 customer projects concurrently. The question, then, was whether these 20 projects could also be managed directly at the divisional level. With this in mind, the divisional management concluded that the branch office should not be a level of recursion but only a workplace with a janitor. The division was flattened by one level. A global logistics company used the same method to flatten its organization from five to three levels of recursion, simultaneously reducing costs by millions and gaining agility.

Our world is ailing because the First Axiom of Management is not being fulfilled. Vertical axes either operate in an overly authoritarian, ponderous, and expensive manner, or are too weak to do their job. New or growing entities need a framework to adhere to. Without structure, they collapse again sooner or later. In particular national and supranational institutions tend to have a vertical control system barely able to cope with rapidly growing complexity. They notice this but neither know what the problem nor what needs to be done. Many organizations, therefore, struggle to fulfill their intended purpose.

Tasks

(a) Start from the segmentation you found in the last diagnostic step. It entails a certain number of operational units with larger or smaller overlaps and dependencies. What do these consist of? Write this down and draw your System 1 as realistically as possible.

(b) Evaluate the horizontal complexity of your SIF: the number of units, their diversity, and their ability to control themselves.

(c) Evaluate the vertical complexity of your SIF: the strength of the six channels. Add these to your drawing. We want to create something like a "quantified flowchart" by drawing channels that are stronger, and thus also drawn thicker, and vice versa.

(d) Are the two axes of control balanced and is Ashby's law being satisfied? If not, what can be done to increase vertical variety? If we are not able to do this to a sufficient degree, can we dampen the horizontal variety by adding an additional level of recursion?

(e) On the other hand, if the axes are balanced: What if you eliminated the level of recursion below your SIF (i.e., the R−1 level)? Would your SIF still be manageable? If so, what prevents us from doing this?

Mission-Critical Tasks (Step III) 11

In the first diagnostic step, we determined the basic structure and its levels of recursion, defined our System in Focus (SIF), and checked its segmentation. In the second diagnostic step, we checked whether we could flatten the organization and examined its management in terms of Ashby's law. Consequently, we now know how many operational units we have in our SIF and what they are. *The third diagnostic step aims to better understand these operational units.* To do this, we will study their specific success factors in order to determine what we need to organize in the first place. To do this, we will look at the operational units individually and then also at how they interact. We will apply complexity considerations (see Chap. 9), from which we will derive which tasks are critical for successful functioning and must therefore be organized. This knowledge will enable us to develop the higher level control system of senior management in a tailored and targeted manner in the subsequent steps.

Let us examine *how the operational units function in the SIF.* In doing so, we should not make the classic mistake of delving into individual processes because otherwise we will lose ourselves in details. We must stay on our level of recursion. From its point of view, what happens in managing and operating an operational unit is a *black box* (cf. Chap. 5 "Russian Dolls"). We are not interested in what exactly the management of the operational unit does or what happens in the operation in detail. Once again, we are only interested in how an operational unit deals with complexity, that is, in matching varieties between its environment, operation, and management. If we know how the operation deals with environmental complexity, and how the management deals with operational complexity, we begin approaching the *success factors of the operational units.*

In most cases, we are dealing with a homogeneous segmentation of System 1. This means that all operational units belong to the same segmentation category and are, for example, regions, product areas, or customer groups. If we understand one of these operational units, we understand all units because they function more or less the same. If, on the other hand, we are dealing with a hybrid structure in which a level of recursion comprises different types of operational units, all types must be

M. Pfiffner, *The Neurology of Business*, Management for Professionals,
https://doi.org/10.1007/978-3-031-14260-4_11

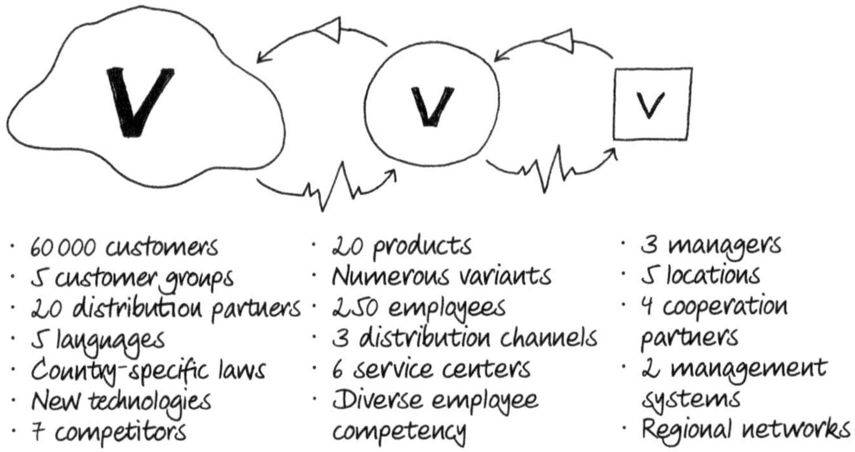

Fig. 11.1 Complexity drivers in environment, operation, and management

examined individually. For example, some units in this case are regions while others are product areas. Hence, it is not enough to only know the region: We must also understand the product area. The same holds true for unrelated businesses or for innovations managed at the same level of recursion.

We first need to better understand the operational unit's environment. What actually is in this environment? And what makes that environment complex and challenging? We look for the complexity drivers in all relevant environmental spheres and influence groups (e.g., state, customers, competitors, suppliers, employees, investors, media, technology, demographics, ecology). In considering these questions, we try to concretize and, as far as possible, quantify everything that comes to mind. The point is to make the perceived complexity visible and to write things down: How great is the market potential? How large are market volume and the market being served? Which and how many customers, competitors, authorities, sales partners, cooperation partners, languages, and so on are included? How many and which customer groups do we serve? Usually, a handful of executives familiar with the business come up with a good answer within 15 min. Next, we do the same for operations and management, again trying to be as specific and as quantifiable as possible: What does the operation or the management contain, and what makes it complex? This gives us an idea of how powerful the three core varieties—environment, operation, and management—are. Next, we contrast them: How much greater is environmental variety than operational variety, and operational variety than managerial variety? Answering these questions helps us develop an awareness of the size of the *control task*.

According to Ashby's law, these varieties will somehow balance out. Thus, the arrows in Fig. 11.1 must begin to work so that they balance out as we would like them to. The arrows are channels for amplifying or attenuating variety (see the examples of soccer or the police in Chap. 9). Reinforcing factors increase latitude

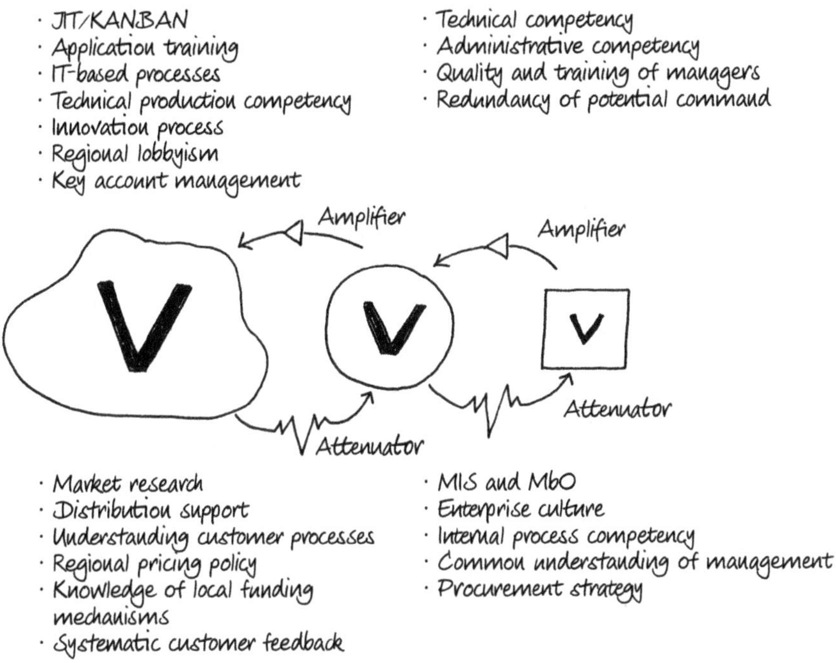

Fig. 11.2 Working out the principal complexity amplifiers and attenuators

and opportunity and therefore lead to instability. And yet, we need to reinforce variety. Attenuating factors diminish the world of possibilities, and thus information, and therefore are dangerous. This risk, too, must be taken. Thus, we had better know what we are doing and consciously perform this *variety engineering*.

Definition

The First Principle of Organization[1]

Managerial, operational, and environmental varieties, diffusing through an institutional system, tend to equate; they should be designed to do so with minimum damage to people and to cost.

We now need to find the amplifiers and attenuators with which the operational unit can actively control complexity so as not to end up losing customers as the shoe store did in Chap. 9. We want to balance complexity so that we can reach and maintain a certain *target value*. We write this into our diagram between the variety blocks (Fig. 11.2). *Behind the required amplifiers and attenuators lie tasks that are critical to success and that must be organized.* Someone must take care of them and

[1] Stafford Beer, *Diagnosing the System for Organizations: The Managerial Cybernetics of Organization* (Chichester, New York, Brisbane, Toronto, Singapore: Wiley, 1985), p. 30.

be responsible for them. We need to focus on them when we organize because, after all, we can neither leave everything to itself nor organize everything. Fortunately, we do not have to. Most things work by themselves if left to do so, or result from reflex, routine, or acclamation. Many decisions do not need to be taken but also take themselves, due to the normative force of facts. *We do not need to manage and organize everything.* Of course, someone still needs to water the plants in the office but nothing really serious happens—except to the plants—if the watering is not organized. Today, however, protecting itself against cyberattacks can be critical for an enterprise's success. In the end, we want to have worked out for our SIF, in accordance with the *Pareto principle*, those *20% of tasks that account for 80% of success.* In the spirit of the "science of simplification," we want to concentrate on the few, yet essential things.

The challenge lies in creating enough variety in service provision. Remember: Environmental variety can only be as large as operational variety allows. Therefore, the environmental variety needing to be absorbed must also be actively reduced as much as possible. How might we do this? We use various management techniques, which are not necessarily associated with complexity management. Just-in-time, total quality management, market research, advertising, modular systems or training, to mention but a few, ultimately act as attenuators or amplifiers. Everything we do can be reduced to the question of whether it amplifies or attenuates variety. The advantage of this view is that we can assign all techniques according to their *effect on the complexity equation.* This makes us aware of what we are actually trying to achieve and gives us a choice between alternatives with the same effect. If one technique does not prove effective, it can be replaced by another. In this way, we can weigh up options. For example, a popular variety amplifier of operations is the use of modular systems, where the combinatorics of a few modules, simple in themselves, provides great variety and thus great power. Further examples are listed in Table 11.1.

Some factors take effect on both sides of the equation, as two sides of the same coin, so to speak. On the one hand, Management by Objectives amplifies variety by opening up the employee's scope of action and thus better utilizing his or her competencies. On the other, it attenuates variety by setting an annual target, and thereby excludes all other possible targets. Advertising amplifies variety by reaching more potential customers through communicative measures, and has an attenuating effect by determining offerings. "You can have a Ford T in any color as long as it's black." The slogan stood for the introduction of standardized painting in assembly line production by Henry Ford and served as a strong variety attentuator because no one asked for a red model anymore. Investment can have an amplifying effect by developing capacity but can also have an attenuating effect because it determines what you invest in and what not. Market intelligence, on the other hand, serves to clearly to make the unknown environment smaller by learning more about it and thus reducing variety. If you know what lies ahead, you no longer have to adapt to all sorts of things. This explains why professional athletes study their opponents meticulously before boxing or playing against them. Every operational unit must

Table 11.1 Examples of variety amplifiers and attenuators

Environment—operation	Operation—management
Amplifiers:	*Amplifiers:*
Modular systems	Management by objectives
Number of variants	Empowering and further training
Cooperations/acquisitions	Consultants or assistants
Customizing/individualization	Networks
Advertising and communication	Technical equipment
Lobbying	Multiplication of experience (expert groups)
Key accounting	Management conferences
Attenuators:	*Attenuators:*
Advertising	Training/education/culture
Market intelligence/market research	Standardization/guidelines/rules
Opening hours	Investment policy and prioritization
Patents	Key success factors
Pricing	Auditing/compliance
ABC customer segmentation	Job design and promotions
Service-level agreements	MIS management information systems

Note: The same factor can sometimes work both ways

ask itself whether to use the new possibilities offered by digitization to amplify or attenuate variety, or to tackle both tasks at the same time.

Thus we write down all the important amplifiers and attenuators that come to mind for the operational unit under consideration. It is quite useful to discuss matters in a 1-h brainstorming session with two or three people familiar with the operational unit. The point is not completeness but ultimately to somehow quantify the variety blocks. Once more, it is about proportions: *Are our amplifiers and attenuators strong enough to balance the lacking variety and to attain our envisaged objective?*

Distinguishing amplification and attenuation is important for quantifying the variety blocks, for factor completeness (have both sides been thought of?), and for our awareness of what we want to achieve. On the other hand, the distinction is no longer important for further diagnostic work. In fact, we now ask *which task behind an amplifier or attenuator* must be fulfilled and organized and write this down. Which of these tasks will the operational unit perform itself in order to act autonomously? Which tasks should be performed by the senior management in the SIF? And which other levels of recursion might also be involved in a mission-critical task? We will deal with these questions in the next diagnostic step (see Chap. 12 "Central or Decentral?").

Beforehand, though, we need to consider something else. So far, we have only looked at the individual operational unit. However, mission-critical tasks also result from the *interaction of all units in System 1*, that is, where they exhibit environmental *overlaps* and operational *dependencies*. We must also elicit these because they also give rise to mission-critical tasks (Fig. 11.3). For example, access to shared customers or suppliers in the environment must be neatly organized, or irritations and conflicts will arise. So which overlaps exist between which environments in our SIF? And what control tasks result from these overlaps? Where do operations

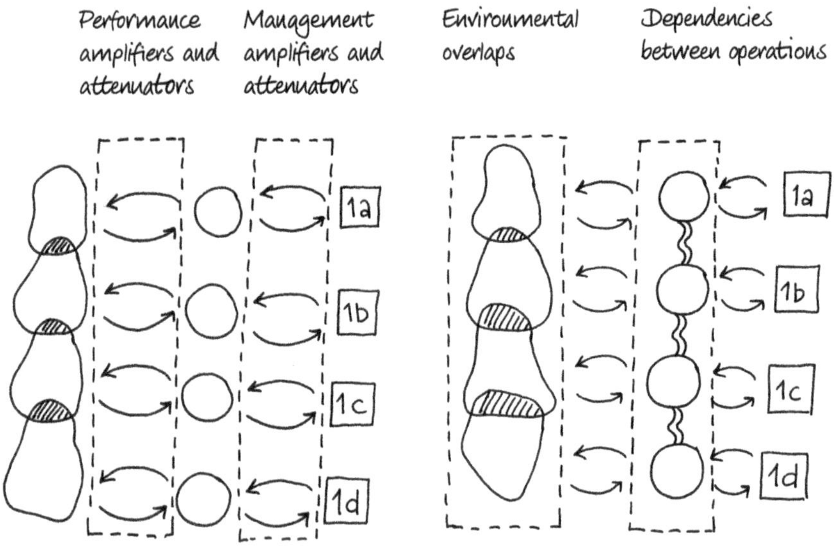

Fig. 11.3 Who handles organizational needs?

Table 11.2 Examples of mission-critical tasks (from interactions in System 1)

Environmental overlap…	*…and corresponding tasks critical to success*
Supraregional customers	Key account management
Supraregional employee potential	Central recruiting
Common competitors	Competition monitoring
Common suppliers	Framework contracts
Cooperation partners	Partner management
Trade fair appearances	Trade show planning and coordination
Operational dependencies…	*…and corresponding tasks critical to success*
Joint manufacturing	Production planning and control
Central distribution	Sales planning and control
Shared offices	Local "janitor"
Pooled technical experts	Access and internal billing mechanism
Centralized purchasing	Global purchasing processes
Central IT	IT support and joint IT strategy
Joint development	Coordination/prioritization of development needs

depend on each other because they need to share certain infrastructures, for example, and what are the resulting control tasks? This, for example, concerns controlling production on shared manufacturing facilities, as well as controlling joint sales or joint purchasing. Table 11.2 presents some examples and the derived mission-critical tasks.

Only when we have compiled all mission-critical tasks from considering the operational units, on their own *and* in terms of their interaction, do we have the *raw material for the further diagnostic and design steps.* We will be adding to the steadily growing list of tasks as we continue to diagnose Systems 2 through 5. The list is a live document and can always be adjusted. Typically, our SIF needs to perform about *20–40 mission-critical tasks.* Distributed among Systems 1–5, this again amounts to our meanwhile familiar seven plus/minus two mission-critical tasks per control system.

Tasks

Focus on System 1 of your SIF and make the complexity considerations discussed in Chap. 9. Which mission-critical tasks do you need to organize?

(a) Take one operational unit in your SIF (*pars pro toto*) or several units (if they function differently). Consider what the environment, operation, and management comprise and what the important complexity drivers in each of them are. Make a drawing as in Fig. 11.1 and write down the factors. How strongly imbalanced are the varieties?
(b) Enter target values between the variety blocks environment-operation and operation-management that you are aiming to achieve.
(c) Consider the techniques the operational unit uses to amplify and attenuate the varieties accordingly to achieve the target values and write them into your drawing (Fig. 11.2). When you think you have found the necessary amplifiers and attenuators, reformulate them as tasks.
(d) List the environmental overlaps and operational dependencies in your System 1 and consider the resulting tasks. Now supplement the list of critical success tasks that you compiled in (c).

Tip: You might confuse levels of recursion already at this stage of diagnosis. Make sure that you always remain on the level of your System in Focus. If you make a drawing, label it clearly (e.g., SIF R0: Division Green).

12 Centralized or Decentralized? (Step IV)

According to the Pareto principle, the 20–40 mission-critical tasks available after the last diagnostic step should comprise those 20% of all control tasks in the enterprise that account for 80% of its success. In other words: If we neatly control these tasks, not much that is crucial can go wrong because the most important part of the enterprise is working. We will therefore focus on controlling these tasks in the following diagnosis. We ask the same question with each task: Who controls this, in coordination with whom, based on what information, and who must be informed about decisions? To this end, we incorporate the existing mission-critical tasks into our model of control, thus individualizing and tailoring it to the enterprise.

To find out which tasks our System in Focus is responsible for, we first return to our levels of recursion: What should the operational units do themselves? What should be done at the level of recursion of our SIF? And what should other levels of recursion do? In *diagnostic Step IV, we assign the tasks from Step III to levels of recursion.* This also means assigning competency and responsibility: Who is allowed to decide what? Control, after all, means continually taking many small and larger decisions.

This brings us back to the old question of *autonomy versus cohesion* (see Chap. 6). We thus return to an area where wars of ideas are fought and where one fashion supersedes another. Discussion focuses on the *perennial question of "centralized or decentralized,"* and thus once again on freedom, hierarchy, and power. In fact, people will be arguing and fighting over whether the horizontal or the vertical axis of control is more important. This resembles the question of whether we should steer more to the right or to the left in road traffic. Instead, both are needed in the right measure and at the right moment. It also depends on where we are and where we want to go. We, therefore, do not ask in any generic way whether we should allocate tasks more centrally or more decentrally but instead *which task needs to be performed by which level of recursion.* For every task, allocation may look different: Fortunately, we have limited ourselves to those tasks that are critical to success.

M. Pfiffner, *The Neurology of Business*, Management for Professionals,
https://doi.org/10.1007/978-3-031-14260-4_12

Task allocation should not be about beliefs or fads but must follow a clear principle and logic. Our approach must take into account the specifics of this enterprise in its current situation. Remember: We did not define the management span generically in Chap. 10 either but adapted it to the enterprise according to its specific situation. Thus: How do we arrive at a tailored solution and what principles should guide us?

The Viable System Model tells us that we should design operational units so that they can develop by themselves (autopoietically). That is, they should constantly reinvent themselves, intentionally and decidedly. They should adapt to the circumstances, strengthen themselves, grow, and fulfill a purpose of their own. They should do this on their own, as independently as possible from other units, to enable us to build a robust and flexible organization. In principle, they should perform as many tasks as possible themselves. Once more, the reasons are:

(a) The principle of *relative autonomy* tells us that the operational units should handle as many tasks as possible themselves in order to maintain their own existence in the long run (cf. Sect. 4.2).
(b) The aphorism *"hierarchy from the relevance of information"* and the principle of *"the redundancy of potential command"* tell us that decisions should be made where the relevant information is and that control must be distributed (cf. Chap. 6).
(c) We thus establish *self-responsibility, self-control*, and a stabilizing *negative feedback loop* (cf. Chap. 9).
(d) *Ashby's law* (cf. Chap. 9) and *The First Axiom of Management* (cf. Chap. 10) show us that most of the complexity must be absorbed where it arises and that only the residue can be absorbed by the higher level of recursion.

These four points are summarized in the aforementioned *principle of subsidiarity*. Depending on the country, this is applied more or less consistently in political systems with federal structures.

Definition
Subsidiarity
Tasks are only taken over by the superordinate level if they can no longer be performed by the subordinate level, the one closer to the task.

Applying the principle of subsidiarity is a *conditio* sine qua non for implicit control and "self-control" in the enterprise and thus also a prerequisite for complexity capability. Operational units control themselves if they manage those tasks themselves that are important to them. Insofar as we give them these tasks and the associated competencies, we can also hold them responsible for results, because responsibility for results presupposes that decisions can be made about what influences results. In this way, we cut off all escape routes for management if the unit does not function. We thus create the necessary negative feedback loop that leads to self-control and stabilization.

Remember: "Negative" feedback does not mean that this feedback has to have unpleasant consequences for the originator but merely that these consequences are coupled "back" in a negative direction in the flowchart. The consequences can be pleasant or unpleasant. It is only important that a control loop is created in which management recognizes deviations in its own interest and can also correct these itself immediately. For this feedback loop to work, we must be able to clearly localize responsibility: *Task, competence, and responsibility* must be brought together *in one place* for this purpose.

To make the management of an operational unit responsible for its results and to enable self-control, we must therefore give it those tasks and competencies that are crucial for its success. As mentioned, an operational unit should perform as many tasks as possible itself. However, it makes no sense to assign a unit many tasks if we do not include the mission-critical ones. No military commander would want to go into battle without having the resources necessary for success. No lawyer would want to enter a legal dispute without having control over the most important arguments. Nor would a surgeon want to operate if he or she first had to ask a central office about every important decision (after all, the office might be unavailable or busy, and therefore would have either no time or other worries). No organization needing to function works like this. But this is precisely how many organizations in which we live today or have around us work.

Critical to success and *crucial for success* are two different things. In the last chapter, we identified the tasks that are critical to success and that need to be organized in our control system. These tasks determine the majority of success, yet not all of them are also crucial for success. Those tasks that are crucial for success are those without which success is impossible or difficult to achieve because they directly influence what the customer pays for. We have already compiled the customer's purchase-decision criteria in Chap. 8.

Definition

Mission-Critical Versus Crucial for Success

Mission-critical tasks are crucial for success if they have a relevant influence on the customer's purchase-decision criteria.

If, for example, it is important for the customer that our service desk responds quickly and competently in the local language, managing local service technicians becomes not only mission-critical but also crucial for success. This task should be performed by the operational unit itself, which requires the necessary competence to do so. Translated into the logic of nonbusiness organizations, these tasks have a direct and relevant impact on the service recipient. The more tasks crucial for success that we can allocate directly to the operational units, the greater their influence on customer benefits and the better they can move independently in their environment, "home in on" new needs, and adapt flexibly. This makes them agile and viable. *We anchor responsibility for customers by creating the opportunity to absorb their variety.*

Table 12.1 Three sequential questions for assessing "Central or Decentral"

1	*Can we even afford* to hand this task over to the operational units?	*If yes*, then continue with Question 2. *If no*, no further discussion is needed. The task is assigned *centrally* to a higher level of recursion.
2	Does the task have a relevant *influence on any of the customer's purchase-decision criteria*?	*If yes*, then we have also found a solution. The task is assigned *decentrally* to the operational unit because it is crucial for success and because we can afford to do so. *If no*, then continue with Question 3.
3	Can we achieve relevant *synergies* with this task?	*If yes*, then the task is assigned centrally. We could have the operational units control it themselves, but we achieve more together without any relevant reduction in autonomy. *If no*, then it does not really matter where we assign the task. It is neither crucial for success nor can we use synergies with it. In this case, we assign it to the *operational unit* because of the principle of subsidiarity.

There are two reasons why a task that is crucial for success must nevertheless be centralized, that is, performed by a higher level of recursion. The first reason might be that one simply cannot afford to allocate certain resources to the operational unit for its sole disposal. Often, offices, IT departments, or manufacturing facilities are shared because it is simply not possible for every unit to maintain and utilize its own infrastructure. Thus, this reason arises from economic conditions alone. The other reason is to seek cohesion or synergies in the interaction of multiple operational units so that the whole can be more than the sum of its parts. Synergies can result in lower costs or higher capabilities. To achieve this, the corresponding task must also be superordinate (i.e., centrally controlled). Synergy is the energy that comes from working together and thus always reduces individual autonomy. We should therefore exercise caution with synergy. If we keep following our previous logic, *we should not curtail the influence of operational units on purchase-decision criteria even if this creates synergies.* Primacy lies with the autonomy and viability of System 1, because what is not robust and viable at the bottom can never be stable at the top.

For our assessment, we therefore subject all mission-critical tasks from Step III to the three questions in Table 12.1, which follow the logic of a decision tree.

If we answer the first question with "no," we may be living with a compromise that we ought to know about: A task cannot be assigned to operational units because we cannot afford to. If, however, that task influences a customer's purchase-decision criterion, we need to know this because we must resolve this compromise as soon as the situation changes and as soon as the enterprise has become strong enough. For example, an association of general medical practices is unable to afford equipping every practice with a laboratory, ultrasound, and X-ray machinery. But as soon as they can afford to, they will decentralize these competencies because they are crucial to successful patient care. If in another enterprise the product areas cannot have their

Mission-Critical Task	Lead	R+1 (Group)	R0 (Market Units)	R-1 (Subsidiary)
Sales Tools (IT) technical design (offer creation, order processing, accounting..)	Com ExC	Initial concept and development, programming, training, rollouts, cont. improvement, support	Annual request and planning of roll-outs together with Excellence Functions; participant in final roll-out presentations	Local adaptation, usage, key user assistance, local conceptional input within guidelines
Sales Support Packages -> Products (Handbooks, Videos, documentation)	PM	Initial concept and development, design, training, cont. improvement, support; → Internal Sales	-	Adapt support packages to the local / regional needs; usage
Standardized Contracts, Terms and Conditions	Com ExC/ Legal	Provide corporate templates	-	Adapt to local demands, local government requirements
Guidelines for International Cooperation	Sales	Definition and control of central guidelines, policies, strategies (Clearing)	Coordination of the execution, coordinate between the MU`s (Clearing)	Local adherence
Key Account Management for International Customers	Sales	-	-	Key Account Management only on local level
Define Product and Service Range	PM	Central Portfolio Management giving generic guidelines (i.e. menu for services and framework of what we generally and at least offer)	Define Regional Product Range together with R0	Local decision on the portfolio within the guidelines
Market Intelligence (project, competitors)	CD	Consolidation, interpretation, everything what is important for the group needs to be done centrally	Consolidation, interpretation, everything what is important for the MU needs to be done centrally	Largely decentralized
Pricing Policy	Com ExC/ Pricing	Central guideline, central tools, support on list price definitions for neighboring countries	Regional harmonization of the price levels	Autonomous decisions on list prices and net price

Fig. 12.1 Allocation of tasks to levels of recursion (example)

own distribution and service units today, we will probably have to live with that compromise. But as soon as the situation allows, we will allocate these resources directly to the product areas if they are crucial for the customer's purchase-decision. Hence, we must always also ask ourselves the second question.

Purchasing is a typical example of a task being centralized for synergy reasons, that is, assigned to a higher level of recursion. Many enterprises could probably afford to provide every operational unit with its own purchasing department. However, that department will have a relevant influence on purchase-decision criteria only in very few enterprises. If you buy a car, for example, you do not care where and how the manufacturer bought the car battery. You will consider other issues. Thus, purchasing need not be assigned to the operational units. But its centralization enables using synergies by increasing our joint purchasing power and thus reducing costs. The task might be assigned to several levels of recursion in the sense of subtasks, so that lower levels of recursion might, for example, purchase whatever is not meant to be bundled. Likewise, middle levels of recursion might perform key purchasing functions because they are close to the best suppliers, leaving the top level to solely define purchasing strategy and policy. Other mission-critical tasks (e.g., key account management) can often be assigned directly and as a whole to a single level of recursion.

In diagnostic Step IV, we now first consider which levels of recursion we want to consider in addition to our own SIF (R0). These are at least the two levels of recursion above (R+1) and below (R−1) our SIF. We arrange these as columns in an assessment table (Fig. 12.1). We enter the mission-critical tasks from diagnostic Step III in the rows. Next, we *go through each task* individually and answer the three questions listed in Table 12.1. Depending on the question, we allocate the *entire task* to a single level of recursion. Or we divide the tasks into *subtasks*, which we allocate to two or more levels of recursion.

This creates both a new and more concrete picture of our control organization. If at the end we consider the levels of recursion individually with their assigned tasks, we will see how every level contributes to the control system of the enterprise. The control system of the whole must keep under control the six key success factors (which we came across in Chap. 8 when considering the assessment criteria for segmenting the basic structure). Thus: Which level is primarily responsible for market position? Which for innovativeness? Which for productivity? Which for attracting good people? Which for liquidity/cash flow? Which for profitability?

Looking at our own SIF in the table, as well as at the mission-critical tasks and subtasks gathered there, shows us what primary contribution (in terms of control) our own level of recursion makes to the whole. Looking at the entire table, we can assess whether *all six key success factors are covered overall, and which level of recursion makes which contribution.* For example, the primary contribution of the group level in an enterprise might be to manage liquidity and innovativeness, while the divisional level focuses on productivity and profitability and that, within these, individual market units ultimately ensure customer value and the attractiveness of the enterprise for good people. On the one hand, this concluding overall view is useful because it allows us to detect any "loose ends": Are there key success factors to whose control no level of recursion makes a relevant contribution? Who should take care of these key success factors in this case? Or, vice versa, are there levels of recursion that make no relevant contribution to at least one of the six key success factors, and could we, therefore, perhaps eliminate these levels (which would bring us back to the questions raised in Chap. 10)? On the other hand, we also need to know what each level of recursion should focus on and what it should primarily be measured against when it comes to *agreeing on goals, assessing performance, and incentivizing those responsible. When we design the enterprise's control system, we also change its management system.*

Tasks

(a) Create a table and in the rows enter all mission-critical tasks from Chap. 11 (Fig. 12.1).
(b) Enter into the columns all relevant levels of recursion of your diagnosis. Consider at least your System in Focus (R0), as well as a level of recursion above (R+1) and below (R−1).
(c) For every mission-critical task, check the three questions in Table 12.1. Based on your answers, allocate the whole task or only parts of it to the levels of recursion.
(d) In your final deliberations, what do you notice when you look at the respective contribution of the levels of recursion to the control system of the whole? Are your findings consistent with your current management and incentive system? Don't be surprised if they aren't.

Tip: Always label the levels of recursion in your diagnosis in the same way (R0), (R−1), (R−2), … also in the table. It is useful to not simply take notes on the mission-critical tasks but also to elaborate on them a bit so that you know exactly what you are talking about.

Diagnosing and Designing the Control Functions (Step V) 13

Diagnostic Step V brings us to the *vertical control axis*. It is the control axis of the *senior management in our System in Focus (SIF)*. Systems 2–5 are located and operate on this axis (Fig. 13.1). In the organization we are designing, the operational units have already absorbed most of the complexity of the business themselves. Senior management only needs to attend to the remaining complexity, that is, the hitherto unresolved issues and open questions. To absorb this cloud of remaining complexity, senior management uses its vertical control channels. With its control systems 2–5, it coordinates, optimizes, and audits the whole, determines the rough direction, and defines the policies. With Systems 2, 3, and 3*, it controls the enterprise's *"Inside & Now,"* and with Systems 4 and 5 the *"Outside & Then."* System 3, sandwiched between System 1 and System 4, balances present and future in a special process overseen by System 5. Since we will be using the nomenclature of the Viable System Model (VSM) more frequently from now on, it is worth looking back at Chap. 4 to recall the five control functions of the model.

We know from our considerations in diagnostic Step II (Chap. 10) how large this remaining complexity cloud is and therefore how strong the vertical channels need to be. From our considerations in diagnostic Steps III and IV (Chaps. 11 and 12), we also know which tasks must be controlled in our SIF. Finally, from the VSM, we know which control functions we need to design around our System 1 and how this integrated control communicates. *We now have all the ingredients for designing the neurology of business, the third dimension of organizing.*

Below we take the perspective of senior management as a whole, with all its supporting functions, departments and divisions, rather than the perspective of a single department such as HR, because we want to develop a control system for the whole. However, as explained in Sect. 8.2, the head of HR can also make any further diagnosis only for his or her own department. In this case, he or she is not interested in senior management as a whole but only in Systems 2–5 of HR. He or she examines the interaction of staff policy, staff strategy, and all other tasks for optimizing, coordinating, or auditing staff issues. He or she is responsible for all of this and therefore needs a control system. Since the head of HR is responsible for a

M. Pfiffner, *The Neurology of Business*, Management for Professionals,
https://doi.org/10.1007/978-3-031-14260-4_13

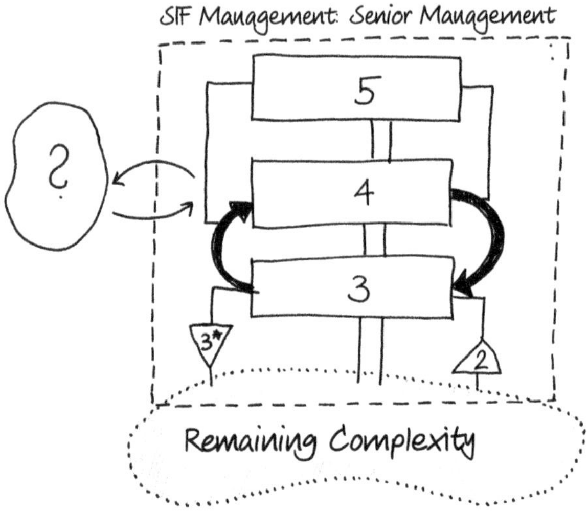

Fig. 13.1 Senior management tackles the remaining complexity

supporting function, he or she must also consider how HR policy fits into corporate policy, how HR strategy contributes to business strategy, and how HR's operational plans and coordinating functions fit with those of the other specialist areas. Following his or her diagnosis, the head of HR must integrate their own subject-specific control functions into the senior management's control system.

Whether a supporting function creates value directly or indirectly is irrelevant for our purposes. Only the distinction between operational and supporting functions is relevant for control. Production, for example, can be organized as an operational or as a supporting function. In diagnostic Step I, we needed to decide on a primary control dimension of the enterprise. So, for example, we chose regions as the segmentation criterion for our System 1, although perhaps products would also have been conceivable. Our operational units are therefore now regions in this example. Unless we have distributed and decentralized the production of products to the operational units themselves in Step IV, it will be the responsibility of and controlled by a department in senior management as a supporting function. In this case, as in the case of human resources, production also has its own purpose-related control system, that is, its own Viable System Model, as it were, in the control system of the whole. Like HR, production also serves the regions, is interwoven into the control system of the entire enterprise, and must therefore fit into senior management like all other departments.

Normally, these alignment (i.e., coordination) processes are only carried out in System 3, which ensures that departments work together and coordinate their plans, goals, and budgets for the purpose of interaction. We might also be familiar with coordination processes in System 4, for example, when the joint strategy is developed in the form of projects with the participation of all departments. Depending on the enterprise, in addition to System 3, overall responsibility is also more or less clearly organized for System 4, which ensures that all areas are integrated into

System 4 issues. System 2 and System 3*, on the other hand, usually seem to have no one in charge. In practice, they are, therefore, also those systems that are most poorly integrated and function the worst.

Thus, it is worth making someone responsible for each of the five control functions to be diagnosed and designed below. A System 2-"Directorate," for example, would ensure that the operational units are not inundated with requests and bureaucratic tasks from all departments at once, but that communication occurs in digestible chunks and actually works. It would regularly clean out System 2, streamline it, and review its usefulness. As a rule, System 3 has a clearly identified person in charge, for example, the COO (Chief Operating Officer) or the business manager. The names for these positions can be confusing, as designations vary depending on the type of enterprise, its legal form, Anglo-Saxon or German law and, above all, the level of recursion. A CEO may be understood as responsible for System 4 but also jointly responsible for System 3. A supervisory board, advisory board, or board of directors certainly performs System 5 tasks but partly also System 4 tasks. It, therefore, makes sense not to rely on the names of bodies and committees, because their actual function can be very different. Rather, we should begin with the control function and speak, for example, of a person responsible for System 3, because that includes all nomenclatures. We know what we are talking about when we talk about System 3. We know what function is meant, what kind of decisions are made, and what responsibility is involved. What the position is called is beside the point.

13.1 S2: Coordination and Support

Let us first design System 2 in our System in Focus. It is located at the *interface between the horizontal and the vertical control axis* and thus can be allocated to System 1 as well as to senior management. System 2 includes all the coordinating, oscillation damping, and supporting functions that ensure that the operational units in System 1 work smoothly and can concentrate on their business. It, therefore, encompasses much more than just the "office" or "shared service" function it is sometimes referred to as. In Sect. 4.3, we talked about the fact that practiced, rehearsed behaviors, that is, cultural elements, are also part of System 2 and therefore also need to be included in the diagnosis, as well as designed and promoted as far as possible. Other things with a coordinating or oscillation-damping effect, such as the common understanding of leadership or the corporate ethos, rites, symbols, and traditions, also influence the enterprise and exert great control without us normally recognizing them as part of the control system. For example, in the early 2000s, the Daimler Group did not produce the Maybach to do business with the ultimate luxury limousine, but primarily to prove to management and employees that the enterprise could build such vehicles. Production thus aimed to promote pride, conviction, and confidence in one's own abilities in System 2.

System 2 is the strongest gateway of complexity available to senior management. A well-designed System 2 performs *70% of its tasks through self-coordination* and another *20% through active coordination* in the form of meetings, committees, projects, or individual agreements. Ultimately, only the remaining *10%* should require defining a new rule of the game or an *individual decision* in System 3. In contrast to their importance for absorbing complexity, the Systems 2 are massively underdeveloped in most enterprises. Their design is left to chance. Their real importance is either not recognized at all (because they do not appear in the first or second dimension of organizing) or they are underestimated, with their potential remaining unused as a result. Poorly designed Systems 2 are a curse of our time. They slow down instead of speed up, cause conflicts instead of avoiding them, absorb management with unimportant things, cause unnecessary costs, and gnaw away at people's motivation.

If coordination and alignment at the interfaces do not function smoothly, the system starts oscillating. For example, a joint customer of operational units A and B demands a discount from operation A, which it grudgingly grants. However, this causes a conflict with operation B, which intervenes with its management, which in turn must contact management A. These exchanges are prone to delays, misunderstandings, and other irritations that trigger new fluctuations. As a result, each element continually tries to adapt to every other element and nothing comes to rest. The system begins to oscillate, with factual problems soon exacerbated by unpleasant, human attitudes, which create even greater tensions. Attenuating these fluctuations or, even better, preventing them in the first place, is the core task of System 2. The better it attenuates these fluctuations, the more it *relieves senior management* of issues and problems it should not be concerned with anyway nor really has time for. A well-functioning System 2 works like our bodily reflexes. For example, when we put our hand on a hot cooker, we pull it back before realizing what has happened. If we trip up on a flight of stairs, we reflexively catch ourselves before higher level management receives the corresponding message. If we waited (or had to wait) for a conscious reaction from our mind, we would burn our hands and break our legs.

Ideally, we will have designed the operational units so that no environmental overlaps and operational dependencies whatsoever occur. In practice, this happens, for example, in enterprises where life and death are at stake. At Swiss Air-Rescue (REGA), the operational units on the lowest level of recursion are the individual rescue missions. As projects, they form a viable unit until they have fulfilled their purpose (e.g., rescuing mountaineers and airlifting them to hospital). Afterwards, this operational unit disappears back into System 1 and a new one is created. As a rule, one rescue operation has little or no environmental overlap with others. Operationally, it is also completely independent of all other operations. It is equipped with all the resources and competencies that are crucial for success. If environmental overlaps occur because several helicopters fly to the same accident, on the other hand, a comprehensive and well-regulated System 2 immediately arises between the pilots, the operations control center, and those responsible on the ground.

Matters are similar with military operations. They, too, are designed so that operational units perform their tasks largely independently. Where overlaps and dependencies nevertheless cannot be avoided, they too have a strongly developed System 2. A fine example occurs in the movie "The Guns of Navarone" (1961): During World War Two, an allied secret operations unit is assigned to blow up two gigantic guns of the German Wehrmacht on an island in the Aegean Sea. The five protagonists of the international commando team have different tasks, because they are all experts in a mission-critical discipline: one in climbing, another in blasting, the third in navigating, and so on. Together, they have all the skills crucial for success and are independent of other operations. Within the team, however, they are interdependent. In System 3, they jointly forge their tactical plan, which becomes a binding, coordinating System 2 function once decided. Since the means of communication are limited and the enemy is listening in, the plan cannot be changed once the action is underway. At this stage, the experts have lost their autonomy to the plan. Only minimal freedom is left on the horizontal axis of control, and the vertical axis of control has a very strong effect. Since the plan does not work out, forcing the team to improvise, ultimately their common will and experience, as well as the military ethos in their System 2, hold everything together and eventually lead to success.

System 2 supports the operational units and enables their self-coordination through platforms such as committees or forums, through computer systems fitted with databases and archives, and through overviews, hotlines, and all sorts of information. It enables units to access resources they do not have themselves, for example, through shared service centers. It maintains common infrastructures. It provides training and development opportunities and allows staff to share and learn from each other. It contains all applicable regulations and plans, whether written down or not. If the environmental overlap is common customers, it provides the relevant set of rules or establishes key account management for a managed process. If the overlap is common technical problems, it may establish a center of excellence or a group of experts to learn from each other and jointly solve problems.

For the most part, System 2 is designed by the management of the operational units themselves. These people know best where the shoe pinches. But as long as they find a common solution, there is no need for senior management; senior management becomes active solely in a subsidiary capacity, for example, if policies need to be implemented, if joint learning needs to be organized, if a new rule needs to be established due to a new conflict, or if a System 2 channel needs to be strengthened. System 2 is thus shaped on the one hand by System 1 and, on the other, by System 3.

Two communication channels emanate from System 2. On the one hand, they connect it downwards with the operational units (more precisely, with their System 2); and on the other upwards with System 3 (Fig. 13.2). *In such a line, communication always flows in both directions.* From the bottom up, the operational units communicate their coordination and support needs and provide information about themselves to System 2. Top-down, System 2 communicates the binding plans and rules and its support services. Communication also flows in both directions between System 3 and System 2: Operational management defines its information needs for higher level controlling and defines its System 2 elements, which are needed to optimize the whole and exploit synergies. System 2, conversely, reports on the status

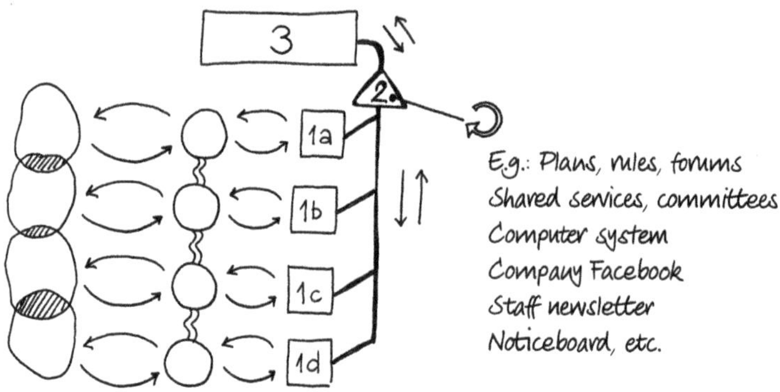

Fig. 13.2 System 2: coordination and support

of System 1 and the ongoing activities by providing a digestible and comprehensible overview.

As mentioned, every department has its own System 2 for this purpose. Marketing provides its sales support resources via System 2. IT provides IT support in its System 2 and communicates the applicable IT policies. HR bundles employee administration in a shared service center. And perhaps there is a central production or sales department that communicates its plans via System 2. Each department wants to be informed by the operational units in the form of surveys. It invites others to meetings and communicates its contents. A good control system bundles these activities and prepares them in a homogeneous package with which the operational units and senior management can cope despite the inhomogeneous content. The widespread feeling of being hopelessly inundated with different information or reporting requests from ten different departments at the same time and being kept from working usually stems more from the rampant diversity of communication channels and formats than from the inevitable diversity of their content. System 2 must be constantly updated, systematically decluttered, and cleaned out so that it does not mutate into a suffocating bureaucracy. Otherwise, time is wasted on useless formalisms, operational units are inundated with emails, reports, phone calls, and meetings they cannot digest, and management still remains poorly informed. *A well-designed System 2, therefore, provides most enterprises with enormous performance reserves.* However, very few enterprises can judge whether their System 2 is too weak or, on the contrary, bureaucratically inflated. They do not recognize where it needs to be developed and strengthened, nor where it can be dismantled and thus relieve the operational units and save costs.

What to do? First, we gather all the tasks known from diagnostic Step IV that require a System 2 function. On the one hand, these tasks stem from the variety engineering of the operational units (amplifier/attenuator) and, on the other, from the needs to coordinate environmental overlaps and dependencies (cf. Fig. 11.3). If necessary, we supplement these tasks with further System 2 tasks (i.e., ones not evident or forgotten in the previous diagnosis). In the end, we want to have compiled the seven plus/minus two most important System 2 tasks to which special attention should be paid. Since each department makes its own System 2 diagnosis, going into depth in the process, this level of detail is sufficient for the enterprise as a whole.

Next, we consider which channels are used to communicate with System 1 and System 3 and how well they are functioning. For now, we only roughly assess these channels to establish what our diagnosis needs to pay attention to. We will consider these channels in more depth in Chap. 14 ("Diagnosing and Designing the Communication Channels"). For the moment, it is enough for us to recognize, in terms of a tendency, whether our System 2 is strong enough and well-managed, and where communication needs to be improved. Where we have identified a concrete need for action, we note down appropriate measures.

Tasks

(a) Draw the control system of your SIF, starting with System 1. Be creative with the Viable System Model but ensure you adhere to its logic. Draw larger operational units larger and smaller ones smaller. Draw planned operational units as dotted lines. Shade environmental overlaps and draw them as large as they actually are. Draw dependencies between operations as wavy lines so that the diagram also conveys an impression of the strength of these dependencies. In the end, we also want to be able to see the control system in terms of "iconic quantification" and to understand matters visually not merely rationally. Our diagram should represent reality as realistically as possible, to ensure our diagnosis involves both hemispheres of the brain.

(b) Look at the mission-critical tasks that you assigned to your SIF in the last diagnostic step and check which are System 2 tasks. If necessary, supplement these with other System 2 tasks that were forgotten in the previous diagnosis.

(c) For each task, write down which communication channels are mainly used for this and which of them need to be looked at more closely.

(d) Establish a sense of your System 2 as a whole: Is it strong enough, well-designed and also well-maintained? Do we need to clean it out? Are departmental requirements being integrated or is everyone working on their own? Does communication work or does it overload the operational units? Does the System 2 deliver action-relevant information? Which tasks are not yet covered or need to be expanded?

(e) Can we identify or establish an overall responsibility for System 2 in the sense of a "Coordination Directorate"? How would you describe its tasks and responsibilities?

Tip: Label your diagram again with: *SIF, R0: Name*. In our further discussion, we must always be able to clearly recognize which level of recursion we are currently on. This is especially important when several colleagues are involved in the discussion, or misunderstandings and errors may otherwise arise quickly.

13.2 S3: Optimizing Today's Business

In a functioning control system, management is not created by exercising authority or by flooding the vertical control axis with variety-attenuating regulations. It distributes competence and responsibility among the operational units and exploits synergies that are recognized in a synoptic view of the whole. As we saw in Chap. 10 ("Manageable or Not?"), management intervenes only there and only as strongly as is necessary to optimize the whole.

System 3 is responsible for *utilizing the existing potential for success.* A high market share, for example, is one such potential. It increases the possibilities of reducing costs but for the time being remains a potential until costs are actually worked on. Section 2.2 has already mentioned the effect of the experience curve, which is undisputed both in theory and in practice. Every market is saturated sooner or later. Then the endgame (final stage) begins, in which supplier performance no longer differs greatly, and in which competition is fought out mainly on the basis of price, thus reducing the number of suppliers. To survive in this phase of falling prices, the enterprise must have its costs under control in good time. Enterprises with higher market shares have more possibilities to reduce their costs because of the experience curve effect.[1] Their long-term lowest achievable basic cost margin is, therefore, lower than that of competitors with smaller market shares. Thus, even if prices are low, margins can still be achieved. The problem is that costs do not lower themselves, nor can they be lowered overnight. In practice, there are a manifold reasons why costs should not be cut at all, or not here, or not now. Exploiting market shares comes at a price, namely, restricted autonomy and reduced variety.

Behind costs may lie an enterprise's strengths. It would be stupid to curtail them. However, costs may also assume the form of accumulated "fat reserves." Finally, there are avoidable costs and unused performance potentials because synergies have not been exploited. Thus, System 3 needs to figure out where costs are actually muscle, where unnecessary fat, and where *potential synergies* are hidden. Our considerations in diagnostic Step IV, "Central or Decentral?" (Chap. 12), have already provided clues about what these might consist of. Our criterion for the central allocation of a synergetic task was that the operational unit is not slowed in its ability to satisfy customers. Synergies can reduce costs, take non-mission-critical tasks away from the operational units (allowing them to focus more on the customer), or bundle competence and expertise centrally to enhance performance on the front line. Existing potential for success can therefore be exploited not only in the form of lower costs thanks to higher market shares, but also in the form of superior customer benefits, greater innovative strength, better productivity, or greater attractiveness for good potential employees thanks to optimized cooperation between all units.

[1] Bruce D. Henderson, *Die Erfahrungskurve in der Unternehmensstrategie* (Frankfurt, New York: Campus, 1974). English edition: *Perspectives on Experience* (1972).

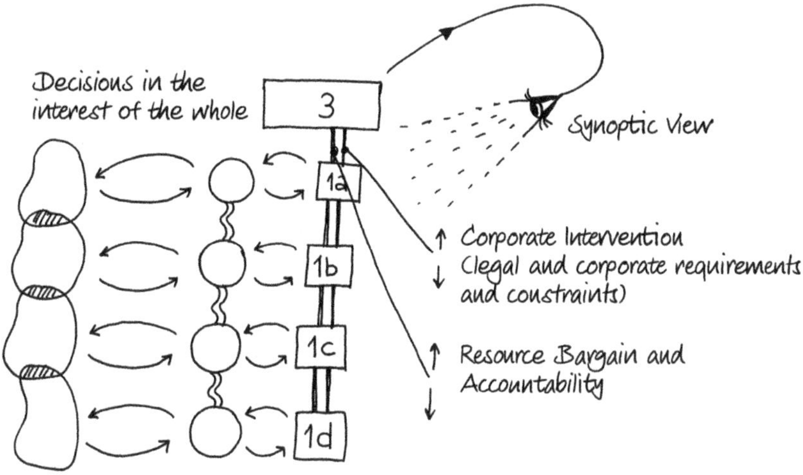

Fig. 13.3 Optimizing today's business

System 3 always makes its decisions for the good of the whole. It exploits synergies, sets priorities where they need to shift between operational units in the short term, and ensures that the operational plans of all units and departments are integrated into a logical whole. It ensures that the change processes identified as necessary in consultation with System 4 are implemented, and that System 1 adheres to the policies adopted by System 5. To enable it to make well-informed decisions, and to implement these effectively, it has a total of *four vertical communication channels* at its disposal. Through System 3*, it can discover hidden synergies and check compliance. Via System 2, it can implement its decisions on coordination issues and gain an overview of System 1 as a whole. Then it is left with the two communication channels that directly connect System 3 with System 1 (Fig. 13.3). The management box of every operational unit is directly connected to System 3, which is of course difficult to represent in a two-dimensional diagram. It communicates with every operational unit both directly and independently of the other units.

These two vertical communication channels have a different character. We call the channel on the left the *"Resource Bargain and Accountability"* channel. It is used to negotiate resources and takes responsibility for them. This communication takes place through agreements between the operational units and System 3. It is mainly the operational planning process that connects and aligns the intentions of the operational units with the intentions of senior management. This includes annual goals and their financial manifestation in budgets. The operational units apply to System 3 for their plans, including any intended investments and required funds. Ideally, they pay for both from their self-generated profits, but may also request support to cover these. Besides compiling these plans, System 3 prioritizes, corrects, or supplements them based on a synoptic view of the whole. In the end, it bindingly establishes these plans also for System 1 and thus anchors responsibility for the allocated resources. Communication runs in both directions in this negotiation process. The operational units report regularly on their goal attainment, on the opportunities that have meanwhile opened, and on the obstacles encountered.

System 3 also includes planning during the year. These are the short-term control cycles that run permanently between specialist departments and operational units in accordance with the defined processes. These include, among others, sales control or production control. If an enterprise is divided into sales regions (System 1), it may have to control central production, which may consist of a few plants in different countries. To do this, the regions first plan their own annual sales targets, which overall pre-steer production targets. These are reconciled in System 3 with the targets of the production manager: Do we have undercapacity or overcapacity? How should production and productivity develop? Do we want to relocate plant sites? Where do we invest and disinvest? And do the targets for the regions therefore need to be adjusted downward or upward? While the production plan is decided in System 3, a *continuous communication loop exists between Systems 1, 2, and 3.* System 2 makes these resources accessible to the operational units. These adjust their targets based on actual events and results. In turn, System 3 collates these adjustments and decides on the current priorities. These in turn flow into System 2 of production, and so on.

Besides negotiating resources and responsibility, a functioning control system also enables imposing binding requirements. The *"Corporate Intervention"* channel restricts the autonomy of the operational units through strict parameters, so-called *"legal and corporate requirements and constraints."* In the second channel, this is used to control purpose fulfillment. As always, communication flows in both directions. System 3 communicates the binding parameters to System 1, which in turn reports back on their compliance. However, the same channel can also be used as a command channel. It is the channel through which, if necessary, a fist can be banged on the table, and the whole can be committed to a binding decision. This proves necessary in some situations, for example, when a rapid turnaround must be initiated in an emergency, or when the managements of the operational units cannot find a solution themselves in case of conflict. Any functioning system may explicitly exercise authority as a last resort (i.e., failing other options). However, it avoids this scenario as far as possible for the sake of the organization's relative autonomy and viability (already mentioned several times). Autonomy is restricted only when and to the extent that it is unavoidable for safeguarding the good of the whole (cf. the First Axiom of Management in Chap. 10). In this regard, we recall the previous examples (REGA and the secret operations unit in Navarone). The freedom of action of the operational units, and thus their variety, must be kept as large as possible.

What do we need to do? We first return to the tasks identified in diagnostic Step IV, which we allocated to our System in Focus and that have a System 3 character. These are the tasks through which we make decisions for the good of the whole and whose purpose is to optimize the current business. We supplement them with other System 3 tasks, ones not yet discussed but mission-critical. In particular, we now return to our *segmentation table from Step I* (Chap. 8). The segmentation variant that we chose in the example in Fig. 8.5 has clear advantages but also some weaknesses. In this example, regions can play to their strengths in terms of response speed and logistics performance. They also make optimal use of personal networks, are attractive for good employees, and have advantageous financial sizes. *This table, however, also shows what the operational units are unable to do.* In our example, they are poor at ensuring engineering and field service quality and innovation performance. If the operational units are not good at managing those factors that are crucial for success themselves, then System 3 must perform these tasks in accordance with the subsidiarity principle. Because *System 3 must focus on these tasks*, we add them to its list of tasks. According to the Pareto principle, in the end, we need to have identified the most important seven plus/minus two System 3 tasks. As every department performs the same diagnosis for itself, thus differentiating its specific tasks, we need not go into detail again.

Next, we examine the two vertical communication channels and consider how well they are functioning today compared to the force that they should unfold according to our diagnosis in Step II (Chap. 10, "Manageable or Not?"). We ask which channels exactly are used to communicate System 3 tasks and which ones require special attention in the next diagnostic step. Sooner or later, the question of who performs these tasks always arises. For the reasons mentioned in Sect. 2.6, however, we ask this question only at the end, in diagnostic Step VII. However, it is inevitable and quite deliberate that diagnosing System 3 automatically also provides an overview of its actors in the form of persons, bodies, and committees. Almost every System 3 that I have come across included some form of "Operations Directorate" that could make binding decisions for the whole. How does this work in our SIF? And who else is involved in our System 3?

Tasks

(a) Collect the tasks from diagnostic Step IV ("Central or Decentral") that have been assigned to your SIF and select those that affect System 3 because it is through them that decisions are made to optimize the whole.
(b) Supplement these tasks with other tasks, above all those that emerged as weaknesses in the primary control dimension during segmentation assessment in diagnostic Step I.
(c) For every task, check which of the two communication channels to System 1 it affects, how communication occurs, and whether the two channels are powerful enough. Only make a rough assessment for this purpose.
(d) For every task, check what information or support needs it entails vis-à-vis System 2. If necessary, supplement your notes on System 2.
(e) Develop your SIF diagram further by entering your System 3 and the corresponding communication channels according to their actual size and strength.
(f) Have we established clear overall responsibility for System 3 in terms of an "Operations Directorate"?

Tip: Continue to take notes on the need for action that you identify for your SIF.

13.3 S3*: Real-Life Information and Auditing

The fourth channel available to senior management for managing operations is System 3*. Its task is to enrich System 3 with unfiltered information directly from operations so that better decisions can be made and compliance ensured. To do this, it connects System 3 directly to every operation in System 1 (Fig. 13.4). Through this channel, senior management knows what is really going on outside.

In search of synergy potentials, senior management can initiate studies to find out, for example, how many variants of electric motors are used in the group's products, in order to reduce them and cut costs, or to determine the benchmark in some area within the enterprise from which others should learn. If it discovers a need for action, senior management sets up a corresponding System 3 project, which is communicated through the corporate intervention channel and implemented in cooperation with operations managers. It may also want to discover potential operations managers, who need to be nurtured outside their own operational unit. It conducts ongoing compliance health checks and audits, systematically detecting open issues, ones needing to be discussed with operations managers. It orders investigations where it finds indications of things not working at all or not properly. Finally, it keeps spending time in operations, to discover, even by accident, what might be improved. With the help of System 3*, senior management retains so-called "groundedness"—a feeling for the reality of the business, which is more easily lost by managers the larger the enterprise.

Here, too, communication flows in the form of circuits: from operations in System 1 to System 3*, from there to System 3, then to operations managers, and from there back to operations. Once again, information flows in both directions in each channel. System 3 formulates its information needs for the attention of System 3*, based on its performance of its mission-critical tasks. System 3* then conveys reports,

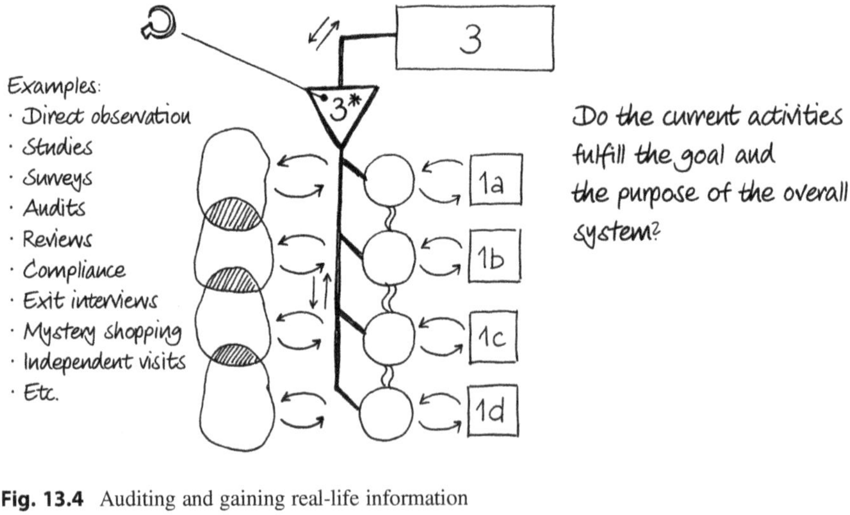

Fig. 13.4 Auditing and gaining real-life information

evaluations, and findings back to System 3 and as a rule also straight back to operations. Information needs arise from every task in System 3. For every information need, we need to consider which channels are best suited to purpose. Channels vary considerably depending on the type of enterprise, size, and situation. For example:

- One reason why the Catholic Church tolerates religious orders (e.g., Jesuits, Dominicans, or Franciscans) is probably because they form an excellent System 3* for it. Geographically located in the Church's dioceses, they can directly inform its highest level of recursion (i.e., past the bishops).
- In very large enterprises, Systems 3* are mostly institutionalized. Thus, in a state, an independent judiciary performs a 3* function by judging operations past their managements in terms of applicable legislation.
- Large companies proceed similarly, through compliance and auditing departments, but their systematic audits are usually limited to financial variables and to spot checks conducted for compliance and quality assurance purposes. System 3* works neither according to the principle "Trust is the beginning of everything" nor according to the principle "Trust is good, control is better." Rather, it discerns where trust is possible and where control is required. It establishes self-regulation via random check because often knowing these are possible suffices to remain within the desired limits (e.g., traffic speed checks). Through systematic checks, it ensures that nothing critical can go wrong.
- In times of upheaval in an enterprise, operations staff can report on the actual implementation status of change projects as so-called "change agents." This is probably the more important part of their work than converting colleagues. After all, it is particularly important in change projects to recognize deviations from the goal at the point of truth in order to make corrections.
- When Daimler's "Smart" innovation project ran into trouble at the turn of the millennium, Andreas Renschler, the project head, held so-called "Frankly Speaking" evenings at the Smartville plants. He would listen to employees in person and on-site. Instead of explaining or justifying the project, he wanted to gain as much information as possible about how the rank and file saw matters.
- We have already discussed mystery shopping, customer visits, as well as announced or unannounced visits by senior management to the operations of operational units as System 3* channels (Sect. 4.4).
- Employee exit interviews are also an effective System 3* channel. Through these conversations, senior management receives information directly, unfiltered, and unadorned from operations because these employees have nothing to lose. I have met top managers who systematically use this channel (as well as the information provided by customer complaints).
- Currently, enterprises are also increasingly using social media not only for their Systems 4 and 2 but also as a strong System 3* channel. To this end, they are creating in-house Facebook pages where employees from all over the world post their unfiltered photos, videos, and reports about special events.

Tasks

(a) For every mission-critical task in System 3, consider the resulting information needs for System 3*.
(b) Note the channels through which System 3 meets those information needs and make a rough assessment of these channels.
(c) Does this enable System 3* to identify the relevant, potential deviations? Is it able to detect potential synergies? What is the overall strength of System 3*?
(d) Knowing what we do about the six channels on the vertical control axis, can we actively absorb horizontal complexity? If not, what needs to be done?
(e) Further develop your SIF diagram by entering your System 3* and the corresponding communication channels according to their actual size and strength.
(f) Can you identify or establish overall responsibility for System 3* in terms of an "Auditing Directorate"?

13.4 S4: External Communication, Adaptation, and Renewal

The environments we have dealt with so far have been the environments of the operational units in our System in Focus. These environments have their own System 4, with which they orient themselves and adapt to their specific environment. In accordance with the principle of recursion, the SIF also has its own environment. This encompasses these environments but is larger than them. Higher levels of recursion always encompass more than the sum of the levels of recursion they contain. System 4 deals with this total environment. It connects the enterprise to that environment in order to communicate with it, to learn to understand it, and to adapt, evolutionarily, to it.

Strictly speaking, the overall environment consists of two different environments: a known environment, which we have accepted as such and are familiar with; and an *unknown environment*, which holds opportunities and threats for the enterprise (Fig. 13.5). This second, problematic environment is contained in and part of the first. Each of these two environments has its own control and communication circuit in connection with the enterprise's System 4.

Let us recall Jack Welch's words: "If the rate of change outside exceeds the rate of change inside, the end is in sight." We can now also understand this insight against the background of Ashby's law of requisite variety: the greater the variety of the environment, the greater the variety of our System 4 must be. In other words, the more turbulent, dynamic, and complex the environment, the more powerful System 4 must be to keep pace with and manage everything. Systems 4 have assumed a new meaning in today's *multi-option and mini-obligation society*,[2] and in the global and multilateral *VUCA world* (acronym for Volatility, Uncertainty, Complexity, Ambiguity). We need to carefully design these systems today. As in diagnostic Step III

[2] Peter Gross, *Die Multioptionsgesellschaft* (Frankfurt am Main: Suhrkamp, 1994).

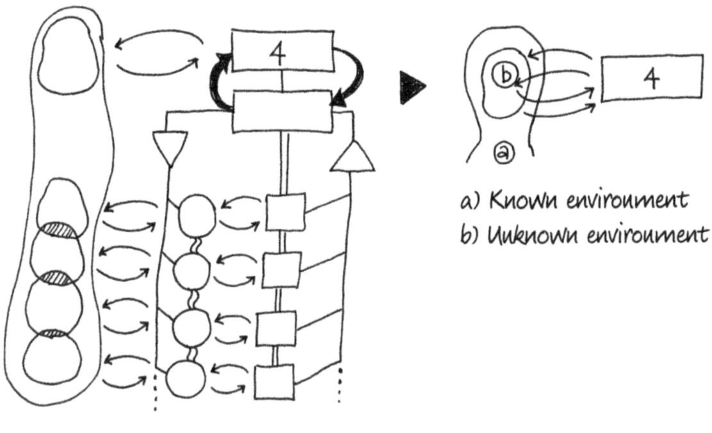

Fig. 13.5 External communication, adaptation, and renewal

(Chap. 11), where we established the desired balance of complexity in the operational unit by means of variety amplifiers and attenuators, and thereby identified the mission-critical tasks of the existing business, we must now also find those tasks for the future business, in order to balance the present and the future. Both worlds have their needs and require entreprise resources.

As in Step III, we consider (1) what the relevant overall environment consists of, (2) work out the most important complexity drivers, and (3) again try to quantify as much as possible. Next, we gather the elements of our current System 4: What does it consist of? How large and how strong is it today? Once more, the environmental variety is inevitably greater than the variety of System 4. We, therefore, again need to find the right balance with our complexity tools.

We do this first for the *known environment*. It comprises the country in which the enterprise is operating, as well as investors, the media, suppliers and competitors, potential customers and employees, and much more. Which of these factors are relevant depends on the enterprise and the level of recursion. System 4 establishes communication with this known, familiar environment. The desired balance of complexity lies in us learning everything from these stakeholders that matters to us and, vice versa, in them knowing everything about us that we think matters to them. For this environment, we need to find the appropriate amplifiers and attenuators, and thus those tasks that are critical to the success of our System 4. These can include corporate communication tasks (e.g., PR, sponsoring, social media, websites) but also participating in associations, lobbying, stakeholder and shareholder management, cooperation management, cooperating with trade unions, market and competition monitoring, recruitment, as well as cultivating personal networks (and perhaps even the local golf club).

We now repeat this for the *unknown environment*. This is more difficult because this environment exists only in the subjunctive. When we study it, our conclusions are also merely hypothetical: "The company would…, could…, should…, and might…" Besides communicating with the known environment, such clarification is the second purpose of System 4. It serves to explore what *opportunities and threats* exist in this unknown environment and how the enterprise should respond. They may be hidden in new technologies, new business models, changes in the legal system or in politics, economic developments, potential new businesses or possible acquisitions. To learn as much as possible about these opportunities and threats with the limited resources of a System 4, we also need to find appropriate amplifiers and attenuators here.

Since the surplus variety of the unknown environment is huge, it is particularly important to properly attenuate complexity. This happens via our models of this environment (i.e., how we conceptualize it). Thus, the challenge is to *work out shared and good-quality models of this environment* (cf. Conant-Ashby theorem, Chap. 9). Such models contain the essential variables and their circular interaction so that we can identify the vicious circles and leverage effects on which we should focus our actions (for details, see Chap. 18, "Balancing Present and Future"). Creating a good model of the unknown environment is therefore an important variety attenuator and thus one of the mission-critical tasks in System 4. It determines which signals we pay attention to and which not. The majority of enterprises that run into financial difficulties recognize the seriousness of their situation far too late because they focus solely on the financial indicators of System 3.[3] While these tell us that we have a problem, they do not tell us where it comes from nor what to do. Most importantly, they do not enable us to look into the future.

Once we have gathered all the mission-critical tasks from examining the known environment and the unknown environment, and once we have added the System 4 tasks that we identified for our SIF in Step IV (Chap. 12), we ought to have gained a good overview and, on this basis, be able to determine the seven plus/minus two most important tasks.

A System 4 task can never be found via a *time horizon* because its time horizons can be very short or span decades, depending on the level of recursion. In our example of REGA helicopter rescue operations, the time horizon for System 4 in a single rescue mission is 15 min. The mission-critical tasks include clarifying weather conditions and the situation and injuries on-site. However, if we move up one level of recursion at REGA, we are talking about System 4 of the "Helicopter Operations" division, and thus clarification involves asking how accident statistics, competition, hospitals, and (helicopter) technology will develop in the coming years. As observed, *not the time horizon makes one issue strategic and another operational, but whether we are considering the enterprise's current or future potential success.* For example, planning sales development with today's products may be long-term, but that does not make it strategic. System 3 is responsible for planning, not System 4. The time horizon of System 4, on the other hand, is determined by how long it will take to correct a strategic mistake: If we back the wrong technology, how long will correcting matters take? If our next product flops, how long will launching the model after next take?

---

[3]Cf. Observa/Eco'Diagnostic, Studie 2001c.

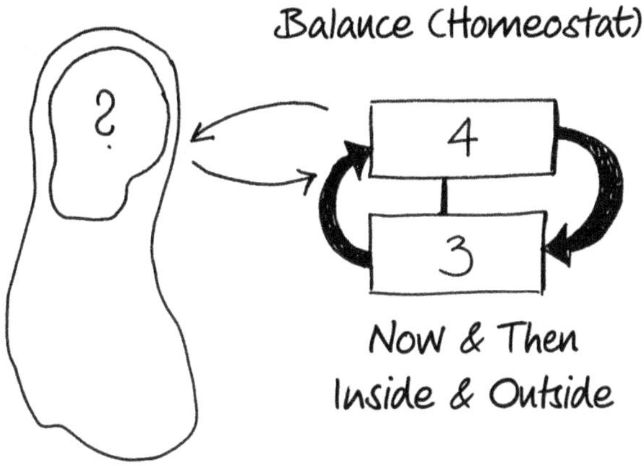

Fig. 13.6 Evolutionary adaptation by balancing Systems 4 and 3

Even in a medium-sized enterprise, many actors contribute to System 4. Once more, every department has its own System 4 tasks. Marketing, for example, collects market information, surveys customers, and observes competitors. R&D conducts technology studies and tinkers with new products or services, while HR is looking for new managers. Every functional area also does its own strategic planning as a contribution to the overall strategic plan. These functional strategies are brought together in System 4 through projects, workshops, or meetings, because if the overall plan calls for growth, the head of HR needs to ensure the enterprise recruits additional managers, the head of finance needs to ensure enough liquidity, the head of IT needs to expand the infrastructure, and the head of production needs to build a new plant or production line. If, moreover, the head of production wants to digitize production facility control, the head of IT also needs to know about and incorporate this plan into his or her strategy. In turn, someone should be responsible for integrating all strategic plans into a logical whole. Thus, in addition to the Operations Directorate, the Coordination Directorate, and the Auditing *Directorate, our senior management also needs a* "Development Directorate" in order to integrate these plans and ensure their effectiveness. Such a Development Directorate is concerned not only with developing new products and services but also with developing the enterprise as a whole. It pursues this goal by taking into account all cross-connections with topics and areas of expertise. *Among others, it is also responsible for designing the third dimension of organizing, the neurology of business.*

In Fig. 13.6, besides the communication channels that connect the enterprise with its known and unknown environment, we recognize a vertical channel that connects System 4 with System 3. *Through this channel, strategic planning becomes the framework for operational planning.* In practice, we often find an open issue in the control system: Because although we have strategic plans on the one hand and operational plans on the other, they have almost nothing to do with each other. This should not be the case *because operational planning must contain the intermediate steps on the way to achieving the strategic goals.* After all, System 3 is meant to implement strategy. It, therefore, regularly reports the corresponding progress to System 4 via this channel. As with every communication channel, information therefore flows in both directions.

System 4 should clarify matters and exercise strategic control. It should build the enterprise's *future success potential*: Because if we want not only to do business but also to remain in business long-term, we must constantly renew ourselves. New demographics, new needs, new technologies, or new business models give rise to new businesses, which displace the old ones. At some point, therefore, it is no longer of any use to be operationally good if the existing business is displaced by new and better solutions. The last suppliers of road maps and typewriters had a comfortable market share—until navigation devices and computers entered the market. The largest video store in town was probably doing great before people started streaming their movies. Such *substitution threats* need to be identified in time.

Still, recognizing new solutions and their substitution trajectories alone is not enough. We need a *mechanism in the enterprise that ensures some sort of evolutionary adaptation*, and we need to organizationally anchor this adaptive capacity in our control system. This adaptation mechanism is drawn in our diagram (Fig. 13.6) as a circuit with two thick arrows to the left and the right of Systems 3 and 4. It connects the enterprise's "Outside & Then" with its "Inside & Now." So what does the mechanism actually consist of in our SIF? What exactly are we doing to make the right decisions between today's business and tomorrow's business?

In diagnostic Step II, we encountered the First Axiom of Management on the vertical control axis (Chap. 10). This tells us that the vertical complexity of senior management must be equal to the horizontal complexity of the operating business that it is supposed to manage. Now we encounter the Second Axiom of Management, which is also situated on the vertical control axis and grounded in Ashby's law. This states that *Systems 3 and 4 must be equally strong*.

Definition

Second Axiom of Management[4]

The variety disposed by System 3 resulting from the operation of the First Axiom equals the variety disposed by System 4.

Normally, our Systems 4 are less pronounced than our Systems 3. Especially when our existing business is very successful, we tend to become arrogant. Since arrogance is a type of ignorance associated with pride, it acts as a strong and dangerous variety attenuator. One tends to continue doing what has delivered success in the past. Figure 13.7 shows a *double substitution time curve (S-curve)*. The lower curve shows the spread of the present business for which System 3 is responsible. The upper curve shows the expansion of the future business and thus the substitution of the old business. System 4, which is responsible for this, examines the

[4] Stafford Beer, *Diagnosing the System for Organizations: The Managerial Cybernetics of Organization* (Chichester, New York, Brisbane, Toronto, Singapore: Wiley, 1985), p. 118.

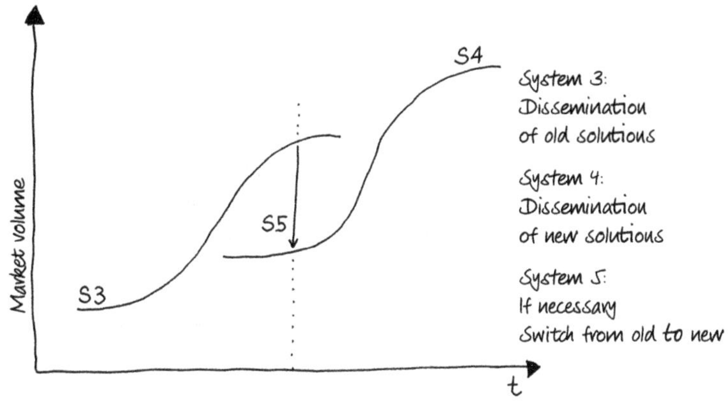

Fig. 13.7 Adaptability: when do we change?

consequences for our own enterprise if trends already recognizable today are thought further into the future. At the height of its success, Kodak was the world market leader in equipment for analog photography and thus excellently positioned on the lower curve. Its System 4 recognized early on that digital technology was going to change everything. Kodak even pioneered this next S-curve by launching the world's first digital camera. Twenty years later, the company, meanwhile over a 100 years old, nevertheless failed. Its System 4 existed and worked well but too weak to really be heard by System 3 and to assert itself. The management (mainly chemists) knew about yet completely underestimated digitalization. Eventually, providers from a completely different business (telecommunications) took over the market. Kodak had not fulfilled the Second Axiom of Management.

Reallocating human and financial resources from the old to the new business (i.e., from the lower to the upper curve) is probably the most difficult and at the same time the most important task of senior management. It can only devote sufficient attention to this task if it is organized in such a way that the operational business does not absorb all its attention. These issues are delicate. If we change course too early, we still have too little information, the uncertainty still remains too great, and we run the risk of a flop. It is only when trends toward implementing a new solution become apparent on the market that variety is reduced and decision certainty increases. Vice versa, if we wait too long, other suppliers will already have gained market share; we need good arguments to take market share back from a competitor.

Designing this built-in and helpful schizophrenia between today and tomorrow is crucial for the enterprise to function long-term. If this mechanism of self-questioning and self-renewal in the control system does not work, viability will not last until purpose fulfillment, but only until the rules of the game in the environment have changed. Thus, for our SIF, we need to carefully consider how this mechanism works for us. Chap. 18 ("Balancing Present and Future") will introduce methods capable of satisfying even the most complex requirements. Only when the System 3–4 mechanism becomes unstable and reallocation decisions cannot be made in time, will System 5, which also supervises the mechanism, intervene in a subsidiary manner.

Tasks

(a) What does the known total environment of your SIF comprise? What are its complexity drivers? What does your current System 4 consist of that communicates with this environment, and how strong is it? Find the most important variety amplifiers and attenuators to make communication with the known environment work.
(b) What is the unknown environment made of and what are its complexity drivers? What in System 4 helps us detect those drivers and to identify the relevant opportunities and threats in time? Find the most important amplifiers and attenuators.
(c) Which other mission-critical tasks do we transfer into System 4 from diagnostic Step IV (Chap. 12)? Compile the most important seven plus/minus two System 4 tasks.
(d) Is the vertical communication channel between System 3 and System 4 functioning? Does strategic planning provide the cornerstones for operational planning? And does strategic controlling exist in addition to operational controlling?
(e) What circular communication channel exists to balance System 3 and System 4? Is the Second Axiom of Management fulfilled? If not, what needs to be done?
(f) Take notes on the action required and expand your diagram to include the overall environment and System 4. Draw System 4 as large as you see it in relation to System 3. Draw strong channels strong and weak channels weak.
(g) Who is responsible for focusing System 4 activities? Can we identify or establish a "Development Directorate"?

13.5 S5: Identity, Norms, and S5-S3/4 Interaction

While System 3 controls operational issues and System 4 strategic ones, System 5 deals with the normative side of the enterprise. It creates identity by clarifying what the whole exists for, and calibrates the control system by setting the basic direction. Besides continuous self-questioning, an enterprise also needs *continuity and stability*. This is provided by System 5. This does not make decisions itself in Systems 3 or 4 but provides a framework for their activities and oversees the steady state (homeostasis) between them. System 5 thus operates in a superordinate way. In our model, it is located above all control elements. This might imply that it is the most important control element. This is correct in a certain sense because it exercises great control: *It controls what controls.* On the other hand, we remember that all Systems 2–5 serve System 1, because only there is purpose fulfilled. We can also imagine the Viable System Model as having three dimensions (see Fig. 4.4), with System 5 at the center surrounded by System 1 and the environment: The control elements and the communication channels remain the same, and the logic of the model is preserved.

In a two-dimensional representation, System 5 has no direct line of communication into the environment. This might puzzle us because System 5 also needs to know what is going on outside. Remember, however, that we are not talking about an organizational chart but about a model of control. System 5 is not supposed to control anything in the environment because that is what Systems 1 and 4 do. It is meant to pre-steer and supervise Systems 3 and 4, for which it needs communication channels into these systems, not into the environment. On the other hand, those making decisions in System 5 live in this environment and are part of it. This is better expressed by the three-dimensional model.

A first mission-critical task is to develop and regularly review the *business mission*. This defines why the enterprise exists (see Sect. 4.6). On the one hand, we thus attentuate variety by defining what we want and do not want. On the other, we do not know what the future holds and must therefore keep our options open (cf. cybernetic imperative in Chap. 9). As observed in the previous section, today's solutions can quickly be displaced by new solution techniques or technologies for the same customer problem. Therefore, when we define the purpose, we do not start from existing solutions but from the *original customer problem*, or we would lose sight of the danger of substitution. We would destroy too much variety if we focused our field of vision on a current solution.

A good business mission contains nothing about today's solutions and technologies, nor about shareholders and expected returns, because we should not limit ourselves to monetary quantities either; neither in measuring results, nor in defining responsibility, nor in defining purpose. No enterprise exists to make money; conversely, money is the measure of how well it fulfills its real purpose and serves as a framework for its viability. Or as Peter Drucker noted: "The essential thing about profit is there is no such thing. There are only costs ... costs of doing business and costs of staying in business ..."[5] Not shareholder value, but customer value, not the value of the enterprise, but its competitiveness must be at the center of System 5. If you have satisfied customers or service recipients, you will also earn sufficient returns and have satisfied shareholders. This does not work the other way around, as economic history has shown over the last 30 years. A good business mission focuses on the customer problem, describes it as an invariant solution, and thus becomes the enterprise's fixed star.[6]

The second mission-critical task is *enterprise policy*. This clarifies the fundamental issues regarding the environment, the enterprise and its management, as well as pre-steers its performance and competitiveness. It provides the parameters for the work performed in System 3 and System 4. Like a state *constitution*, it applies to all levels of recursion. The cybernetic approach to defining parameters is not to define as many provisions as possible for as many cases as possible, but to *define policies (basic statements) with a large scope of application and thus high complexity*. This

[5]Peter F. Drucker, *Management: Tasks, Responsibilities, Practices* (Oxford: Butterworth-Heinemann, 1974).

[6]Aloys Gälweiler, *Strategische Unternehmensführung* (Frankfurt, New York: Campus, 1987).

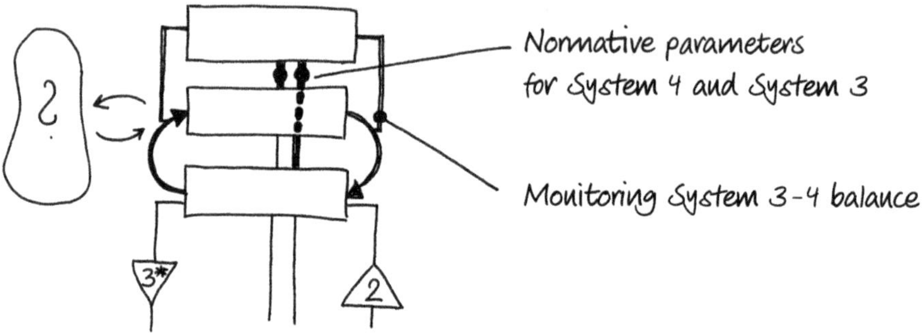

Fig. 13.8 System 5: creating identity and defining basic principles

maintains the variety of the problem at a high level, at least initially, after which vagueness is removed slice by slice with the help of a few principles until clarity emerges. A policy is thus a basic statement that applies to many situations (variety-amplifying) and equally to all levels of recursion (variety-attenuating). In road traffic, the right of way is such a policy. It exerts enormous regulative power through a simple statement. In his management concept, one my clients anchored the basic principle that the Viable System Model be used at all levels of recursion to design the control and communication structures. His policy resulted in strong self-organization and self-control.

Defining policies is one matter. To be effective, however, they must also be communicated. To this end, Fig. 13.8 shows a vertical channel connecting System 5 to System 4, and a vertical channel connecting System 5 directly to System 3. Normative control is thus *linked to strategic and operational control*, through which it implements its mission and corporate policy. Too often, these channels do not work as they should in practice. We might have a business mission, or a corporate policy in the form of documents and brochures, but no one knows this. When I was still an inexperienced consultant, I once made the mistake of not asking for the normative parameters before starting a strategy project. At the end of the project, the management had worked out three strategy variants with me, but the owners rejected all of them. The strategies were feasible and promising but not those that were wanted... We could have saved ourselves the effort. Thus, at this point in our diagnosis, we must establish how clearly and how comprehensibly the business mission and the corporate policy are defined, and whether they are impacting the enterprise right down to its smallest capillaries.

Figure 13.8 also shows a second channel, which intervenes from System 5 on the left and the right in the steady state (homeostasis) between Systems 3 and 4. *System 5 fulfills its supervisory duty through this channel and ensures that this homeostat, which balances the future with the present, actually works.* This oversight is the third mission-critical task in System 5. Most major business failures can be traced back to the failure of this homeostat: the crisis of the Swiss watch industry during the 1970s (after missing the trend toward quartz technology); the collapse of Rolls Royce (after investing too heavily in developing aircraft engines); the grounding of Swissair or Kodak (see above).

In the whole control system, morevoer, System 5 also acts as a sponge that absorbs the last bit of complexity not yet absorbed by the other control elements. *Every open question is answered and decided normatively.* This is expressed by the Third Axiom of Management:

Definition

Third Axiom of Management[7]

The variety disposed by System 5 equals the residual variety generated by the operation of the Second Axiom.

Thus, our system must be strong enough to oversee the balance of System 3 and 4 and, if necessary, to make a timely and final decision. This is represented in Fig. 13.7 by a vertical line between the two S-curves of the old and the new business. Because we never have enough information in this balance, stalemates may occur when a question is not yet ready to be decided but must nevertheless be decided now. In this case, System 5 must take a normative decision. *Making a final decision at the end of all deliberations and discussions* is a vital capacity to prevent an organism from being paralyzed by remaining variety and uncertainty.

If the owner of an enterprise is also able to say "That's enough" at some point, this is a strong variety attenuator. Sometimes this is necessary to provide the enterprise with direction and security. The principle of papal infallibility in the Catholic Church or a referendum in a democratic state also absorbs the last vestige of variety. However, the Systems 5 of many enterprises are too weak. Their representatives do not really manage to oversee the balance between Systems 3 and 4 and to make final decisions when necessary. They know too little about the factual issues, have too little time, and if they do have some degree of assertiveness, ignorance therefore once again becomes the great absorber. What about our SIF? How powerful is our System 5? Which bodies, committees, and individuals are active there? Besides supervisory boards, boards of directors, partners, or shareholders, for example, an advisory board, a council of elders, or a works council might also be active in System 5. How do they work together? Is responsibility for System 5 being taken as a whole, an *"Identity Directorate"* that integrates these entities and is able to make decisions? And can they work together to fulfill the Third Axiom of Management?

Tasks

(a) Consider what your System 5 is doing today and which bodies, committees, and people are involved there. Gain an impression of the strength of System 5.
(b) Collect the mission-critical tasks for System 5 in your SIF from diagnostic Step IV. Supplement them with other mission-critical tasks that you consider

[7] Stafford Beer, *Diagnosing the System for Organizations*, p. 130.

important, and from these again determine the seven plus/minus two most important tasks.

(c) Assess the vertical communication channels between Systems 5, 4, and 3: What is being communicated through which channels? How well is this working?

(d) How does System 5 oversee the steady state (homeostasis) between Systems 3 and 4? Does it notice when things are out of balance and can it act on its diagnosis?

(e) Is the Third Axiom of Management satisfied overall? Is System 5 strong enough? Does it have enough variety to clarify and conclusively decide all unresolved questions and issues? What would enabling it to do so require?

(f) Can we identify or anchor clear accountability for some form of "Identity Directorate"?

Tip: If you are dealing with a rather small SIF, where one person is performing the senior management functions more or less single-handedly, ask how much time you spend on each function, and how you manage to do that. Likewise, in a large enterprise, you can elicit how much time senior managers are spending overall on each of the control functions 1 through 5. The results are usually amazing.

14 Diagnosing and Designing Communication Channels (Step VI)

We have meanwhile defined all the boxes in our Viable System Model. If we now screen them for a moment, what remains are the lines connecting the control elements. These are the communication channels, which converge to form a single, large information circuit. Only they connect the whole into a *"Total Integrated Control and Communication System."*

Earlier we emphasized that the lines are more important than the boxes, because what matters is how the control elements are connected. This applies to all systems. Depending on what we connect and how, completely different behavior results, completely different properties emerge, and the previously nonexistent emerges. This can be experienced most impressively in music. If the instruments in an orchestra perform one after another, different music emerges than if they are connected, that is, allowed to perform simultaneously. While the musical score determines which instrument is connected to which and when, the musicians determine how the individual instruments respond to each other in the system. From the right interaction emerges the beauty of music.

We also remember that the lines of communication in the Viable System Model should always be thought of as control loops. Most processes occurring in an enterprise are not the linear, cause-effect relationships that we draw so readily in our model as simple value chains. Causality, instead, is circular. *All control processes are information cycles rather than linear flows of information.* Our model of control consists of many such interactive control loops which, on the one hand, can take place on a small scale between two control elements (e.g., between System 3 and the management of an operational unit). Or, on the other hand, they may connect several systems in a large loop, as shown by the example of a production control system in Sect. 13.2.

But there are many more such control loops in the enterprise than we are able to diagnose. Not that we need to diagnose all of them. It suffices if we focus on the essential ones and only examine the problematic ones in more detail. To this end, we received indications from diagnostic step V, where we also briefly assessed the communication channels in Systems 2–5. Where we suspected that a channel was

M. Pfiffner, *The Neurology of Business*, Management for Professionals,
https://doi.org/10.1007/978-3-031-14260-4_14

not functioning properly, we isolated it and examined its communicative performance.

14.1 Communicative Performance

In diagnostic Step III, we asked whether taken together the amplifiers and attenuators between the variety blocks (environment, operation, and management) are strong enough to achieve the desired balance. From the most important amplifiers and attenuators, we derived mission-critical tasks, prioritized them, supplemented them, and distributed them among the control elements. In Step VI, we now ask in detail through which communication channel these tasks are performed. Whether a channel does its job depends on its communicative performance, and this consists of three elements: channel capacity (i.e., how much information can be conveyed through it), comprehensibility, and timeliness of content. Once more, our measure of performance is variety, our benchmark Ashby's law: "Only variety can absorb variety."

14.1.1 Channel Capacity

Since Shannon's seminal work in information theory, we have become accustomed to the idea that communication channels can convey only a certain amount of information per time unit, and that this can be measured in bits per second. Shannon's tenth theorem states that channel capacity must exceed the required bit-handling capacity in order to resolve ambiguities in the channel caused by "noise." What does this mean? Different channels have different capacities. If we want to inform the customer about product features, we can do so through a text, a brochure, a video, a face-to-face meeting, or a demonstration. A text clearly has less capacity to convey information than a personal conversation or a demonstration. This raises the question: How powerful does this channel need to be to really get the message across? Does it have the necessary variety?

Definition

The Second Principle of Organization[1]

The four directional channels carrying information between the management unit, the operation, and the environment must each have a higher capacity to transmit a given amount of information relevant to variety selection in a given time than the originating subsystem has to generate it in that time.

Some tasks can be completed via a text message or an e-mail, others require a telephone call or a meeting. Even more complex issues might demand a retreat, a

[1] Stafford Beer, *Diagnosing the System for Organizations: The Managerial Cybernetics of Organization* (Chichester, New York, Brisbane, Toronto, Singapore: Wiley, 1985), p. 45.

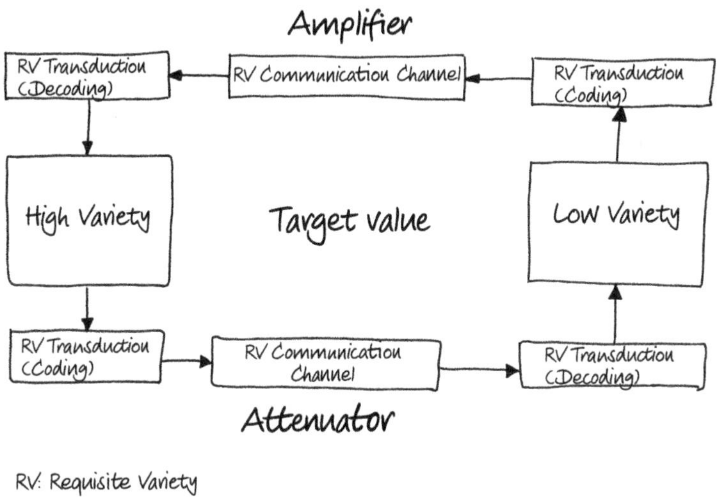

Fig. 14.1 Diagnosing communicative performance

workshop, or an IT system. To set a production goal for the current month in the Resource Bargain and Accountability channel (Systems 3 and 1), one meeting suffices. But to translate the target into a production plan (Systems 3 and 2) requires a complex production control system that specifies exactly which machine needs to do what in which shift. Either way, the channel must have more variety than what is to be communicated, so that no lack of clarity arises in the form of gaps, misunderstandings, errors, or ambiguities. Thus, we should be generous rather than stingy with channel capacity. When in doubt, we should choose channels with too much capacity rather than too little.

In one reorganization project, the issue was how to communicate the new organizational structure to thousands of employees scattered across the world. Many communication channels (e.g., e-mail, newsletters, or PowerPoint presentations) do not lend themselves a priori to conveying such a complex and important message. They have too little variety and therefore are too weak as a channel. Among others, it was eventually decided to produce a professional half-hour video featuring animations and graphics, in which the management explained matters personally and in detail, and which was broadcast worldwide at the same time. Afterwards, local managers answered employee questions.

14.1.2 Intelligibility

Communicative content must be encoded by the sender and decoded by the receiver (Fig. 14.1). Depending on the channel, these are different processes. If the channel is a brochure designed to inform the customer about the product, encoding involves putting one's message in the brochure. Does this enable clearly conveying the intended message? As for decoding, the question is whether the recipient can understand the content. If written in German, the brochure will not be understood in China. If written in "gobbleddygook" (i.e., technical jargon including foreign words, abbreviations, or specialist terms), the German customer might not understand them either.

Transferring content into a transportable form, and thereby producing information for the recipient, is called *"transduction"* (from Latin *transducere*, "to go over, to transfer"). Transduction is also but not only "translation." Essentially, it involves giving content, in the form of facts or data, a semantic meaning able to become effective. Remember: *"Information is, what changes us"* (cf. Chap. 9). For this purpose, transduction, like the channel itself, must possess the necessary variety. If communication is to function, not only must the channel be strong enough to transmit the message, but both sides must be able to comprehensibly express or read the message. In other words, it must be transformable.

Definition

The Third Principle of Organization[2]

Wherever the information carried on a channel capable of distinguishing a given variety crosses a boundary, it undergoes transduction; the variety of the transducer must be at least equivalent to the variety of the channel.

Regarding the lines of communication, we ask which channels are used to communicate the content of mission-critical tasks, whether they have sufficient capacity, and whether the transducers on the sender's and the receiver's side are working. Too often, communication is grossly lacking. The resulting data cemeteries do not really inform the receiver. Reports are produced that include a lot but not what is of interest. People speak and write thinking first or thoughtlessly draft e-mails that lead to queries or errors due to poor transduction.

Thus, we need to ask whether we normally manage to convey important content in digestible portions, and whether these messages are understood and prove useful at the other end. If they do not, they will simply be ignored. One seminar participant told me that at some point, he began inserting the sentence "Anyone who reads this will receive a first-class bottle of red wine as a gift from me" somewhere in his weekly reports. Every week he added an additional such sentence. In the end, he said, he drank the bottle himself. He saw this as proof of senior management wasting its time producing useless reports. However, he did realize that the problem was not only the recipients: The lack of communication may also have arisen from choosing the wrong communication channel or misdesigning the report. Many lines of communication work poorly. Not because their messages are essentially unimportant, and could therefore be neglected or ignored, but because communication is ill-considered and poorly designed. If we find ineffectively communicated mission-critical tasks, we have discovered an important need for action.

---

[2] Stafford Beer, *Diagnosing the System for Organizations*, p. 47.

14.1.3 Timeliness

Third, we check the timeliness of communication. All communication lines are supposed to work in *real time* but usually do not. As a rule, we face delays that sometimes complicate control. Even in the world's most developed countries, economic data still arrive very late. Hence, economic decisions are made out of step with economic reality—potentially right decisions are made at the wrong time. This is how systems can work themselves up to destructive levels. We need to design our control system to work in sync with events as they occur in the environment and in the operation. Each operational unit has its own dynamics and therefore its management also enjoys relative autonomy. Meanwhile, the general dynamics in the System in Focus result from the synchronization of the vertical axis. Through it, an enterprise can be accelerated or decelerated. When we evaluate communication channels, we must, therefore, also pay attention to their operating speed: Are things happening in real time or are delays causing problems?

Definition

The Fourth Principle of Organization[3]

The operation of the first three principles must be cyclically maintained through time without hiatus or lags.

Due to deficiencies in the control system, yet sometimes also due to an excessive orientation to legally determined time horizons, the time lags on the vertical control axis of senior management are often too large. *The time axis is one of the most important parameters in management.* It plays a vital role in many management issues. Whether something happens now or 6 months from now can make a significant difference and determine success or failure. If System 4 spots an acquisition opportunity but System 3 cannot act on it in time, the enterprise misses out. And whether the cost-cutting project takes effect now or 6 months from now can save a company or not. Neurologically, this is understandable: If we decide to start running to avoid missing the bus, we cannot first take our blood pressure, check our adrenaline levels, and consult our heart and lungs. It is of no use to management if the control system takes months to produce information in the form of studies, statistics, and discussion groups when it has to decide now. *The control system must adapt to the reality of management, not vice versa.* Following widespread digitalization, today's technological possibilities make real-time control possible to a considerable extent. Nevertheless, most enterprises still plan with fixed time horizons.

While diagnosing the control system, the management of a high-tech corporation hypothesized that the vertical channel between Systems 4 and 3 was not functioning properly. Closer scrutiny revealed that neither the communication channel nor the transduction was the problem, but the timing. Corporate requirements demanded that

[3] Stafford Beer, *Diagnosing the System for Organizations*, p. 55.

operational units submitted their budget plans for the following year in September of the current year. In addition, strategic considerations had to be made every year and strategy forms had to be completed. The deadline was the end of November, that is, 2 months after the deadline for operational planning. This arrangement effectively ensured that no strategic consideration was ever incorporated into operational planning, and therefore no strategy was ever implemented. The vertical channel between Systems 3 and 4 worked flawlessly in terms of content, but was utterly useless due to its asynchrony. For years, strategic planning had merely churned out paper.

Other enterprises conduct a major strategy exercise every 5 years to move the colossus in a different direction in a sluggish implementation project. By the time the results are visible, however, the environment has changed so considerably that these are now the wrong results. These fixed planning cycles are asynchronous with actual changes in the environment and in the operation. Control is a continuous and adaptive process that requires *reacting when something relevant happens*. The response does need not be as fast as possible, but it should not cause delays. The control system, therefore, needs real-time information.

Task
Look back at your results in diagnostic Step IV. You have briefly assessed all the communication channels in SIF and should have gained a sense of which ones are problematic and need closer examination. Diagnose only those channels. To do this, write down the mission-critical tasks. For every task, consider what to do if . . .

(a) The communication channel being used lacks sufficient capacity to transmit messages unambiguously.
(b) Transduction is not working at one end or at both ends, and therefore messages are neither effective nor beneficial.
(c) The channel is not operating in sync with events and is causing harmful delays.

Tip: Use Fig. 14.2 to diagnose the communication channels.

14.2 Communication Security

Since this book is not about communication in general, but about control, communication security is an important issue. Now this does not mean protection against eavesdropping, hacking, or information misuse, because such matter extends beyond the normal and legal functioning of an enterprise. Nor does it mean normal, everyday communication about this and that. Rather, it means that communication succeeds where it must succeed, because the tasks concerned are critical to success.

Anyone who has worked in an enterprise knows how often communication works poorly, badly, or not at all, even in normal operations, and what effort and costs are incurred as a result. The most common communication failure is misunderstanding *because information never consists of one message, but always of a number of*

SIF: ....

			Observations; Variety Check		
		Mission-Critical Tasks / Responsibility	Channel Capacity	Intelligibility	Synchronicity
Communication Channels	TWO-ONE	Coordination/Oscillation Damping/Support/Policies • ...			
	THREE-ONE	«Corporate Requirements and Constraints / Intervention» • ...			
		«Resource Bargain and Accountability» • ...			
	THREE-TWO	Information Needs/Coordination Instructions ... • ...			
	THREE*-ONE	Real-Life Information/Audits • ...			
	FOUR-ENVIRONMENT	Familiar Environment (Communication/PR, Networks Stakeholder Management) • ...			
		Unfamiliar Environment (Opportunities/Threats, R&D, Intelligence, Recruiting) • ...			
	THREE-FOUR	Strategic Parameters • ...			
	¾ HOMEOSTAT	Balance (Homeostatic State) TODAY versus TOMORROW • ...			
	FIVE-FOUR/THREE	Normative Parameters for System 4 (Outside & Then) • ...			
		Normative Parameters for System 3 (Inside & Now) • ...			
	FIVE- ¾ HOMEOSTAT	Monitoring ¾ Homeostats (TODAY versus TOMORROW) • ...			
	ALGEDONIC SIGNAL				

Fig. 14.2 Overview of communication channels

possible messages. A friend of mine, who ran a hotel management school on Lake Geneva, told me he had dictated the monthly orders to an apprentice. Among others, the order included small-squared writing pads for students. But *Hüslipapier*, the Swiss German word, also has a second meaning: toilet paper. Two weeks later, a truck stacked with toilet paper parked outside the hotel. Now that is a reasonably charming example. Other examples lead to more serious, sometimes even tragic situations. When life and death are a stake, no room remains for faulty communication. Enterprises having to function at all costs establish the principle of *"Zero Defects Communication,"* just as others establish the "Zero Defects" principle in quality management. They get things right the first time, and anchor responsibility for them with the sender.

A message may be mispronounced or misunderstood. It may be mistranslated, distorted, shortened, or halted. It may arrive too late or not be sent at all. The room for interpretation is large, and the variety on the receiver's side is immense. Since the work of Claude Shannon and Warren Weaver, we know that communication originates in the receiver.[4] *Not what I said is communication, but what the other person understood.* As a consequence, the sender is responsible for making themselves understood by the receiver. Only the sender knows the meaning of what they want to say, and therefore only they can judge whether communication has

[4]Claude E. Shannon and Warren Weaver, *The Mathematical Theory of Communication* (University of Illinois Press, 1949).

succeeded. They, therefore, remain responsible for communication until they have convinced themselves that it has succeeded.

Important

Communication takes place in the receiver

The sender is responsible for successful communication: They choose the right channel, ensure timeliness, comprehensibility and usefulness, and close the communication loop to check whether they have been understood correctly.

The sender's first responsibility is to choose the right communication channel. Can this issue be communicated via e-mail or is a conversation needed? Will a telephone call do or is a meeting needed? Do other people need to be involved or informed? Can this channel be used to communicate in a timely manner?

Second, the sender is responsible for comprehensibility (i.e., transduction). They must make the message suitable for the recipient. If the recipient is an engineer, they will probably understand matters more easily via graphics. If they are a lawyer, they will need text rather than images. And if they are a mathematician, they will need numbers and percentages to understand. It is also important to speak in the recipient's language: How does something need to be expressed? And what context is needed for them to understand?

Messages should be designed ergonomically. An e-mail, for example, must tell the recipient in the subject line whether "Action: ..." is required, or whether it is merely "Information: ..." It should cover only one subject so that the sender can process and save it in an orderly fashion. It must be clearly structured and unambiguously numbered so that the reply can refer to parts of it. In the end, the recipient must know what is expected of them and by when.

If we are honest with ourselves, even these basics are often handled carelessly. A 100 years ago, when it still took months to receive a reply to a letter, misunderstandings simply could not be afforded. Inevitably, a lot of thought had to be given to the ergonomics and comprehensibility of a letter. It is against this background that we should understand the following words, which have been attributed to Blaise Pascal, Voltaire, Goethe, Churchill, or even to Mark Twain: "If I had had more time, I would have written you a shorter letter." We must regain this communicative competence. It has become even more important since messages can be multiplied so easily, quickly, and abundantly. Today, we often communicate too rashly with the wrong means, which, moreover, have too little variety for the message we wish to send.

Third, senders must convince themselves that communication has been successful. To do this, they must close the communication cycle. We apply these cybernetic feedback loops reflexively in technology, but too seldom in interpersonal communication. Far too often, we communicate linearly, in terms of "fire and forget": We simply say or write something and forget about it afterwards. Since communication originates in the receiver, we have not yet communicated if we communicate in this way. It is only when we have heard our counterpart's response that we know what we have said. Only feedback makes communication effective. Hence, operations that must function need to apply two principles to close the communication loop: *order acknowledgment* and *completion report*. Both principles are well known from the military, firefighters, hospitals, or aviation. They ensure that misunderstandings can be detected and corrected immediately. We can implement the principle of order acknowledgment in our own System in Focus (SIF), for example, by having the person whom we have given a verbal instruction record this order in writing. First, this saves time, and second, the recipient's summary shows what he or she has understood. The completion report is also important. It should be self-evident that every employee immediately reports order execution in a short message. Only then is the second cycle closed and does the client know that they can erase the matter from their mind and consider it closed. As long as the client receives no feedback, on the other hand, they remain responsible, because not receiving a message can mean many things: The job is done; or it is not done yet but well on its way; or there are difficulties; or the recipient has since died. Automatic completion reports kill this variety, which might otherwise stress the client.

When the environment changes significantly, communication within the enterprise must also adapt: Which channels are used, how they are timed, which rules apply to maintain ergonomic communication, and which security level is needed for communication to succeed also has to do with the current state of the enterprise. We recall Ashby's law: If the environment becomes more dynamic, the control system must also become more dynamic. It is therefore worth considering how long it takes to move the enterprise from one *mode of operation* to another.

In today's enterprises, three different modes of operation are usually enough: normal, increased activity, and crisis. In the normal mode of sustained activity, communication, and control occur as usual. In the operation mode of increased activity, the availability of certain people must be shortened and the cycle becomes faster. E-mails, for example, now have to be answered within 24 h and one or the other communication channel has to be changed in order to increase message density. In the crisis mode, even stricter rules apply: The whole team is on deck, everyone can be reached immediately, communication channels and rhythms are as short as possible, and the vertical control axis limits the autonomy of the operational units via the corporate intervention channel, together with the System 3* channel, so that the whole can react quickly and compactly. Ensuring communication through closed loops becomes mandatory. In practice, other modes of operation of control systems can be observed, such as "growth," "retreat," or even "moribund," that is, dying and expiring, for example, when a market disappears or a technical solution becomes obsolete. Depending on the mode, individual control elements 2–5 receive a different weight and individual communication channels become stronger or weaker. *Diagnosing and designing the third dimension of organizing thus not only involves functioning in the status quo, but also prepares the enterprise to be able to switch immediately to a higher mode of functioning if necessary.*

Task

(a) Basically, the principles of effective and secure communication apply to every type of communication and at every level of recursion in the enterprise. Have we established these principles in our SIF as part of our System 2?
(b) For every mission-critical task, we can say which channel is used to communicate and at what frequency, who is responsible for it, who takes care of comprehensibility, and who closes the loop at the end. For which tasks do we still need to clarify this responsibility? Use Fig. 14.2 to gain a better overview.
(c) In what mode of operation is our SIF currently operating? Are we prepared to quickly move it to a higher mode if necessary?

14.3 Connecting Several Levels

Besides communication performance and communication security, connecting different levels is important. *We first look at how the various specialist areas are connected in our System in Focus and how their control elements are integrated into the overall control in senior management.* Every specialist area controls itself in the SIF via the same Systems 2–5. Marketing, for example, takes care of brand policy in System 5; in System 4, it controls the marketing mix and conducts market research; in System 3, it defines marketing targets and controls marketing projects; in System 2, it coordinates the marketing activities of the operational units and supports them with materials and training; and in System 3*, it checks compliance with corporate identity. Nevertheless, the control system of marketing differs from that of HR or IT. It includes other tasks, uses other channels, and is timed differently. As discussed in Chap. 13, the tasks of the various specialist departments need to be integrated into a logical whole in each of the Systems 2–5. Moreover, the proposed "Directorates" in each system are responsible for this interconnection (Fig. 14.3).

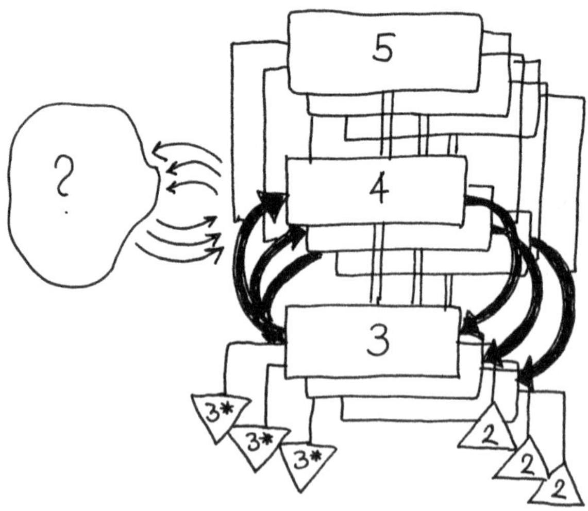

Fig. 14.3 Integration of departments into the control system

In diagnostic Step VI, we leave the level of recursion of our SIF for the first time and link the higher and lower recursion levels with it. Thus, our System 3 must talk to that System 3 of which it is itself the management of an operational unit (R+1), and to the Systems 3 in the management box of its own operational units (R−1). Figure 14.4 shows the Viable System Model at three recognizable levels of recursion, each of which having its own System 3. The communication between these levels concerns how the operational plans of each level can be integrated into a meaningful whole at the next higher level and, vice versa, where the operational planning of the higher unit constrains that of the lower units. *This planning across levels of recursion is the organizational glue that provides cohesion.*

Most people understand planning as a professional activity that results in products called plans. However, we must see planning as a permanent decision-making process through which investments are allocated today so that the future may be different. Because newer information is available at every moment than in the previous moment, it is actually crazy to implement plans—professional products—later than when they were made. If we produce a plan with a certain date, and implement it down to the last detail, we will see stupid action. Or as the Prussian Field Marshal Count von Moltke the Elder put it: *No plan survives enemy contact.* By introducing command tactics, Moltke gave his commanders great autonomy, and thereby gained the upperhand over other armies at the time, which were still strongly commanded along the vertical axis of command. *Planning, then, means continuously modifying or abandoning current plans as soon as the environment has changed in a relevant way.* It is exactly the opposite of sticking to fixed plans, whether operational or strategic. As soon as relevant factors have changed—and they do all the time—a plan must be updated on the central command axis. Otherwise, it no longer serves the needs of the organization as a whole. If the current situation is not recognized in real time, time-lags occur that can send the organization into uncontrollable oscillation. Therefore, all levels of recursion must be required to continuously update, integrate, and communicate their plans to each other.

In most organizations, the linkage of operational planning in System 3 with the higher and lower levels of recursion works well. These are the well-rehearsed annual target agreement and budgeting processes, as well as the more quickly timed processes for updating and reconciling operational plans such as incoming orders or sales expectations. But what about System 4 (Fig. 14.5)? Here we find an open issue in many enterprises. Often strategic planning takes place on one or even a few levels, but they are not effectively integrated. If, however, the enterprise is to function not only today but long-term, this is necessary because the strategy of the higher level of recursion must be implemented via the substrategies of the lower levels of recursion and must make sense at these levels. From operational planning, we know how this interconnection across levels of recursion works. What actually prevents us from applying this to strategic planning as well?

Finally, System 5 must also be interconnected across the levels of recursion to form a logical whole (Fig. 14.6). Systems 5 must also communicate with each other. The System 5 of the higher level of recursion provides the framework for the Systems 5 of the lower levels of recursion. In practice, we find that System 5

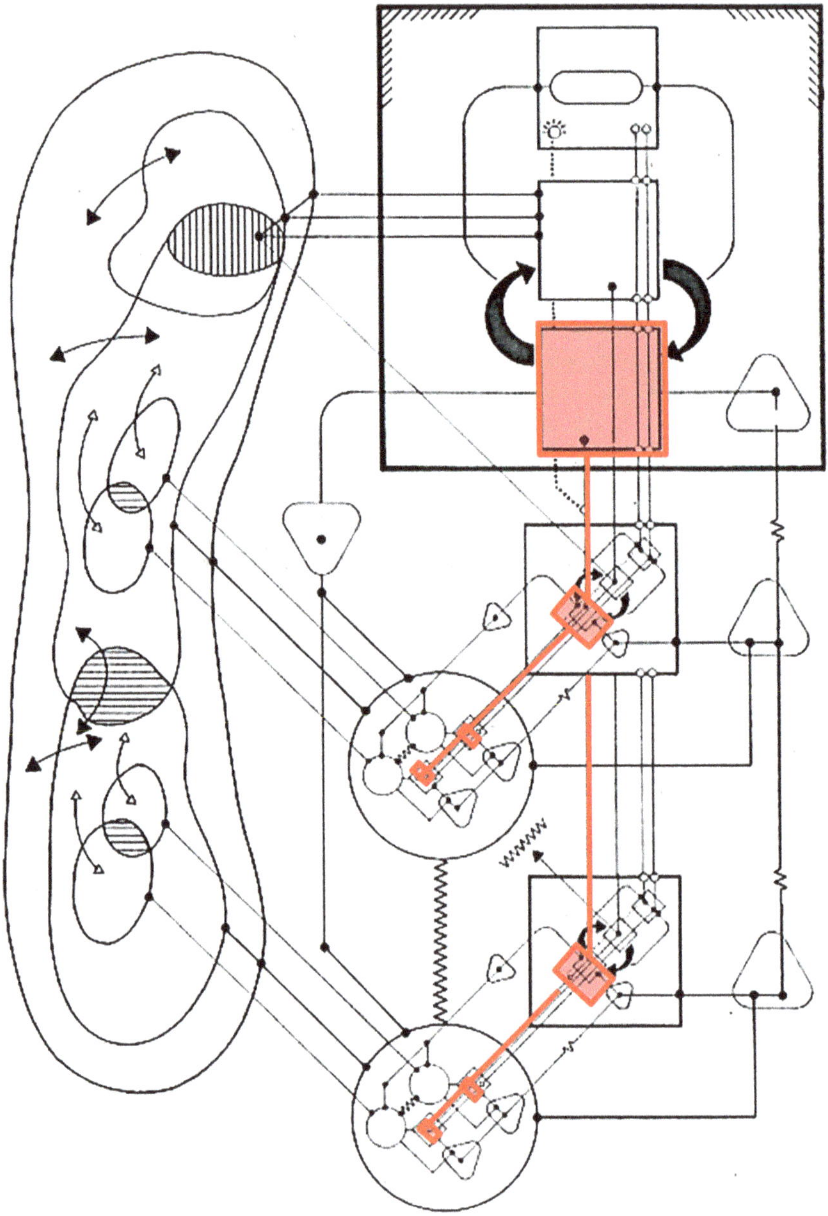

Fig. 14.4 Interconnection of System 3 via three levels of recursion. Source: Beer, *Diagnosing the System for Organizations* (1985)

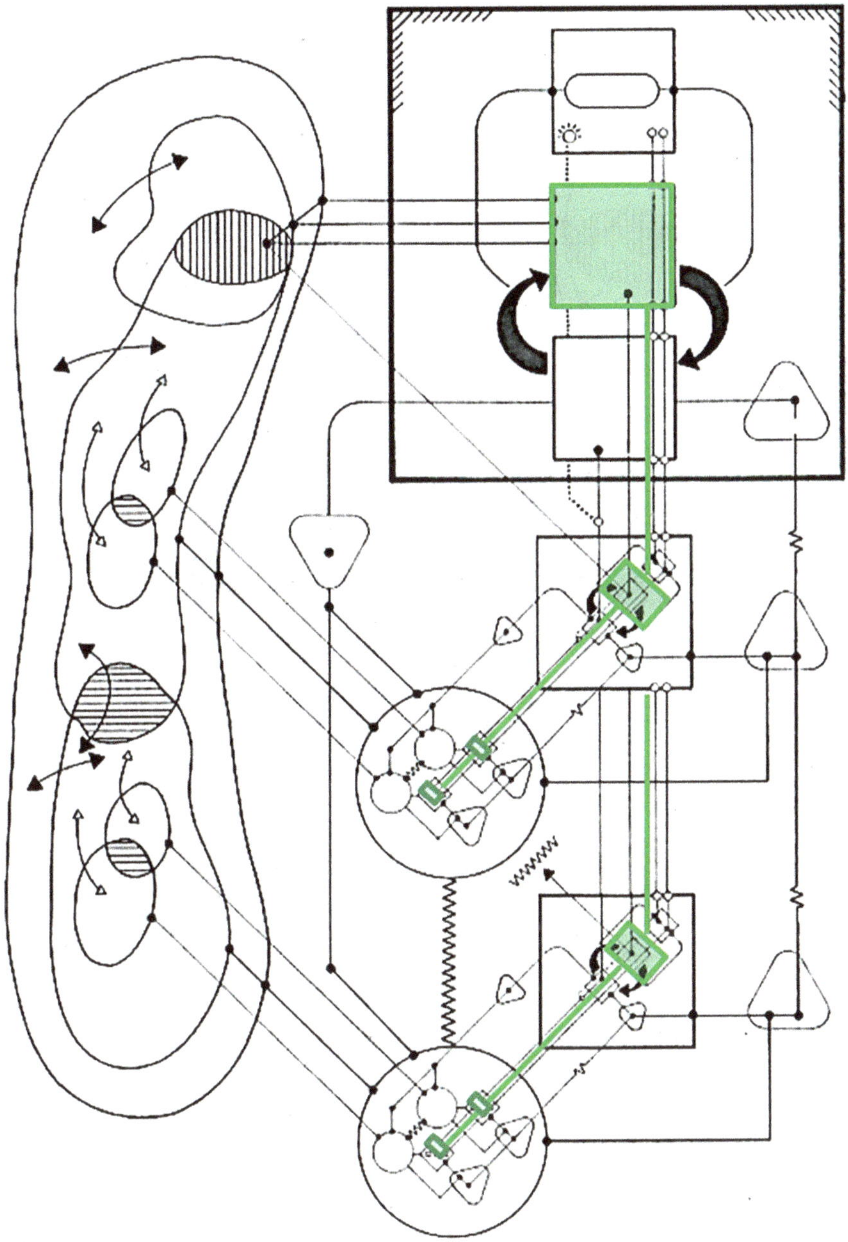

Fig. 14.5 Interconnection of System 4 across three levels of recursion. Source: Beer, *Diagnosing the System for Organizations* (1985)

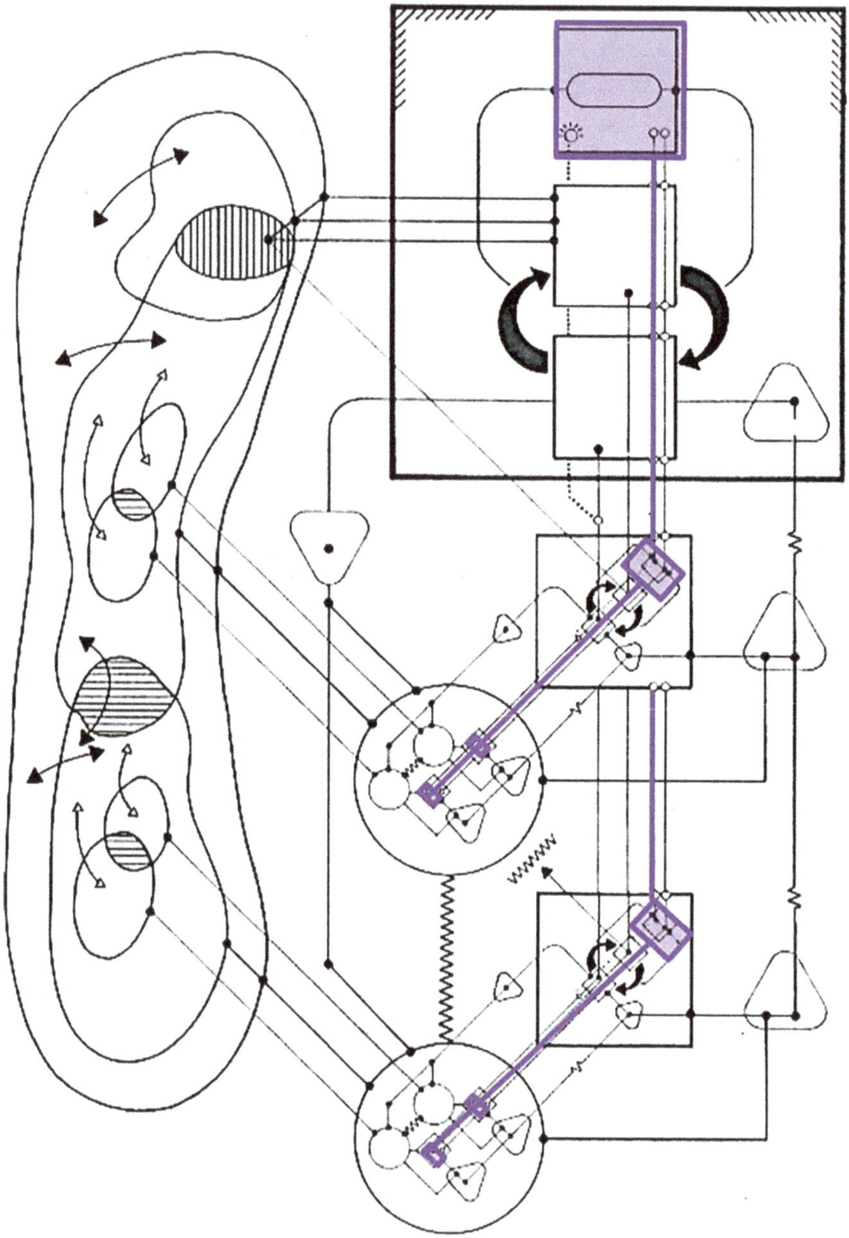

Fig. 14.6 Interconnection of System 5 across three levels of recursion. Source: Beer, *Diagnosing the System for Organizations* (1985)

activities are visible only at the highest levels of recursion of the enterprise, especially when they are enforced by legal regulations. This is not enough, because lower levels of recursion must adhere to the parameters of the higher level, but must be more fine-grained. The state constitution is far too coarse-grained for a family, and also irrelevant for the family in many respects. The family must also adhere to the state constitution, but must flesh out this framework for itself. Deeper levels of recursion must ask themselves what exactly the overarching business mission and corporate policy means at their level, and what additional normative parameters should apply to their own SIF. Every unit needs its own identity and thus its own System 5.

In practice, the linking of systems via levels of recursion sometimes does not work via written communication, but via one and the same person performing several functions. For example, members of the management team on the higher level of recursion often sit on the committees of the operational units on the lower level of recursion and thus interconnect these in one and the same person(s). The challenge, then, is to distinguish the different hats worn by these people. A common understanding of the organizational model helps them to do this.

Tasks

(a) How does the interconnection of disciplines per system function 2–5 work in our SIF? Who is responsible in each case?
(b) How is our System 3 connected to the System 3 of the higher and lower level of recursion? Is the communication channel used powerful and secure enough? Make the same considerations for System 4 and System 5.
(c) Finally, assess how well each of Systems 2 through 5 interconnects both, the departments and the levels of recursion, into a logical control subsystem.
(d) If your assessment of the last point is critical, ask yourself again whether some form of "directorate" should not perhaps be established per system function to take care of this.

14.4 Does the "Algedonic Signal" Work?

The purpose of the algedonic signal (Fig. 14.7) is to make us aware of significant events. Algedonic is composed of two ancient Greek words: *algos* (pain) and *hedone* (joy). Thus, a pain-or-joy signal is conveyed to the highest level of consciousness when its attention is required. In our own organism, such signals wake us up at night, for example, when we come down with a fever, when our stomach hurts, or when mosquitoes bite us. Such signals are the *only signals able to penetrate all levels of recursion* on the vertical control axis, all the way to the uppermost level. This level must know that something relevant is happening in order to take action if necessary. Without the algedonic signal, we would run the risk of dying of thirst or poisoning ourselves, because we would only become aware far too late that we are harming ourselves with our current behavior. If we filter out the information with painkillers,

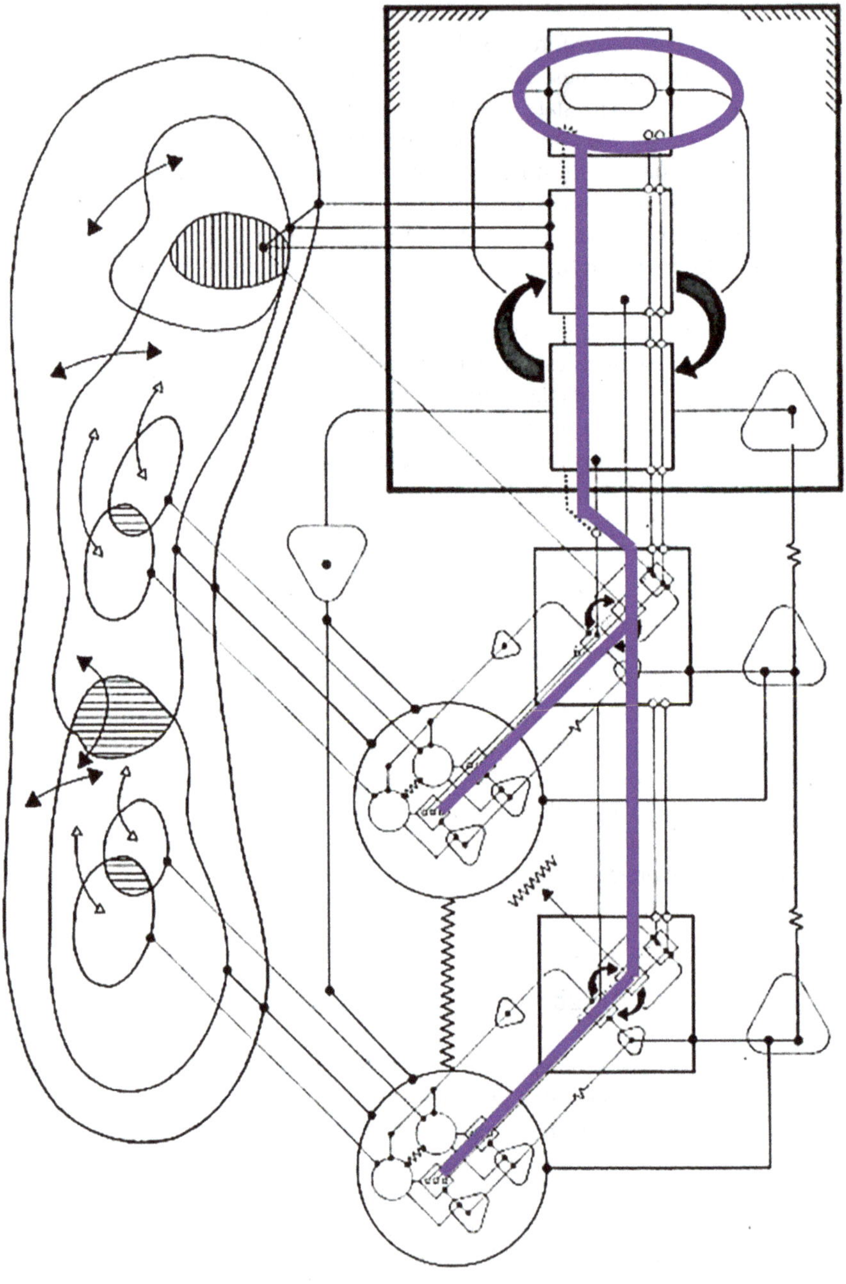

Fig. 14.7 The algedonic signal. Source: Beer, *Diagnosing the System for Organizations* (1985)

we do not realize that we should stop what we are doing. Vice versa, it is important that the organism feels pleasure when something life-enhancing, beneficial happens.

The same applies to our enterprises. Its highest organ needs to know about positive or negative events to be able to react to them. *The most important information is often found in the unusual and the unexpected:* What works much better or completely differently than we expected? If so, what does that tell us? Especially in larger enterprises, people are very careful and cautious when dealing with the representatives of the highest bodies. Who is allowed to say what to whom is actively controlled, and thus useful information is filtered out. Aware of this, these people therefore need to consider how they can still obtain the relevant information. How might an employee at the lowest level of recursion in the enterprise inform the highest supervisory body? And how do we ensure that this algedonic channel is not abused?.

Essentially, the same rules and laws apply to the algedonic channel as to all other communication channels: its capacity, intelligibility, and synchronicity must be checked and adapted to the situation in the System in Focus (SIF). The most difficult question is probably that of the appropriate communication channel. It should be a channel that can be used by everyone across all levels of recursion. It should have enough variety so that it can clearly convey an important message. And it should work in the short term. An enterprise might establish a works council (employee representation) on the supervisory board for this purpose. Its members are known as trusted representatives of the workforce, and they know that they can inform the supervisory board through these trusted contacts if necessary. Conversely, a member of the supervisory board can also be made a trusted contact for all employees. Or an independent ombudsman's office can be established. The enterprise can actively collect this information sporadically via employee surveys or mood barometers. Today, IT offers many such possibilities. These are still used far too little at the state level, for example, to find out what people want (popular will). The enterprise can conduct so-called "corporate identity tests" to assess the effectiveness of its work in System 5. It might set up a physical or virtual mailbox for messages to the management, or use the intranet (moderated or unmoderated), apps or social media platforms for this purpose.

We have now reached *the end of the diagnosis and design process* per se. Step VII considers how we can effectively communicate and implement the

results of our redesign. From the smallest operation at the lowest level of recursion to the most senior committee at the highest level of recursion, the enterprise is riddled with the same control issues and problems. The symptoms manifest in different ways. And yet, the *recipe for success*—the precepts, principles, and laws of effective control and communication discussed so far—remains the same. The *principles of functioning* apply at every level of recursion. Only the concrete content changes. In particular, we should think more often about the stabilizing effect of *negative feedback loops* in complex systems. In doing so, we realize that errors, as long as they can be kept under control within reasonable limits, are not the long-suspected enemy. On the contrary, they are the prerequisite for survival, if—and only if—we actually learn from them with the appropriate feedback loops and continuously adapt and improve. This does not mean that mistakes should be accepted and even welcomed in the enterprise, as certain corporate mission statements would have us believe. Rather, we need to ensure that they cannot have a critical impact. This corresponds to the motto with which this book began in the Prologue:

> Ever tried. Ever failed. No matter.
> Try again. Fail again. Fail better.
> (Samuel Beckett, *Worstward Ho!*)

Task
Check whether an algedonic signal can reach the top level in your enterprise to rouse it if necessary. If not, how could you build an appropriate communication channel—at least for your System in Focus?

Later in the Bar

Sandra: Quite complicated.
Marc: What do you mean?
Sandra: Controlling a company. Somehow I believe this is possible without all of this.
Marc: Sure, otherwise many enterprises would have stopped existing long ago. I found several serious open issues when I diagnosed my insurance company. But the company works all the same.
Rachel: The greatest danger in times of upheaval is not upheaval itself, but taking action based on yesterday's logic. Peter Drucker.
Sandra: Which means?
Rachel: Even those companies that work do so in the mode of the old world, and that's slowly going under. Everything is getting faster, more interconnected, and more complex. Companies aren't yet playing in the league they should be with their current control systems. Those who don't make the grade, that is, get promoted, in time will be relegated.
David: Just like in soccer ... This reminds of a saying on the wall in my grandmother's kitchen: *Wie sturen kan zeilt bij elke wind.*
Marc: Oh, and what does that mean?
David: If you can steer, you can sail in any wind! We Dutch should know. We are simple but complex.
Marc: Simple but complex—so are we insurers. With our insurance modules, we also create diversity through simplicity. Everyone can put together the package they need. But the company itself seems rather complicated to me. Just being in our modern office building, you can easily go missing.
Rachel: Unlike Notre-Dame de Paris or Cologne Cathedral. They may look complex, but you can't get lost in them.

David: Or poetry: Do you know Japanese *haikus*? Poems consisting of just a few simple words but prompting lots of thoughts, feelings, and associations in the reader.

Rachel: Careful, David is getting romantic again. But you're right: Things should be complex but simple. Even the control systems in companies. I think self-control makes things simple but complex.

Sandra: So you're saying if I did everything that way in my company, I would find everything simpler afterwards?

Rachel: Exactly. And most importantly, you'd have time for what's really important. What do you reckon: As a CEO, how much of your time do you spend in each of Systems 2–5?

Sandra: 90% in operations. And then a supervisory board meeting every now and then.

Marc: You're exaggerating.

Sandra: I'm constantly cleaning up after others—just like at home with the kids.

Rachel: At least now you can explain to them why they always have to tidy their room.

Sandra: And why?

Rachel: Cybernetics: There are countless states in which the room can be in disarray, but only one in which it is tidy. Like the families in the Tolstoy quote. So there must be chaos in the room most of the time. Sheer probability calculus. It's not your kids' fault. You need a negative feedback loop to stabilize the whole thing.

Sandra: I've been looking for that for a long time.

David: It's complicated ... Once again: Something is complex if it can take on different states. And we measure that in terms of variety. But when it comes to quantification, that's where you lose me.

Sandra: Well, that makes sense to me. Quantifying is not counting, it's just comparing quantities. Instead of counting the five fingers on one hand, I only have to hold the fingers of the other hand against them. Things match and that's that.

Rachel: You mean Ashby's law is fulfilled.

Sandra: Exactly. That's what I like about it. And I think it's in line with how we manage in our company. You know the phrase, you can only manage what you can measure, don't you? It's been bugging me for a long time. As long as you can measure something and one number is bigger than the other, my secretary can decide. You don't need me for that. There's many things I can't measure, but I can judge them. And the more important they are, the more I depend on experience and my sense of judgment. For example, a staffing or investment decision. You can't measure anything anymore.

Marc: I'll go along with that. But I understand even better what you mean by soccer: If a researcher is tasked with preventing eleven players from scoring, he either starts a large research program to study player behavior, creates a thousand electroencephalographic diagrams, and makes statistical forecasts—or simply puts eleven players on the field. Ingenious!

Sandra: That's what practitioners do.

Rachel: And cyberneticists. But mostly it's more like starting research programs. Especially when companies have too much money.

David: For me, that's what's so appealing about it. The connection to practice. When I was married and the children were small, we preferred to invite friends to dinner who also had children and asked them to bring them along. Now I know why: Variety absorbs variety and we could talk over dinner. Thanks, Ashby!

Rachel: The same simple law in different manifestations, crucial to success or failure—and suddenly you see it in action everywhere once you know it.

Marc: Amen. That's what I was thinking at lunch today: A buffet has much greater variety than a set meal. I think I've already caught the bug, too . . .

David: I recognized myself more with the closed communication loops. In aviation, those are important. You can't function without them. We pilots, unlike you managers, have always had ergonomic jargon and clear rules.

Sandra: In your aircraft computers?

David: Yes, of course, the electronic systems do most of the work today, but we also have to be able to fly without them. And then we also need order acknowledgments and completion reports. The tower gives an order, which I acknowledge, and only when it says "correct" is the loop closed. And when I've done that, I report "completed."

Marc: I know this from the military. In artillery, you don't fire without target acknowledgment—for good reasons. And reporting executed orders is a reflex. Otherwise, you're in trouble.

Rachel: I'm not an army buff like you, but I do wonder why we don't communicate better in companies. Probably because it seems to matter less. You can afford to make a lot of mistakes. Things will have to change.

David: That's not an issue for us.

Sandra: Are you kidding? Swissair went bankrupt!

David: Oh, I meant in the airline business. Yes, perhaps they should have learned better from air traffic control how to deal with complexity. You can't have anything go wrong there.

Sandra: Definitely. And Swissair's System 5 probably didn't have the variety to oversee the 3–4 balance either. Wrong strategic decisions and then also a liquidity pool of all companies. No de-networking—no robustness, only profit-driven thinking. After all, only politicians sat on the board because of their networks and connections.

David: You really seem to have absorbed this Viable System Model by now.

Sandra: There's only one thing I don't like. When I drew the Viable System control system for my company, I noticed that I can't find our two production plants anywhere. I drew the operational units, the regions in our case, but I can't find our central production anywhere. It's the largest box on the organizational chart.

David: Isn't it in System 2?

Rachel: Stop! We're talking about a control system here. So you'll need to find production control there, but not the plant itself. And central production is controlled not only by System 2. For example, it also needs to write a production strategy in System 4 or develop new products on behalf of the regions.

David: True. Supporting functions have their own Systems 2 through 5 and must coordinate with the other supporting functions. Operational units, on the other hand, can do whatever they want. I'm glad that a flight is an operational unit.

Marc: Right, you can't do entirely what you want either, but have quite a bit of autonomy. Aren't you even allowed to marry people on a flight?

David: Yes. Or unload a drunken hooligan on an unscheduled stopover.

Sandra: All right, so that means that I can find the production plant in the organizational chart because it's about organizational units, people, and committees. But in the third dimension of organizing that's no longer the case because it's about control instead of objects? Right?

Rachel: Exactly. In the control system, the lines of communication are important. If you cut the wire, nothing works.

Marc: Thousands of control loops. For us in cybersecurity at our insurance company, those are quite critical. The system diagrams look like a bunch of nematomorpha in our company—you know, those thin string worms. But in managing the business, we don't seem to get a grip on them. It seems like an unsolvable tangle.

David: Nemawhat . . .?

Sandra: Not for the practitioner. It's not about finding and controlling all the control loops, but just the most important ones. And I think I've already found the three most important ones in my company's diagnosis. Anyway, I'll take another look at those.

Rachel: There it is again, the Pareto rule: Don't control everything, but only control what controls.

Marc: It's crazy that we're already doing in technology what should be done in the company itself: neatly and tidily defining the control loops. They're what holds the world together at its core.

David: Are you saying that Dr. Faust was actually looking for control loops?

Marc: And didn't find them, because you can't see them. Now I finally understand the meaning of the dragon biting its own tail.

Rachel: The oroborus?

David: Sure, it symbolizes a closed loop or rather a communication loop, something that controls and balances itself.

Rachel: A homeostat. In technology, for example, thermostats regulate room temperature. You can see the device, but what you can't see is the oroborus behind it. It's a closed control circuit. Set the temperature, measure it, detect the deviation, correct it.

Marc: That's why no surgeon has ever found a thermostat in a human body. The control loop itself is the thermostat. It keeps us in balance when we go into cold storage. In the military, by the way, we used to say "command, control, correct"—it's the command and control loop.

Rachel: You with your military. Okay, that's a closed loop as well. But the interesting thing for me about the Viable System Model is that for once it's not about managing people, but about managing the entire enterprise with its huge complexity.

Sandra: Right. I've been to hundreds of management and leadership seminars and read books on communication. But they always deal with communication between people in management relationships or in teams.

Marc: And with the ideal manager. How people should be and how they should interact with each other. But you never find these great leaders in companies, but instead an impertinent boss who is just protecting his own mite and wants to maintain his power.

Rachel: And the only guidelines you get are turnover and return on investment.

David: So what good is a Viable System Model if you have a boss like that?

Rachel: Wait, that's unfair. The model is not the model of an ideal manager, who only exists in books but never in real life. It's the model of ideal control. It doesn't say anything about how people should be, but what they should do to be successful. That's different.

Marc: Sometimes I get the impression, at least with us, that they can't even believe that it's possible to become more successful and at the same time more free by letting go. That's why they cling to everything they have. They believe that they have to do everything themselves and do precisely that.

Rachel: It's a self-fulfilling prophecy. Paired with a good dose of narcissism!

Sandra: That's life. But life is also about evolution and improvement. I find the idea exciting that the potential for the next big evolution lies within the organization itself. Everyone seems to be looking for it, but so far they haven't really found it.

David: Because everyone's still looking for new managers or is stuck in the old categories of thinking about organizing. It's just a question of how the company needs to be wired to make control work.

Sandra: Sounds a little technocratic to me.

Rachel: But also biological. I'm more interested in how the company needs to be wired than whether Heiner gets along with Kati or not, and whether the boss is forgetful or selfish. That's why there's wiring after all. Heiner, Kati, and the boss leave at some point, the organization stays.

Marc: It's slowly dawning on me that while organizing includes the building blocks, it's the relationships between them that matter most. We renew our cells in the body every 7 years, but the relationships between them remain the same. That's why we can still recognize an old friend.

David: I agree. A hospital can be a 100 years old, and the people who work there are always different. The elements change, but the relations remain the same. Organizing is dividing and putting together.

Sandra: That's nicely put . . .

David: (laughs) Thanks. Right, I'm breaking up the party and retreating.

Marc: Yes, friends, I'm also switching to operation mode "retreat." Gotta be up early . . .

Rachel: Beware: The early worm gets eaten by the bird. Or something like that . . .

Part IV

From Knowledge to Implementation

Making the Organization Understandable (Step VII) 15

The amount of control is proportional to the amount of information the system has—about itself. (Stafford Beer)

Our diagnosis has meanwhile examined the levels of recursion and possibilities for flattening the organization, the segmentation into customer-oriented operational units, the control functions, and the corresponding communication channels both within our System in Focus and to the lower and higher levels of recursion. We now know precisely where our control system is working, where it is not, and what needs to be done. However, knowledge is as worthless as crude oil as long as it remains unused. Part IV, therefore, explores how we might proceed *from knowledge to implementation*. After a brief or even detailed diagnosis of the control system, we have gained a lot of knowledge that we can implement immediately and independently of other things. For example, we improve our System 3*, improve the communication channel from our System 4 to the superordinate System 4, abolish a meeting in System 2, and call another one into being. No one finds implementing such individual measures difficult. If, on the other hand, we realize that other matters urgently need our attention—which is almost always the case—we must communicate our diagnosis to others, and make them understand the control organization as we see it.

The most effective way of doing this would be to explain our observations with the help of the Viable System Model. As a rule, however, our bosses, colleagues, and employees are not familiar with the model and would therefore need to be trained in advance. After diagnosis, many enterprises include the model in their management training. As a result, more and more employees become familiar with the model over time. By combining training and simultaneous application in their own area of responsibility, our bosses, colleagues, and employees continue to refine and continuously expand the control organization. They learn by practical example, and at the same time, with a little help from the experts, create concrete benefits within the enterprise. They also develop a common language so that they can effectively discuss with each other the most important management model in the enterprise.

M. Pfiffner, *The Neurology of Business*, Management for Professionals,
https://doi.org/10.1007/978-3-031-14260-4_15

We have already talked about the great importance and effect of meaningful, shared models in Chap. 3. Experience shows that leaders pick up the Viable System Model very quickly and retain its language when discussing organizational issues. Perhaps this happens because the model is intuitively understandable. After all, it is how we are organized as humans ourselves, and also, based on my own observations, because practitioners find its language useful.[1]

Other enterprises simply want to implement the lessons learned. And sometimes you just cannot wait until enough employees understand the language of the Viable System Model. Since there is no "One Minute Manager" for this, nor will there ever be one due to the Conant-Ashby theorem, we use the usual *onboarding tools* for communicating the organization: *organizational charts, function diagrams, and job descriptions.* This is enough for implementation. Ultimately, employees do not primarily need to understand the model; first and foremost, they need to know what their job is. Thus, in the final step of our diagnosis and design process, we consider how to present the findings about our control system in a generally understandable way. The same communication requirements apply here as we discovered in Sect. 14.1. We are designing the user interface of the control system, so to speak.

15.1 Representing the Control Organization

Organizational descriptions are fundamentally problematic because they usually have little explanatory power, are difficult to understand, and quickly become obsolete. They are also so boring that no one reads them unless they absolutely have to. Most people avoid instruction manuals and prefer trial and error. Neither organizational manuals, nor regulations, nor process descriptions meet our requirements for channel capacity, transduction, and synchronicity of good communication. In practice, we must nevertheless use the means at our disposal to make the organization understandable. Even if we use them a little differently than usual, they still do their job.

For a simple, yet meaningful (complex) representation of our control organization in the System in Focus (SIF), the *function diagram* has proven worthwhile. It enables clearly presenting the entire control organization of an operational unit on a single A4 page. It is easily and quickly adapted or updated. Further, a function diagram allows linking tasks to organizational units and determining which unit is involved in which task and how (i.e., which function it assumes in the task) (Fig. 15.1).

In Step VII, we therefore first create a *control function diagram* for our SIF. In the *columns* of this diagram, we enter all *organizational units*. These are the current bodies, departments, divisions, or committees. But watch out: Do not enter the

[1] Martin Pfiffner, "Five Experiences with the Viable System Model," *Kybernetes*, Vol 39, No 9/10, Emerald (2010), pp. 1615–1626.

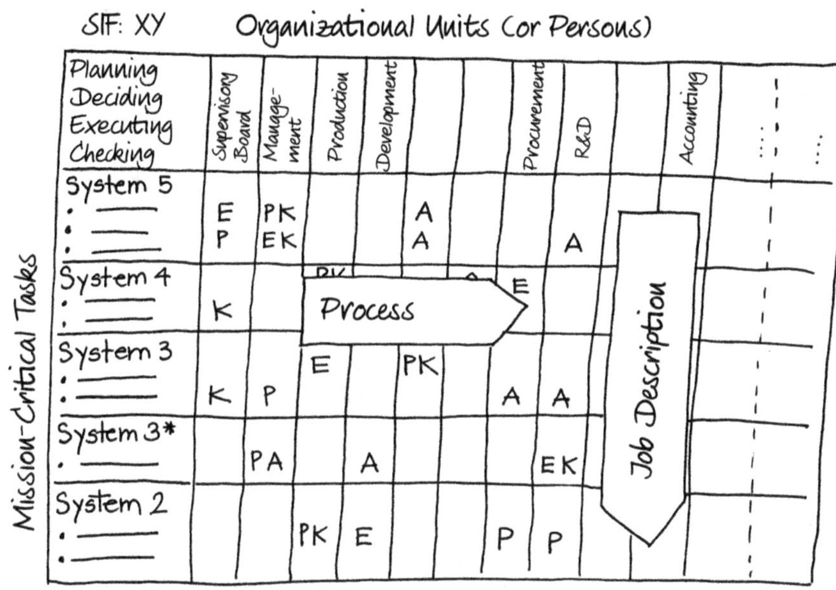

Fig. 15.1 Control function diagram

operational units in our SIF. I wonder why not? (. . .see the end of this chapter for an answer).

Depending on the level of recursion, we enter organizational units for which someone is responsible and which normally also appear in the organizational chart. Or we enter individuals who may no longer be managing areas or departments at lower levels of recursion but who are performing relevant tasks. Organizational units can also take the form of committees, large projects, regular meetings, or conferences. They are the organizational entities in which technical or general tasks are pooled.

In the *rows* of the diagram, we enter the *control tasks for each of the Systems 2–5* in our SIF (we defined those tasks in diagnostic Step V, based on Steps III and IV). If we have done well so far, we should have no more than 20–40 tasks. Next, we determine who does what. To do this, we consider for every individual control task which organizational unit (or person) in our SIF should be involved in it and how: Who should plan this task? Who should decide it? Who should execute it? Who should control it? We enter this in the center of the diagram. To enable us to depict the control organization on one page, we abbreviate the functions; for clarity's sake, use no more than three to four different abbreviations. The following have proven useful:

P *Planning:* Is responsible for this control task as a process. Initiates the process and develops process quality. Prepares decisions.

D Decision: Has the authority to make decisions and has overall responsibility for the task.

I Implementation: Is involved in the task, informed about the results, and if necessary asked for its opinion before a decision is made. Implements the decision.

C Control: Checks the result and whether the task is completed. Normally, this unit is responsible for the process. However, in some situations control should lie with the decision-maker or the person performing the task.

Read horizontally, the diagram shows the *cornerstones of the process* behind every control task and the essential interfaces: Who needs to work with whom? Who initiates? Who prepares? Who decides? Who executes? Who controls? At the end, we go through every control task line by line and check whether it is sufficiently organized. It should now be clear who makes which contribution to which control task and who ensures that it works.

Next, we go through all the columns and look at the organizational units. An organizational unit or person may perform none, one, several, or even all functions per task. Reading the diagram vertically is particularly interesting: This shows where every unit makes its main contribution, and what kind of contribution it makes in the first place.

The *supervisory body*, for example, mainly performs System 5 tasks, but is probably also involved in some System 4 tasks. It shapes the principles and content of corporate governance as well as stakeholder relations. It reviews and previews the business, elects and leads the members of the highest executive body and determines its rules of procedure. It should not include active or former executive members or persons with active business relationships, because no one can or should control themselves. For it to develop power and work effectively, its members must be able to devote sufficient time to it, possibly also at short notice. Large bodies are therefore not suitable because they become ineffective. Coordinating work schedules may take longer than the matter actually requires.

The *top executive body* in the SIF chiefly fulfills System 3 and 4 tasks. It focuses on implementation and results. It communicates externally and staffs key positions. It provides strategic and operational planning and ensures that resources are properly allocated in terms of balancing Systems 3 and 4. However, it may also help shape the business mission in System 5 and the concepts of corporate policy.

The tasks of the *departments or divisions* (e.g., human resources, marketing, IT) are usually distributed about equally across all Systems 2–5. Sometimes they perform very specific tasks (e.g., a compliance department will only have functions in System 3*). Not all departmental or divisional tasks will appear in the control function diagram of our SIF because they do not all belong to the 20% of tasks critical to the success of the SIF. *Every department or division can create its own control function diagram to represent its mission-critical tasks in more detail.*

If more diversity, perspective, experience, or networking is needed, then work with *boards, panels, or committees*. They perform specific tasks, prepare decisions, or pool technical expertise for tasks such as learning, training, or leveraging experience. For example, the contribution of the Momo committee in one bank was to coordinate divisional managers with the board on Monday mornings (hence the so-called "Monday morning" committee). They act as variety amplifiers for those committees that are in charge and make decisions. As a rule, these types of organizational units do not appear on the organizational chart, nor do *conferences*, large *projects*, or *meetings*. But if, for example, a meeting is held regularly, it should appear in our control functions diagram. This enables us to check whether it makes a relevant contribution to our SIF. Normally, audits prove worthwhile because much time and energy are wasted in such historically grown, small organizational units. Sometimes this happens because they are badly prepared, poorly chaired and, most importantly, rarely followed up, and sometimes because a meeting, committee, or body would not really be needed if it did not already exist. Often too many or the wrong people are involved (those who have time), and no one maked things work because no one is really responsible. Precisely because many unproductive or unnecessary entities exist in practice, and whose purpose degenerates into intellectualizing, let us visualize them in the control functions diagram and subject them to scrutiny. This enables us to gain further insights, even in the final diagnosis and design step.

Finally, for every *organizational unit or person* on the vertical axis of the diagram, we can check how important their *contribution to the whole* is and what it consists of. Glancing at the corresponding column and the functions it contains is enough. If we find columns that remain empty, we should ask ourselves whether these units are really needed or whether the organization can be simplified here: Can we dissolve the unit and allocate its remaining, obviously less important tasks, to another organizational unit?

One of the great advantages of the control functions diagram is its clarity and flexibility. It can be easily updated when changes occur in the control organization, because as a rule the control tasks do not change. Besides, any changes in organizational units or responsibilities can be quickly adjusted. The functions in the diagram (PDIC) can be changed immediately and effortlessly. It can be posted next to people's desks and shows at a glance who is involved in which task and how.

Tasks

(a) Create the control functions diagram for your SIF. To do this, enter all organizational units (or people, depending on the level of recursion) existing today in the columns.
(b) In the rows of the diagram, enter the control functions you established in Step V for Systems 2 through 5 in your SIF. Be sure to maintain the allocation to Systems 2 through 5.
(c) For every control task, consider which entity (or person) should be involved and how. Enter the appropriate abbreviation (see above) in the diagram.
(d) For every control task, check at the end that it is sufficiently organized and that accountability is established.
(e) For every organizational unit, check what its contribution is and try to reduce organizational units not making a significant contribution.

(f) Check that accountability for Systems 2 through 5 is established. See below for a job description of such "directorates."

Tip: Ensure you remain on your level of recursion in your control functions diagram. Do not enter organizational units or people in the diagram that neither really belong to that level nor are managed there. Leave out System 1.

15.2 Job Descriptions

The columns also include the key points of the job descriptions for the organizational unit or person in question. We can see which mission-critical tasks a unit or person is involved in, in what form, and for which tasks they have responsibility and decision-making authority. Although these are merely the *key points of a job description*, they are defined concretely and precisely where they matter most for functioning. Job descriptions have the advantage that they show individual employees clearly and concisely what their tasks, competencies, and responsibilities are. Since jobs are sometimes and over time also adapted to the strengths of the jobholder, it makes sense to compare them with the control functions diagram and to review and update them[2]: Is the job well designed? Does it fit the strengths of the jobholder? Is it neither too large nor too small? Does it allow the jobholder to be effective and does it offer a chance to succeed? Especially in large enterprises, positions often exist whose *raison d'être* is worth questioning. For instance, what exactly was the "Chief Assistant to the Assistant-Chief" whom I came across in an EU institution responsible for? What does an "Implementation Officer" or a "Cost and Productivity Tracker" do? Do we really need every "aide" or "advisor"? Or can we create real jobs for these people, where they can play to their strengths but also take responsibility for their own contribution? Thus: We take the key points of a job description from the appropriate column in the control functions diagram and, after a review, we add any additional tasks of the job beyond the mission-critical ones.

Job descriptions are conceived primarily for *individuals* but it also makes to formulate them for *organizational units*. After all, the purpose for which an organizational unit was created too often remains opaque because both the tasks and the unit have changed over time. When I ask an enterprise about the purpose of a committee or regular meetings, as a rule they list the standard agenda and members. The purpose of a system is—what it does. That is true. But we often struggle to state the intended purpose because we do not know it. It, therefore, makes perfect sense to question and clarify this purpose every now and then. We might also inquire in some detail whether a meeting or committee in its present form is still the right medium for fulfilling the task in question. Communications technology is evolving so rapidly

[2]Fredmund Malik, *Führen, Leisten, Leben: Wirksames Management für eine neue Zeit* (Frankfurt, New York: Campus, 2006), pp. 298–303. English edition: *Management: The Essence of the Craft* (2010).

that more suitable channels—with better capacity, comprehensibility, and timeliness—might be available. Or we might conclude that an organizational unit has served its purpose and is no longer needed. Considering that complexity works exponentially, we usually struggle to clean out the organization and make room for the new.

A job description, even for a board, committee, or meeting, should start with its *purpose*: What contribution to the whole does this organizational unit make? Besides the *members*, and what is required of them, the *duties, competencies, and responsibilities* of this entity must be stated. A good job description also regulates the flow of information by describing from which entities the organizational unit obtains information and whom it must inform. The *rhythm* at which the organizational unit meets and achieves results must be defined. Most importantly, someone must be responsible for every organizational unit. *Negative feedback loops* can only work if the responsibility for a task and the competence to perform that task are anchored in a single place. Only this clearly establishes who must take action, who decides, and where responsibility lies. Too often, this kind of stabilizing feedback is dispensed with by dividing up responsibility: "We'll do it together." Nor can an employee have two bosses at the same time; as the saying goes: "He who has two bosses is a free man." Self-control only works if the control loop is closed and if there is *a clear point of responsibility*.

As argued in Chap. 13 and Sect. 14.3, it makes sense to *clearly define responsibility* not only for the organizational units but also *for all control systems 2–5*: Who ensures that the individual control system and its communication function properly? Even if several organizational units perform different tasks in most control systems, responsibility can, for example, be assigned to the most actively involved unit. We can certainly be creative, as long as the law does not impose any restrictions. For instance, we must clarify whether the supervisory body or the executive body should be responsible for System 4. In doing so, we must take into account that different types of enterprises have different regulations in different countries. Where there is room for maneuver, for example, in anchoring responsibility for System 2 or 3*, use existing strengths: System 4 tends to need different strengths and a different set of people than System 3, as well as different people than System 2. We can also summarize the tasks of such a *"directorate"* in a job description:

Tasks of a System × Directorate (per Control Systems 2–5)

1. To verify and ensure that all tasks included in the control functions diagram are performed and take effect for the control system concerned.
2. To check and ensure that communication with the connected control systems (according to the Viable System Model) is working.
3. To integrate the departments within their own control system, in relation to the mission-critical tasks.
4. To integrate the planning processes between the higher and lower levels of recursion and to verify and ensure that communication is working.
5. To keep the system function lean and transparent, and to free it from inherited problems.

6. To maintain data on filing systems and to keep data-up-to date and lean.
7. To keep up-to-date the control functions diagram within its control system and to align that diagram with the job descriptions of the organizational units or individuals involved.
8. . . . other specifics of the system function.

Thus, after creating or checking the job description for all organizational units in our control functions diagram, and after specifying its work rhythm, we can make another interesting observation. If we juxtapose all the larger, regular meetings held in one and the same year in a single *meeting diagram*, we create a *cardiogram of the enterprise*. With many decisions being made in these meetings, clearly mapping their rhythm shows how the enterprise is paced, and how quickly or how slowly it works and reacts. A enterprise's meeting calendar is like its pacemaker: It allows us speed up or slow down the enterprise. It also enables us to discern how meetings influence each other information-wise. The decisions of one session serve as the input for other decisions in other sessions. Normally, these meeting diagrams are designed very unergonomically, because no one is responsible for overall control. Meetings are therefore entered more or less randomly in calendars according to their members' availability.

Tasks

(a) Create a job description for every organizational unit in your SIF (or for every person). Start with the functions found in the corresponding column in the control functions diagram. Add other duties, authorities, and responsibilities as appropriate.
(b) For every organizational unit, write down who is responsible for it and ensure it is only one person. Describe its purpose and contribution to the organization, mode of operation, any standard agendas, members, roles, authorities and responsibilities, information flow, and work rhythm.
(c) Adjust the units if you conclude that they are not fulfilling their intended purpose, if there are more appropriate ways of accomplishing the task, or if the current design does not promise success.
(d) Create a concerted meeting calendar for your SIF. Check that the rhythm at which the organization operates is timed in sync with its relevant environmental changes.

15.3 Organizational Chart

This, finally, brings us to organizational charts. Section 2.1, as you may recall, stated that we should not begin with these charts but finish with them. Let us do precisely that by adjusting our organizational chart where changes have resulted from diagnostic Steps I and II, from testing the control functions diagram, and from our considerations about jobs and their descriptions. Organizational charts are important because they tell employees where their organizational home is, who their boss is, and who their colleagues and collaborators are. It is the first dimension of organizing, which, figuratively speaking, describes the anatomical units of the organism.

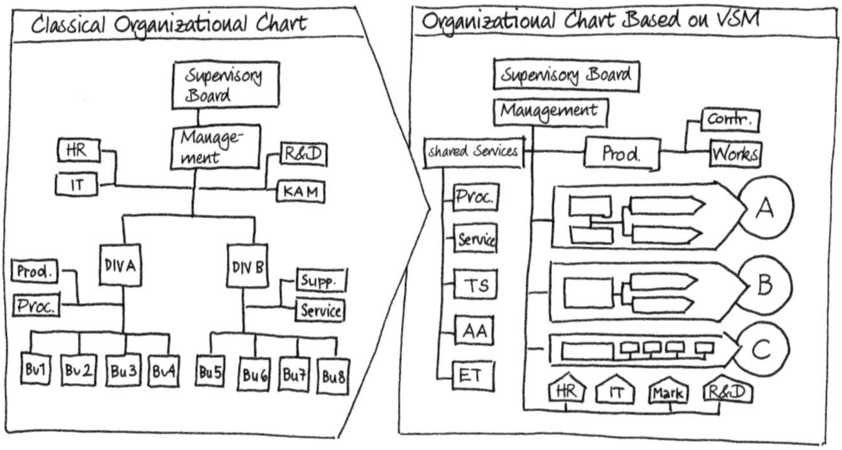

Fig. 15.2 Organizational charts

Although their explanatory power is limited, organizational charts can be enriched with a little more information (Fig. 15.2). For example, we can use the five control functions to classify the anatomy somewhat. Visually distinguishing operational and supporting functions immediately doubles the information content of any organizational chart. In addition, the *customer* or *service recipient* can easily be entered in any organizational chart, akin to us drawing the environment into our model of control. Being slightly creative, we draw non-value-creating *supporting functions* below the operational units, so that they also provide visual support from below, whereas we draw value-creating supporting functions (key specialisms) above. We must, however, understand that we are not drawing a control system, but an information-enriched organizational chart. We can write names in the individual boxes to clearly establish contacts. If we have defined responsible persons for Systems 2–5, it makes sense to visualize them also in the organizational chart (which is easily doable graphically). Even organizational units such as *boards, committees, panels*, or important *meetings* can be included in the organization chart if considered relevant enough after comparing them with the control function diagram and after checking the individual positions.

Controlling an organization becomes easier, the more managers and employees know about their own organization. Or as Stafford Beer was quoted at the beginning of Part IV: "The amount of control is proportional to the amount of information the system has—about itself." Digitization opens up new possibilities in this regard. We can use the Viable System Model not only as a thinking tool, but also as a *navigation interface* through control-relevant information. Most enterprises today do not have good classification systems for their information. This is a problem because it is easier to file something than to find it again. How often are you unable to access information that is actually available in timely fashion because you do not know where to find it, or because only another organizational unit has access, or because the information is duplicated, incorrect, outdated, or available in different versions. No factory operation handles raw material as messily as knowledge organizations handle information.

A *navigation system for information* must follow the laws of complexity discussed in Chap. 9. It attenuates complexity, first, by the principle of recursion. One knows at which level of recursion of the overall enterprise something needs to be looked for. Second, it reduces complexity to manageable sizes by means of the five control subsystems. With a mouse click, the searcher first selects the right level of recursion and then the right control subsystem according to the classification into coordinating, optimizing, auditing, clarifying, and identity-creating functions. We thus also remain on the level of the seven plus/minus two manageable elements and thus on a fast search path. On the other hand, such a navigation system increases variety for the searcher. It is simple, yet complex. Another mouse click takes him or her to the daily updated information about all the mission-critical tasks being performed in this system. In System 3, for example, the minutes of meetings and presentations are stored; in System 2 coordinative information such as regulations, lists, plans, overviews; in System 4 communication documents, strategic plans, and studies; and in System 5 the business mission, policies, and so on. It is important not to build a shadow repository of information for this navigation system, but to link it directly to data wherever they are stored. Other systems would need to be maintained. As no one has time, they become obsolete immediately. These few remarks only scratch the surface of the available technical possibilities. The best technology, however, is of no use if the navigation model falls short.

By representing the control organization, we have now gone through all seven steps of the diagnosis and design process. We have distinguished levels of recursion, examined flattening and manageability, segmented and designed the operational units, filled the control elements with content, and examined the communication channels between them and between higher and lower levels of recursion. Finally, we presented the results in the form of a control functions diagram, as well as through job descriptions, a meeting cardiogram, and a much more robust organizational chart. We are ready for implementation.

Tasks

(a) Match the updated organizational units in your control functions diagram with the organizational units found in your organizational chart. Adjust and add where necessary.
(b) Use design elements based on the Viable System Model as described above to make your organization chart more meaningful. *Answer to the question in Sect. 15.1*: What we want to represent is the control system of our SIF with its Systems 2–5. System 1 with its operational units is the object, not the subject, of this control. The operational units in System 1 control themselves. According to the principle of recursion, they have their own Systems 2–5 and thus will create their own control function diagram on the lower level of recursion. Therefore, the operational units are not entered in the control functions diagram of the SIF.

16 Successful Implementation

Not all enterprises implement equally well. Weak implementers spend a lot of time on *analysis phase*. They conduct studies, launch surveys, collect statistics, and run workshops with lots of people, because they want to base their decisions on facts and to broadly underpin them. Somewhat less effort is spent on the *options phase*, in which design options are explored. Such enterprises invest least effort in planning and designing the *implementation phase*. Only when plans have been approved do they start thinking about implementation and setting up a project according to the usual standards. Since they are only now considering implementation, they have already made so many mistakes that implementation becomes sluggish. In the end, a lot of paper is produced, yet little changes in the enterprise. It is, therefore, worth devoting a separate chapter to implementation, also because some specifics are particularly important for implementing organizational projects.

It is worth *reversing the funnel* and investing most time and effort in the implementation phase. While empirical evidence is important, our mental models guide and constrain our fact-finding, and how we interpret the evidence. More important than a broad and detailed evidence base, therefore, is working with the right diagnostic models. These narrow our search radius for decision-relevant information and direct our attention to the crucial questions. Provided that we concentrate on the essential variables at the beginning of a project aided by the Viable System Model, and thus proceed purposefully, the often very long and detailed analysis phases can be significantly shortened. Apart from their ultimate benefit being small, because amassing even more detailed facts about the really difficult questions does not provide greater certainty, today's dynamics means in-depth analyses outdate faster, the longer they take.

Just as the helmsman on the ship stuck in fog needs to manage without precise facts on position, currents and azimuth, our reorganization process can also function largely independently of precise facts. *It is about direction, not precision.* Much can and must remain open at the beginning of implementation. The goal must be clear and the cornerstones (key points) must be binding, but continuous adjustments can be made during expansion. If the direction is right, precision will follow naturally

M. Pfiffner, *The Neurology of Business*, Management for Professionals,
https://doi.org/10.1007/978-3-031-14260-4_16

over time. The implementation phase itself needs the most time and attention. The individual steps in a reorganization project must be well thought out and designed from the beginning and carefully planned through completion. The identifiable difficulties, hurdles, and obstacles should not be resolved later, but anticipated so that they do not arise in the first place. Thus, what needs to be done and what considered? The following points have proven worthwhile in practice.

16.1 Incremental Change or Reorganization?

Diagnosis may produce two types of results. First of all, the first two diagnostic steps have shown that the building blocks of the organization are basically in order. The number of the levels of recursion and segmentation remains unchanged, and thus the operational units remain the same. *This first case is unproblematic* because the organization is only adjusted *incrementally* (i.e., in small steps, and only here and there). We might conclude that in the current mode, the supervisory body cannot adequately assess the System 3–4 balance and takes action to improve it. We might realize that a coordination mechanism for joint learning is missing, or decide that an existing committee has become useless and should be abolished. These measures are easy to implement and require neither a project nor extensive communication. Nevertheless, they also need to be followed up consistently. Especially abolishing organizational entities, which actually seems simple, can sometimes take longer and turn out to be more difficult than expected.

The second case is problematic. Diagnostic steps I and II have revealed that segmentation must change, or that certain levels of recursion must be eliminated or established. In this case, the building blocks of the organization do not remain unchanged. We are adjusting the anatomy of the enterprise, and thus are dealing with *reorganization*. This case is problematic because it affects the functioning of the entire enterprise. A large number of people and opinions need to be reconciled. Individual interests can no longer be ignored and solutions must be found for certain things. A reorganization can therefore be compared to a surgical intervention in the anatomy of an organism. Yet unlike surgery, the patient is wide awake (fully conscious and *unanesthetized*) during reorganization: He or she sees what is coming and reacts accordingly. Since a reorganization cannot be performed in the maintenance hangar as with aircraft, but instead takes place in full flight, few executives have any real first-hand experience of this challenge. They may have witnessed two or three major reorganizations in the course of their careers. They may even have been responsible for one themselves, but often years ago.

Enterprise *productivity* is expected to decline throughout the reorganization phase and somewhat beyond. Reorganizations immediately receive the greatest attention from all employees because almost everyone is affected in one way or another. They lead to massive uncertainty due to fears, misunderstandings, and misinterpretations. The word "reorganization" alone can cause turmoil in the enterprise, among others, because as a rule (at least in the English-speaking world) it means large-scale layoffs, and not necessarily the adjustment of the organizational structure. Thus, as soon as employees hear through the grapevine that their enterprise is facing reorganization, they focus on themselves, rather than on the market and customers. They imagine all the scenarios that might affect them and gather all the available and purported information to shed light on the situation. The fear of change means that information tends to be interpreted negatively rather than positively, thus setting off the rumor mill. Moreover, the danger of intrigue grows the longer reorganization lasts. The longer there is doubt about fundamental decisions, or uncertainties become apparent in the determination to implement, the more opportunities arise for employees to perhaps shift the outcomes in their favor or at least influence them somewhat.

Such a phase is fatal for the mood in an enterprise and for team motivation. *Reorganization is more likely to succeed, the less long it takes.* Even in large enterprises, not much more than half a year should lapse between the first discussions and focusing a new organization. Instead, every practitioner has probably experienced reorganizations that drag on for years. In one large European aerospace company, employees unofficially christened their reorganization project "Dolores"—the Painful One—when, even after 2 years, the end was still not in sight.

Chapter 3 has already emphasized that structure and culture are closely related. Every structural change *impacts enterprise culture* in its own way, but it is difficult to shift or change that culture as a whole. Fortunately, this is not even necessary because we do not need to change the culture as a whole but only *individual, concrete behaviors*. This is possible by practicing them over a long period of time and following up time and again. This requires time and patience. In this regard, however, it is much more a question of whether we have the people needed for that structure, and who we might lose if it is implemented. Not everyone goes along with everything. The critical question that we therefore must ask at the end of diagnostic Step II concerns people: *Do we have enough managers, and also the the right ones, to implement the new organization?* The best structure is useless if we lose too many key people and competencies or, in the end, if we do not enough managers to bring it to life. Thus, if we are not dealing with incremental change but rather with real reorganization, we somehow need to find the right balance between the structure that the business requires and what people are capable of and want.

16.2 People Versus Things

If we are lucky, we will have the managers we need for the new structure. Usually, we don't. In this case, should we build the organization around the available people? Or should we insist on the right organization—even if this means losing key people or being unable to fill positions? These questions concern the conflict between people and things. In other words, what is right for the enterprise and what for the individual employee. Both sides are important, and the equation is difficult to solve. Section 2.6 argued why it is mistaken to start with people. Therefore, to start our organizational diagnosis, we only looked outward: at purpose and at customers or service recipients. Our first question was: What is right for the enterprise and its customers?

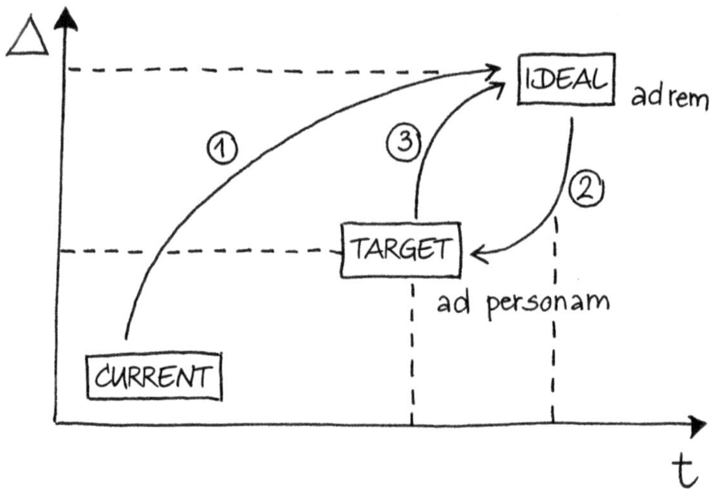

Fig. 16.1 People or things? The right sequence!

At the same time, we know that things will not work without the right people. How, then, do we reach the right compromise? Figure 16.1 goes back to Walter Krieg, one of the founding fathers of the St. Gallen Management Model. It shows that the path from the CURRENT organization to the TARGET organization implemented in the end is not direct but proceeds via an IDEAL organization. This organization is said to be correct ad rem (Latin, "for the matter"). The organization fulfills its purpose with the customer and not with the employee. Therefore, the organization that best serves the customer should be favored. The customer's rather than the employee's needs come first and therefore determine the IDEAL organization.

We have worked out this IDEAL organization in diagnostic steps I and II. It serves as a point of orientation. Only when we have found it do we consider whether this organization is also correct *ad personam* (i.e., "for people"). In most cases it is not, and compromises need to be made. To this end, we need to know what would be ideal: From all possible compromises, we need to choose that one that most closely approaches the ideal. This is the good compromise, as opposed to the many bad compromises that might also be possible but lead us further away from the ideal. *This compromise is the TARGET organization that we will implement.*

Therefore, in diagnostic Steps I and II, we force ourselves not to think about specific people at first. We also disregard our personal interests as much as possible for the moment, knowing that sooner or later, we will attend to these issues in detail. At the end of Step II, we write down our IDEAL organization, which we have developed based on the facts (ad rem), and ask ourselves whom we want to fill key positions with. The first question is whether we even have *enough managers* to fill all the necessary key positions, or how long developing or finding those people might take. Certain positions can be held by other managers for a limited period of time. In the mid-term, however, all key positions must be filled, or the enterprise will strangle itself.

The second question concerns *individuals and their individual situations.* Every considerable change produces winners and losers. As a rule, the winners cause no problems, which raises the question: Which managers might lose out or see themselves as losers? Among these people, some are unproblematic, either because they do not see themselves as losers or because the enterprise could cope without them. Which leaves those key people with whom solutions must be found in personal discussions. Where no solutions can be found for these people, or if key positions cannot be filled, the IDEAL organization cannot be implemented or at least not yet.

A TARGET organization is usually an intermediate step. It is followed by further approaching the IDEAL organization as soon as certain compromises are no longer necessary or problematic cases have solved themselves. Thus, these further intermediate steps no longer represent a reorganization as such, but merely incremental changes, which can be implemented uncritically. However, the TARGET organization and the IDEAL organization should not be too far apart. If they did, too many compromises would have to be made and the reorganization effort would be superfluous because it would not really allow reaping the benefits of the change.

Thus, we make these considerations after diagnostic Step II, before working on the future building blocks of the TARGET organization in Step III. Quite possibly, at this stage, we might conclude that the CURRENT organization fits or that reorganization would not achieve significant improvements given the necessary compromises. In this case, we continue diagnosing the control system with the current building blocks and focus on expanding and improving it. As mentioned, such incremental and unproblematic changes to the organization can be implemented without the implementation phases and success factors addressed below.

16.3 Four Implementation Phases

But if we must reorganize, correctly designing the implementation phases and the communication in these phases is crucial. In practice, a four-phase approach has proven successful (see Table 16.1). The duration of the individual phases and the number of people involved may diverge from this standard depending on enterprise size. But even in large enterprises, reorganization should not last longer than 9 months in employees' perception, from first mention to completion of the implementation project. Everyone accepts a 9-month "pregnancy" if the outcome holds water.

In *Phase A*, no reorganization project exists yet. Organizational diagnosis has been initiated to find out whether such a project is necessary. We should not make this kind of diagnosis on our own, but in a small team of three to five trusted people who, taken together, know the business sufficiently well and can bring the project, if there is to be one, to completion, first as a core team and later as a steering committee. We need these different perspectives and opinions to ensure our

Table 16.1 Four implementation phases

Phase	Duration	What	With Whom	Communication
A	3 months	Develop the IDEAL and the TARGET organization up until diagnostic step IV	Core team (3–5 people)	None
B	4 days	Discuss and refine the TARGET organization and distribute mission-critical tasks (central vs. decentral)	Core team plus key people (20–40 people)	Brief communication to the entire company
C	3 months	Take diagnostic steps V–VII and prepare implementation	Core team	Updates for key people
Focusing the TARGET organization				
D	6 months	Implementation and fine-tuning	Core team plus line managers	Detailed information for the whole enterprise

deliberations have the necessary substance and depth. This core team goes through diagnostic Steps I and II together and develops the IDEAL organization (Fig. 16.1). Next, this organization is examined *ad personam*: Do we have the key people and can we fill all positions in a reasonable time? What else could fundamentally jeopardize or call into question this IDEAL organization? When we reach this point after about 1 or 2 months, we must and can decide whether to:

(a) *Stop discussing organizational structure*. We have meanwhile established that change would not significantly improvement matters, that we do not have the people necessary to implement change, or that we would lose too many critical key people as a result. Therefore, nothing should be communicated up to this point, because communication would only unnecessarily unsettle the enterprise. Three to five trusted people can meet a few times over two to 3 months for a half-day meeting without this already becoming an issue in the enterprise.
(b) *Keep the CURRENT organization*, but complete diagnosis in order to *improve the control organization*. In this case, we are dealing with unproblematic, incremental changes that the core team can diagnose, design, and implement on its own. Based on the CURRENT organization, the core team jointly works through all further diagnostic Steps III to VII. We skip Phase B, since neither the commitment nor the knowledge of a larger number of colleagues is required for the remaining diagnostic steps. It is advisable to briefly inform employees that we want to ensure the enterprise functions better by improving the control organization in individual, well-targeted places and by closing gaps. We thus prevent the rumor mill from churning, which is inevitable at this stage, however, secret we keep matters. Information has begun leaking and is being interpreted incorrectly and negatively. We, therefore, need to keep communication in our hands and actively manage it.
(c) *Adjust the CURRENT organization* and whether the expected improvements justify the effort and expense of *reorganization*. If reorganization goes ahead,

we must decide which compromises we should make *ad personam* and therefore what the TARGET organization will look like. The core team works through diagnostic Steps III and IV on this basis. Only in this case does it continue with *Phase B*.

As of now, we are dealing with reorganization. We need to consider whom we involve in the discussion, for what purpose, how, and when. So far, only the core team has been involved. At the *start of Phase B*, we will know how many levels of recursion the enterprise will have in the future and how they will be segmented. This corresponds to the *raw building* (shell). We know the foundation, the number of floors, and the rooms per floor. Next, we turn to *interior design* (fittings) and establish the commitment of those who will 1 day occupy these rooms. We, therefore, need to involve those people in the enterprise whom we envisage will occupy these future key positions. We also need to incorporate additional knowledge into the solution in order to uncover as many white spots and as many consequences of the new organization as possible that we have not thought of so far. We are looking for a relatively broad-based "high variety" discussion in Phase B. In particular we are looking specifically for dissent, because sustainable solutions emerge from *enacted dissent* rather than from hasty consensus. In most cases, when we list these key people, we end up with 20–30 people from all different functions and levels of recursion in the enterprise. Together with the core team, these are the people we need to win over to the new solution and who we, therefore, involve in designing the solution. Implementing change succeeds only if a critical number of key people and opinion leaders in the enterprise support and really want it. We need to create a *robust management coalition* and ensure that the key people involved understand the need and the purpose of the reorganization, because they will either drive implementation or simply want to prove why it is unfeasible.

On the other hand, we do not want to encourage discussion of the *cornerstones of the new organization* (which we designed in Steps I and II). We define these as *binding*. In these two steps, and within our normative parameters, we have designed how our organization does justice to our customers' needs and our strategy. We have used variety engineering to check flattening and manageability and know that we have the people needed for implementation. We communicate and justify the need to change the CURRENT organization to the defined key people in terms of these points. We also show them the results of Steps III and IV and suggest which mission-critical tasks should be performed by which level of recursion (central vs. decentral) in the future.

On this basis, the key people should discuss what they consider the most difficult obstacles and the greatest barriers with the core team—and they should *jointly develop solutions*; that, after all, is what managers to do. Aside from the given cornerstones, these people may question everything—provided they propose better ideas. How we involve these key people is basically open. Whichever form we choose, it must enable generating concrete solutions and commitment within a few days in a concentrated manner. Most conventional methods do not prove useful in this respect. They take too long and produce too few results. Section 18.1 presents one tried and tested method, which Stafford Beer developed for the balancing act between Systems 3 and 4. Either way, it is important to carefully minute the discussions in Phase B. This ensures that the essential arguments and good ideas surfacing unplanned during discussions are not lost again and can later be used to comprehensively communicate the new structure to all employees.

Since we have now involved and briefed more than a handful of people, we can assume that the information about reorganization has spread across enterprise, even if we requested discretion. Journalists and intelligence agencies know that nothing remains secret beyond five people at the latest. This explains why we now need to inform all employees directly about what is being worked on, who has been involved, and when further information can be expected. Do not yet communicate contents or solutions: Although available in principle, no definitive decisions have been taken.

We develop this communication in *Phase C* before focusing the organization as part of preparing implementation. We now further refine and decide the cornerstones and the solutions developed in Phase B. This work can be done again by the core team, supported by key people from Phase B where necessary. Normally, Phase C also lasts about 3 months, because the implementation phase needs to be thoroughly prepared. Measures are put together, priorities are set, the implementation organization is designed, and the communication concept for implementation is devised. Typically, interviews are also held with individuals at this stage to fill any remaining vacancies. Incidentally, communication in Phase C is limited to occasionally updating key individuals from Phase B. However well-prepared implementation is, many issues still need to be left open for the moment because there is no solution or answer to them yet, or because they must first be piloted. In addition, some issues can only be recognized and grasped once we have worked in the new organization for some time. However, we must adhere to the cornerstones defined in Phase A, because uncertainties about these open the door for delays, whispering and intrigue, and thus jeopardize reorganization. Experienced employees can "smell" such uncertainties immediately.

Finally, the day comes when *Phase D* begins and we must throw the lever. We have considered matters long and hard and must now act quickly. On that day, the old organization will be abolished and the new one will come into existence. Introduction should happen snaplike rather than piecemeal; full throttle than with a grinding clutch, as is too often observed. Employees must know what goes and what does not. If, however, they are expected to work partly in the old organization and partly in the new one, this causes confusion. They will seek refuge in the old organization whenever they feel uncertain. If you want to introduce something new, you must do away with the old for good. Even if much must be left open when the new organization is focused, it can be launched nevertheless. This puts the *new managers in the driving seat* and enables them to fill the remaining gaps during the 6-month implementation phase. This is the time for detailed testing, learning, fine-tuning, and correcting. After these 6 months, the implementation project should be completed. From then on, the normal decision-making processes in the new organization apply to all outstanding issues. Otherwise, reorganization projects become never-ending stories.

Communication in Phase D is crucial. From the start, we must make it clear to employees first-hand, as simultaneously as possible and bypassing all hierarchies, why the organization is being changed, what goals are being pursued, and how the new organization is to function in principle. At the end of Phase D, and from Step VII onward, organizational charts, control function diagrams, and job descriptions will be available for this purpose. The requirements for good communication described in Chap. 14 also apply here. We must avoid the popular waterfall approach, where senior management informs the divisional heads, who inform the department heads, who inform the team heads, who inform the employees. This cascading communication takes too long and leads to something other than what was meant. Good communicators communicate directly and pay close attention to choosing the appropriate communication channel. They think long and hard about how best to make themselves understood. They consider possible misunderstandings in order to avoid them from the start. They start with undisputed matters, neither justify nor look back, but emphasize the goals and the new mode. They lay out the communication for the entire duration of the implementation phase and continuously communicate the big picture time and again in weekly, small and digestible installments. They make the first successes visible as soon as possible in order to drive implementation. Finally, they ensure that communication is again two-way. The steering committee (as a rule the board) must learn what is not yet working, as well as misunderstandings or undesirable developments exist. It must build trust by listening. In addition to effective implementation controlling, the steering committee creates a suitable System 3* and an algedonic channel in the implementation project for this purpose.

16.4 Four Success Factors

Executives with strong implementation skills give particular attention to four success factors. Besides taking these points into account, success requires nothing more, yet also nothing less, than the usual tools of good project management.

16.4.1 Adapt the Management and Incentive System

Especially in the implementation phase, the principle of "control what controls" is important. Besides the customer, the behavior of managers and employees is determined most by whoever decides their salary, bonus, and progression at the end of the year. Who discusses performance with whom and who decides whose career is relevant for most people in most enterprises. They usually do what their superior expects them to do. That is the control mechanism that we have to control. We have adapted the anatomy to a new, *dominant control dimension*. Now we also need to control via that dimension and orient the neurology of the enterprise toward it. If, for example, we have moved from a functionally structured System 1 to a regional structure, the strategic and operational planning process must take place in the same dimension (i.e., also in the regions). Because then, the regional managements and no longer the functional areas agree targets with operations staff and assess their performance.

By adapting the management processes, we establish the negative feedback loops provided for this purpose in the control system. Those responsible should feel the consequences of their actions in their new areas of responsibility both positively and negatively. The more we can involve them in their own success (which includes, yet is not limited to, money), the more we create not only rapid change but also the entrepreneurial culture required today, as well as motivation for good people. Therefore, the fastest and most effective way of implementing organizational change is to immediately adapt the management and incentive system to the new, dominant control dimension. A new anatomy comes to life only when properly innervated. Neglecting the neurology of the enterprise is, therefore, one of the cardinal errors of organizing (Sect. 2.10).

16.4.2 Pull Instead of Push: The Principle of "Powers Reserved"[1]

Managers with strong implementation skills require new managers to utilize the the room for maneuver resulting from reorganization. They know that it is easier to rein in their people a little where necessary than having to push them. If someone oversteps their authority, as a rule we realize this quite quickly and can take action. If, however, someone does not use their scope of action and remains idle, we may not notice this until after much valuable time has been lost. This explains why strong implementers establish the principle of *"Powers Reserved"* from the first day of implementation: *What is not forbidden, is permitted.* Reservations about decisions are defined in the job descriptions for every level of recursion and for every organizational unit. Everything else should be decided on a subsidiary basis. Some enterprises live the opposite principle: Only what has been explicitly permitted is permitted. Anyone who has understood the essential principles of correctly handling complexity will immediately recognize the error. This approach worked in old-school, deterministic, and trivial organizations, but is out of place in today's complex organizations. Especially in enterprises where executives have always waited for instructions from the board, clear communication is even more necessary: What is not forbidden, is permitted. Otherwise, nothing happens.

[1] Knut Bleicher, *Organisation – Formen und Modelle* (Wiesbaden: Gabler, 1981), p. 361.

16.4.3 Build Trust[2]

Third, managers with strong implementation skills closely heed communication quality in all dimensions. They ensure that their messages are conveyed via sufficiently strong communication channels, and that they are substantial and understandable. They pay attention to the timeline when communicating. They ensure they are understood correctly. Most importantly, they ensure that they listen as well as talk. They create an algedonic channel through which they can establish contact with every employee and through which they can receive signals. They build trust in their team by being responsive and listening, but also by meaning what they say, thus demonstrating integrity. They are fair and avoid playing games in which employees only stand to lose. They refrain from applying mechanisms where employees stand no chance of winning. Finally, they go hard on the matter but soft on people.

16.4.4 Perseverance and Positive Thinking

Managers with strong implementation skills have the right attitude and demand the same from their employees. They are not optimistic, but realistic and positive. During their careers, they have learned to draw enough strength from the 10% of daily success (sense of accomplishment) to tolerate the 90% of daily trouble. They focus on the positives and force themselves to always find unexpected opportunities in problems and difficulties. They bolster what is going better than expected. They accept the principle of "no resistance, no change." They also know that a new solution will attract a small number of outright supporters, an equally small number of outright opponents, and a large number of employees who see reorganization like 160-year-old, bearded, Bavarian engineer: "Schaungmer mal, dann wermer scho sehn" (Let's wait and see). Such more or less indifferent employees wait to see what happens.

Hence, managers with implementation experience pay little attention to outright detractors to avoid signaling that implementation is worth opposing. They know that they, their management team, and their employees will undergo various psychological phases (resistance, uncertainty, reorientation, and consolidation) in the new organization. Precisely because they know this, they have enough perseverance to endure these phases. They adjust to the fact that long-established (entrenched) behaviors will not change overnight. They also acknowledge that many members of the enterprise are still struggling with the new situation, which proves that they are experiencing "change" that will bring real change. Finally, they try to find *that* example that proves things can be done as quickly as possible. More effective than

---

[2] Fredmund Malik, *Führen, Leisten, Leben: Wirksames Management für eine neue Zeit* (Frankfurt, New York: Campus, 2006), pp. 147–156. English edition: *Management: The Essence of the Craft* (2010).

presentations are people who demonstrate things, because what one person can do, others can do too. In 1919, British pilots Alcock and Brown demonstrated that non-stop transatlantic flights were possible; a few years later, Charles Lindbergh, the "Flying Fool," followed suit; yet another few years later, Pan Am launched the first transatlantic airline. And shortly after Reinhold Messner and Peter Habeler climbed Mount Everest for the first time without oxygen, many other mountaineers suddenly managed to do likewise.

17 Quick Diagnoses

Recognizing patterns is a key skill of effective managers. In everyday conversations, meetings, and observations, they do not assess situations based on analysis but recognize patterns based on their experience and without lengthy deliberation. If they have enough experience, these assessments are usually correct or at least capture the essential point. Experience means that the patterns we have experienced and learned condense in our minds over time into a model that we use to explain the world to ourselves. Whenever we observe, understand, and explain something, we do so with the help of our mental model of that thing.

Therein also lies a danger: We would rather doubt our observations, especially if they do not fit our model, than question the model itself. How often, for example, do we squeeze someone into our model of them: When our child does something that does not fit our model of it, we tell ourselves that our son or daughter is not quite themselves at the moment. Or we ignore our observation. As noted in Sect. 1.5, Copernicus did not see what the most experienced astronomers before him had seen, even though they were observing the same sky. The model determines what we see and what we miss, and thus gives meaning to perception. Thanks to his improved model of astronomy, Copernicus reached very different conclusions than his predecessors. Einstein, too, gave us a new view of the world by shifting axioms that now enabled parallel lines to cross. However, most people tend to adapt the facts to their model. If that model is too simple, blind spots arise. Logically, we remain unaware of these as long as we do not change our model. This leads to poor situation assessments and wrong decisions.

Experience alone therefore is not enough, not even in organizing. According to the Conant-Ashby theorem, we must be prepared to expand our model of a good organization due to the higher complexity and dynamics of the world, and due to all the unsolved problems—and also because, according to Einstein, we can never solve the problems with the same thinking that created them. In the current transformation phase, from the old world to a new one, as described in the Prologue to this book, choosing the right models is crucial.

M. Pfiffner, *The Neurology of Business*, Management for Professionals,
https://doi.org/10.1007/978-3-031-14260-4_17

Hence, well-managed enterprises pay meticulous attention to which management models are used and that all managers use the same model. This is the only way of creating harmonious and effective management teams that not only pull together but also pull in the same direction. These companies consciously protect themselves against mental pollution caused by managerial fads and fallacies. In medicine, too, great importance is attached to the *quality of models* in training physicians. As part of scientific discourse, the existing models are constantly questioned and improved based on new findings. Nowadays, for example, a general practitioner can make a relatively accurate diagnosis in a short time based on the patient's symptoms and clinical picture. The physician recognizes the pathological pattern, which leads to the principal causes and indicates where he or she needs to look more closely. Similarly, we can use the Viable System Model to read an organizational situation in detail and quickly assess it based on recurring patterns. We make the same observations, yet reach different conclusions than by applying the models of the first two dimensions of organizing. *Practical experience and a powerful model thus complement each other to produce a spot-on diagnosis.*

In my work as a management consultant, I have repeatedly encountered several organizing patterns, which are described below as examples. My goal is to show how the Viable System Model (VSM) can be used to identify what otherwise would be overlooked. I also show that the VSM serves to make amazingly accurate quick diagnoses whenever we are looking at an organizational structure—be it our own enterprise, a customer, a supplier, or a recreational association. Like a chess player competing against 20 opponents at the same time, the VSM allows us to quickly grasp the situation, as well as recognize the underlying patterns and the corresponding options.

I refer to the following seven patterns in a figurative sense as physical or mental pathologies. While this enables focusing on the neuralgic points in the respective structure, it does not mean that the enterprise in question is doing badly or is "sick." Enterprises are often surprisingly robust because they offset organizational weaknesses with management performance or favorable circumstances. It does, however, mean that the enterprise has relevant weaknesses or gaps in its control organization that will most likely manifest sooner or later. When the first symptoms become evident in the form of control and communication problems, we can locate them and know what to do.

For every pathological pattern, I briefly highlight how this situation arises, what symptoms to expect, and what the path to recovery looks like. Anyone who finds themselves and their organization caught in one of these patterns should not be alarmed: The majority of today's organizations fit one or even more of these patterns. In our public enterprises, we have resigned ourselves to the fact that we often make things harder for ourselves than necessary. In a market economy, as we all know, you do not need to be good, but simply better than your competitors.

17.1 Dissociation

17.1.1 Situation

The pattern of dissociation concerns the *functional organization*. It often arises in an early phase of the enterprise, when being consciously designed for the first time. The whole is subdivided into specialist disciplines or functions according to the principle of "combine what belongs together," so that specialists are among themselves. The organization thus becomes coherent, responsibilities are clear, and specialist knowledge is bundled. Especially in the early stages of an enterprise, this can be necessary in order to strengthen the individual functions. For example, Leo Fender, the famous pioneer of the electric guitar, initially performed most of the functions in his company himself: workshop manager, buyer, salesman, accountant, and above all developer. All at the same time. Growth and success forced him to give up some of these functions. He hired the best specialists in their respective fields that he could find. They boosted success by bringing technical expertise and experience to the enterprise. The workshop manager optimized production processes, the buyer ensured good purchasing prices, and the accountant optimized taxes and capital costs. In a functional organization, professional expertise can be used and developed in the best possible way in every position. So what is the problem?

The purpose-fulfilling, operational units become functions (e.g., production, sales, development, logistics, service). Looking at this organization in Fig. 17.1, we are first struck by the large environmental overlaps. The operating units are mutual *"internal customers,"* all sharing the same external customer in the same

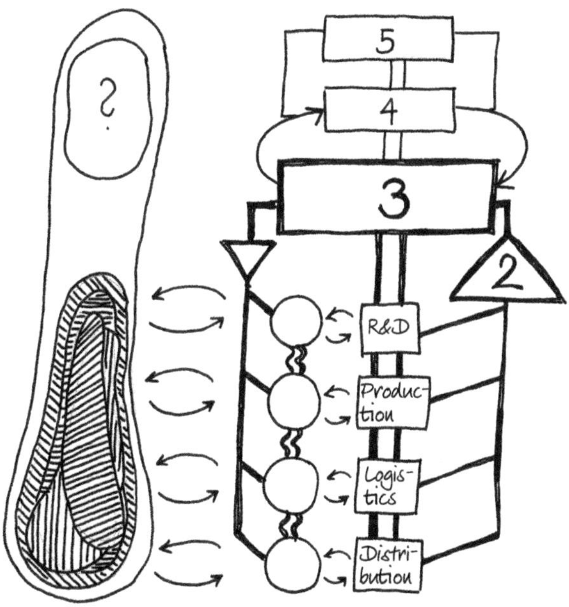

Fig. 17.1 Dissociation (functional organization)

environment with the same competitors. In reality, however, there is only this single, *external customer* to which all functions are oriented, because customers are defined by the fact that they can also say “no” occasionally. Internal customers cannot. All possible environmental overlaps between the functions must now be precisely controlled, or irritations will occur. For example, the customer calls the sales department to inquire about the delivery of his product. Because it is still in quality control, he or she is put through to that department, from there to spare parts, then to logistics, and at some point, the customer hangs up, frustrated. Although we have all experienced such situations, many environmental overlaps must and can be managed well. Digitalization, in particular, provides Systems 2 with powerful new tools to ensure coordination. Nevertheless, overlaps remain a weakness of the organization. The more complex the enterprise becomes, the harder the job gets—to the point where, as business grows, complexity becomes so rampant that it overwhelms management.

And yet, it is not only large environmental overlaps, but also powerful operational interdependencies (the squiggly lines) that place the highest demands on control. They are so strong that we can no longer speak of viable units, because no unit can succeed without the other. In this respect, the functional organization functions like a rowing team, in which all rowers are rowing toward the same goal; or like a ballet company whose dancers perform the same choreography in sync and according to their roles. With the piece given and the script fixed, there is little room for interpretation and spontaneity. This organization is strongly controlled by the vertical axis. This is fine as long as we are dealing with a stable goal, or if the audience has clear expectations about the piece of music being performed. In a more volatile environment, however, the operational units have too *little room for maneuver* and, above all, they cannot assume real *responsibility*. Negative feedback loops are broken by departmental boundaries. Self-stabilization is difficult, and the system tends to work itself up.

17.1.2 Symptoms

Due to these significant dependencies and environmental overlaps, the onset of the *“blame game”* is one of the first symptoms of the functional organization reaching the limits of its controllability. In this phase, no one wants to take responsibility for anything anymore, and problems are externalized (i.e., blamed on others). Dissociation sets in: Production points the finger at sales, the latter at R&D, the latter at quality control, and the latter at production.

Another symptom is increasing *bureaucratization*, with which the supporting, indirectly productive functions (e.g., HR, marketing, auditing, or IT) seek to make their task easier for themselves. However, process formalization is either not taken seriously by the operational units or generates rising costs, followed by decreasing productivity and motivation. Systems, committees, and meetings spring up like mushrooms. Excessive bureaucracy (“bloatedness”) emerges, in an attempt to absorb the exponentially growing complexity of the enterprise, but is increasingly unable to do so. This limits the self-organizing power of the operational units and shifts the focus away from the customer to internal coordination.

System 3 has to manage a large part of the operational business itself. Whenever System 2 is overwhelmed, it has to put out fires, resolve conflicts, and make decisions. Senior management often loses itself in *micromanagement* in such structures. It inevitably takes over functions that should be performed by the operational units. This is exacerbated by the fact that many managers love exactly that. Thanks to their success in an operational unit, they have been promoted to senior management, where they prefer to continue doing what has made them successful: Manage the operational unit. That is where they know their way around, and where they feel comfortable.

Notably, the *vertical communication channels are very thick*. Variety is largely absorbed by these channels, since it cannot be absorbed by System 1 itself. The functional organization thus also places great demands on the functioning of these communication channels. While this might go well for a long time, it remains a weakness of the organization and may take effect when a certain complexity threshold is reached.

Since operations largely absorb the capacity of senior management, there is little time to work on Systems 4 and 5. The enterprise tends to focus inward, (i.e., conservatively on itself). It looks at the market from an *"inside-out" perspective*. It develops products and services and asks itself who might need them and how best to distribute them. It is—probably quite rightly—proud of what it does and can do. In the case of dissociative disorder, however, *adaptability* suffers. Orientation toward the product rather than the customer and too much inward focus can land the enterprise in trouble, especially when the target begins to move and audience expectations have changed.

17.1.3 The Path to Recovery

Remedial action begins here. The successful, functional organizations that I have seen have made *focusing on the customer their preeminent guiding principle*. They forced themselves, throughout the organization, from senior management to operations staff, to constantly ask themselves how they could make the customer's life even easier. Customer value was their uttermost priority, to which they subordinated everything else. They staffed their System 4 with strong people, whose sole task was to monitor trends and changes (in markets, competitors, and technologies), and to prepare the business to cope with these with new products and services. These organizations focused on something they were really good at provided they were functionally structured.

Once the business becomes large enough, the autonomy of the operational units needs to be strengthened to enable them to take responsibility and absorb complexity. This requires *examining segmentation*, as we did in Chap. 8. If, as can be expected, a segmentation variant has clear advantages over the CURRENT organization, we need to check whether reorganization is possible. Equally important is diagnostic Step IV (i.e., checking the allocation of mission-critical tasks to central or decentral units). The functions previously performed centrally must be distributed to the operational units as far as possible in accordance with the criteria mentioned in Chap. 12. This requires a certain size.

From the functional organization, we must distinguish the functional distribution of business in a board of directors. Senior management can easily divide itself up by function, and normally does so. It is only when the operational, purpose-fulfilling units are divided by functions (which only together amount to a business) that we diagnose potential dissociative disorder. Although serious, this is part of corporate teething problems. Most larger companies have experienced such a disorder at one time or another. In many cases, it even boosted their development.

17.2 Schizophrenia

17.2.1 Situation

Schizophrenia is a dysfunctionality that tends to happen at a later stage of corporate development. It occurs primarily in the adolescent stage of enterprises, when they are experiencing their strongest growth and need to figure out who they really want to be. In the example in Fig. 17.2, the enterprise used to be organized in terms of sales regions in order to bring the sought-after product to the regional markets as efficiently and accurately as possible. In fast-growing markets, this can be important in order to quickly occupy terrain through customer proximity and better service. In a later phase, the strategic focus (of our sample enterprise) shifted to innovation, brand, and product because the markets were now saturated. Product range, marketing, discounting, new products, and new business models thus became more important than the short distance to the customer. Therefore, product divisions were created, which were supposed to once again generate more product innovation, cohesion, and cost awareness. Here begins the pathology.

Because "regional princes" have become the strong people in the enterprise, we cannot plonk product heads in front of their noses. After all, the regional managers are key figures on whose competence the enterprise wants to keep relying. *As a result, it shirks what has meanwhile become a necessary decision: Should the product or the region take the lead?* Product-oriented, global business units are established and assigned the same rights and duties as the regions. In this way, no one is deprived of anything and everyone can—supposedly—only win. If other dimensions need to be optimized, for example, the diverging needs of different customer groups, these are also turned into operational units. The most challenging anatomy that I have ever encountered was at a large supplier to the automotive industry. The company was trying to optimize four different control dimensions simultaneously. Its System 1 consisted of four different types of operational units, all sharing the same environment. Section 2.5 has already discussed this popular escape into the matrix.

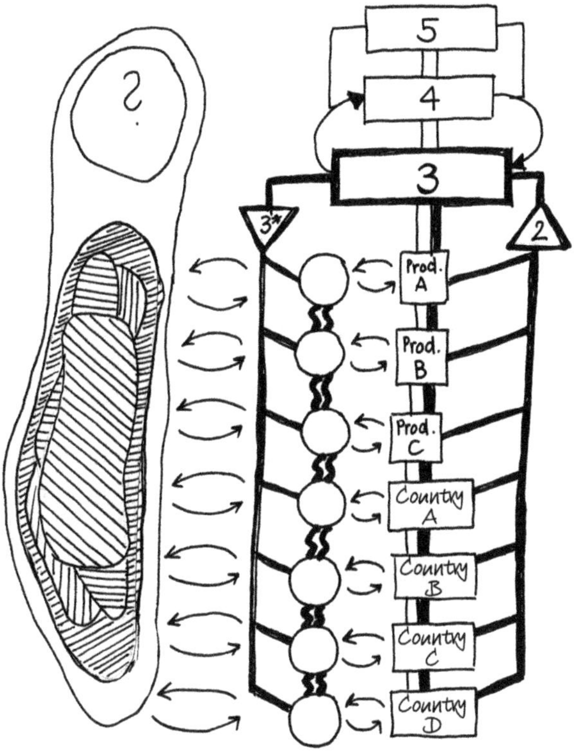

Fig. 17.2 Schizophrenia (matrix organization)

17.2.2 Symptoms

The problems of the *matrix organization* resemble those of dissociative disorder: large environmental overlaps, strong operational dependencies, and thus very little agility in the operational units. However, the clinical picture is even more pronounced because we double the number of units responsible for results by introducing the additional, equivalent control dimension. The matrix organization, therefore, not only has very different operational units, but also a many of them, all unable to manage their problems independently due to their interdependencies. Sooner or later, the *manageability of the enterprise* is inevitably put to the test, because the variety of the horizontal control axis increases enormously and exceeds that of the vertical axis. The First Axiom of Management is violated (see Chap. 10).

Coordination effort increases exponentially because the *number of interfaces has been maximized*. It absorbs managers in vast amounts of major and minor coordination meetings, thus demanding enormous discipline and emotional robustness. Besides the *increasing number of meetings*, the symptoms of schizophrenia in the enterprise include the simultaneous *loss of productivity, loss of transparency, and loss of responsibility*, because, once again, the negative feedback loops have been ruptured by departmental boundaries. Consequently, the entrepreneurs in the enterprise grow frustrated and demotivated, and good people leave the organization. Self-organization is hardly possible. As a result, the enterprise collapses sooner or later if it continues to grow. Or it hits a wall due to its strategic myopia, because there is no time to work on System 4 nor on enterprise development. Senior management capacity is again absorbed by operations.

As with dissociation, vertical control channels are necessarily strong. In particular, the *corporate intervention or command channel* is very likely to be heavily used to occasionally crack down and impose order. It is, however, difficult to hold the operating units responsible for anything because responsibility has disappeared somewhere between the dependencies. Sometimes, the command channel is then used even more fiercely. As a rule, these interventions are not sustainable. On the contrary. In larger enterprises, this creates the impression of autocracy and ivory tower behavior among employees, since senior management no longer knows the many operational units sufficiently well to intervene competently in concrete issues—unless it has established a sufficiently strong System 3*, consciously and in good time. This, however, is usually not the case.

17.2.3 The Path to Recovery

Remedying corporate schizophrenia requires deciding according to which control dimension the enterprise should primarily be managed. Do we allow regional management, product management, or customer group management take the helm? The enterprise must figure out what it wants to be: a service world champion, a product or technology leader, a sales channel specialist, or whatever other segmentation options come to mind (Chap. 8 discussed how to work this out). Only by taking this decision does the enterprise again focus on optimizing customer value and on strategy implementation. Thus, the chosen primary control dimension provides the operational units in System 1. These develop their strategies, make operational plans, and account for results. All other units become supporting functions. These are not expected to grow autonomously but to provide efficient service.

Here, *the challenge is primarily human*. In our example, the former "regional princes" (country managers) must be turned into globally responsible product managers. Are they willing and able to do this? The opposite is also conceivable: Product areas were first established yet later lost their strategic importance to regions. In this case, key people at headquarters must be prepared to move abroad with their families. Otherwise, executives previously responsible for a business will become division or department heads of central functions. For some of them, this can be a problem. We, therefore, need to examine which key people we might lose as a result of reorganization and what that means for the enterprise. We will manage to offset losing some of them, as we are usually already dealing with larger, adolescent companies. The good people, however, will be pleased to see responsibilities clarified again, the focus turned outward again, and room for maneuver reestablished.

All other changes can easily be made because they simplify the enterprise. As with dissociative disorder, System 2 and the supporting units, which have meanwhile presumably become bloated, are purged. Freed-up resources are used to reinforce System 4, which presumably has been neglected, while the management systems and internal accounting modes are adjusted. The physiology of the enterprise (i.e., the second dimension of organizing) remains largely unaffected because the core business processes essentially remain the same, even if responsibilities have shifted to a new control dimension.

17.3 The Bottle-Neck

17.3.1 Situation

Another pattern often encountered in markets in their initial or final stages is the bottleneck organization. It is characterized by a particularly strong, authoritarian System 3 that controls primarily through the command channel. In a fast-growing, dynamic market, this can be important to quickly set the enterprise as a whole on a different course and to shift priorities. In a saturated endgame market, where competition is mainly squeezed out on price, it can be important to reduce costs. However, I have also encountered the bottleneck for completely different reasons, as in a globally active medium-sized company in the capital goods industry. This family-owned company, meanwhile in its second generation, experienced its heyday in the last 10 years. It quickly developed from a European market leader into a world market leader. At the same time, the operational management in all divisions was replaced twice in the past 10 years. The owner's son was the owner and, since his father's death about 15 years ago, the sole managing director. He knew the business from scratch and had driven the company's success to date.

17.3.2 Symptoms

I first spoke to the owner. He told me about his company's successes and about his pride in leading his father's factory into a good future. But he also told me that he would not be able to bear the strain much longer. The long working hours and absences from home had taken their toll on his health and had wrecked his private life. He was proud of the company and its successes, he said, but one thing really bothered him: He had to do everything himself. The divisional heads kept running to him, and he was having to spoon-feed them. Nothing worked without him. Change was urgently needed with the divisional heads, because he had become the bottleneck of the company's development.

Next, I spoke to the divisional heads. They also first highlighted their great successes and their pride in the company and its products. Only one thing bothered them: the boss. At times, his authoritarian behavior was very unpleasant. They had enjoyed far more entrepreneurial freedom in their previous management

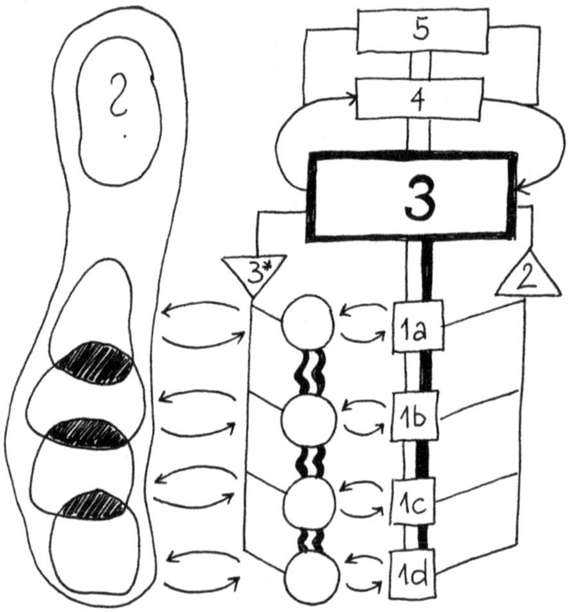

Fig. 17.3 The bottle-neck

positions. He took decisions in their areas of responsibility, but was now so far removed from the operational business that most of these decisions were at least dubious. Three out of four divisional heads were, therefore, already considering their resignation.

The next day, the divisional heads and the CEO conducted a quick diagnosis of the company with the Viable System Model. The resulting diagram corresponded roughly to Fig. 17.3. After 2 h of discussion, the situation was clear. The root cause of the company's problems was located in a completely different place than everyone had previously thought. It transpired that the divisions had significant environmental overlaps and were highly interdependent in terms of production and development. Many functions were also located at headquarters for purely historical reasons. This had never been changed despite the increasing maturity of the divisions, which had grown strongly as a business. The company as a whole had also developed strongly in recent years. New business areas had been added and service had been professionalized. The company's System 2 had not been able to keep pace with this rapid development. It was severely underdeveloped and in some cases nonexistent. Its IT systems were outdated and had drifted apart in terms of content in the divisions, making it difficult to gain an overview. Personnel development tried to satisfy individual wishes, otherwise doing only what was necessary. The rulebooks were obsolete or nonexistent, and almost no committees or meetings existed for coordination or learning purposes.

Thus, divisional structure and the centralization of many very formal services already limited the divisional heads' scope of action from the outset. An underdeveloped System 2 means that conflicts arise and that the system starts oscillating.

Since System 2 cannot perform its attenuating task, the next system must try to do so. This is System 3. In our example, this was the owner, in his capacity as the sole managing director. And here a vicious circle began: The owner had to spend more and more time "troubleshooting" the business and putting out many small but delicate fires. As a result, he had less and less time for his System 3*, that is, to visit the shopfloor, customers, and suppliers, as he had learned from his father, and which he had done, often and gladly, in the past. He thus somewhat lost his feel for the business. He had also long since withdrawn from all the associations and committees outside his own company in which he had previously played an active role. Since there was also no other time to work on System 4, there was a lack of clarity about the strategic goals that the entrepreneur had sketched out in his head yet never clearly formulated and communicated. At times, moreover, he was not sure himself whether the company was developing in the right direction. It was really only driven by opportunity. The divisional heads felt that their boss was making decisions arbitrarily, without no discernible consistency, and therefore saw major challenges ahead for the company. All this, coupled with the boss's autocratic behavior, had increasingly led to conflicts on the System 1–3 channel.

17.3.3 The Path to Recovery

What makes this example interesting is that both sides, the owner and the divisional heads, had *looked for the problem in the people involved instead of in the structure*. The owner felt that his divisional managers were no good, while they saw him as the cause of all evil. It was only when they looked at the jointly developed diagram that they realized what the real problem was. Neither their organizational charts nor their process descriptions had adequately captured the situation over the past few years. The managers' mood changed immediately after drawing their company's Viable System Diagram and after diagnosing the situation. As long as they had located the problem in people, they considered changing or even solving matters impossible. Yet no sooner had they identified the structural cause than the solution was already in sight.

The subsequent joint examination of segmentation according to Step I had revealed that the overlaps and dependencies were unpleasant yet unavoidable. The business was uncompromisingly focused on the customer—which might explain its successes despite internal squabbles. The solution, then, was to systematically develop System 2 around the areas of mutual dependencies. The rules of the game were jointly defined, coordination meetings were created, and IT was placed on a new footing so that it could support operational management much better. As far as possible, tasks crucial to success were shifted to the divisions, which helped streamline head office. The autonomy of the operational units was thus strengthened, enabling them to respond better and faster to important events. To strengthen System 4, a joint strategic planning process was developed, and overarching System 4 responsibility established. The divisional heads were involved in an extended management team in which they had to take the view of the company as a whole.

From this bird's-eye view, they began to understand the unpleasant measures that affected their division and that they would otherwise have tended not to support from the divisional manager's frog perspective. Last but not least, the owner was once again able to do more of what he actually liked best, namely, visiting customers and employees to learn from them what could be further improved in the company, and to actively contemplate all of this on the golf course.

17.4 Uncontrolled Growth

17.4.1 Situation

Figure 17.4 shows a company with strong operations. Here, the foundation of the house is right, and thus the most important aspect of the entire organization is right from the start. The operational units enjoy great autonomy. They manage the complexity of their environment independently. Also, their overlaps with and dependencies on other operational units are manageable. System 2 works and is sufficiently developed. However, the other control functions of senior management are only very weakly developed. In reality, the environment of the whole company is no greater than the sum of the environments of all its operational units. Hence, the operational units mainly optimize themselves, the company is only concerned with today's business, and senior management lacks its own, higher level view, both outward and into the future.

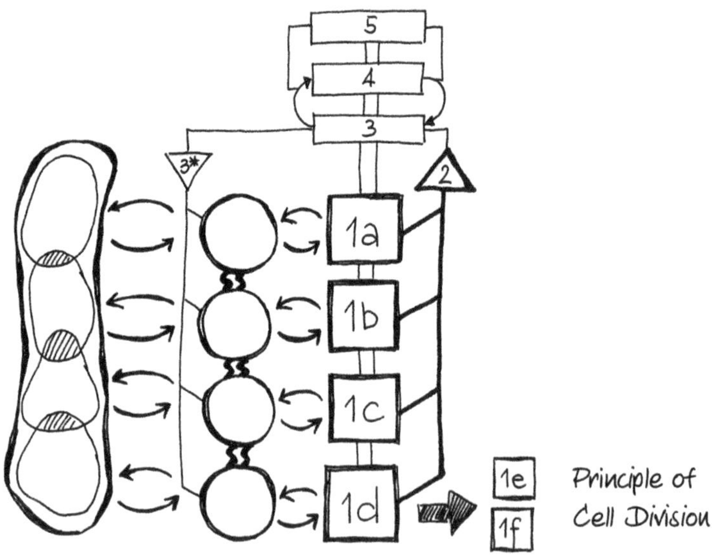

Fig. 17.4 Uncontrolled growth

I have often encountered this pattern in companies in the high-tech sector or in the consumer goods industry. It is often caused by dynamic, short-lived, or fast-growing markets. These require autonomous units that can quickly zero in on different customer benefits and adapt agilely to environmental changes. In dynamic markets, acquisition opportunities arise from direct contacts from within the operational units. In this way, they discover suitable businesses and acquire them. Or they split into several businesses because they have grown so quickly. In this sense, System 1 operates on the principle of cell division, as we would expect from a healthy organization, but grows in an uncontrolled and opportunity-driven way. Innovations only emerge from today's businesses. The strategy of the whole company is the sum of the strategies of all operational units. *The whole is no more—yet also no less—than the sum of its parts.*

17.4.2 Symptoms

The problem is the *cohesion of the whole* because *overarching control is missing.* Senior management is almost imperceptible. The organization's strong centrifugal forces in the dynamic market are not countered by a sufficiently strong centripetal force to hold the parts together as a meaningful whole. The business grows, as it were, from below and in different directions, and thus increasingly loses strength and identity. It becomes bogged down. Looking at the horizontal control axis shows that the number of businesses is increasing, that they are increasingly diverse, yet can at least control themselves sufficiently well. The high level of horizontal diversity needs to be absorbed. This requires an effective senior management team, or this company will sooner or later destroy itself. Its operational units do not support each other today and will fight each other in the future, because sooner or later conflicts will arise from the environmental overlaps. The enterprise also exhibits large duplications in all functional areas. Synergies are not exploited because no one feels responsible.

In a young, growing market, it is possible to live with these symptoms. Long-term, however, the enterprise will not be able to survive like this. Long before the markets reach their saturation phase, the enterprise must *learn how to be stronger together* to ensure it will be strong enough when it enters the endgame phase. Saturated markets have too many suppliers and as a rule refocus on the remaining seven plus/minus two suppliers, each having a large enough market share to drive costs down to the required level. Exploiting this market share requires a strong System 3. The enterprise as a whole (yet not the divisions) is also *strategically short-sighted* and only innovates on its own merits. While it might take note of basic innovations, it will not take them seriously if they require adjusting the business portfolio. The enterprise focuses on today's product or service, leaving innovations to emerge in terms of "more of the same." The enterprise does not use its own potential and risks breaking apart sooner or later due to the egos of its operational units.

17.4.3 The Path to Recovery

Building control systems takes time. Hence, it is better to start sooner rather than later. Some of the enterprises that I have supported have hit the road and begun building up senior management functions. The operational units realized that every unit would have to invest resources in this build-up, although ultimately their own autonomy would come under pressure as a result. Since the business is managed chiefly by the operational managers, they are the strong people in the enterprise. Normally, they are reluctant to give up their autonomy if their unit cannot benefit from doing so. In enterprises that have successfully broken out of this pattern, the *heads of the operational units have therefore been integrated into senior management functions and feedback loops have been established that have encouraged their self-interest in collaboration.* The previous entrepreneurs in the enterprise were promoted to the next higher level of recursion in addition to serving as operational managers. First, they participated in committees and later in governing bodies. In this System 3 role, they were concerned mainly with synergies that benefited their own business, among other things.

Forums were developed for the *self-coordination of decentral functions* (e.g., R&D, production, sales or quality assurance), through which they could learn from each other where they needed to learn. The functions themselves remained within the competence of the operational units so as not to weaken them. Only where functions were neither critical nor crucial to success were they merged and professionalized. Eventually, first projects were created, and subsequently permanent central functions, which began to work on the common future issues in System 4. Human resources development began tentatively at first, later systematically, in order to discover and facilitate opportunities for employee development in other operational units. In this way, these companies preserved their leaders for the future and established the *redundancy of potential command* early on (cf. Chap. 6). They also systematically train their managers to have a common understanding of management.

In sum, this pattern concerns a viable enterprise that is performing well on the front lines. However, striking the right balance between the autonomy of the individual unit and the cohesion of the whole may be difficult and might cause turmoil. Therefore, we should not wait too long to intervene, to enable proceeding incrementally before painful interventions become necessary. In particular, we must ensure that development does not stop at System 3. The *System 4 function* is not fundamentally in the interest of the operational units, because they have their own System 4. At the overall enterprise level, they feel that money and personnel are only spent on highly questionable things anyway. Decisions made from this overall System 4 perspective can ultimately threaten their own existence. For this very reason, it is also important to train managers to embrace a common understanding of these mechanisms, and thus to develop a language within the enterprise with which these issues can be meaningfully discussed. I have seen a number of enterprises, also ministries or NGOs, which had no significant System 4 in place for similar reasons. In such cases, System 5 collapses into System 3. Executives in

System 5 become involved in purely operational issues because they used to work in these areas themselves and still like to grapple with them. Without a System 4, an enterprise will behave like a brain-amputated animal: It is alive yet only responds to stimuli.

17.5 Dominance

17.5.1 Situation

The next pattern often arises in enterprises that have *grown up in their home market* and expanded beyond regional borders into foreign countries. At a certain stage, their positions in regional markets differ significantly, and even the regional markets are suddenly so different that they can become a challenge for managing the enterprise. Figure 17.5 shows a dominant, operational unit. It is much larger and much stronger than the other operational units. It is the traditional home market, alongside which a number of relatively small operational units are serving other regions.

The dominant unit has all the functions required by a viable unit, because only this unit existed in the past. The other regions, on the other hand, started out as pure sales organizations. They have few resources and little autonomy. Except for sales,

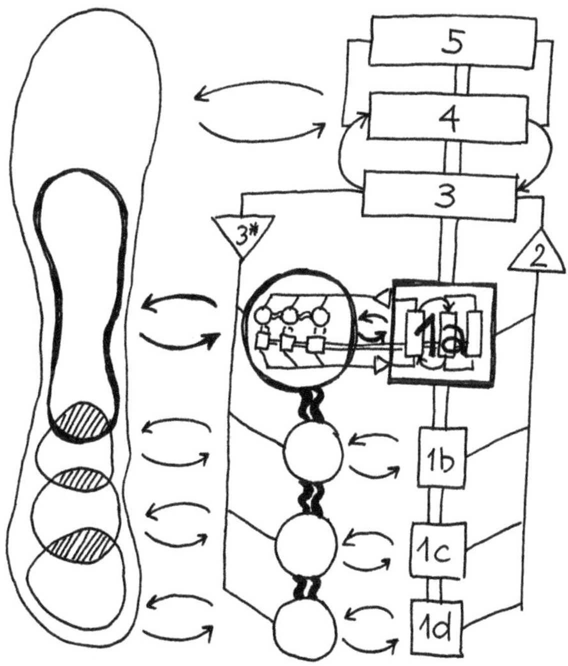

Fig. 17.5 Dominance

they must request everything needed to function from the dominant unit. There, decisions are made from the perspective of the home market.

Deciding to expand abroad creates a new level of recursion. Setting up operational units also in other regions turns the home market into one of several operational units, albeit the most important and largest one. At this stage, some things often are confused. Instead of designing a new level of recursion, the enterprise pretends that the home market is also this new level. Legally and politically, this is the simplest way, but it remains mistaken. It has not worked long-term in any enterprise that I have encountered. Typically, the management of the home market remains what it has been in the past: the management of that operational unit. Managers do not move physically or mentally to the next level of recursion. The lines between headquarters and home market are blurred, and responsibilities are unclear.

17.5.2 Symptoms

As a result, *dominant decisions are made in favor of the home market* wherever overlaps and dependencies are perceived as unfair and arbitrary. Senior management spends 80% of its time in the dominant unit. This is where money is made, while the other operational units still cause more trouble than pleasure. In the dispute over internal resources, therefore, the home market regularly wins. This is understandable, yet dangerous. For instance, a medical goods supplier was deliberating the right color for support stockings. For cost reasons, the company only wanted one color, although regional tastes differed. In the home market, marketing demanded that the stockings should be white. In contrast, marketing in southern Europe insisted on black stockings because white does not sell in southern countries. Such conflicts paralyze and burden an organization, or, at best, create a tendency toward the lowest common denominator. In the case of support stockings, people were on the verge of agreeing on gray stockings to keep the peace, which probably would not have sold in either market.

These problems are also familiar in other industries that are structured regionally due to different cultures and tastes. In Spain, an oven must have a roasting spit because it is part of Spanish cooking culture. But a roasting spit is not a typical feature of a German oven. In Italy, savory cookies must be seasoned according to a different recipe than those in England, because otherwise no one in Italy will eat them. While the price-performance ratio may have to be adapted to the local market, having a strategic discussion about prices and quality with the home market is difficult. These differences elude this market (or rather its management). After all, one believes one knows the business sufficiently well. The autonomy of the smaller, operational units is severely restricted by the ignorance of the dominant unit. Accordingly, they tend to receive too little attention from senior management, which is still primarily controlling its home market and seeking success there.

Consequently, building up new markets takes a very long time and is characterized by many internal disagreements and difficulties. There is a tendency to lose good people in the regions because they do not feel like constantly clashing with the stronghold-like, dominant unit. Conversely, it is difficult to persuade good people in the home market to take on management tasks abroad, especially if they have to fear that their envisaged position in the enterprise will suddenly be occupied when they return at some point.

17.5.3 The Path to Recovery

The enterprise must first establish what it really wants. It needs a thorough System 3–4 decision to balance today's business and tomorrow's, which must be overseen and guided by System 5. It is important that the owners also back the decision: Should the regions have the character of excursions into new areas, in order to sound these out and take advantage of any opportunities? Or are they part of a necessary and thus well-targeted entry into a new phase of the company's development, which entails relevant potential, but also conversion effort and investment?

In the latter case, *senior management* must first be staffed so that it can devote its time and *attention away from the home market to the new whole*. This initiates and becomes the most challenging task in the next phase of the business. Typically, this requires restaffing the appropriate functions in the home market. This can be achieved if the redundancy of potential command has been ensured in good time. In addition, mental relocation often also requires physical relocation. Otherwise, it is too easy to overlook nesting and to mix levels of recursion. We discussed this cardinal error of organizing in Sect. 2.7.

So far, the distinction between decentral and central functions and tasks has not been a major issue. Now, on the other hand, we must decide which functions and tasks should be performed at the newly created level of recursion. *Tasks crucial to success* needing to be centralized because they are otherwise unaffordable must be elevated to the new level of recursion. Failing this, the inevitable egoisms of the dominant unit prevent the whole from developing. For example, a central production unit serving all regions can no longer be controlled by the dominant, operational unit, where it was located previously, organizationally and perhaps also legally. What else might be expected than that this unit, which like all others is pressured to perform, would not first solve its own problems with all the resources at its disposal before thinking of the whole?

Tasks crucial to success that one afford to decentralize must be handed over to the operational units. These units must have the competencies needed to build up their region in their own hands. Only this will ensure they have sufficient *room for maneuver* to confront the complexity of their market. They must be measured and judged by *different standards* than the home market. They need the *full attention and full support* of senior management as the situation demands. Thus, looking at its organization tells us whether an enterprise is seriously expanding into new markets or instead pursuing a dubious "try it once" strategy, whether it is dabbling instead of "going for it."

Dominance as an organizational pattern occurs not only for these reasons and in this form. In a sense, the same mechanisms occur in other segmentations and other types of enterprises and lead to the same control problems. History, for example, shows that no republic, federation, or confederation survived for any length of time if one country or state was much larger and stronger than the other member states.

17.6 Multiple Personality

17.6.1 Situation

A multiple personality disorder is *as common in the nonbusiness* sector as in the business sector. It occurs when an enterprise joins forces with one or more other enterprises, for example, to optimize their shared value chain, to jointly manage a large project, or to achieve other, higher level goals. The enterprise contributing most to this value creation or that is closest to the customer or service recipient takes the lead. In effect, this creates a new level of recursion with its own identity, in which the collaborating enterprises each form an operational unit in their shared System 1. As a result, *Systems 2–5 must be developed jointly* for the project to succeed, and for matters to become manageable and viable.

However, to simplify matters and save effort, the enterprise does not build its own level of recursion but insteads attempt to control everything through that enterprise that has taken over the *management of the consortium or syndicate*. Greek *syndikos* means administrator. Accordingly, this enterprise takes over the administration for all other members—and integrates their performance into its own existing control system.

Figure 17.6 shows the de facto new level of recursion thereby created, with its operational units. Systems 1a and 1b are the two existing operational units of the leading enterprise. Systems 1c and 1d are two additional enterprises that are participating in the consortium. The senior management is no different from the senior management of the leading enterprise. It has no right to intervene and thus no vertical command channel and no System 3* that would reach into Systems 1c and d. These are integrated solely through a weak System 2 (meetings and project contracts) and slightly through a weak Resource Bargain and Accountability channel. *That aside, they float freely in the control organization.*

17.6.2 Symptoms

The complexity of the enterprise's own business on the horizontal axis increases because external operational units are added. Every operational unit now makes a different contribution to value creation. This increases the number of units and their diversity. Since at the same time essential control functions on the vertical axis are missing or are severely curtailed, the whole becomes unstable (cf. Chap. 10). The partners' various contributions are integrated at the level of the individual deal,

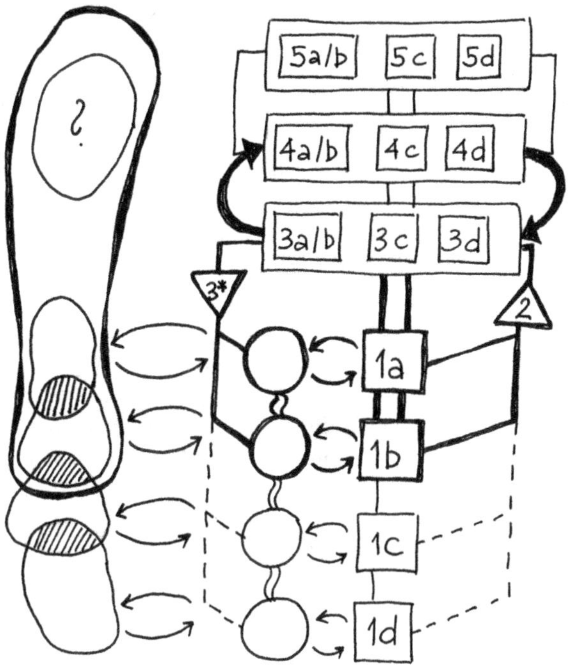

Fig. 17.6 Multiple personality

where, however, there is great potential for conflict: Will the partner really perform? And will they abide by the rules of the game—insofar as these exist?

System 2–5 functions are taken over by the management of the controlling enterprise, which, however, has too little variety because it does not understand the other enterprises in the consortium well enough and therefore takes too little account of their interests and possibilities. The corporate intervention channel from System 3 to System 1 is missing. It can hardly restrict the autonomy of the units involved where it would be necessary to optimize the whole (e.g., the value chain). Ultimately, the well-being of its own operational units is more important to this management than the consortium. The whole is actually only held together by an equally weak System 2. The first shocks overwhelm this structure. Moreover, the other structural elements are missing so that the enterprise can settle down again.

17.6.3 The Path to Recovery

As mentioned, the problem is that while a separate level of recursion with its own identity is needed, it is in fact missing. If the consortium is led by one of the participating enterprises, the latter will find itself in a difficult position. It is supposed to maintain its own identity while at the same time providing a common identity for all the other personalities now joining it eye to eye, so to speak. Identities compete and a *struggle for hierarchy based on interest and power* rather than on the relevance of information begins (cf. Chap. 6). The controlling enterprise subsequently protects itself from this with the help of *ignorance*, a well-known variety attenuator, by simply screening out the other personalities whenever possible. This, however, does not resolve the conflicts, but merely pushes them down to the level of the deal (e.g., a project).

The consortium has a different identity than its members. This must be respected by establishing bodies and committees outside a leading enterprise in which all partners are equally involved. A common System 3 must be built to consider and balance all interests, as well as a common System 2 in which the mechanisms for cooperation are bindingly regulated, and a System 3* that gives all members mutually defined insight into joint operations. Likewise, a common System 4 and System 5 are needed that account for all the characteristics, perspectives, and interests of the participating enterprises and thus provide the necessary variety. One way of achieving this is presented in Sect. 18.1. In all these control functions, the leading enterprise must also be perceived as no more than a primus inter pares.

17.7 Mindlessness

17.7.1 Situation

Mindlessness often occurs after failed reorganizations. While a new strategy or evolving customer needs change the anatomy, the neurology is not adapted to the new anatomy. One NGO, which first operated nationally, was originally founded to help reduce unemployment and alleviate suffering. Thanks to the enthusiasm and determination of its employees, the NGO grew over several decades. It multiplied its donation income and launched ever more extensive and ambitious projects that attracted positive attention. Later, international offshoots were established to coordinate international projects in different countries. These offshoots also worked successfully. In fact, they played a decisive role in project success because they were more familiar with local conditions and knew how to deal with local people and authorities. When asked how the enterprise had to organize itself to focus on what mattered to beneficiaries, the answer was clear: *The region rather than the issue* had to become the dominant control dimension. It was therefore decided to use the international offshoots not only for project coordination but to turn them into operational, viable units that would increasingly carry out their own projects in their own environment with their own donations.

In another NGO, active in the field of science, grant money was allocated to regional research centers and institutes to promote and fund research. Also operating successfully, this enterprise continuously expanded its budgets and the scope of its activities. The individual regional centers flourished, and numerous science awards and Nobel Prizes were won. With the increasing complexity of research projects, on the one hand, and increasing competition for scarcer funding on the other, it became ever more important to occupy few yet essential topics strongly favored by taxpayers and thus by the ministry of education and research. These types of projects are almost always interdisciplinary, and so managing a topic area or project now including many representatives from many research centers became a challenging task. It became evident that the primary control dimension, therefore, had to move *away from the region*, or away from the individual research center. The management of the individual thematic field in which one wanted to achieve an effect moved into the foreground and was recognized as the primary control organization. It was therefore decided to create an organizational entity per thematic field in the form of a program management that would control the center and institute representatives.

In both examples, for strategically correct reasons, *the primary control dimension* was turned around and responsibility and competence were assigned to new organizational entities. In both examples, moreover, the existing organizational entities continued to operate exactly as before. They continued to report directly to the senior management of the enterprise, as in the past, just as the latter continued to have the same discussions with them on the Resource Bargain and Accountability channel. The newly created operational units now followed suit.

17.7.2 Symptoms

Figure 17.7 shows the situation from the *perspective of the newly created program management* of a subject area in the science organization. As a primary control dimension, such areas must be operational units and as such viable. They acquire their own funding and ensure attractive programs whose results have an impact on society. They are responsible for results and develop their own strategic and

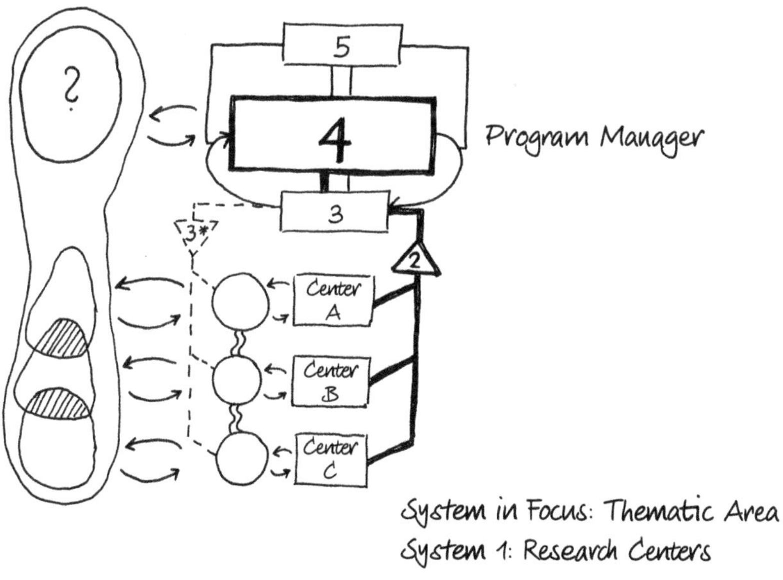

Fig. 17.7 Mindlessness (structure defeats strategy)

operational plans within the enterprise's parameters (flanking measures). The units active in the thematic field in the participating research centers and institutes thus become the operational units in its System 1. Since the management system was only expanded, yet neither revised nor adapted, the centers remained de facto as before as operational units at the same level of recursion at which the newly created program managements were added. Consequently, program managements had *no effective access to the resources* in the participating centers and institutes.

Although the situation in the organization as a whole resembles the pattern of schizophrenia discussed above, the dysfunctionality from the perspective of the program management one level of recursion lower is quite different. The lack of penetration into the centers (i.e., into its own operational units in the regions) makes it a management eunuch. It depends on the goodwill of the centers, which in case of doubt tend to optimize their own interests. This makes it almost impossible for program management to implement its thematic area strategy. Although program directors have taken on the task and the responsibility, they have not been given the authority to do so. The danger is that this consumes promising managers in the enterprise, unknowingly and without any malicious intent. They first take pride in being promoted to program managers. If they are still inexperienced, they do not realize until it is too late that they cannot achieve results in this structure. They are a thorn in the side of the previous center directors because they are seeking to exert influence, whereas the latter have their own plans.

By way of compensation, the program directors typically bloat their System 4 in order to balance the lacking penetration of their System 1 with even more technical competence through studies, expertise, and network vis-à-vis the centers. If they cannot decide and issue instructions, they must convince others in terms of substance. In addition, they inflate their System 2 in order to exert influence via manifold regulations. Toward the management, the centers use the resulting *bureaucracy* as the main argument why no program management is really needed.

Analogously, the same happened in the first example (the NGO in the field of unemployment), where the regional managements in vain opposed the established program managements, which are still best equipped financially. Figure 17.7 shows matters from the perspective of a region. Its operational units are the themes, that is, the individual projects, over which they have no control until they are funded and launched in their own countries.

17.7.3 The Path to Recovery

The cure is the same in both cases: The neurology must adapt to the changed anatomy. With the science organization, this means that, for legal reasons, the centers still prepare their budgets and balance sheets, but these may *no longer have any control relevance* for the enterprise. Management looks solely at the results of the program directors, their strategies and operational plans. *Center staff are allocated to programs*, but help each other out when necessary on-site, at the centers and between programs. They no longer have their *management and goal-setting meetings* with the center or institute director on site, but with the program director, who also evaluates their performance. Results are attributed to the programs. Essentially, the centers merely do the groundwork for the programs. *Staff development* (i.e., which researchers should be involved in which programs in the future or should lead which projects) no longer takes place in the centers but across the centers in the program. This does not suit the regional centers. Without such competencies, however, the new strategy remains a piece of paper.

Some of the previous management members in the centers will now manage a program. Since the centers already had certain thematic focuses and specializations in the past, allocation is straightforward. Some center and institute directors are retiring, while others are happy to take on a role with slightly less responsibility or to move to another center. Only when the management system is adjusted and staff issues are resolved do calm and traction return to the organization.

Strictly speaking, this pattern is not about headlessness, but tetraplegia, that is, the disconnection between the enterprise's head and organs. These function on their own, but make volitional control impossible. A similar, yet reversed pattern was widespread about 20 years ago: the cephalopod. During the "New Economy," the existing economic rules were discarded. Highly optimistically, new patterns were assumed according to which trees would suddenly grow into the sky. The startups subsequently traded at the stock exchange at dizzying amounts consisted mainly of heads. They had no body to speak of. Their purpose was to generate expectations that were then sold on the stock market. To do this, they had large development departments in System 4 and prominently staffed boards of directors and advisory boards in System 5. What they did not have was a System 1, that is, customers who bought their products and services. Enormous sums of money were earned, only to be lost in a single swoop after the dotcom bubble burst. *Most of all, viability requires a functioning System 1. Visions are not enough.*

The patterns of dysfunctionality discussed in this chapter do not amount to an exhaustive list. They are common examples intended to demonstrate the diagnostic power of the model. In each example, the problem was assumed to lie elsewhere prior to diagnosis. Only in the course of working with the Viable System Model were the real, structural causes recognized. However, the most neuralgic points were already recognizable in each case after the quick diagnosis. In this sense, the model resembles a pair of glasses that we put on when dealing with organizational issues. These enable us to see more *and* also more sharply than other lenses.

18 Balancing Present and Future

One of the most difficult tasks for senior management in the current transformation phase, in which so much is changing so rapidly, is to find the right balance between the necessities of today's business and those of the future business. The final chapter of this book, therefore, considers the *balance between the present and the future,* as well as between the *outside and the inside* of the enterprise. We have already discussed the System 3–4 homeostat and its importance for viability in Sects. 4.5 and 13.4. When it works, the enterprise learns. It renews itself and adapts to the changes in its environment at the same pace. This self-renewal mechanism ensures that the enterprise adapts and evolves in terms of a continuous steady state (homeostasis).

But what do the concrete mechanisms in such a homeostat look like? Which procedures favor correct answers to the question of when the enterprise should shift its resources from today's priorities to those of the future? And with what structures does it find its course despite adverse conditions ("bad weather") and lack of information? As humans, we can react immediately when confronted with an unexpected opportunity or danger. We recognize what is going on, consider the implications, weigh up the options, choose one option, take action, and make corrections if we have missed the target. We are able to catch a ball flying at us unexpectedly in a flash (or adeptly conquer our first love). These functions are engraved in our nervous system, run automatically and unconsciously, and make us excellent cyberneticists without our intervention. In our enterprises, on the other hand, the nervous system is fragmented, and therefore it may take a very long time from stimulus to decision-making (i.e., choosing one course of action rather than another). The necessary, neurological structures do not arise in the enterprise by themselves; we must consciously build and shape them. In practice, most enterprises struggle to make this mechanism work reliably and long-term. Three problems make this task difficult:

1. *We tend to see the old in the new.* What we have thought, seen, or done so far resembles a track in deep snow. The probability that our thinking follows the

M. Pfiffner, *The Neurology of Business*, Management for Professionals,
https://doi.org/10.1007/978-3-031-14260-4_18

beaten track is much greater than it striking out on a new trail. Once created, links in our brain resemble these tracks in the snow, so that our perception is shaped by what we have done or seen so far. We perceive changes only with a certain delay. The more successful the past was, the more likely what does not fit into what has worked will be suppressed or not perceived at all. This phenomenon is also known as *"perceptual hysteresis"* (Greek for deficiency or lagging behind). The problem with blind spots is that we are unable to locate them. Most executives struggle to "become empty," in order to see new things and allow new answers to take effect.

2. These are the most difficult issues facing the enterprise and which it needs to decide. Senior management is confronted with the entire complexity of these issues, in which professional, specialist viewpoints play as much a role as economic, social, or political ones. None of these decisions can be viewed in isolation, neither within the enterprise nor on the time axis. The issues are interconnected and the consequences of decisions can only be predicted to a very limited extent. Since, according to Ashby's law, we cannot ignore these interconnections and transversal (cross-cutting) effects, many perspectives must be taken into account, and therefore many people from different functions must be involved in finding solutions. *Knowledge is distributed throughout the enterprise, and people do not talk to each other of their own accord.* Every department works for itself. R&D does not talk to market research, nor does HR speak to IT, just as divisions do not talk to each other. Yet neither we can simply stick them in the same room. If we do, only those shouting the loudest will end up being heard. We need a method that uses the intelligence distributed across the enterprise.
3. This must happen quickly. With the old methods, we analyze and discuss matters ad infinitum, as well as act too little and too late. The numerous studies and planning reports sitting on people's shelves become outdated faster than they can take effect. No one has time to read them. Thus, we need to jettison the old planning methods, which were created for a less dynamic environment and have not infrequently degenerated into planning bureaucracies, and to become *faster and more effective.* With the help of new technologies, we are basically able to control in *real time.*

The simplest way to balance System 3 and System 4 is through meetings. Agendas control which meetings deal with System 3 issues throughout the year and which are deliberately dedicated to System 4 issues. *Projects* such as a strategy development project also focus all relevant functions and key people in the enterprise on a System 3–4 issue for some time. That alone, however, will not suffice in the future. We will have to prepare for even more complex questions, which we will need to answer even faster and more comprehensively than meetings and projects allow for. The enterprise's brain capacity is exhausted with conventional methods. Nevertheless, we are only at the beginning rather than at the end of our possibilities. Two of these, presented below, have proven themselves in practice, across the world and in all types of enterprises.

18.1 Beyond Dispute

How can we find even better answers to even more complex questions in even less time? Answers that take into account all the relevant interconnections and ones that can actually be implemented? The most powerful computer available to us is still our brain. Nevertheless, one person alone can do little. He or she is trained and experienced in one or two specialist areas, adopts a certain perspective according to his or her responsibilities, and is subject, like all of us, to the perceptual hysteresis described above. Thus, to focus expertise from all relevant disciplines and perspectives on an issue, we need to bring several people together. And since we also want to implement these solutions, will-formation must take place among a critical mass of key people in the enterprise. But how do we bring these people together so that they can really use their *collective intelligence* and reach agreement? This is not simple. If, however, we succeeded in connecting 20–40 brains so that they function as a single brain, we would have created an immensely powerful computer able to consider all professional, economic, social, and political points of view.

How do we structure a large group of people without forcing them into the customary, deadly straitjackets (hierarchy or method)? After all, they are supposed to arrive at a comprehensive answer to a complex question within a few days, while developing the common will to actually implement this solution. Which *communication structure* and what *self-regulatory mechanisms* ensure that this system ultimately produces more than the sum of its parts—instead of ending up, as is so common, either in dispute or with the lowest common denominator? How often is consensus the solution that no one really wants and is therefore doomed to failure from the start? What structure instead brings about consensus in terms of the greatest factor shared by all of those involved?

Beyond Dispute: The Invention of Team Syntegrity: Titled thus is a book by Stafford Beer in which he describes his interpretation of cybernetics as applied to this question.[1] To this end, participants attend a *2–4-day retreat* and follow a cybernetic (instead of ecclesiastical) protocol, as in a papal conclave, which leads them to the solution of their issue. However, we are not merely electing persons, the path to the white smoke (signaling election) is much more complex. The crucial question is: How do we interconnect those involved to enable something new to emerge? Different *networking patterns* lead to very different results. The "silent mail" pattern, for example, in which one person passes on something to another, inevitably leads to nonsense. In enterprises, the so-called "layers of clay" between the levels of recursion alter or impede message content. Other networking patterns are conducive to quickly convey a message. If, on the other hand, we want to share knowledge and experience and arrive at new ideas and insights, this requires two-way communication, or conversation: a process of mutual learning,

[1] Stafford Beer, *Beyond Dispute: The Invention of Team Syntegrity* (Chichester, New York, Brisbane, Toronto, Singapore: Wiley, 1994), pp. 210–224.

understanding, and inspiration. This requires a networking pattern that allows everyone to hear everyone else and to respond immediately, as in a jazz combo. This works well with small groups (up to five people). How, though, might this work in a *large group of 30 odd people*?

Such retreats or conferences take place every day in countless domains across the world: Within individual enterprises, between multiple enterprises, and in political committees and bodies. However, the procedures, methods, and protocols applied normally tackle variety from the wrong side. They destroy variety so drastically before it even begins, leaving no room for truly innovative ideas during retreats. They merely dampen but do not amplify. I have experienced the resulting frustration several times over the past 20 years, as a participant at scientific or political conferences or in business conferences.

For instance, at a Middle East peace conference on Lake Geneva in Switzerland, some 30 high-ranking representatives of the Jews and Palestinians gathered for 4 days to resume talks for the first time after a long hiatus. Just 2 h after the conference began, the first crisis arose because neither side agreed with the agenda, although it had been prepared with great diplomatic instinct by the organizers (members of the inviting institution). The guests wanted to discuss other matters. By defining an agenda, most common conference protocols curtail variety to such an extent that everyone knows the outcome in advance. An experienced assistant can use the meeting agenda to write the minutes before it even begins. As for scientific conferences, at some point, people began publishing the results (the conference proceedings) before the conference took place. In corporate retreats, as a rule one presentation follows another, so that the only time participants get to talk to each other is during the breaks and over a beer in the evening—which turns out to be the most productive part of the event. Nothing new can come from such protocols. They only replicate yesterday's thinking and logic. Beer, therefore, dedicates *Beyond Dispute* "to the open mind" and quotes a piece of ancient wisdom at the beginning: "He that answereth a matter before heareth it, it is a folly and shame unto him."[2] *We want to master and utilize complexity—not simply reduce it.*

Back to our peace conference: After a compromise on the agenda had very skillfully been reached, over the next few days participants convened in a large hall somehow recalling Versailles. The chair was clearly identifiable by its position on an elevated platform. Every seat had its own microphones and the tables were arranged in a large U. Topics were dealt with sequentially according to the same pattern: Discussions began with a keynote address. Next, participants listened to speeches, which they could respond to by raising their hand. A moderator guided the ensuing discussion. Because everyone sat at the conference tables knew that with 30 participants they would get at most one chance to say something, no one stopped talking once it was finally their turn. As 10 min had usually already passed since the show of hands, no statement was related to the previous one. Instead, people spoke to position themselves and their opinions. Not those who had something to say spoke,

[2] Book of Proverbs 18:13 (King James Version).

but those who had not yet had their turn. The communication channel was completely overloaded, and misunderstandings, impatience, and anger soon arose even among the most attentive participants. Instead of a conversation, an argument ensued, with the divisions between the parties growing deeper and deeper the longer the conference lasted. During the breaks, there were small discussion groups and groupings, in which presumably the essence of this conference emerged, so that the official protocol seemed like a useless, even rather disturbing frame. During one break, a senior and experienced Jewish representative, who had already attended the Camp David negotiations in the late 1970s, told me that not people and lacking opportunities were to blame for such events never producing viable results, but their protocols. Having seen similar meetings fail so often, he had given up expectations, but never hope.[3]

I made a similar experience at a climate conference in Brazil. Participants soon felt manipulated: They suspected that the organizers knew the outcomes of the conference in advance and only needed the participants to claim that the results had arisen from proceedings. Participants felt they were being used for purposes that were not their own. Again, nothing common or new emerged after 4 days. The old-style protocols were not designed for collaboration, but for speeches and presentations. The executives with whom I spoke about their retreats and will-formation processes in enterprises also judged the benefits to be too insignificant, apart from networking.

Thus, we are attempting to solve twenty-first-century problems with sixteenth-century communication processes. Although conference and meeting organizers are aware of this, they nevertheless choose the established path to avoid being accused of making mistakes. The danger of falling victim to contrived creativity techniques or computer gimmicks, or other fads on which many providers ride their luck, is too great. This is how expertise is wasted and, above all, how opportunities are missed.

At such retreats, variety should not be destroyed from the outset by prefabricated categories in the form of a fixed agenda and presentations. Instead of answers, we first *search for the right questions*. For if we already had the answer, we would not need a retreat. Participants must find those topics that, in their view, need to be discussed in-depth. Only this enables them to contribute their knowledge, perspectives, and interests so that proceedings produce something worth implementing.

For every participant to subsequently be able to exchange ideas with every other participant on every topic, we need to *maximize connectivity between all participants*. The complexity of getting 30 people under control to accomplish this is staggering. It corresponds to the number of functioning or nonfunctioning relationships between those involved. Thus, according to the formula described in Chap. 9, these are two states (that learn something from each other or not) squared by the number of relationships. For 30 people, this amounts to $n(n - 1)$ relationships.

[3]Between 1992 and 1995, when Yitzchak Rabin was Israel's Prime Minister, Stafford Beer's method was used in the peace process between Israel and Palestine with great success.

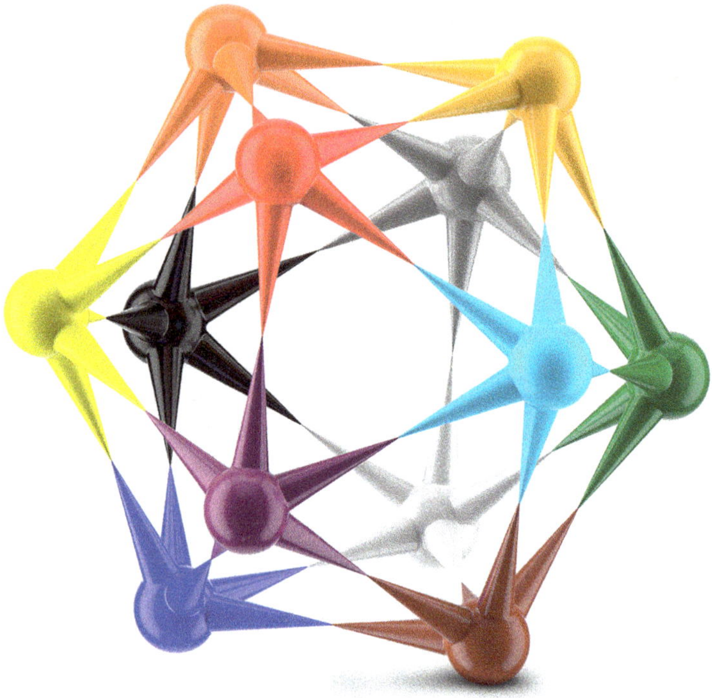

Fig. 18.1 The icosahedron: 3D communication structure

Hence, the formula for the variety of the control task is $2n^{(n-1)} = 2^{870}$. A conventional method would take an infinite amount of time to do proper justice to this enormous variety. Or it would use such massive variety attenuators as described above, which would also completely destroy the potential solutions contained in the variety. To harness the existing potential, we need maximum connectivity over the course of a few days. In addition, for good ideas and insights from individual discussion topics to cross-fertilize and inspire each other, we need to *minimize the information distance between all topics.*

The trick is to network the system of 30 people *not linearly but three-dimensionally*. This means curving the system into a ball (or globe) and closing it so that information, arguments, and good ideas can circulate within it. Stafford Beer found the ideal structure for this in the icosahedron (Fig. 18.1). Along with the cube, tetrahedron, octahedron, and dodecahedron, this is the most complex of the five Platonic solids. The symmetry and visual beauty of these regular polyhedra suggest their interesting mathematical properties, which we will exploit. For example, the icosahedron is known as the mother of the golden section, whose aspect ratios are repeated between all vertices. It also contains other important geometric shapes (e.g., the mystical enneagram used by Sufists and Jesuits).

In this three-dimensional communication structure, the cornerstones are the topics to be discussed. They are determined jointly by the participants on the first half-day of the retreat in a process specially designed for this purpose. The connections or braces between the cornerstones are the participants themselves, with *every brace representing one participant*. These connect, so to speak, the topics and their contents through their own person. This structure is *nonhierarchical*, because a globe has neither top nor bottom. It is also perfectly democratic, because every participant has the same possibilities to influence the outcome.

This is exactly what we need in this phase, because we want to use everyone's knowledge equally to reach a solution. Participants are only invited to the retreat if they have relevant knowledge or if they are key actors in implementation. We want them to stand by the solution in the end because they have developed it themselves. Whether the democratic form is also used for democratic decisions is an open question. In most enterprises where I have applied this method, the board reserved its right to decide but wanted to know the integrated opinion of its key people before deciding. In almost every case, about 70% of proposals were accepted, about 20% were revised, and about 10% were rejected or replaced with something else. If it were not so, and if the key people saw the world quite differently from the board, something would be fundamentally wrong with the enterprise.

To quantify this three-dimensional communication structure, Stafford Beer uses the so-called Bavelas measures. These were developed by Alex Bavelas at the time of the Josiah Macey talks to describe social structures as networks and to make them measurable and comparable.[4] The icosahedron achieves maximum values in all categories: Group Dispersion, Relative Centrality, and Periphality. These units measure how many steps it takes for every participant to reach every other participant, depending on the protocol, and how centrally or how peripherally participants are positioned in that network by the protocol. These factors influence the chance of individual participants making good proposals heard, as well as the intensity of networking and the emergence of working morale and combative spirit.

Besides the step from two-dimensional to three-dimensional space, we also move from a 90° to a *60° angle*, which exists in the icosahedron between all braces. The icosahedron consists entirely of *equilateral triangles* and therein lies hidden an interesting property. We humans normally build at 90° angles and stabilize our architecture via compressive forces: Something is held upright because something is pushed down. If we look around us, all 90° angles in our environment are made by humans. We live—and think in a certain sense—in a Euclidean space and in a 90° style. Nature, on the other hand, prefers to build in a 60° style because evolution favors the equilateral triangle for designing robustness and efficiency. The shells of microorganisms in the sea, called diatoms, stabilize so much with this style of construction that Alfred Nobel used them to tame nitroglycerin and make it robust

[4] Alex Bavelas, "Communication patterns in problem groups" (1952), In: *Cybernetics: Transactions of the Eight Conference*, 1951, Josiah Macy Jr. Foundation, New York.

enough for his dynamite. Even our own cellular tissue is arranged in a 60° rather than in a 90° style.

Richard Buckminster Fuller, the American Leonardo da Vinci of the modern age, employed the 60° principle to build geodesic domes consisting solely of equilateral triangles, which became more stable the larger he built them. He thus overcame the previous maximum size of about 45 m in diameter of a classical dome, whose masonry is stabilized by compression. Today, the largest geodesic domes have diameters of over 200 m, with minimal use of materials. The structure is stabilized not by compression, but mainly by the *tensile forces emerging between the 60° angles. The triangles transform, so to speak, the pressure into tensile force, and vice versa.* Buckminster Fuller suggested that nature exists in an omnipresent equilibrium between tensile and compressive forces. While the two forces were long known to exist, the fact that they coexist and cooperate in all physical systems was not known. Buckminster Fuller called his design principle, by which a structure is held together primarily by tensile forces, *"tensile integrity"* or *"tensegrity."*

We can imagine that push and pull also work in a discussion group. It wants to reach agreement and therefore pushes toward a common point, but also pulls the whole apart time and again through arguments and counterarguments. The communication structure of the icosahedron distributes these forces evenly across the whole, thus ensuring stability and robustness. Vice versa, group members are under pressure to find a solution for every topic, but the structure keeps tearing asunder hasty and superficial solutions to gain depth. The tensile forces result from every participant performing three different functions. They are members of certain topics, and as such responsible for results. With other topics, they are critics, observing, questioning, criticizing, and adding to the discussion being conducted by its members. Finally, they are observers of other topics, where they merely listen and quietly reflect. The imperative to listen and reflect gives participants the chance to understand other views and to broaden their own understanding. In addition, the three different functions (member, critic, and observer) attenuate the variety of 12 topics to a level that is digestible for the individual. Tensegrity is created primarily by the critic function, which connects all 12 topics inside the icosahedron, stabilizing the structure through traction.

The integration of different viewpoints through tensile forces occurs synergistically, which explains why Beer called his method *"Syntegrity" (synergistic tensile integrity).* In fact, the properties of the icosahedron produce an effect known as "reverberation." The synergistic engine ensures that several people are smarter than a single person—which is normally not necessarily the case. The world of information works differently from the world of energy in this respect: If you harness two donkeys to a cart, they are automatically twice as strong as a single donkey. If, however, you harness two brains to a task, they are not automatically twice as smart as a single brain. Fully exploiting the potential 870 personal relationships among 30 key people requires reverberation.

Reverberation works as follows: When any of the 12 topics are discussed, members sit at the table, critics in the second row, and observers at the very back of the room. Every group meets in this configuration three times for 1 h each. The

Fig. 18.2 Reverberation

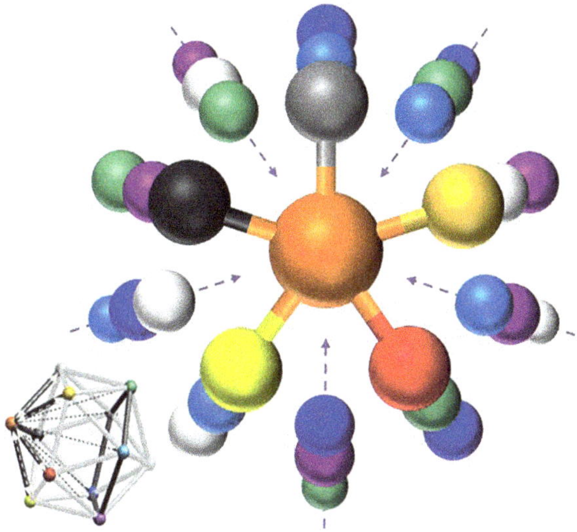

topic members at the table are accompanied by a "facilitator," who supports the group, as well as mirrors and summarizes their discussion, so that the members only need to think and talk. They do not have to operate computers or follow creativity techniques, but simply do what they always do: talk to each other. Reverberation occurs automatically because of the structure, which formats the groups so that the *most up-to-date knowledge from all other thematic discussions is available in every discussion.* The presence of the members and critics alone means that the knowledge from all other topics exists, redundantly, several times in every group and can be used for further discussion. In particular, this includes the good ideas, good arguments, or aspects to be coordinated. These are brought from one topic to the other via participants' short-term memory. What impressed them in one topic, in the shape of new insights and ideas, they carry continuously from one topic to the next. They select and filter out what is good, interesting, and useful from all the discussions. Every good idea and every important insight thus begins to enter the three-dimensional structure, is multiplied and distributed and, as if by itself, seeks its place in those topics where it can make a contribution. To illustrate this: Someone expresses a good idea about one topic, which is heard by all members, critics, and observers in the room. Some of them carry this further into other topics, from where it is, in turn, carried further into other topics until it hits the person where it started in the neck again from behind. In practice, participants feel how good ideas multiply in the course of the retreat and how topics begin to grow together and coordinate themselves as if controlled by an invisible hand.

In Fig. 18.2, the circle in the center represents one of the 12 topics being worked on by its five members. Each of the five members is itself a member of a second topic (large circle), a critic of two other topics (smaller circles), and an observer of four other topics (not shown). Also indicated (with dotted lines) are the five critics of the topic, who are also critics of a second topic and members of two additional topics. Thus, when the topic is discussed in the middle, all the information from the other groups is available in *multiple, redundant* ways. If an idea from another group is useful, or if two topics need to be coordinated in terms of content, someone will bring that into the discussion. The effect of reverberation is therefore that the topics coordinate themselves and that sensible proposals multiply, complement each other, and develop from group to group over three rounds without anyone controlling this. The process controls itself.

As with the Viable System Model, a structure based on cybernetic principles ensures self-control and self-coordination, because communication in a large group of people must also be organized to enable higher levels of performance and *"control by communication."* As a rule, such retreats begin with an opening question that describes the greatest challenge currently facing the enterprise. This may concern very different issues, such as developing a strategy, shaping the organization (cf. Sect. 16.3 Phase B), post-merger integration, cost reduction, conflict resolution, or lauching a major project. Based on this opening question, participants are selected and invited. During the first half-day of the retreat, they then whittle down the still immense variety of the opening question to 12 topics that they think need to be discussed. Next, each of the 12 groups, each comprising five members, five critics, and some observers, discusses their topic for an hour and produces a first interim result, which is written down by the facilitators. This is followed by a second and a third round of discussions, which build on the previous ones and develop the topic further. After three rounds, the structure has distributed 90% of the information across all topics, which can be calculated in terms of the so-called *eigenvalue*.[5] The *eigenvalue* involves the system in continually returning to itself, that is, to what it contains. It is a measure of how much a system can calculate itself or, in our case, observe itself and become self-aware. In fact, by the end of such a retreat, the emerging group consciousness might be called *"alignment."* The group has generated a 90% common view and a common will.

In the end, we have an answer to the opening question in each of the 12 topics, which *fit together like puzzle pieces to form an overall picture*. All relevant perspectives have been incorporated into this answer. The result is actionable because it is comprehensive, concrete, and not only understood but desired by 30 key people. In my personal experience of over 200 such retreats on all five continents and in all different types of enterprises and cultures, expectations have been positively surpassed every time. The method is so robust that it works with top managers at the corporate level as well as in federal ministries, in SMEs with practitioners, in scientifically oriented NGOs, or even with illiterates. It does not depend on technology, creativity techniques, particularly good facilitators, or especially disciplined people. It works with the people we meet in our organizations. And it is almost infinitely scalable to smaller or larger forms. In their recent book

[5] Stafford Beer, *Beyond Dispute: The Invention of Team Syntegrity*, pp. 210–224.

Cracking Complexity, David Komlos and David Benjamin call this method "the breakthrough formula for solving just about anything fast."[6]

18.2 The Operations Room

The enterprise can balance its "Outside & Then" and its "Inside & Now" with very simple means, meetings, and projects. It can do so more elaborately, if necessary, by bringing 30 key people together for 4 days to solve their respective greatest challenges. And third, there is the middle course presented in this section. What these three forms of balancing have in common is that each establishes a particular structure so as to elicit a desired behavior on its own. On one occasion, it is the structure of the agenda so that System 4 issues receive sufficient attention and space in the minds of senior management. On another, it is the communication pattern that enables discussing a complex issue among many key people. Or it is a physical structure: the so-called *Operations Room.* This is a *decision-making space* where senior management works on its System 3, 4, and 5 issues and whose physical design fosters correct decisions. All three structures use the same cybernetic principles.

The design of those rooms where important decisions are made today goes back to the old world of the twentieth century. These are large, prestigious rooms with a large oak table at their center and a projector and whiteboard fitted on a wall. Information is distributed via large documents in emails and via long presentations. However, the users of these rooms are subject to their own neurophysiological limitations. Thus, it makes no sense to flood them with data they cannot digest, assuming they read the documents and follow the presentations. It is absurd to present these data in such a way that the relevant patterns remain hidden within. Just as it is dangerous to operate with outdated data. And yet, precisely this happens.

Today's boardrooms are also too often preoccupied with the past. Especially in publicly traded companies, senior managers tend to think short-term: Good quarterly figures must be delivered to keep shareholders happy and the company's stock value up. Such thinking reduces board members to past-oriented data, such as incoming orders, sales, profit, and profitability ratios. Yet executives in other types of enterprises are also primarily concerned with the past in these spaces. They look in the rearview mirror to see what has happened in recent weeks and months. But we can only manage the future (however near), not the past (however recent). Our job is to manage, and that requires previews that reach beyond the usual level of expectations for the next 3 months.

If the enterprise has planning departments that a priori should not exist, we often find them at the end of a branch in the organizational chart. They are engrossed in their models and frustrated by their inability to influence the thinking of managers. Typically, such departments have a communication problem with senior

[6] David Benjamin and David Komlos, *Cracking Complexity: The Breakthrough Formula for Solving Just About Anything Fast* (Boston, London: Nicholas Brealey Publishing, 2019).

management or the Operations Directorate. Report creation, formal committees, or informal conversations between them seem too weak to have any real impact. Departments are perceived as troublemakers vis-à-vis what operational management is trying to accomplish. Their reports are not read, and the informal conversations, while effective, can also be suspected of seeking to take political influence. Thus, success depends on personal relationships—and thus on coincidence.[7] In this situation, such departments at least try to contribute with standards, defined processes, and ready-made tools. In the end, this escalates into a planning bureaucracy, whose real benefit must be questioned, even if all data were regularly tracked in the system.

What we need, however, is not unthinking plans, but thoughtful planning. If you ask those concerned how they experience such planning processes, they complain that it means going through the mill and that the effort could be minimized as long as last year's data are still reasonably accurate, because no one ever looks at these again. That might be overstating matters, but I have seen many larger companies work precisely like this. Jack Welch (CEO of General Electric) reportedly eliminated his entire strategic planning department for this very reason. He demanded that people think, not administer. He did not want "long-term planning," which gets its name from sitting around on shelves for a long time. Instead of routinely and diligently tracking forms, we should automatically recognize when and where something really needs fresh treatment and spare ourselves the rest of the effort.

Corporate planning cannot be delegated to a planning department. It must be done by senior management itself because this is its most important task. But we need better control centers in our enterprises to do this, to take work off our hands, to support our thinking and understanding in a brain-friendly way, and to focus on the relevant points. Once again, we are lagging behind the state of the art here, because the control centers of our enterprises are nowhere near as sophisticated as the control centers of our technical systems. Compared to air traffic control centers, the control centers of aviation companies (e.g., an airline or catering company) look pathetic. In both areas, the Conant–Ashby theorem applies equally: A system can only be brought under control to the extent that the control system has variety. Vice versa, *to the extent that the control system lacks variety, the system to be controlled will be out of control.* We are technically sophisticated at controlling logistics, production, or air traffic, but not yet good enough at controlling the enterprise.

This *lack of variety* in enterprise control first became apparent during World War II in the form of drastic information overload. The combined action of countless land, sea, and air forces in major battles produced an uninterrupted flow of reports that arrived at headquarters in an uncoordinated fashion. From the ever-changing picture that emerged from these reports, resource allocation decisions had to be made. In this situation, the British developed the so-called *"war room,"* where all military branches looked together at the same situation map, discussed matters with each other, and simulated options, while the incoming information was made

[7] Stafford Beer, *Brain of the Firm: The Managerial Cybernetics of Organization*, 2nd ed. (Chichester, New York, Brisbane, Toronto, Singapore: Wiley, 1972), p. 193.

immediately visible in real time on maps spread out on large tables.[8] This first interdisciplinary attempt to create an overall reality among all decision-makers by having them develop a common situation model based on real-time information had a major impact on the course of Britain's integrated defensive battle. The structure of modern *situation rooms* (e.g., of emergency and crisis teams) resembles these "war rooms." Enterprises whose business requires up-to-date overviews and rapid responses also use such rooms today. In most enterprises, on the other hand, we still find the standard boardroom, even though disruption has become the norm there as well. Thus, it would be time to reverse the logic and to build war rooms not to manage crises, but to use these room in such a way that crises do not arise in the first place.

Stafford Beer called his cybernetic interpretation of such war rooms the *"Operations Room."* Its role is to continuously balance Systems 3 and 4. It is where all formal senior management meetings take place. As the *control center of the enterprise*, it operates permanently and acts when something relevant happens. Its structure must take into account some key principles and include four building blocks. These can be designed in a very simple and "low-tech" way. They can be found in their most primitive design, for example, in the command post of a village fire department or on the armored personnel carrier of an infantry company camped out in the forest. The simplest means are used to post overviews and situation maps and to bring together the lines of communication. Even if the means are simple, they nevertheless fulfill their function. At the time of President Allende, Beer used the simplest of means to set up an operations room for the Chilean government. It was run in real time in the 1970s with a single, primitive computer and, with its learning filters, was able, although never quite completed, to prevent one crisis or another before the definitive coup in 1972.[9]

Meanwhile, countless "high-tech" versions of operations rooms exist (e.g., NASA's Mission Control Center in Houston) or government situation rooms (e.g., the White House in Washington). Most organizations are neither dependent on "high tech" nor limited to "low tech," but require a healthy middle ground. The structure of an operations room, whether high- or low-tech, remains invariant. The principles by which it is designed include a *factual logic, a sociopsychological logic, and a chronological logic.*[10]

Regarding *factual logic*, the question is which essential variables need to be balanced in the first place. We should not be satisfied with the available data, but must ask ourselves what we really need to control and design IT accordingly. Our market share is relevant whether we know it or not. So we should know it better. Normally, what we really need to know is much less than what we accumulate in our systems and reports anyway. Chapter 8 has introduced and justified the truly

[8] Stafford Beer, *Brain of the Firm*, pp. 241 ff.

[9] Stafford Beer, *Brain of the Firm*, pp. 162–166.

[10] Sebastian Hetzler, *Real-Time Control für das Meistern von Komplexität. Managing Change durch kontinuierlich richtiges Entscheiden* (Frankfurt, New York: Campus, 2010), p. 22 and 45ff.

necessary factors. They are based on Aloys Gälweiler's strategic navigation system,[11] as well as on the findings of the empirical strategy research program PIMS,[12] and have been summarized by Fredmund Malik as *key success factors*:[13] market position (consisting of market share and relative customer benefit), innovation performance, productivity, attractiveness for good people, liquidity and cash flow, and profitability.

On their own, operational data and financial metrics, on the other hand, are strategically misleading. Alone, they tell us nothing about viability—only about survivability, and merely for a short time. In the short term, we can minimize costs and maximize profits by, for example, postponing necessary investments or write-offs. We survive, and possibly even reap rising share prices and bonuses, but damage our viability. Vice versa, there may be great potential for success that is simply poorly exploited by the current management and explains why our operating figures also look bad on their own. Thus, it always takes both sides—the operational information of System 3 and the strategic information of System 4—to see the full picture and to make the right decisions in terms of long-term viability. Precisely that is the task of the operations room: to show senior managers information from both areas and thereby provide them with a comprehensive picture of the health of the enterprise as a whole. For nonbusiness enterprises, these factors can be adapted mutatis mutandis.

The principles of *sociopsychology* ensure that interaction behavior and the characteristics of human perception are taken into account and supported. They recognize the limited ability of humans to absorb and process information, but also take advantage of their ability to recognize patterns. An operations room is intended to be what for the Greeks, translated into Latin, was a *phrontisterium*, a thinking room. Paper and laptops are therefore banned from the room because otherwise people will hide behind them and undermine communication. Instead, large, interactive screens are positioned on the walls for users to work together. Great emphasis is placed on how information is presented. Everything we know from psychology about perception, pattern recognition, and consciousness tells us that we should form our judgments based on relative sizes and shapes, colors, and movements. Our brains, on the other hand, are not good at dealing with large sets of numbers. It should leave that to computers, which present information in a way that is appropriate for the brain, in the form of graphs and in relative motion. Our brains are not analyzers, but recognizers. For example, a balance sheet, itself a simplified representation of complex content for the otherwise overburdened brain, can also be shown more ergonomically as a quantified flow chart with thicker or thinner lines, or

---

[11] Aloys Gälweiler, *Strategische Unternehmensführung*, 2nd ed. (Frankfurt, New York: Campus, 1990), pp. 23–52.

[12] Robert D. Buzzell and Bradley T. Gale, *Das PIMS-Programm: Strategien und Unternehmenserfolg* (Wiesbaden: Springer, 1987). English edition: *The PIMS Principles: Linking Strategy and Performance* (1987).

[13] Fredmund Malik, *Strategie: Navigieren in der Komplexität der neuen Welt* (Frankfurt, New York: Campus, 2011). English edition: *Navigating the Complexity of the New World* (2016).

Fig. 18.3 The operations room

as an "iconographic model" with larger or smaller circles and boxes. Only the symbolization (icons) and animation of content makes data become meaningful and actionable information.

Regarding *chronology*, it is important to make planning independent of fixed time horizons, artificial rhythms, and periodizations. It must be set up as a permanent process. Today, it no longer suffices to conduct a strategy process every few years, because the half-life of strategies becomes shorter, the more dynamic the environment becomes. This does not mean that we must constantly develop new strategies, but we do need to constantly review the premises on which our strategy is based. New strategic considerations are needed when the premises change. And we need these considerations immediately. In operational planning, too, plans must constantly be adapted based on new information. Certain planning cycles are prescribed by law, such as budgeting, accounting, or certain meeting cycles. Functioning planning complies with these regulations, without succumbing to their bureaucratic standards and fixed time horizons. It updates plans when this has become necessary (cf. Sect. 14.1). In an operations room, therefore, both operational and strategic information must be available permanently, simultaneously, and up-to-date so that it can be kept in view.

Four walls in the operations room, which need not be square, are dedicated to four specific control topics (Fig. 18.3). How strongly these walls are supported by information technology is, as observed, not the crucial point. But it is important that they keep irrelevant information away from the user. The problem in our decision spaces is not primarily the lack of information, nor the lack of relevant information, but the flooding with irrelevant information—which is often compounded by misused information technology.

18.2.1 Information and Alarm

On the first wall, the *control variables* listed under *factual logic* above are displayed. Advancing digitalization is making it increasingly easier to show all variables in their current state. Today, we should not make decisions with data representing the world as it looked 1 month or several months ago. In a dynamic environment, control must occur in real time, which it can today. Section 14.1 has already considered synchronicity, as well as the problem that our control systems have long been unable to keep pace with the rate of environmental change. Already in 1967, the Six-Day War between Israel and Egypt was over before the UN could even convene a meeting. We need the same real-time control for our enterprises that we have already established for our technical operations, for example, in the form of production control based on the Kanban principle or a subway control center that has contact with and access to all trains and whose reservation system is interconnected online. Today's technology also enables controlling the enterprise itself in real time.

Second, data must be filtered to avoid drowning in them. The logic needs to be reversed: *Not managers should have to look for information in systems or reports, but systems should alert managers when something requires their attention.* If productivity is dropping in a plant, the control system should alert us that we need to act and provide ourselves with additional information to be able to take action. Thus, the control center is not supposed to measure the past, but to *detect instability*. If something is out of balance, we need to look at it and act.

Filtering, however, always also reduces variety and must therefore be done correctly. The most common way of filtering is to form averages and sums. This may enable filtering out what is decisive and really interesting from the data. For example, if one hospital patient has a temperature of 40 °C, the second a normal temperature of 36°, and the third is suffering from hypothermia (32°), on average everything seems fine and in order. So we need *intelligent filters* that detect instabilities and changes and that direct our attention to where management needs to act. Modern statistical techniques interpret incoming data against the background of an indicator's past behavior, and they are able to learn. Time-series data at a given point in time can either match expectations based on past history (no change), be an outlier, indicate an unexpected change in degree, where something stabilizes at a new level, or changes its gradient (i.e., trend). Only with changes in degree and trend changes do the filters in the operations room generate *alarm signals* that draw the attention of management to these developments.[14]

Special attention must be given to *algedonic information*, that is, recognizing the unexpected. Most common reporting systems tend to filter out surprises. For senior management, however, it is much more important to know what is unexpected than what went well or poorly. Every surprise must be taken seriously and analyzed, even if this sometimes turns out to be merely an insignificant anecdote. Surprising and

---

[14] Sebastian Hetzler, *Real-Time Control für das Meistern von Komplexität. Managing Change durch kontinuierlich richtiges Entscheiden*, pp. 152–154.

unexpected success is especially significant. We must discover it, ask ourselves what it means, and take advantage of the opportunity that may be hidden in it. After all, the easiest way of surviving problems is to make them irrelevant through successes.

The *Triple Index* proposed by Beer to measure performance is also interesting.[15] It consists of three indicators: actuality, capability, and potentiality. Actuality encompasses what we actually achieve with today's means and constraints. Capability describes what we could achieve if we got the most out of things under the existing constraints. Finally, potentiality encompasses what we should do to develop our resources and reduce constraints within the limits of what is possible. Productivity, then, is the relationship between actuality and capability. The relationship between capability and potentiality is latency, and the relationship between actuality and potentiality is performance. This can also be calculated from the product of productivity and latency. This triple index is useful because it integrates *the views of both System 3 and System 4*. Contrary to orthodox reporting schemes, it shows the damage a manager can cause by optimizing only the present, thus destroying the company's market reputation, which will be needed in 3 or 4 years. Neither the income statement nor the balance sheet indicates this nonperformance.

18.2.2 Memory

The second wall is dedicated to the *enterprise's memory*, the *"model of itself."* It must show a model of the enterprise to which everything we know about the enterprise is allocated, and which guides us through that memory as a navigation aid. The Viable System Model (VSM) is particularly well-suited to this purpose, as it encompasses all the information relevant to control, assigns it to levels of recursion, and categorizes it into the five subsystems. The VSM, as discussed in Sect. 15.3, thus breaks down variety into manageable units in a manner that is comprehensible and appropriate for the control system.

We also need the memory system to provide an overview of our resources and of the decisions and actions we have already taken. Whenever we want to know something more specific about ourselves, we can access the memory system. This is where, for every level of recursion, we can find the applicable regulations and policies, the annual calendars and other overviews in System 2; the annual goals, budgets, meeting minutes, and operational plans in System 3; the strategy, functional strategies, and market intelligence reports in System 4; and the corporate policy concepts and business mission in System 5.

When we plan and weigh up options, we need to know what resources are available to us so that we can actually implement a plan in the end. Planning, after all, is not about future states, but about actions taken today so that the future will be different. All planning ends up with measures or actions that someone has to take care of. Thus, first of all, we need to remember what we have already decided in the

[15] Stafford Beer, *Brain of the Firm*, pp. 162–166.

past, which projects, actions, and measures are being implemented, what their current status is, and who is taking care of what. This gives us an overview of the available resources and thus serves as a prerequisite for planning and prioritization. Second, in addition to this *operational controlling of measures*, we also need *strategic controlling*, which keeps our strategic premises, goals, and the distance to success permanently in our sights. And third, an enterprise should recognize events, topics, opportunities, or problems above a certain criticality and significance as an "issue," define them and assign responsibility for them to someone.

The memory system ensures that all these premises, measures, actions, projects, and issues are not forgotten. After all, as discussed in Chapter 16, implementing things once they have been decided is difficult for many managers because they lose sight of and forget them. The operations room supports managers in maintaining focus and the necessary overview so that priorities are set correctly when resources are too scarce—and when are they not?

18.2.3 Planning and Simulation

After the model of the company itself, the model of the outside, that is, the environment, is displayed on the next wall. It contains the relevant complexity drivers and the current trends in technology, customers, demographics, politics, or economics affecting this enterprise. But this model also describes the interconnections between these factors and their interplay. Section 13.4 has discussed the complexity drivers of the environment. And yet, as Saint-Exupéry said: The essence is invisible. Not the drivers themselves but above all their interactions determine a situation. If we now manage to recognize the right interactions, we create a *"model of totality"* of this enterprise in its environment, with which we can simulate options, run through scenarios, find leverage effects, and engage in self-reflection so that we stop doing the wrong things and do the right things.

Our brain is quickly overwhelmed by the *representation of impact cycles,* which occur between the connections of these drivers. These, however, determine whether the system is unstable or stable, whether the situation can be changed only with difficulty or quite easily, how much initial thrust is needed at which point for anything to move at all, and in which impact cycles the powerful "virtuous circles" or "vicious circles" are hidden, in which the greatest danger, but also the greatest levers and the best approaches for strategic thrusts lie. Here, too, computer support can and must be resorted to. MIT professor Jay Forrester developed *"system dynamics"* for this purpose as early as the 1960s. This computer-aided method, which enables simulating and quantifying the interaction of drivers and their reaction to measures taken by the enterprise, has since been used successfully to model industries, cities, or even global issues. In Germany, Frederic Vester also popularized interconnected thinking in the 1970s. His approach is called *sensitivity modeling*. Unlike system dynamics, it focuses more on the quality of connections and impact cycles than on their quantification. Easy-to-use programs are now available for both methods, enabling the management group to create its own "model of totality" with which it will discuss the future and options.

This model also needs to be worked with continually, because everything soon changes a little again, and most of all because the discussions held while working on the model move something in the management group. If senior managers regularly update and further refine their model, its control power increases in accordance with the Conant–Ashby theorem. Senior management begins to better understand and develop a common notion of its environment and the enterprise within it. Over time, it finds the pivotal points from which the decisive changes emanate, while remaining stable themselves. And senior management locates ever more precisely the success factors for the enterprise and invests all its energy in these factors. This conversation turns managers into a team. However, the model can only act as a catalyst for this if it is permanently visible to everyone in the operations room, so that spontaneous discussions can kick off at any time.

This kind of continuous engagement with the future is better than relying on forecasts that very likely are expensive (first) and wrong (second). Our world is changing at breakneck speed, and interconnections and effects are emerging that did not exist previously. "Forecasts are difficult," the physicist Nils Bohr reportedly said, "especially when they concern the future." In our planning, therefore, we must also reverse the logic: *Rather than relying on forecasts, we need to ask ourselves where things are heading if the trends already evident today continue, and what we therefore need to do today.* The development and interconnectedness of trends can be simulated, creating scenarios that help us test how strategic thrusts will play out in order to develop the best options. We will then be prepared for certain scenarios and will have resolutions and plans in the drawer for others. Strategic action also takes place in sync with changes in the present, because strategic planning is also not about decisions that will be made in the future, but about how today's decisions impact the future. Like operational planning, strategic planning takes place continuously. And, in accordance with the cybernetic principle, strategy is also not about precision, but about direction.

The premises for the scenarios and for our strategy are continuously updated in the operations room in terms of strategic monitoring or a strategic radar by senior management based on ongoing developments. If relevant changes occur, the scenarios are discussed again and, if necessary, new alternatives or plans are run through and tested: What is the effect of doing this instead of that? Here we are helped by the memory wall, which we use to check whether we have the necessary resources for each alternative.

18.2.4 Attention Focus

The fourth wall is quickly explained. It is used to focus everyone's attention on a particular topic. On this wall, presentations, pictures, video clips, or Internet pages about a particular issue are displayed, in order to enrich ongoing discussion with information. We may also want to integrate the expertise of professionals abroad into

Fig. 18.4 Example of a firm's operations room

our discussions via video conference. The wall can be used for many things and basically serves as a reserve should we need more or different information. Finally, we should also be able to draw and write on this wall by hand, in order to visually (and visibly) support our discussions with sketches and models.

Figure 18.4 shows the operations room of a global enterprise with several thousand employees. It was set up after the diagnosis of the control system had revealed relevant gaps in System 4 and in System 3–4 interaction. As in many other enterprises, business review meetings were held regularly with the divisional heads, but they dealt almost exclusively with operational issues. Strategic issues were systematically superseded by operational issues, partly because the enterprise was undergoing a strong growth phase. Management recognized the danger and acted by creating a structure in the form of the operations room that changed the behavior of managers. In addition to the usual operational issues, the physical structure meant that strategic issues now became the focus of discussions. Divisional management first reported on one wall on the status of business (Information and Alarm) and on the status of the implementation of measures and projects already decided (Memory). Second, the Information and Alarm wall was used to look for the unexpected or surprising and to review and discuss any changes in strategic premises (Planning and Simulation). If no action was needed, the meeting was closed. Otherwise, options were worked out and tested against each other (Simulation and Planning), and actions were decided and anchored (Memory). In between, following the nature of our sometimes erratic thinking, we jumped back and forth from one wall to another. The executives worked together on the walls in this room. When certain issues proved to be particularly complex, the method described in Sect. 18.1 was used to bring executives together in different places around the world to let them work together on the way forward. Over a period of 10 years, the enterprise developed so strongly by applying this approach that it became a dominant operational unit within the enterprise and was therefore later split into several, smaller companies.

Later in the Bar

Sandra: Whew . . . that was a long day!

David: You can say that again. But now it's done.

Rachel: No, now the work is just beginning.

Sandra: Again, the same question crosses my mind: It's always about cybernetics, cybernetics, cybernetics, . . . If this is really so important for our society, why do we never hear about it? I for one have never heard of cybernetics before, except when it comes to the Terminator or bitcoins and espionage.

Marc: Never caught on as a science.

Rachel: Because as an interdisciplinary science, it doesn't fit into the categories of universities. It's like with an agenda: What doesn't fit into the given categories has no place.

Marc: And that's why nobody can make an academic career in cybernetics. There are only journals, but no interdisciplinary journals through which you can earn academic merit.

Sandra: Excuse me?

Marc: I once considered an academic career. If you want to get ahead, you have to publish as often as possible in recognized journals. Everything has to be watertight in terms of expertise for publications to be accepted at all. Something interdisciplinary has no chance. So there are no chairs of cybernetics at universities. At best for control technology on engineering programs, because that's obvious.

David: Yes, cybernetics is about practice. Somehow we're all good cyberneticists. When we're in love, we know not to run straight at the target because these systems behave in complex ways. So, with great finesse, we start designing the control process with the right framework and conditions so that the desired result is created and, in the end, we are both talking about love.

Rachel: Or take artists. They're high-variety athletes. Brian Eno, the genius of rock and pop music in the 70s and 80s, said his work was most influenced by Stafford Beer's cybernetics. Eno writes that music is not created by replicating a goal, but rather by designing the process so that music can emerge from it. The result remains open at first, and the goal is movable. David Bowie also listed Stafford Beer among those five books that he would take to a desert island.

Sandra: And yet neither boys in love nor artists talk about cybernetics. Well, most people don't know that they can speak prose.

Rachel: (laughs) And besides, the Americans abandoned the word "cybernetics" after they were overtaken by the Russians in its technical application. You remember the Sputnik shock of 1957, don't you?

David: Remembering would be saying too much.

Rachel: From then on, the word was avoided in America. People tended to talk about IT or AI, applications in computer science. In Russia, on the other hand, cybernetics has become hype. There are cyberneticists in Stanislav Lem's famous novel *Solaris*, published in 1961, which was turned into a film a few years ago starring George Clooney.

Sandra: You don't say ...

Rachel: Every engineer knows that. You managers should probably look into it instead of always juggling ROCEs and EBITs. For you, cybernetics stops at cybersecurity.

David: Or with cybersex. Every digital doppelganger today seems to start with "cyber."

Marc: Nothing against cybersecurity. We have our hands full at our insurance company. And it's really not technology that makes the job difficult, but what's going on in the company. Something has to change, otherwise the best technology is of no use. It just makes everything even faster, which already doesn't work as it is. Nothing is worse than doing the wrong thing even better.

Sandra: Anyway, I'm glad there's a simple representation of the control organization at the end. I like this diagram: the whole organization on one page. And that's it?

Rachel: Well, I guess the real work is to fill the diagram. You don't see the control loops and communication channels themselves there. You only see them when they don't work. Therefore, the result of organizational diagnosis is probably a set of measures that grind the edges and fill the gaps at various corners and ends of the control system.

David: Almost sounds like carpentry. Craft.

Sandra: I wonder if it's that easy. At least now I don't have to explain the Viable System Model to my whole company.

Marc: Sure, it's enough if you have the measures and show control with the diagram. That's all it takes. But I'll also teach my people the model. I want them to learn that language and understand what they're doing and why. Like engineers, IT specialists are close to that way of thinking anyway and won't struggle with it.

Rachel: And then they can continue to diagnose themselves. They probably do that in the learning process anyway. It seems to me that once you have the model in your head, you automatically start diagnosing everything around you. And suddenly you'll also see Ashby's law in action everywhere.

David: Speak for yourself. But seriously: Isn't this, as is so often the case with you managers, once again simply nothing more than old wine in new bottles?

Marc: What makes you think that?

David: Control and communication are management. The control organization and the communication organization are nothing other than the management organization. And that's what we've been dealing with for a long time, isn't it?

Rachel: Yes, but not from the point of view of the underlying science: the science of control and communication. And the fact that everything that wants to grow and thrive needs not only a structure, but a very specific structure—and one that is always and everywhere the same. Now that's also new.

Sandra: To be honest, I don't know of any other model that could be used to diagnose a management or control structure. Instead, there are just a few models for subareas like MbO and a few principles.

David: And you'll find different ones in every book.

Sandra: Right. But that's pretty arbitrary. Everybody's talking about something different and the latest recipe. That bugs me every time. A little more science would be helpful. But why are you interested in management, David?

David: Well, there have always been pilots who founded their own airline, haven't there?

Sandra: Like Moritz Sutter with Crossair, you mean? Or Nicki Lauda?

David: For example. I'm sure he was a master of practical control engineering, and I'm sure he took what he knew about how things worked into management somehow.

Sandra: I wasn't aware of how close communication and control are. I had a gut feeling, but I didn't know how to deal with it. I've since realized quite a few things about my own company.

Marc: Yes, and complexity as a benchmark. That's also new. And insightful, I think. Diversity is strength.

Rachel: Wait, diversity is just diversity to begin with. Whether it's strength depends on how you deal with complexity. That has also broken companies in the past.

Marc: Right. Diversifications gone wrong abound.

Rachel: Or adventures that were recognizably doomed in advance by their sheer complexity, like Edzard Reuter's technology group. Too much horizontal complexity, so unmanageable.

Marc: Or the Daimler-Chrysler excursion. Okay, so the art is where you contain or avoid diversity, and where you promote it.

Sandra: So far, it's been a matter of feeling. Mind you, it's true, it helps to have a model of these things in your head.

Marc: What do you mean by that?

Sandra: So far, I couldn't talk to my managers about these things. I sometimes couldn't sufficiently justify my gut feeling about a decision. In the future, I'll be able to do that better. If everyone knows Ashby's law, you can discuss things differently.

Marc: But I found the disease thing distasteful.

Rachel: Why? Are you afraid of diseases?

Marc: It bothers me that words are used carelessly that might carry a lot of meaning for some people.

Sandra: That doesn't bother me. I think that companies can also be sick, and that you have to call a spade a spade. Otherwise, nothing changes. We wouldn't have medical progress if we didn't articulate unpleasant things.

Marc: But unlike medicine, these are metaphors.

Rachel: Hold on! Not the word matters per se, but the disease mechanism it's used to describe. Words don't heal, only understanding the influencing factors and connections does. And that's what's behind these metaphors. I agree with McCulloch: Don't bite my finger—look where I'm pointing.

Sandra: I agree. The diesel scandal could have been prevented if Volkswagen had been diagnosed with dissociation in time.

David: In hindsight, everyone is always wiser. But what do you mean by that?

Sandra: Well, if Volkswagen, as a technology-driven company, had been divided into functional areas, then according to the pattern of dissociation, either Systems 2 would have had to work great, or then problems would have been flushed up to executive floors, where they would have to be decided without enough expertise. Or have I misunderstood that?

Rachel: No, that's quite true. You mean Piëch and his executives behaved that way because the organization forced them to?

Sandra: I wouldn't exactly say forced, but it certainly had an influence on the culture. And then, after all, it's the executives who shape the organization.

Marc: I'll go along with that but still don't like the disease labels. But okay, sometimes you have to provoke to get a discussion going.

Sandra: That's right. Managers can't afford to be Wittgenstein.

David: What does that mean?

Sandra: He's quoted as saying: "If you can't talk about it, you should keep quiet about it." But we have to act. A manager simply can't simply remain silent like a poet.

Rachel: I'm beginning to understand why you like this model.

Sandra: But I think the operations room and the retreat method are a bit over the top. If I lock up thirty of my executives for a few days, I can shut the place down.

Marc: If that's really the case, then you would have to study the redundancy of potential command again. Do you remember that principle?

Sandra: Well, I'm probably exaggerating a little. But it's time-consuming.

Marc: It depends, compared to what? When I think about how much money and effort we could have saved in the last 2 years if the right people had talked to each other from the beginning. I'm telling you, for us it's not the technology …

David: A structure that ensures that in the back and forth of conversation, things fall into place by themselves and good things multiply. It sounds too good to be true.

Rachel: If it really works, it's the best example of how cybernetics deals with complexity.

Marc: You need to see the effort in relation to the benefits.

Rachel: Or to the alternatives that you have. Most of the time there's just no alternative to talking to each other.

Sandra: That's kind of comforting.

Rachel: Yes, more and more people need to talk to each other, the more complex everything gets. The future is no longer what it used to be ... Karl Valentin.

Marc: The alternative is hundreds of meetings. You talk, but sequentially and for months, and don't get anywhere. But there's no cost center for that. Costs only come in the form of pastries, milk, and sugar.

David: (laughs) But if I imagine thirty high-ranking UN officials in a negotiation session ... or the thirty prima ballerinas in a corporation. I'd rather fly.

Marc: That raises an interesting question.

Rachel: Which?

Marc: What if your boss is such a prima ballerina and doesn't want that kind of structure? Bosses usually have their own agenda.

David: You mean if they're just interested in their career, their bonus, their power? I raised that question yesterday.

Marc: Not even that. Self-interest might sometimes play a role as well. But they might just see the priorities very differently.

Sandra: I'm with Theodore Roosevelt on that.

David: Remind me.

Sandra: Do what you can, with what you've got, where you are!

Marc: How right he was.

Sandra: I demand the same from my managers. I hate it when they whine about all the things they would like to do, but unfortunately can't. There're enough things they can do within their own sphere of influence. I give them every freedom to do that. Sometime I'd really appreciate them using it more.

Marc: May God grant me the serenity to accept things I can't change, the courage to change things I can, and the wisdom to distinguish one from the other.

Sandra: (laughs) I'll raise my glass to that! And if you succeed with what you can tackle yourself, then your influence will grow by itself, you needn't worry about that.

All: Cheers everyone!

Epilogue: The Proof of the Pudding is in the Eating

> We are aware that the many techniques of cybernetics ... will transform our whole society. With this knowledge, we are wide awake, alert, capable of action; no longer are we blind, inert powers of fate. (Pierre Trudeau, Canadian Prime Minister 1968–1984)

The models and methods presented in this book are not new. Nor is the fact that the rapid development of technology since the 1950s has led to a wealth of new possibilities and an enormous increase in performance. Digitization is its provisional culmination, and its consequences cannot be foreseen. What is new, however, is that we must now respond to this situation. Until now, our organizations have mainly reaped the benefits of this technological development. Since the 1950s, markets have grown, resulting in low unemployment, high tax revenues, and much prosperity in an economic climate that for decades was mainly characterized by fair weather.

The two recessions, in the form of the oil crises in the 1970s and 1980s, can be seen as periods of respite amid a unique economic boom. In the meantime, however, technical systems have taken a striking lead over social systems. On a larger scale, this first became visible in the new economy and high-tech crises at the beginning of the new millennium, but at the latest in the financial and economic crises starting in 2008. These crises were caused by overstretched or mismanaged control systems in firms, in nongovernmental organizations, and in governmental organizations.

The ongoing euro crisis is also ultimately due to a failure of control systems in firms and at the state level, leading to their massive debt overload—not after difficult times, however, but after an incredibly long period of fair weather. Together with all the other challenges, this crisis, in which we are still mired, is neither a financial nor an economic crisis. It is a crisis of society and its organizations, which have reached their performance limits in their current mode of functioning. This applies equally to industrialized nations and to developing countries, because as Peter Drucker observed: "It can be said that there are no 'underdeveloped countries.' There are only 'undermanaged' ones."[1]

In turbulent times, we often hear the call for strong, charismatic leaders, despite history showing us that they have often turned out to be seducers rather than leaders.

[1] Peter Drucker, *Ecological Vision: Reflections on the American Condition* (Routledge, 2000).

M. Pfiffner, *The Neurology of Business*, Management for Professionals,
https://doi.org/10.1007/978-3-031-14260-4

The call for better managers, and leaders, is heard again these days. And yet, we only have the leaders we have—and there is no hope that this will ever change. But the alternative is interesting: If we must already assume that our society has to function even with normally gifted leaders, we should not look for better people, but for better control and communication systems around these people that make it easier for them to succeed. In the twenty-first century, organizations will have to function better if we are to retain our freedom of action. A new functioning of economic and social organizations is needed—a functioning under today's conditions.

It is therefore time to apply the fire of Prometheus not only to technology, but also to our management systems. Where negative feedback loops work well, namely, a priori in the realm of entrepreneurially managed family businesses, good management systems have evolved out of necessity and through talent. But we need to bring the performance of all our organizations, large and small, public and private, business and nonbusiness, up to the same level of performance that technology itself has achieved. The next revolution, therefore, must no longer be one of machines, but one of organizations.

Ashby's law works here, too: If we are to control and harness technological development, our control system must have at least the same level of complexity—and we are miles away from that today. If technological opportunities and advances are left unmanaged, they will do harm. They will lead to uncontrolled pollution, total surveillance, consumer manipulation, damage to health, and even greater dangers. On the other hand, we also need to control them so that we can place their potentials at the service of people and use them, because they also lead to unmatched efficiency, understanding, welfare, justice, transparency, enlightenment, knowledge, and many other good qualities. When properly used, they increase our choices instead of decreasing them, as Heinz von Foerster's ethical imperative demands (cf. Chap. 9). The practical problems in the economy and society will only be solved, and technical progress will only bring social progress, if we design our social systems better. It is they that develop, deploy, use, and regulate technology. How well they do this and in whose interest depends on the quality of organizations.

We do not need to demand the agile organization, nor the hierarchy-free, innovative, intelligent, or productive organization. If we design the neurology of the organization correctly and wire it properly, these characteristics will emerge on their own. Conversely, it is of no use to have agile, innovative, or productive units if overall control and communication do not work. Will cybernetics really help us here? A science that has seemingly disappeared after an initial euphoria? If we do not want to wait for the strong leader, our best bet seems to be to apply the recipe that gave us a massive technological push 70 years ago and produced wonderful new capabilities to our organizations, which are also in desperate need of new capabilities. Stafford Beer was the first to begin applying the insights of cybernetics, which I called the "recipe for success" in the Prologue, to the management of social systems. For him as a pioneer and innovator, there was no beaten track. He was therefore particularly fond of and frequently recited the following verses by the Spanish poet Antonio Machado:

> Caminante, no hay camino
> Se hace camino, al andar
> (Wanderer, there is no path
> The path is made by wandering)[2]

In the meantime, the path to the third dimension of organizing is open and mapped out. With the Viable System Model, we have the first-ever generic model of control. We also have all the technical prerequisites and possibilities for a complexity-appropriate, robust, fast, and agile type of planning. And we have sufficient practical experience. We must and can now organize the third dimension of organizing. And yet, probably the greatest challenge remains. It no longer lies in finding a path, but in the determination to pursue it. Finding new ways is not easy. In so doing, we face an immense force: the status quo. It is the enemy of anything new. We do ourselves a favor if we stick with the status quo and keep doing what everyone is doing. No one will blame us if we cling to what is. We therefore paradoxically limit ourselves precisely because we want to succeed. Heinz von Foerster expressed this beautifully in his First Theorem: "The more profound the subject you ignore, the greater your chances of fame and success."[3]

However, the evolutionary principle of mutation, selection, and adaptation will certainly work here as well. Not only does it produce optimized solutions, but it is itself the optimized solution for progress, as the German bionicist Ingo Rechenberg proved in the 1970s. Already many enterprises around the world are working on their third dimension and breaking new ground in control and communication. The successful ones will certainly give their competitors a run for their money and sooner or later will simply oust them. Until these ideas prevail, and until the new itself becomes self-evident again, we need to be convinced that we are taking the right action. This conviction makes the difference between whether we allow ourselves to be stopped by doubts and difficulties or not. In this sense, a passage from another poem fits here. The American poet Robert Frost often went for walks with his friend Edward Thomas, a Welsh poet. The latter is said to have regretted time and again that they had not taken a different path where they could have marveled at the perhaps even more beautiful flowers and landscapes. Frost made fun of the fact that his friend always ended up sighing, no matter which path he took. Like all true poets, he transformed this everyday episode into something much larger, which we find articulated in the last lines of "The Road Not Taken"[4]:

> Two roads diverged in a wood, and I—
> I took the one less traveled by,
> And that has made all the difference

[2]Emilio J. Garcia-Wiedemann, *Los Proverbios y Cantares de Antonio Machado* (Editiones Dauro, 2014).

[3]Heinz Von Foerster, *Understanding Understanding: Essays on Cybernetics and Cognition* (Springer, 2003), pp. 191–197.

[4]Robert Frost, *Mountain Interval* (New York, Henry Holt and Company, 1916).

If this book contributes to developing the growing worldwide community engaging with the application of the Viable System Model (VSM) and other applications of management cybernetics in conferences, internet forums, tutorials, books, and articles, it will have served its purpose. I hope it has sparked an enduring thought in the reader: What if my company could control and communicate as effectively as my own nervous system, and what fantastic properties could we evoke? I hope that readers will realize that while applying the VSM requires rocket science in a sense, it is not itself "rocket science." Rather, it proceeds in a relatively simple and pragmatic way. I welcome any feedback, opinions, questions about application, or even experience reports on applying the VSM, especially from anyone who decides to establish the third dimension of organizing in their sphere of influence and now ...

... lays aside the manual and ventures out into the traffic.

Glossary

Ashby's Law	Only complexity can absorb complexity. See Chap. 9.
(Relative) Autonomy	The self-determination and freedom of action of one's own existence or identity, which, however, remains more or less dependent on other existences or identities—and hence is "relative." See Sect. 4.2
Algedonic Signal	Ensures that critical information, whether negative or positive (pain or pleasure), bypasses the usual reporting structure and reaches the top level unfiltered and quickly. It is the only signal that penetrates all levels of recursion. See Sect. 14.4
Aphorism	An insight or realization.
Autopoiesis	Self-production, self-creation, and self-preservation. See Sect. 4.2
Axiom	A credible basic assumption or premise.
Axiom of Management (First)	The sum of horizontal variety disposed by all the operational elements equals the sum of vertical variety disposed on the six vertical components of corporate cohesion. See Chap. 10.
Axiom of Management (Second)	The variety disposed by System 3 resulting from the operation of the First Axiom equals the variety disposed by System 4. See Sect. 13.4
Axiom of Management (Third)	The variety disposed by System 5 equals the residual variety generated by the operation of the Second Axiom. See Sect. 13.5
Black Box	A system whose internal structure is of no interest. Investigation and description are

M. Pfiffner, *The Neurology of Business*, Management for Professionals,
https://doi.org/10.1007/978-3-031-14260-4

	limited to external behavior (input/output of the black box). See Chap. 5
Conant-Ashby Theorem	Every good regulator of a system must be a model of that system. That model must have requisite variety. Applied to management, it says that the outcome of any management cannot be better than the model on which it is based—unless by chance. See Chap. 9
Complexity	Behavioral variety of a system that arises from the fact that its elements can interact in different ways. The measure of complexity is variety. See Chap. 9
Control (Self-)	Mostly used here in the sense of the English word "control," i.e., in the sense of steering. Whenever possible, this should occur in the sense of self-control, i.e., implicitly or intrinsically. This requires a negative feedback loop. But it can also be explicit or extrinsic ("Go and see"). See Chap. 9
Control Function	What control does, divided into the five control elements or Subsystems 1 to 5, which perform five different control functions. See Chap. 3
Cybernetic Imperative	Always act in a way that increases the number of choices. Also called ethical imperative, when an action increases the number of choices available to others. Formulated by Heinz von Foerster based on Immanuel Kant's categorical imperative. See Chap. 9
Crucial for Success	Tasks critical to success that have an influence on purchase-decision criteria. See Chap. 12
Critical to Success	The twenty percent of all tasks that together account for 80% of the company's success. See Chap. 12
Enterprise	All types of organizations, business or non-business, large or small. Any viable, operational unit is called a business for simplicity's sake.
Emergence	New properties of a system that cannot be traced back to properties of its elements, but arise from their interaction. See Sect. 1.4 and Chap. 14
Essential Variables	Vital factors that the control system must keep well under control and/or within

	defined limits. See Chaps. 3 and 12, and Sect. 18.2
Function Diagram	Assigns competencies to jobs (people or organizational units) for individual tasks in the form of a two-dimensional matrix. Links the first dimension of organizing (structure) to the second dimension (flow/processes). Also called function matrix or activity distribution chart. See Sect. 15.1
Information	"What changes us." A difference that makes a difference. See Chap. 9
Homeostasis	The maintaining of a state of equilibrium. Stability of a systems' internal environment in an external, unpredictable environment. A steady state. See Chap. 9, Sect. 13.5, and Chap. 18
Homeostat	A homeostatic system.
Law	Laws are based on axioms.
Law of Cohesion	... for multiple recursions of the Viable System: The System 1 variety accessible to System 3 of recursion x equals the variety disposed by the sum of the metasystems of recursion y for every recursive pair. Autonomy may be restricted only to the extent necessary to preserve the identity of the whole. This also means that decisions are made at the lowest possible level. See Chap. 5
Leadership	The same as good and proper management. Conversely, good and proper management automatically leads to leadership.
Manager	Any person with responsibility for a relevant contribution to the enterprise. Regardless of the number of employees who are managed
Management	The function that transfers knowledge into benefits. Leading people and leading an organizational unit.
Miller's Number	"Seven plus/minus two," limited by cognitive valence. See Sect. 8.3
Mission-Critical	See "Critical to Success"
Operational Unit	An element in System 1. Endowed with relative autonomy, responsible for results, for purpose fulfillment, and self-directed. See Sects. 4.1 and 4.2

Policies	Statements of principle that can be applied to many different situations. Example: The right of way in road traffic. See Sect. 4.6
Purpose	The purpose of a system is what it does. Corresponds (only) in a functioning system to the enterprise's purpose as defined in a business mission. See Chap. 8
Principle	Something that must be considered, studied, and thoroughly understood. Principles are important things that we cannot ignore.
Principle of Organization (First)	Managerial, operational, and environmental varieties, diffusing through an institutional system, tend to equate; they should be designed to do so with minimum damage to people and to cost. See Chap. 11
Principle of Organization (Second)	The four directional channels carrying information between the management unit, the operation, and the environment must each have a higher capacity to transmit a given amount of information relevant to variety selection in a given time than the originating subsystem has to generate it in that time. See Sect. 14.1
Principle of Organization (Third)	Wherever the information carried on a channel capable of distinguishing a given variety crosses a boundary, it undergoes transduction; the variety of the transducer must be at least equivalent to the variety of the channel. See Sect. 14.1
Principle of Organization (Fourth)	The operation of the first three principles must be cyclically maintained through time without hiatus or lags. See Sect. 14.1
Principle of Potential Command	Power resides where information resides. See Chap. 6
Redundancy of Potential Command	Each level of command is trained to command the next higher level of recursion. Command can thus be performed in different places, depending on where the relevant information is. See Chap. 6
Regulatory Aphorism (First)	It is not necessary to enter the black box to understand the nature of the function it performs. See Chap. 5
Regulatory Aphorism (Second)	It is not necessary to enter the black box to calculate the variety that it potentially may generate. See Chap. 9

Recursion	A repeated application of the same function to itself. See Chap. 5
Recursive System Theorem	In a recursive organizational structure, any viable system contains, and is contained in, a viable system. See Chap. 5
Level of Recursion	Management level. The next level, which includes all levels below. See Chap. 5
Senior Management	The management of the System in Focus. This refers to the responsible persons who together as the management of some operational units fulfill their System 2 to 5 functions. The superordinate (meta-) control system. See Introduction and Chap. 13
SIF (System in Focus)	The operational unit we want to diagnose and design. The SIF is always on level of recursion
Squiggly Lines	Dependencies between operations. See Sect. 4.3
Subsidiarity	Organizational principle according to which tasks are only taken over by a higher level (of recursion) if they cannot be taken over by the subordinate, relevant level.
System	A set of elements that interact with each other and with the environment. Through the interrelationships, the whole is something other (hopefully more) than the sum of its parts. A system is defined by an observer according to his or her interest.
System 1	Includes all operational units at a level of recursion that together fulfill the purpose of the whole, are accountable for results, have relative autonomy, and are self-directing.
System 2	Provides coordination and oscillation damping. Also contains supporting functions.
System 3	Optimizes the "Inside & Now" of the enterprise.
System 4	Provides the "Outside & Then" of the enterprise.
System 3-4-Homeostat	Ensures fluidity between the "Inside & Now" and the "Outside & Then" of the enterprise and the evolutionary adaptation to a changing environment.
System 5	Provides identity and parameters.
System in Focus (SIF)	The level of recursion being diagnosed.

Subsidiarity	Tasks are only performed by a higher level of recursion if the lower level is not able to perform the tasks itself. See Chap. 13
Theorem	Something that can be demonstrated and proven.
Theorem (First)	The more profound the subject you ignore, the greater your chances of fame and success (Heinz von Foerster).
Transduction	A process by which information is transformed into a suitable form so that it can be understood, used, or transported by another system. See Sect. 14.1
Variety	The number of different states that a system can assume (from the point of view of an observer). Measure of complexity. See Chap. 9
Viability	"Able to maintain a separate existence." See Sect. 1.4 and Chap. 3

Selected References

Chonological List of Studies on the Viable System Model

1. Beer, Stafford (1972). 2. Auflage. Brain of the Firm. The Managerial Cybernetics of Organization. Chichester, New York, Brisbane, Toronto, Singapore: Wiley.
2. Beer, Stafford (1979). The Heart of Enterprise. The Managerial Cybernetics of Organization. Chichester, New York, Brisbane, Toronto, Singapore: Wiley.
3. Malik, Fredmund (1984). 10. Auflage. Strategie des Managements komplexer Systeme. Ein Beitrag zur Management-Kybernetik evolutionärer Systeme. Bern, Stuttgart, Wien: Haupt.
4. Beer, Stafford (1985). Diagnosing the System for Organizations. The Managerial Cybernetics of Organization. Chichester, New York, Brisbane, Toronto, Singapore: Wiley.
5. Espejo Raul und Harnden, Roger (1989). The Viable System Model. Interpretations and Applications of Stafford Beer's VSM. Chichester, New York, Brisbane, Toronto, Singapore: Wiley.
6. Espejo Raul und Schwaninger, Markus (1993). Organisational Fitness. Frankfurt, New York: Campus.
7. Beer, Stafford (1994). Beyond Dispute. The Invention of Team Syntegrity. Chichester, New York, Brisbane, Toronto, Singapore: Wiley.
8. Fuchs, Jürgen (Hrsg.) (1994). Das biokybernetische Modell – Unternehmen als Organismen. Wiesbaden: Gabler.
9. Paetzmann, Karsten (1995). Unterstützung von Selbstorganisation durch das Controlling: Eine systemorientierte Untersuchung auf Grundlage des „Viable System Models". Peter Lang.
10. Espejo Raoul, Schuhmann, Werner und Schwaninger, Markus (1996). Organizational Transformation and Learning. A Cybernetic Approach to Management. Chichester, New York, Brisbane, Toronto, Singapore: Wiley.
11. Bachmann, Manuel und Michel, Dieter (2001). Das Pentagramm der Komplexitätsbewältigung. Management-Kybernetik am Beispiel des Schweizer Paraplegiker-Zentrums Nottwil. Basel: Verlag Paraplegie.
12. Schwaninger, Markus (2006). Intelligent Organizations. Powerful Models for Systemic Management. Berlin, Heidelberg: Springer.
13. Hetzler, Sebastian (2008). "Brain supporting environments" für Entscheide in komplexen Systemen. Ein kybernetischer Ansatz für die Gestaltung wirksamer Entscheidungsumfelder. Dissertation Universität St. Gallen, Schlesslitz: Rosch-Druck.
14. Hoverstadt, Patrick (2008). The Fractal Organization. Creating Sustainable Organizations with the Viable System Model. Chichester: Wiley.
15. Türke, Ralf-Eckhard (2008). Governance. Systemic Foundation and Framework. Heidelberg: Physica.
16. Pfiffner, Martin (2010). Five Experiences with the Viable System Model. Kybernetes, Vol 39, No 9/10, pp. 1615-1626: Emerald.

M. Pfiffner, *The Neurology of Business*, Management for Professionals,
https://doi.org/10.1007/978-3-031-14260-4

17. Pfiffner, Martin (2010). Wiedergeburt des Organisierens. MoM-Letter, 18. Jg, 2/2010, Seite 19-38.
18. Pfiffner, Martin (2012). Von der Maschine zum Organismus. Das Viable System Model fördert komplexitätsfähige Organisationsstrukturen. ZFO, 81. Jg, 6/2012, Seite 416-422.
19. Espinosa, Angela und John Walker (2011). A Complexity Approach to Sustainability. Theory and Application. London, Singapore, Hackensack: Imperial College Press.
20. Espejo, Raul und Reyes, Alfonso (2011). Organizational Systems. Managing Complexity with the Viably System Model. Heidelberg, Dodrecht, London, New York: Springer.
21. Leschber, Hendrik (2012). Diagnosing the EU Political System According tot he Viable System Model of Stafford Beer. Master Thesis, MBA Krems, Donau Universität.
22. Rios, José Perez (2012). Design and Diagnosis for Sustainable Organizations. The Viable System Method. Heidelberg, Dodrecht, London, New York: Springer.
23. Grösser, Stefan N. und Zeier, René (2014). Systemic Management for Intelligent Organizations: Concepts, Models-Based Approaches and Applications. Heidelberg, Dodrecht, London, New York: Springer.
24. Frahm, Michael (2015). 2. Auflage. Kybernetisches Bauprojektmanagement: Gestaltung lebensfähiger Baustrukturen auf Grundlage des Viable System Models. BoD Books on Demand.
25. Haberkorn, Nico (2016). Das Viable System Model als Grundlage für Organisationsarchitektur. Studienarbeit. GRIN.
26. Lambertz, Mark (2016). 2. Auflage. Freiheit & Verantwortung für intelligente Organisationen. Das Modell Lebensfähiger Systeme (Viable System Model) nach Stafford Beer. Düsseldorf.
27. Strasser Thomas (2016). Businesspläne vor dem Hintergrund des Viable System Models: Mit dem Fokus auf die Gründungsphase von Start-ups. VDM Verlag.
28. Groten, Marcel (2017). Integrierte Planung von Doistributionsnetzwerken auf Basis des Viable-System-Models. Schriftenreihe Rationalisierung. Apprimus.
29. Blokdyk, Gerardus (2018). Viable System Model the Ultimate Step-By-Step Guide. 5starcooks.
30. Lambertz, Mark (2018). Die Intelligente Organisation. Das Playbook für organisatorische Komplexität. Business Village.
31. Lassl, Wolfgang (2019). The Viability of Organizations Vol. 1. Decoding the „DNA“ of Organizations. Springer.
32. Lassl, Wolfgang (2019). The Viability of Organizations Vol. 2. Diagnosing and Governing Organizations. Springer.
33. Benjamin, David and Komlos, David (2019). Cracking Complexity. The Breakthrough Formula for Solving Just About Anything Fast. Boston, London: Nicholas Brealey Publishing.
34. Beer, Vanilla und Leonard, Allenna (2019). Stafford Beer, the Father of Management Cybernetics. Big Data Analysis. Including Cybernetic Glossary. Amazon Distribution.
35. Gomez, Peter, Meynhardt Timo und Lambertz, Mark (2019). Verantwortungsvoll führen in einer komplexen Welt. Haupt.

www.ingramcontent.com/pod-product-compliance
Lightning Source LLC
Chambersburg PA
CBHW050118180326
41440CB00003B/225
* 9 7 8 3 0 3 1 1 4 2 5 9 8 *